RALEGH and MARLOWE

A Study in Elizabethan Fustian

RALEGH SMOKING BEFORE QUEEN ELIZABETH.

RALEGH and MARLOWE

A Study in Elizabethan Fustian

ELEANOR GRACE CLARK

NEW YORK
RUSSELL & RUSSELL · INC.
1965

REISSUED, 1965, BY RUSSELL & RUSSELL, INC.
BY ARRANGEMENT WITH FORDHAM UNIVERSITY PRESS
L. C. CATALOG CARD NO: 65—13956

PRINTED IN THE UNITED STATES OF AMERICA

PREFACE

THE STUDY which is herewith presented to the public has had a curious history. The second part was largely written about ten years ago, but owing to a severe illness, the manuscript lay on my desk unpublished until 1933, when I had the good fortune to be permitted to read certain chapters of it to Professor H. J. C. Grierson of the University of Edinburgh, who was then lecturing at Columbia University. His interest in the Marlowe Circle was immediate and generous, though he found the argument for a specific fustian intention throughout Marlowe's plays to be so revolutionary in its implications that, in his opinion, a more elaborate investigation of the whole question of Elizabethan topical literature was necessary by way of approach. Accordingly, at his suggestion, and with the help of his constant friendly criticism during a year of residence and teaching in the University of Edinburgh, I wrote Part One in 1934-35. Upon my return to this country, I published this first section of the work under the title *Elizabethan Fustian: A Study in the Social and Political Backgrounds of the Elizabethan Drama,* intending to follow on at once with the second part, which was devoted to the fustian element in Marlowe. By the time the final arrangements for this publication were completed, the original volume, both the first and second impressions, was sold out and was unobtainable. The Fordham University Press decided, therefore, that it would be profitable to the readers of Part Two to have Part One reprinted in the same volume as an introduction to the whole study. I welcomed this suggestion, as it gave me the opportunity to make considerable additions, revisions, and corrections of the text of Part One. Chapter Three has been entirely rewritten.

As it now appears, the whole book may be described as a study in Elizabethan and Jacobean fustian with particular reference to the Marlowe-Ralegh relationship, and I believe that it will at least help to fill in a very serious lacuna in the scholarship of the period. Scientific investigation of the general problem of topicality in the literature of the sixteenth and seventeenth centuries has long been carried on under two serious handicaps: first, a field already cluttered with the debris of reckless or shabby scholarship; and secondly, a lack of co-ordination of the results which have been obtained through sound methods and by careful scholars. In order to overcome these difficulties, I have here gathered together a very good share of the existing contemporary testimony concerning the practice of topicality in the period under consideration; this evidence is surprisingly ample and above suspicion as to quality. Moreover, I have relied for any modern interpretation or analysis of topical puzzles upon only the most reputable and, in the main, the most conservative scholars. Obviously, I have leaned most heavily upon Sir Edmund Chambers, without whose magnificent collection of materials this study could not have been made. I have also depended much upon the editors of particular dramatists, such as Professor Bond for Lyly, Professor Parrott for Chapman, and Professor Lucas for Webster. It is, I believe, the editors who are most likely to know something of the political and social backgrounds of the plays which they must elucidate, though it is not possible to over-estimate the value of such general studies as Dr. Virginia Gildersleeve's *Government Regulation of the Elizabethan Drama,* or Dr. Lily Campbell's *Elizabethan Use of Historical Parallels.*

Concerning the evidence herein reviewed, I confess that I myself am astonished, both at its abundance and at the verdict of approval which has been pronounced upon it by unquestionably competent scholars.

It remains to be seen what will be the verdict of such scholars upon the evidence for a new case of topicality in the plays of Christopher Marlowe. In approaching the second half of this study, it seems only fair that the reader should bear in mind my own conception of the problem and of the evidence. Throughout, I have regarded my task as chiefly an investigation of the social and political milieu in which Marlowe lived and worked, such exploration being undertaken with a view to the *possibilities* of topicality in the plays, rather than as an attempt to *prove* that the plays were fustian. Very much has been written of the men who killed Marlowe, but until now it has been all but impossible for the lovers of Marlowe to know anything about his friends, associates, or patrons. I believe that the interests and manners of this group of men are reflected in Marlowe's poetry; but I believe even more strongly that a knowledge of this brilliant circle should be valuable to students of the period, whether or not they are persuaded that Marlowe wrote as he talked, that is, of the men and interests about him. However well or ill I may have accomplished the task of presentation, I believe that the facts themselves contained in these pages will justify their publication, since they constitute a gratifying documentation of one of the most fruitful human relationships in all English literary history.

I owe the deepest gratitude to the many friends who have helped me during the preparation of this study. Some have supplied information, some bibliography; others have read the manuscript and offered valuable criticism and suggestion. All have been generous in giving advice and warning. For every individual contribution, particularly for every warning, I am acutely and truly grateful.

The greatest of all my debts is to Sir Herbert Grierson. Throughout my residence in the University of Edinburgh I have enjoyed the advantage of his scholarly and vigorous criticism. His personal friendliness, combined with his wariness of the subject, made him the best of critics.

To the following persons also I should like to make specific acknowledgment for having read and criticized the manuscript in whole or in part: Dr. R. W. Chambers, of the University of London; Mr. Henry Harvey Wood, M.A., of the University of Edinburgh; Mr. John Purves, of the University of Edinburgh; Dr. Samuel C. Chew, of Bryn Mawr College; Mr. Kenneth Bell, M.A., of Balliol College, Oxford; Dr. Conyers Read, of the University of Pennsylvania; Dr. Jean Wilson, of Smith College; Dr. Blanche Colton Williams, of Hunter College; Dr. Joseph Reilly, of Hunter College; Dr. Samuel A. Tannenbaum, of Hunter College; Dr. Oscar J. Campbell, of Columbia University.

To former President Eugene Colligan, and to the Board of Trustees of Hunter College, I am also deeply indebted for the grant of a year's leave-of-absence, without which I could not have completed this study.

I should like also to express my special gratitude to Mrs. Wallace de Lagune (Eleanor Renner), my friend and former student at Bryn Mawr College, for the translations of the *Satire Ménippée,* which she has made in connection with her study of that very interesting book; and to Miss Ruth Ogg and Miss Loretta Clifford, also friends and former students at Hunter College, and to Miss Lucy Martin Donnelly. Miss Ogg, together with Mrs. Adelaide D. V. White of London, typed and prepared the manuscript for publication. Miss Clifford prepared the index to Part I, as first published.

To Fordham University Press my gratitude for understanding co-operation in the problems of production of this book.

I need hardly add that the friends who have helped me are in no way responsible for the thesis herewith presented.

E.G.C.

New York, 1941

CONTENTS

ELIZABETHAN FUSTIAN

CHAPTER ONE

Fustian: Its Origin and Practice

IN THE FACT AND NATURE of the censorship of the drama in the sixteenth century lie, oddly enough, the sources of evidence both for and against the thesis of this book. It is therefore necessary for the reader to know something of the nature and development of this institution, that he may appraise the value of the argument which is to follow. The facts in the history of dramatic censorship before and during the reign of Elizabeth have long been known to scholars, but the discussion of the problems involved offers one of the most curious anomalies in the annals of literary research. One may easily claim that the bulk of legislation in this line—Marian, Elizabethan, and Jacobean—was concerned with and occasioned by the presence of topical matter in the plays. Of this truth there can really be no doubt; yet in the face of the onrush of modern investigation concerning this early drama as propaganda, scholarly authority has braced itself to resist the conclusion that the drama was, to any considerable degree, used as a vehicle for propaganda.

One can readily understand the reluctance of a certain school of sentimental and so-called "aesthetic" critics to see their literary god Shakspere dethroned from his exalted position as the highest exemplar of the doctrine of *l'art pour l'art*. For the most part these have never heard of Edmund Tilney or George Buck or Henry Herbert, or of such typical instances of dramatic treatment of contemporary politics as *The Isle of Dogs, Believe As You List, Eastward Ho!, Sir Thomas Moore,* or the *Game at Chess,* to name several at random. But there are genuine scholars, such as Professor H. J. C. Grierson, Professor Alfred W. Pollard, Dr. W. W. Greg, Sir Edmund Chambers, Professor J. Q. Adams, not "of that vile brotherhood" at all, who, though fully aware of the cases of indubitable topicality, are nevertheless exceedingly cautious about accepting mere theories of interpretation, especially those broached by irresponsible persons, such as the gifted but reckless Mr. F. G. Fleay, or, more recently, by such enthusiastic literary historians as Miss Lilian Winstanley.

For the caution which condemns confident assertions based on scanty or contradictory evidence, especially when presented with slovenly documentation, the careful scholar has nothing but respect. It is possible, however, to carry one's disgust at shabby workmanship or amateur enthusiasm further than is legitimate, i.e., into a premature abandonment of the line of investigation. This course has, happily, not been followed by Sir Edmund Chambers, who has, in fact, assembled most of the material I am herewith presenting with a view to extending our notions somewhat to admit of the possibility of a wider scope for the topical play than has hitherto been thought likely.

Much of the evidence concerning the topical play has already been ably presented by Dr. Virginia Gildersleeve in her *Government Regulation of the Drama.* (New York, 1908.) However, inasmuch as she has confined her discussion to plays which had been actually censored by Government authorities, there now needs no apology for a new presentation which shall include a review of cases that escaped the censor, even though they were indubitably topical.

The official censorship was not instituted until 1581; but since it did not get into very efficient working order for several years, it is not surprising that most of the early records of test cases are incomplete or ambiguous. It seems, therefore, expedient to begin the account of the censor's activities by relating a fully developed and indisputable instance of it. Middleton's *Game at Chess* furnishes an elaborate example, not only of the topical play, but of the feeble gesture of resistance on the part of the censor, in this instance, Sir Henry Herbert. The *Game at Chess* was, in fact, the first important case of his administration. I subjoin the account of the play given by Dr. Gildersleeve (*op. cit.*, pp. 118-122):

For years public feeling had been running high against James's feeble policy of friendship with Spain, culminating in the project of the marriage of Charles, Prince of Wales, with the Infanta Maria. In Gondomar, the Spanish Ambassador at London, the people saw the very incarnation of the Spanish and Jesuitical intrigue which they so hated. But the proposed match fell through. In October, 1623, to the joy of the English, Charles and Buckingham returned from Madrid without the Spanish bride; James's policy was finally overturned; and Buckingham now headed the movement against Spain. In March, 1624, war was declared between the two countries, and in August the playwright Middleton seized this opportunity of catching the popular fancy by embodying in a symbolical play the hatred of Spanish intrigue and the joy at its defeat. His famous *Game at Chess,* under the thin disguise of the pieces on a chess-board, sets forth a story of perfidious Jesuit plotting and, more notably, a portrayal of the visit of Charles and Buckingham to the Spanish Court. The White and Black Kings and Queens respectively represent the English and Spanish sovereigns. The White Knight seems to be Charles, the White Duke, Buckingham, and—to omit the other characters—the Black Knight is a scurrilously bitter portrait of Gondomar.*

In spite of the almost unparalleled boldness of this treatment of current events, the play obtained Herbert's official license, and was acted by the King's company at the Globe nine times, amid great enthusiasm. Then, upon the complaint of the Spanish Ambassador to the King, the *Game at Chess* was suppressed. The official correspondence, which has survived, throws an interesting light on the affair. On August 12 Mr. Secretary Conway sent the following letter to the Privy Council:

"His Majesty hath received information from the Spanish Ambassador of a very scandalous comedy acted publickly by the King's

* It is interesting to note in passing that Massinger's *Grand Duke of Florence* is on the same subject. For an excellent discussion of this play, see Miss Johanna Stocholm's edition prepared for a Ph.D. thesis, Bryn Mawr, 1930, especially pp. lxxii-ff.

The following note from the editor of Osborne's *Traditional Memoirs* (Edinburgh, 1811, p. 200) may be of more than casual interest to the readers of Middleton's *Game at Chess*: "The celebrated Lily published an exposition of a (pretended) ancient prophecy, concerning a *White King,* which ran thus: 'When the lion of rightfulnesse is dead, then shall arise a White King in Britain, first flying, and after riding, after ligging downe, and in this lig down he shall be lymed, and after that he shall be led. Then shall be gadred together much fold, and he shall take helpe for him; then shall be sought helpe, and there shall none arise but bed for head. And then shall one gone there, the sun ariseth another, then the sun gone down, &c. &c. &c. After the White King shall fall into a kirk-yard over a wall.' In interpreting this piece of fustian, it cost the astrologer hard work to make out James to be the *lion of rightfulness,* since he very little resembled that magnanimous animal. But Charles I was said to be the White King, because, contrary to former usage, he was apparelled in white at the coronation."

players, wherein they take the boldness and presumption, in a rude and dishonourable fashion, to represent on the stage the persons of His Majesty, the King of Spain, the Conde de Gondomar, the Bishop of Spalato, &c. His Majesty remembers well there was a commandment and restraint given against the representing of any modern Christian kings in those stage-plays; and wonders much both at the boldness now taken by that company, and also that it hath been permitted to be so acted, and that the first notice hereof should be brought to him by a foreign ambassador, while so many ministers of his own are thereabouts, and cannot but have heard of it. His Majesty's pleasure is that your Lordships presently call before you as well the poet that made the comedy as the comedians that acted it: And upon examination of them to commit them or such of them as you shall find most faulty, to prison, if you find causes, or otherwise take security for their forthcoming; and then certify his Majesty what you find that comedy to be, in what points it is most offensive, by whom it was made, by whom licensed, and what course you think fittest to be held for the exemplary and severe punishment of the present offenders, and to restrain such insolent and licentious presumption for the future."

On August 21 the Privy Council replied. They have called some of the principal actors before them, they report, and "demanded of them by what license and authority they have presumed to act" the scandalous comedy. "In answere whereto they produced a book being an original and perfect copy thereof (as they affirmed) seen and allowed by Sir Henry Herbert, Knt., Master of the Revels, under his own hand, and subscribed in the last page of the said book: We demanding further whether there were not other parts or passages represented on the stage than those expressly contained in the book, they confidently protested they added or varied from the same nothing at all." The poet, one Middleton, the Lords report, has "shifted out of the way"; but they have sent a messenger to apprehend him. They have sharply reproved the players, forbidden them to act this comedy any more, or any play whatsoever until his Majesty's pleasure be further known, and made them give bond for their attendance upon the Council when wanted. Instead of telling the King the offensive passages, they sent the book, subscribed by the Master of the Revels, so that Conway or some one appointed by the King, may peruse the play, and "call Sir Henry Herbert before you to know the reason of his licensing thereof, who (as we are given to understand) is now attending the court."

The responsibility of the affair was now shifted to the shoulders of the Master of the Revels, who seems to have interceded at once with his kinsman and superior officer, the Earl of Pembroke, Lord Chamberlain. On August 27 Conway wrote again to the Council, expressing the King's satisfaction with their procedure, and bidding them "examine by whose direction and application the personating of Gondomar and others was done; and that being found out, the party or parties to be severely punished, his Majesty being unwilling for one's sake and only fault to punish the innocent or utterly to ruin the company." Pembroke had evidently been soothing the King's feelings and had settled the affair. On the same day he wrote to the Lord President of the Council, reviewing the history of the case, and stating that the players had petitioned the King that they might be allowed to perform again. "His Majesty now conceives the punishment," writes the Lord Chamberlain, "if not satisfactory for that their insolency, yet such as since it stopps the current of their poore livelyhood and maintenance, without much prejudice they cannot longer undergoe. In consideration therefore of those his poore servants, his Majesty would have their Lordships connive at any common play lycensed by authority, that they shall act as before." But the players are to be "bound" not to repeat the *Game at Chess,* and the Lords are to continue their efforts to find out who was originally responsible for the production of the play.

As Middleton had "shifted out of the way," his son Edward was brought before the Council, but released with the injunction to attend again whenever required. There seems to be no reliable evidence for the story that Middleton himself was imprisoned because of the play, and freed on sending to the King a petition in humorous doggerel. It appears, then, that for this grave indiscretion the only punishment inflicted was the suppression of the company for about two weeks. This leniency is not hard to understand. The players and the poet were absolved from real responsibility by the license of the Master of the Revels, who was, in his turn, protected from serious consequences by his influence with the Lord Chamberlain. Moreover the King's Spanish policy was now reversed, Charles and Buckingham were in command, and the all-powerful "White Duke" must have looked kindly on the play which celebrated the course he was now guiding.

The eagerness with which the public welcomed dramatic representation of such vital current politics is strikingly evident in the great enthusiasm which greeted the *Game at Chess.* This is made vivid by a letter from Chamberlain to Carlton, dated August 21, 1624, in which he speaks of the "famous play of Gondomar, which hath been followed by all sorts of people, old and young, rich and poor, masters and servants, papists, wise men, &c., churchmen and Scotsmen." The exceptional applause which the play won was remembered as a stage tradition for many years. But the authorities continued to frown upon it, and the early printed editions apparently had to be issued surreptitiously, without license, for they are not entered in the Stationers' Register.

This instance is so clear that the point needs no labouring. It proves: (1) that current issues were presented on the stage; (2) that they were thinly disguised; (3) that the popularity of the play was largely dependent upon its topical nature; and (4) that interested "powers" connived at the practice, even though it was discovered and condemned by the King himself.

With this case very clearly in mind, I turn now for a brief notice of the earlier conflicts between the stage and the censor, and between the stage and the Privy Council, to see whether or not this problem of topical matter was an issue during the period which we are specially considering, 1585-1593. Again I quote from Dr. Gildersleeve *(op. cit.,* p. 4ff.):

When Henry VII ascended the throne in 1485, the drama was already flourishing in England. Mysteries were being performed in many towns and parishes, and moralities were common. Noblemen kept among their retainers companies of professional players, and the King himself had a company in his household. But in spite of all this dramatic activity, apparently no necessity for governmental censorship was yet felt. The regulation of plays seems to have been attended to satisfactorily enough by the local civil and ecclesiastical authorities. Not until the troubles of the Reformation and the policies of Henry VIII began to arouse a spirit of revolt among the people, did the royal government feel that there was anything to fear from the content of plays. Then it became evident that the religious nature of the drama at this time, coupled with the religious nature of the questions in dispute, made the stage a peculiarly dangerous weapon.

Most of the early "dangerous, seditious" plays have been lost, particularly the pro-Catholic ones, but the notices of them which have survived place their controversial nature beyond dispute. The following list includes plays on both sides:

1. John Roe's *Lord Gouvernaunce and Lady Publike-Wele,*

known as "the masque and goodly disguising of one John Roe, sergeant-at-arms," containing an attack on Wolsey and played at Gray's Inn in 1526. (E. K. Chambers, *Mediaeval Stage,* II, 219.) Sir William Cavendish says in his life of Wolsey that at no one were political satires and pasquinades launched more freely than at Wolsey, and he mentions his great sensitiveness in this respect. His general course was to endeavour to buy up all copies, a proceeding in which he was, of course, by no means notably successful. Concerning William Roy's *Rede Me and be nott Wrothe,* Cavendish further states that "Wolsey spared neither pains nor expense to have all bought up." This verse satire was by Jerome Barlow and William Roy, two Franciscan friars who wrote their satire in Strasburg. It is usually referred to as "Roy's Satire." (See, Hugh Walker, *English Satire and Satirists,* [London, 1925], pp. 40-45.)

2. Another of these plays satirising Wolsey was written by Simon Fish, a student at Gray's Inn, and, like Roe's play, performed in that place. The Cardinal was so infuriated at this performance that the youthful author had to "fly for his life to Germany." It was while on the continent that "young Fish wrote his *Supplication on Beggars* which, attacking the monastic orders of England, was read and so hugely enjoyed by Anne Boleyn that, showing it to the king, she caused him by her inimitable reading of such passages as echoed his Majesty's views relative to plundering the abbeys, to recall Fish and take him under his royal protection."

3. In the following year the St. Paul's boys acted before the ambassadors from France, a play on the Captivity of the Pope, in which the "herretyke Lewtar" was a character. (Chambers, *Mediaeval Stage,* II, p. 219.)

4. The release of the Pope a year later was dramatised and acted before Wolsey. (*Ibid.*)

5. *The Conflict of Conscience* by Nathaniel Wodes, a minister of Norwich, is described on its title page as "an excellent new Commedie Intituled: The Conflict of Conscience, Containinge, A most lamentable example, of the dolefull desperation of a miserable wordlinge, termed, by the name of Philologus, who forseeoke the trueth of God's Gospel, for feare of

the Losse of lyfe, & wordly goods." Sir Edmund Chambers says of this play *(Elizabethan Stage,* III, p. 517):

> The characters are allegorical, typical, and personal, and arranged for six actors 'most convenient for such as be disposed either to shew this Comedie in private houses or otherwise.' Philologus is Frances Spierd, a pervert to Rome about the middle of the sixteenth century. The play is strongly Protestant, and is probably much earlier than 1581.

6. *New Custome,* published in 1573, but probably dating from about the middle of the century, is a similar "moral of Protestant controversy, with typical personages, bearing allegorical names, arranged for four actors." *(Ibid.,* IV, p. 37.)

7. *Pammachius,* an antipapal play performed at Christ's College, Cambridge, under the very nose of the Loyal Chancellor, Bishop Gardiner. Parts of this "tragedie" were "soo pestiferous as 'twere intolerable!" (Chambers, *Mediaeval Stage,* II, p. 220.)

8. *King John,* possibly John Bale's famous play, performed at Cranmer's house in 1539. The performing of this piece of dictated orthodoxy before Cranmer is interestingly paralleled by the performance of Davidson's *Siege of Edinburgh Castle,* 1571, "quhilk," says James Melville, "I saw playit in Mr. Knox presence, wherein, according to Mr. Knox doctrine, the castell of Edinbruche was besieged, [by Mary's enemies] takin, and the Captan with an or two with him, hangit in effigie." (Chambers, *Elizabethan Stage,* III, pp. 283f.)

9. The plays of the two Wagers, (Lewis and W.), are also orthodox from the Protestant point of view, with biblical and allegorical characters, and, like *New Custome,* arranged for four or five actors. Both plays, *The Life and Repentance of Mary Magdalene* and *The Longer Thou Livest, the More Fool Thou Art,* are approximately the same date as *New Custome.*

10. *Enough Is As Good As a Feast* (c. 1560). Boas describes this play as "a morality with a controversial Protestant flavour."

11. *Lusty Juventus,* by W. Wever, probably in the reign of Edward VI. Hawkins (in Dodsley's *Old English Plays,* II, pp. 43-44) describes this play as follows:

> The design of this interlude is to expose the superstitions of the

Romish Church, and to promote the Reformation. The stage (as the learned Dr. Percy observes) in those days literally was what wise men have always wished it—a supplement to the pulpit. . . . From this play we learn that most of the young people were new gospellers, or friends of the Reformation; and that the old were tenacious of the doctrines imbibed in their youth, for thus the Devil is introduced lamenting the downfall of supersition:

The old people would believe still in my laws,
But the younger sort lead them a contrary way;
They will not believe, they plainly say,
In old traditions and made by men,
But they will live as the scripture teacheth them. . . .

A specimen speech from the lips of Hypocrisy will convince the reader of the truth of these observations:

[*Hypocrisy, bragging of his work to the Devil*]:

I have brought up such superstition,
Under the name of holiness and religion,
That deceived almost all.
As holy cardinals, holy popes,
Holy vestments, holy copes,
Holy hermits and friars,
Holy priests, holy bishops,
Holy monks, holy abbots,
Yea, and all obstinate liars:
Holy pardons, holy beads,
Holy saints, holy images,
Holy body, holy blood,
Holy stocks, holy stones,
Holy clouts, holy bones;
Yea, and holy holy wood.
Holy skins, holy bulls,
Holy rochets and cowls,
Holy crouches and staves,
Holy hoods, holy caps,
Holy mitres, holy hats;
All good holy holy knaves
Holy days, holy fastings,
Holy twitching, holy tastings,
Holy visions and sights,
Holy wax, holy lead,
Holy water, holy bread,
To drive away spirits.
Holy fire, holy balm,
Holy oil, holy cream,
And holy ashes also;
Holy brooches, holy rings,
Holy kneeling, holy censings,
And a hundred trim-tram mo.
Holy crosses, holy bells,
Holy relics, holy jewels,
Of mine own invention:
Holy candles, holy paters,
Holy parchments, holy papers:
Had not you a holy son?

12. *The Interlude of Youth* (c. 1554). Of this play John P. Collier says (Dodsley, *op. cit.*, II, p. 4):

The *Interlude of Youth* is decidedly a Roman Catholic production, and I have therefore little doubt that it made its appearance during the reign of Mary. . . . On the whole, this piece is one of the most amusing and most humorous of the class to which it belongs.

Halliwell also praises it warmly as "probably the most interesting early-printed moral play that has descended to our times." The precise dates of these plays cannot be established, but it seems as if the *Interlude of Youth* were an answer to *Lusty Juventus*. Youth is here made to swagger rudely; with violence he sweeps aside Charity, who pleads with him for the better cause. Thus Youth:

Aback, fellows, and give me room,
Or I shall make you to avoid soon!
I am goodly of person;
I am peerless, wherever I come,
My name is Youth, I tell thee,
I flourish as the vine-tree:
Who may be likened unto me,
In my youth and jollity?
My hair is royal and bushed thick;
My body pliant as a hazel-stick;
Mine arms be both big and strong,
My fingers be both fair and long;
My chest big as a tun,
My legs be full light for to run;
To hop and dance, and make merry;
By the mass, I reck not a cherry,
Whatsoever I do!
I am the heir of all my father's land,
And it is come into my hand:
I care for no more.

13. *A Religious Interlude of St. Thomas the Apostle,* which was written and exploited by "certain Papists" at York for the sake of creating a protest. The King forthwith commanded the Justice to arrest and imprison "any papists who shall, in performing interludes which are founded on any portions of the Old or New Testament, say or make use of any language which may tend to excite those who are beholding the same to any breach of the peace." (Gildersleeve, *op. cit.,* p. 7.) Perhaps the "Papists of York," Wolsey's own See, hated him with a special

fury. Miss Strickland tells us that "Wolsey was hated furiously throughout England because he was supposed to be the originator of the divorce, and one of the popular rhymes of the day sets forth public indignation at the wrongs of the people's darling [Princess Mary]. This rhyme concludes:

> The Carter of York is meddling
> For to divorce them asunder.

This play of *Thomas the Apostle* is particularly interesting as showing the early use of biblical setting and situations as fustian for current issues. We shall have occasion to note many such "fictions" in the course of this study.

A word of explanation regarding the use of the word *fustian* may, perhaps, be timely. The trick of saying one thing and meaning another, of using an historical or mythological episode as a cloak to cover some personal or political allusion, became, as we shall see, a stock device of the dramatists for avoiding trouble with the censor. It went by many names; Cinthio called his little political allegories *myths;* his volume, so often rifled by the English poets, was entitled *Hecatomythi.* Spenser, Chapman, and Lodge used another learned name for the device, the Greek word for masque, *Prosopopoiea.* Lyly called it *Calamance* (see p. 67); but by far the most popular Elizabethan word for it was *fustian.* This word was originally used to designate a coarse cloth made in Holland, often called *Dutch Fustian,* and much affected by the English for topcoats and ulsters. Hence when one said "Absalom" and "Achitophel" when he really meant, as Dryden later did, Monmouth and Shaftesbury, he was said to be hiding under a fustian. Hence any jargon or made-up language for which a gloss was required was called *fustian.* In *Doctor Faustus,* for instance, when Wagner begins to spout Latin to the clown, the latter exclaims: "God forgive me, he speaks Dutch fustian." *Every Man Out Of His Humour* furnishes another example. Clove says: "Monsieur Orange, yon gallants observe us; prithee let's talk fustian a little and gull them." In his dictionary published in 1598, Florio defines *Monelle* as "a roguish or fustian word, a word in pedlar's French, signifying wenches." But *Cynthia's Revels* furnishes the best illustration of the use of the word in precisely the sense in which I use it in this book. The "Third Child" announces: "First, the title of this play is Cynthia's Revels, as any man that hath hope to be saved by his book can witness; the scene Gargaphie, *which I do vehemently suspect for some fustian country.*" [Italics inserted.] I believe that, on the whole, this old sixteenth century word is an apter one for describing the device under consideration than any of the more academic ones in use among modern scholars, such as *topical matter* or *propaganda* or *allegory.**

It is hardly possible to overestimate the contribution made by these early topical plays to the development of the drama. Much, probably too much, has been said of the liturgical ancestor of the drama, to the neglect of its didactic branch. Critics never weary of elaborating on the none-too-sure connection between antiphonal singing and dramatic dialogue, but they rarely allude even by name to the scores of plays that illustrate the certain combination of political or religious propaganda with the "honest mirth" and "comic inventions" to be found so commonly in the moralities of the 60's and 70's. Of course, the degree of didacticism varies all the way from the general to the particular, from types to persons, and from vice to specific crimes, and it is often difficult to say where the allegorical morality ends and the propaganda begins. It is probably for this reason that so many critics have failed to note that an important change in literary fashion was achieved when the subject of the plays ceased to be general causes and became particular issues, when the characters ceased to be abstracts and became rather definite human personages who embodied some precise evil practice that needed correction. Professor George Saintsbury *(Short History of English Literature,* p. 227) has expressed the same protest. He says of those critics who underestimate the importance of plays like *King John* "on the plea that it is only a didactic interlude with a historical subject":

This seems a little hard, for Bale is surely entitled to the credit of seeing that the didactic interlude—that is to say, the play in the only

* For a more detailed exposition of this term "fustian," and of its sixteenth century usage, the reader is referred to my "Reply to Professor Tucker-Brooke," in the *Shakspere Association Bulletin,* vol. xiv, no. 1, January, 1939, pp. 57-59.

state it had then reached—was capable of being applied to historical subjects, and so becoming the historic play in time.

It is to be noted that these situations and characters were no less real because the dramatists, Nathan-like, fearing the wrath of some sinful David, often found it expedient to present them under cover of a parable or historical parallel.*

The style of the non-controversial play is so precisely similar to that of the more specifically motived interlude, that only a careful reading will reveal "the distinction which makes all the difference." Compare, for instance, the early *King Darius,* a non-controversial morality, dating from about 1565, with the definitely Protestant *Apius and Virginia* (approximately 1556). In both cases genuine dramatic characters, i.e., historical or legendary figures, appear side by side with the conventional "vice," (called Iniquitie in *Darius,* and Haphazard in *Apius and Virginia),* which the dramatist was at first obliged to offer in order to prevail upon his audience to attend to the main theme. Whatever the motive behind these early Tudor interludes, the formula for them is ever the same—instruction plus entertainment. The title pages which illustrate this fact are legion; they comprise an outline of the plot, plus an assurance of diverting side shows. A few examples will illustrate:

1. *Common Conditions*: "An excellent and pleasant Comedie, termed after the name of the Vice, Common Conditions, drawne out of the most famous historie of Galiarbus Duke of Arabia, and of the good and evill successe of him and his two children, Sedmond his son and Clarissa his daughter; Set foorth with delectable mirth, and pleasant shewes."

2. *Jacob and Esau*: "A newe and merry and wittie Comedie or Enterlude, newly imprinted, treating vpon the Historie of Iacob and Esau, taken out of the xxvii Chap. of the first booke of Moses, called Genesis."

3. *Locrine*: "The Lamentable Tragedie of Locrine, the eldest sonne of King Brutus, discoursing the warres of the Britaines, and Hunnes, with their discomfitures: The Britaines

* The best of all discussions of the Elizabethan use of historical parallel as fustian for current issues is by Miss Lily B. Campbell, whose observations are published in the *Huntington Library Quarterly,* January, 1938, pp. 135ff.

victorie with their Accidents, and the death of Albanact. No lesse pleasant then profitable."

4. *Cambyses*: "A Lamentable Tragedie mixed full of pleasant mirth containing the life of Cambyses King of Persia."

5. Francis Merbury's *The Marriage between Wit and Wisdom* (c. 1579): "Very fruitfull and mixed full of pleasant mirth as well in the beholders as the Readers or Hearers."

6. *Three Lords and Three Ladies of London*: "The Pleasant and Stately Morall, of the three Lordes and three Ladies of London. With the great Joy and Pompe, Solemnized at their Marriages: Comically interlaced with much honest Mirth, for pleasure and recreation, among many Morall observations and other important matters of due regard."

There has, of course, never been any doubt concerning this pattern of profit with pleasure in the early moralities, but what we do need to emphasize is the growing prevalence of the propaganda element. Indeed, even in plays as late as the early seventeenth century, the propaganda was often enough the real *raison d'etre* of the piece. We may infer that this was the case in the play of William Alabaster, Essex's chaplain in the Cadiz expedition of 1596. On 22 September, 1597, Richard Percival wrote to Sir Robert Cecil (Hatfield MSS, xii, 394), "Alabaster has made a tragedy against the Church of England" and Chamberlain (7, 64) records that he was "clapt up for poperie," but had escaped from the Clink by 4 May, 1598. As late as 1614 Sir John York, with his wife and brother, was similarly fined and imprisoned for having at his house a private performance of a "scandalous play acted in favour of Popery," in which the Devil declared that all Protestants were eternally lost, and carried King James off on his back to the fiery lower regions. (Gildersleeve, *op. cit.*, p. 113.) The authors of these plays were punished, not because they presented current interests under a fustian, but because their presentation was hostile to the existing regime. On the other hand, plays like Dekker's *Whore of Babylon,* the anonymous *Famous Victories,* or the *Troublesome Reign,* all dealing with Catholic intrigues against Elizabeth, and bitterly antipapal, were, so far as we know, in spite of their violence and crudity, never reprimanded by authority.

The result of this bold propaganda on the stage was, at first, general legislation against the practice, and finally a definite system of censorship. Perhaps the first definite legislation concerning the content of plays is to be found in Statutes 34 and 35 of Henry VIII, cap. i, passed in 1543, entitled "An act for the advancement of true religion and for the abolishment of the contrary." *(Statutes of the Realm,* III, 894, quoted by Gildersleeve, *op. cit.,* p. 7.) This is a general declaration against seditious utterances, but it makes a special condemnation of "printed books, printed ballads, plays, rhymes, songs, and other fantasies."

A more direct blow at the stage was contained in a proclamation issued by Queen Mary in 1553, August 18, forbidding all critically disposed persons to preach "after their own brains, and by playing of interludes and printing of false, fond books, ballads, rhymes, and other lewd treatises in the English tongue, concerning doctrines in matters now in question and controversy." Like Statutes 34 and 35 of Henry VIII, this was also intended as "an act for the advancement of true religion and for the abolition of the contrary"; only the reader must keep in mind that Mary's notions of the "true religion" were not those of her father. Both proclamations, however, were meant to condemn the practice of dealing with the problem of the Anglican schism on the stage, in the pulpit, and in printed tracts, ballads, and songs.

Nevertheless, the "abuse" continued, all through the reigns of Henry VIII, Edward VI, and Mary, and, as we shall see presently, throughout the Elizabethan and Jacobean eras. Various disciplinary tactics were tried. For instance, on 6 August, 1549, a royal proclamation announced a suspension of all theatrical activity "in the English tongue" for a space of three months. The wording of this proclamation is of special interest to us *(ibid.,* pp. 9-10):

> For asmuche as a greate number of those that be common Plaiers of Enterludes and Plaies, as well within the citie of London, as els where within the realme, do *for the moste part plaie suche Interludes as contain matter tendyng to sedicion and contempnyng of sundery good orders and lawes,* [italics inserted] where upon are growen, and daily are like to growe and ensue, muche disquiet, division, tumultes, and uproares in this realm; the Kynges Maiestie . . .

straightly chargeth and commaundeth al and every his Maiesties subjectes . . . that from the ix day of this present moneth of August untill the feast of all Sainctes nexte comming, thei ne any of them, openly or secretly plaie in the English tongue any kynd of Interlude, Plaie, Dialogue or other matter set furthe in forme of Plaie in any place publique or private within this realme, upon pain that whosoever shall plaie in Englishe any such Play, Interlude, or other matter, shall suffre imprisonment, and further punishment at the pleasure of his Maiestie.

The three months penance was soon a thing of the past, and the abuse went on as merrily as before. The next attempt at control was the inauguration of a system of license. Under this new regulation, no "common players or other persons, upon like paines" (imprisonment and fine, as in the case of printing unlicensed books) were to be allowed "to play in thenglish tong, any maner Enterlude, play or mattre, without they have special license to shew for the same in writing under his maiesties signe, or signed by vi of his highnes' priuie counsaill." (*Ibid.*, pp. 9-10.) This was obviously a clumsy, not to say an impossible, mechanism of control, for it is certain that the Privy Council could not supervise the texts of all the plays given in the realm, and it is at least unlikely that the managers of public companies would wait about patiently while the text went the round of the six members, awaiting the leisure of each. *The Acts of the Privy Council* from this time forth, however, furnish abundant proof of their attempt to exercise some sort of control. Often enough, however, the real responsibility for the licensing and the task of penalizing fell to the lot of the Justices of the Peace and other local officials. Again and again the proclamations make it clear that the cause of offense in the plays is that they contain "very naughty and seditious matter" touching the state of the realm and the Church. Church and State—these were the subjects upon which criticism on the stage was taboo, be it disguised under any device or allegory whatsoever. It seems incredible to us now that any such criticism, however obvious, could arouse an audience to the pitch of making a disorderly, even riotous demonstration of its sympathetic concurrence; but the evidence that the plays did have this effect is overwhelming. We have already referred to the seditious rising in the city of York at the performance of the "interlude of St. Thomas the Apostle" and to the riots preceding the Interdict of 6 August, 1549. Similar disorders in 1556 caused the Council to direct the Lord President of the North to suppress all "playes, enterludes, songues, or any such lyke pastymes whereby the people may any wayes be steryd to disordre." (*Ibid.,* p. 11.) Of course, every Elizabethan scholar is familiar with the troubles attendant upon the playing of *Richard II* with seditious intent to rouse the people to a demonstration in behalf of Essex, but a full discussion of this play is reserved for a later section.

Dr. Gildersleeve sums up the whole mass of pre-Elizabethan legislation on this subject by observing *(ibid.,* p. 13) that "the censoring was concerned with suppressing sedition and heresy—anything likely to stir up political revolt—and not with matters of decency or morality."

With the accession of Elizabeth, the policies of control became at once more vigorous and more consistent. Almost her first act was to prohibit plays altogether until she had organized a more feasible system of licensing. Her next step was to settle the responsibility for censorship, not upon the Privy Council, but upon the mayor of each city or town, or, in the country districts, upon the lieutenants of the shire. Her proclamation of 16 May, 1559 stated *(ibid.,* p. 15):

> And for instruction of euery of the sayde officers, her Maiestie doth likewise charge euery of them as they will aunswere: that they permyt none to be played, wherein either matters of religion or of the governance of the estate of the commõ weale shalbe handled, or treated; . . .

Imprisonment for fourteen days or more was to be the penalty for disobedience.

Her next step was to bring the London companies under even stricter surveillance by requiring them to submit all their plays to the Master of the Revels before performing them either in London or in the provinces. This responsibility and privilege (for it involved a fee for each licensing act) was secured to the Master by patent in 1581. Dr. Gildersleeve observes (*ibid.,* p. 17):

Since the licensing of plays was a profitable business, it was to the interest of the Master to develop this authority as extensively as possible. This he began straightway to do; but it would be folly to suppose that this patent created at once any revolution in the censoring of the drama. It was years before the Master's licensing authority was thoroughly established in and about London. It could never have been established throughout the rest of the kingdom. But it grew steadily during all our period.

For some time it is clear that the Master acted with the help of the Mayor and the Archbishop of Canterbury. Their constant intention was to permit only such plays "as were fitted to yield honest recreation and no example of evil," ever striking out and reforming "such parts and matters" as they found "unfit and undecent to be handled in plays both for Divinity and State." *(Ibid.,* p. 18.) Dr. Gildersleeve observes that, as a matter of fact, Tilney, the Master of the Revels from 1579 to 1610, does not seem to have established his supreme power in the licensing of plays until the beginning of the seventeenth century. This fact may, probably does, account for the official appearance of comparatively few well-established cases of topical matter in the early Elizabethan plays. It was not that they did not exist, but that the censor had not yet developed a thorough system of detection and apprehension of offenders. So much for the cause and fact and nature of the censorship.

CHAPTER TWO

The Procuring of Plays

WE TURN NOW TO A CONSIDERATION of the play-producing problem from the point of view of the players. It must be clear to the reader by now that the stage was used consciously for propaganda but that, especially in matters of Church and State, every effort was being made to condemn and prohibit the practice. It may perhaps be doubted if the players themselves had these matters so keenly at heart on their own behalf. "Honest recreation" and hard cash are perfectly good professional motives. But again and again the early references to propaganda plays indicate that some persons of high authority or quality "procured" such and such a play to be played, thus combining the simple professional motives of the players with their own more devious intent of presenting propaganda. Such a practice is, of course, to be expected in plays and entertainments given at private houses, of which there is abundant record. The *Device* for the Queen's Day (17 Nov., 1595) furnishes an excellent illustration, in that it provides evidence: first, that Essex procured Bacon to write the entertainment for him; second, that the "show" represented Essex's own suit to Elizabeth; and third, that the satire in it was recognized by the audience as directed against the Cecils. The play or playlet took place "partly in the tilt-yard, partly after supper." It is described as follows by Sir Edmund Chambers *(Elizabethan Stage,* III, p. 214):

> Before the entry of the tilters a page made a speech and secured the Queen's glove. A dialogue followed between a Squire on one hand, and a Hermit, a Secretary, and a Soldier, who on the entry of Essex tried to beguile him from love. A postboy brought letters, which the Secretary gave to Essex. After supper, the argument between the Squire and the three tempters was resumed.

Apparently the Queen was annoyed by the performance, for she said, upon retiring, that "if she had thought there had been so much said of her, she would not have been there that night"; so Rowland Whyte records, *(Sidney Papers,* I, 362), and he adds, "The old man [the Hermit] was he that in Cambridge played Giraldy; Morley played the Secretary; and he that plaid Pedantiq was the soldier; and Toby Matthew acted the Squires part. The world makes many untrue constructions of these speaches, comparing the Hermit and the Secretary to two of the Lords; and the soldier to Sir Roger Williams." Sir Edmund is certainly right in identifying the two lords as Burleigh and Cecil. The Queen frequently addressed Burleigh as "Sir Eremite of Tyball," and in 1594 Cecil (Sir Robert) had based his whole entertainment, on the occasion of the Queen's visit to Theobald's, upon this conceit.

Miss Strickland says (*Life of Queen Elizabeth* [London, 1867], p. 480):

> The character was chosen in allusion to one of the queen's playful letters to Burleigh, in which she styles him the Eremite of Tibbals, and addresses him as "Sir Eremite." In the course of his long hyperbolical speech the hermit addresses this absurd flattery to the royal sexagenarian: "But that which most amazeth me, to whose long experience nothing can seem strange, is that with these same eyes do I behold you the self-same queen, in the same estate of person, strength, and beauty in which so many years past I beheld you, finding no alteration but in admiration; insomuch that I am persuaded, when I look about me on your train, that time, which catcheth everybody, leaves only you untouched."

Whether or not "the world" was correct in its interpretation of these speeches, the fact that such a suggestion was made is an important bit of evidence concerning the prevalence of topicality in court plays. The speeches for this apparently tedious device are to be found in Lambeth MS v, 118 in Bacon's handwriting, though it is possible that Essex himself had a hand in their composition. Sir Henry Wotton, Essex's secretary at this date, says *(Reliquiae Wottonianae,* 21): "For his [Essex's] Writings, they are beyond example, especially in his things of delight at Court . . . as may be yet seen in his Impresses and Inventions of entertainment; and above all in his darling piece of love and self love." But, as Sir Edmund points out, "it is hard to distinguish the literary productions of a public man from those of his staff." Later, when Bacon himself became a "great man," on more than one occasion he caused masks and entertainments to be written by others, but to be directed and financed by himself. Thomas Churchyard is another poet whose services were often engaged by noblemen for providing plays, pageants and, as we shall see later, satirical lampoons. He tells us that he wrote "the devices of warre and a play at Awsterly, Her Highness being at Sir Thomas Gresham's," and among works procured from him by friends whom he is "loath to offend," he includes *(Churchyard's Challenge,* 1593):

> . . . a book of a sumptuous shew in Shrouetide, by Sir Walter Rawley, Sir Robart Carey, M. Chidley, and M. Arthur Gorge, in which book was the whole seruice of my L. of Lester mencioned that he and his traine did in Flaunders, and the gentlemen Pencioners proued to be a great peece of honor to the Court; all which book was in as good verse as euer I made: an honorable knight, dwelling in the Black Friers, can witness the same, because I read vnto him.*

This instance is of special interest, as it shows that Sir Walter Ralegh was one of those who procured a play to be written, perhaps even preparing the "Argument," apparently in direct answer to the avalanche of adverse criticism of Leicester's conduct of affairs in Flanders. We know on other grounds (Ralegh's letter to Leicester, 29 March, 1586), that Ralegh was engaged at this time in inducing the Queen to take a more favourable view of Leicester's actions. It is possible that it was from Leicester that Ralegh got the idea of using the stage for the advertisement of special points of view, though, indeed, he could have got it anywhere; it was as general as the air. The connection between *The Woodstock Entertainment* of 1575 and Leicester's suit has been so generally recognized that it will not be amiss to notice it here, even though there is no contemporary evidence for particular identifications other than Loricus for Sir Henry Lee. The contemporary description (Nichols *Progresses of Queen Elizabeth,* I, p. 590) takes the form of a letter from an eyewitness. (I follow Professor Pollard in believing this eye-

* For a notice of a possible relation between Churchyard and Marlowe, see, Alwin Thaler, *Churchyard and Marlowe, MLN,* 1923, pp. 89ff.

witness to be the author Gascoigne.) The play is called *The Tale of Hemetes the Heremyte.* In the beginning Hemetes has just interrupted a fight between Loricus and Contarenus whom he brings, together with the Lady Caudina, to a bower where Elizabeth is placed, and then begins his Tale, of which the writer says:

He shewed a great proofe of his audacity, in which tale if you marke the woords with this present world, or were acquainted with the state of the deuises, you should find no lesse hidden then vttered, and no lesse vttered then shoulde deserue a double reading ouer, euen of those (with whom I finde you a companion) that haue disposed their houres to the study of great matters.

Upon this hint, the Queen

. . . left earnest command that the whole in order as it fell, should be brought to her in writing, which being done, as I heare, she vsed, besides her own skill, the helpe of the deuisors, & how thinges were made I know not, but sure I am her Maiesty hath often in speech some part hereof with mirth at the remembrance.

The *Tale* was followed by a short comedy, in 991 lines of verse, in which Occanon comes to seek Caudina, [Leicester's wife?] who is persuaded by his arguments and the mediation of Eambia, the Fairy Queen, to give up her lover for her country's sake. In this little drama, we are told "that her Graces passions and other the Ladies could not* . . . shew it selfe in open place more than euer hath beene seene."

The deposition of Augustine Phillips, Shakspere's friend and fellow member of the Lord Chamberlain's company, concerning the supposedly seditious performance of *Richard II,* furnishes an illustration of a later date. The deposition runs (*State Papers, Elizabethan, Domestic,* 1598-1601, p. 578):

February 18
On Thursday or Friday seven-night, Sir Charles Percy, Sir Josceline Percy, Lord Monteagle and several others spoke to some of the players to play the deposing and killing of King Richard and promised to give them 40 shillings more than their ordinary to do so.

This action closely parallels that of Hamlet "procuring" the

* Sir Edmund Chambers (*Elizabethan Stage,* III, p. 402) inserts a hypothetical "but." I believe the sense is correct as it stands.

players, who were apparently bent on "honest recreation" and a livelihood, to include in their performance the highly objectionable topical matter concerning Claudius' murder of the king. In both cases the players were well remunerated for the risk they took. A similar instance is furnished by the *Interlude* at Stirling Castle some time before 14 May, 1567, though our information does not make it clear that the performers were professional. On that date Drury wrote to Cecil:*

> There has been an interlude of boys at Stirling of the manner of the King's death and the arraignment of the earl. . . . This was before the Lords, who the Earl thinks were devisers of the same.

This is obviously an interesting parallel to the *Hamlet* episode and may easily have suggested the whole device to Shakspere. That a play "to catch the conscience" was a fairly common device, is well established by a passage in Heywood's *Apology for Actors.* (Chambers, *Elizabethan Stage,* IV, p. 253.) Concerning the proposition that "plays have discovered murders" he says:

> We will prove it by a domestike and home-borne truth, which within these few years happened. At Lin, in Norfolke, the then Earl of Sussex players acting the Old History of Feyer Francis' drove a townswoman to confess the murder of her husband in circumstances parallel to those of the play. . . . Another story of a woman who had driven a nail into her husband's brain, urged to remorse by a similar incident in "the last part of the Four Sons of Aymon" played by "a company of our English comedians (well knowne)" at Amsterdam.

We have noted the fact that Cranmer had the Protestant *King John* played at his house in 1539, and Cromwell is said to have "found the stage a convenient weapon in the Protestant cause." (Gildersleeve, *op. cit.,* p. 6.) The practice went even further than these illustrations indicate. Many, if indeed one may not say almost all, important noblemen actually maintained one or two poets, often actually in residence, whose precise duty it was to invent these fustian actions and put them into

* Quoted from Miss Lilian Winstanley, *Macbeth, King Lear and Contemporary History* (Cambridge, 1922), p. 87. It is curious that Miss Winstanley makes so little of this parallel in her volume on *Hamlet and the Scottish Succession* (Cambridge, 1921).

dramatic shape. The reader will not need the reminder of the presence of such a poet among the followers of Timon of Athens. Of Thomas Watson, who entered upon his literary career under the patronage of Walsingham during his residence in Paris, 1581-82, William Cornwallis wrote to Heneage that he "could devise twenty fictions and knaveryes in a play, which was his daily practice and his living." (Chambers, *Elizabethan Stage,* III, p. 506.) Years after Watson's death, Harington was accused of aping his tricks in the spurious etymologies offered in the *Metamorphosis of Ajax*. In *Ulysses Upon Ajax,* Harington's anonymous critic says:

> . . . faith, they [the fustian etymologies] are trivial, the froth of witty Tomas Watson's jests, I heard them in Paris fourteen years ago; besides, what balductum [trashy] play is not full of them?

That is, he heard them in Paris when Watson was in the service of Walsingham. In a similar capacity Bacon was attached to Essex; Chapman to Nottingham and then to Somerset; Daniel to Sir Edward Stafford and later to Mary, Lady Pembroke; Massinger to the Earl of Pembroke; Nashe to Lord Strange (later fourth Earl of Derby), Sir George Carey, and Archbishop Whitgift successively; Munday, as well as Lyly, to the Earl of Oxford; Lodge to the fifth Earl of Derby, and so forth. Indeed, the domestic poet was anything but unusual, though obviously there were many poets who preferred—or found it more remunerative—not to be tied so closely to one patron that they could not write for others when invited to do so. Jonson's long list of special patrons (Lady Mary Wroth, William, Earl of Pembroke, Sir Francis Stuart, and others), seems to imply that he belonged to the more independent group. Given such a relationship, with a well-established tradition of topicality upon the stage, it is hardly possible to overestimate the difficulty of the censor's problem.

CHAPTER THREE

The Censor at Work

THE PRACTICE OF STAGE PROPAGANDA was not to be given up lightly, either by the persons of quality who had some cause to present, or by the players who found these plays on local or current issues much the most popular of all in their repertoire. The question was how to go on playing them without colliding with the censor. The use of fustian upon the stage was not a new idea, as we have already seen; but as the century wore on and as the Master got the situation better in hand, the practice developed into an astonishing elaboration and subtlety. A play by Massinger licensed in 1631 when, under the new regime, the censorship was slightly relaxed, furnishes a striking example of the author's procedure and the censor's attitude. The following account of the play is taken from Professor Charles J. Sisson's edition of *Believe As You List* for the Malone Society, 1927:

The play is first mentioned by Sir Henry Herbert, Master of the Revels, in his Office Book: "This day being the 11 of Janu. 1630, I did refuse to allow of a play of Massinger's because itt did contain dangerous matter, as the deposing of Sebastian King of Portugal, by Phillip the (Second), and ther being a peace sworen twixte the kings of England and Spayne" (*Variorum*, iii, 229-31). Herbert does not give the name of the play, but the most cursory examination of this manuscript shows that Herbert is referring to the first draft of *Believe As You List*. The play was revised by Massinger, who substituted the story of Antiochus for that of Sebastian, and it was again submitted to Herbert, in the form of the present manuscript. It had possibly already been prepared for acting by a stage adapter, and the parts assigned and learned. Herbert licensed it unconditionally on 6 May, 1631: "This Play, called Beleiue as you liste, may be acted, this 6. of May, 1631. Henry Herbert."

The reasons for this reversal of judgment on the part of the Master are set forth by Professor Sisson:

The play originally dealt with the adventures of Sebastian, King of Portugal ('the late, & sad example' hinted at in the Prologue, 1. 5), who led an army into Africa and was there believed to have perished in 1578 at the Battle of Alcacer-el-Kebir in Morocco.*

Two years later Philip II of Spain annexed Portugal. Various pretenders arose, claiming to be the lost king and finding support among the discontented Portuguese. Of these the most notable appeared at Venice in 1598. He seems to have persuaded the Republic to admit his pretensions, but was driven thence on the complaint of the Spanish Ambassador. After a chequered career in various countries he was finally executed by Philip III in 1603. He seems to have been a Calabrian named Marco Tullio. His adventures were accompanied by a great deal of publicity and propaganda and by the avid journalism of the time both in the press and on the stage. . . .

* Recognizable to English ears as the Battle of Alcazar. The "general reader" may be grateful for the following brief note concerning Sebastian from the *Encyclopedia Britannica,* 11th ed., p. 566:

"Sebastian, king of Portugal (1554-1578), the posthumous son of Prince John of Portugal and of his wife Joanna, daughter of the emperor Charles, was born in 1554, and became king in 1557, on the death of his grandfather John III of Portugal. . . . He grew up resolved to emulate the medieval knights who had reconquered Portugal from the Moors. He was a mystic and a fanatic, whose sole ambition was to lead a crusade against the Mahommedans in the north-west Africa. He entrusted the government to the Jesuits; refused either to summon the Cortes or to marry, although the Portuguese crown would otherwise pass to a foreigner, and devoted himself wholly to hunting, martial exercises, and the severest forms of asceticism. His first expedition to Morocco, in 1574, was little more than a reconnaissance; in a second expedition Sebastian was killed and his army annihilated at Al Kasr al Kebir (4 August, 1578). Although his body was identified before burial at Al Kasr, reinterred at Ceuta, and thence (1582) removed by Philip II of Spain to the Convento dos Jeronymos in Lisbon, many Portuguese refused to credit his death. 'Sebastianism' became a religion. Its votaries believed that the *rei encuberto,* or 'hidden king,' was either absent on a pilgrimage, or like King Arthur in Avalon, was awaiting the hour of his second advent in an enchanted island. Four pretenders to the throne successively impersonated Sebastian; the first two, known from their places of birth as the 'King of Penamacor' and the 'King of Ericeira,' were of peasant origin; they were captured in 1584 and 1585 respectively. The third, Gabriel Espinosa, was a man of some education, whose adherents included members of the Austrian and Spanish courts and of the Society of Jesus in Portugal. He was executed in 1594. The fourth was a Calabrian named Marco Tullio, who knew no Portuguese; he impersonated the 'hidden King' at Venice in 1603 and gained many supporters, but was ultimately captured and executed."

English interest in this unfortunate king was especially keen because of his connection with the famous (or infamous) Tom Stuckly, English adventurer and traitor, who commanded the centre in the battle of Alcazar and who was killed there in 1578.

[Meanwhile] circumstances had changed considerably between 1601 and 1631. The Spanish Alliance, however unpopular, became an accomplished fact and an established policy under James I, and after an interval of fresh war, peace had again been declared in 1630, Charles I giving way upon the question of the Palatinate. Now the story of Sebastian accused Spain of usurpation and tyranny, and might be interpreted to accuse Charles of pusillanimity in his refusal to succour Frederick of Bohemia, husband of his sister Elizabeth, against Spain and the Emperor. The survival of the word Batavian (1279) lends colour to this view. Such a play would be intolerable to Charles on both counts. On revision the play was transformed into a story of a Syrian king reported to have been overthrown by Rome in Achaia and to have fallen in battle.

The new hero is the Seleucid king known to history as Antiochus the Great, whose conquests in Asia rivalled those of Alexander. . . . In the revolts of his vassals that followed his defeat by the Romans, Antiochus was believed to have perished in Luristan, in 187, though varying accounts of his death are given.

It is evident that, of the "bookes tost and turnde to make it up" (Prologue (15-16) by Massinger), Raleigh's *History of the World* was the chief, though he consulted Plutarch, and possibly also Livy, Diodorus, and Justin, all of whom were available in English as well as in the original. The events related in these histories are skilfully adapted to enable Antiochus to be substituted for Sebastian as far as possible. Plutarch's story of the betrayal of Hannibal to the Romans by Prusian, king of Bithynia, is transferred to Antiochus with this intent. There is no authority for his supposed escape from death, his sojourn in India, his return, and his persecution by the Romans. But this was an essential part of the story of Sebastian and Spain. In the play Antiochus therefore re-appears after twenty years spent in a desert, and seeks recognition and help first from his old ally Carthage, then in Bithynia, and finally, after persecution by the Roman ambassador to Carthage, comes into the power of a great Roman official who, with his wife, was formerly associated with him. Thus Carthage corresponds to Venice, Bithynia to Florence, Marcellus and Cornelia to the Duke and Duchess of Medina Sidonia, the Stoic to the Hermit, and Berecinthius to Sampayo, as the story is told in the various accounts of Sebastian. The hero is represented as a genuine king and a persecuted martyr.

The revision was carried out by Massinger himself, as is obvious, and the manuscript shows the clearest examples both of such errors as arise in a transcript of existing copy, and such corrections as occur in free original composition, as the notes to the passages point out. These two types of correction will serve to indicate which parts of the play were taken over verbatim, and which were written as substitutes for deleted parts of the first draft. For example, the part of Berecinthius seems to have been newly composed in the main. Massinger had apparently endeavoured to save himself trouble as much as possible. For instance, the proper names chosen are such as may serve as the metrical equivalent of the disused name, Antiochus for Sebastian, Carthage for Venice, and even Demetrius, the chirurgeon, for Sebastian Nero.

Further instances of name substitution for the sake of discretion may be seen in the change of Oldcastle to Falstaff (see Part II, pp. 253ff.) and in the timely substitution of "the Grand Turk" for "the King of Scots," said by Barnabe Rich to be possessed of a devil Balthaser. (See the Conclusion to *Riche His Farewell to Militarie Profession,* 1581.) The change was made in the first edition appearing after the accession of James.

I have submitted this full description of *Believe As You List,* (a broad hint title like *As You Like It,* or *What You Will*—with the additional advantage of being ambiguous—i.e., believe as you list about the pretender's claim), not because it is a better case of fustian than many another, but because it shows better than almost any other instance the attitude of the censor toward the use of fustian. Not only did Herbert allow the play in its revised state, though seeing through the whole process of disguise, but the corrections in the revision show that he even cooperated in the business as far as possible. Professor Sisson *(op. cit.* xx,) says: "It is clear . . . that the censor could be helpful as well as critical, and was prepared on occasion to mend what he had marred." Compare the statement of Sir Edmund Chambers *(Elizabethan Stage,* III, p. 233) concerning the MS corrections in Beaumont's *Faithful Friends:* "The MS is in various hands, one of which has made corrections. Some of these seem on internal evidence to have been due to suggestions of the censor." We shall have many occasions to note similar cases in the course of this study.

Be it remembered in this case that Massinger, like Shakspere, wrote for the Pembroke party (Gildersleeve, *op. cit.,* p. 123); that is, he was interested in presenting affairs from the point of view of his patrons, the Herberts, Earls of Pembroke and Montgomery, the "noble pair of brethren" to whom the first folio of Shakspere was dedicated.* Now at the time of the licensing of *Believe As You List,* the Lord Chamberlain of England was this same William Herbert, Earl of Pembroke, and he was the close relative and immediate patron of Sir Henry Herbert, the Master of the Revels. As Dr. Gildersleeve points out *(op. cit.,* p. 19), "the hierarchy of dramatic rulers ran —King, Privy Council, Lord Chamberlain, Master of the Revels; and all the higher powers interfered at will, though for the most part they left the exercise of authority to the Master, the Servant of the Crown." It seems fair, then, to infer that Sir Henry was entirely willing to allow the servant of his great and powerful relative, the Lord Chamberlain, to say what he liked upon the stage, so long as he did it under a fustian or disguise which exonerated the censor in the eyes of the law.

The history of the play of *Sir Thomas Moore* shows us the censor (this time Sir Edmund Tilney) in a slightly less tractable mood. Our discussion of this play is somewhat obscured by our inability to give it a positive date. My own inclination is to place it in the vicinity of 1593,† the date of the *Bill against Alien Straungers selling by way of Retail any Foreign Commodities,* a bill vigorously defended by Sir Walter Ralegh in words and tone agreeing completely with the tenor of the original version of the play. Ralegh had said: "Whereas it is presented, That for Strangers it is against Charity, against Honour, against Profit *to expel them;* in my opinion it is no matter of Charity to relieve them. . . . I see no reason that so much respect should be given unto them. And so to conclude, in the whole cause I see no matter of Honour, no Profit in relieving them." Dr. Gildersleeve *(op. cit.,* p. 93) gives the following summary of the action:

> The play sets forth the rise and fall of Sir Thomas More, portraying him first as the Sheriff of London, suppressing, by his eloquence

* For full discussion of Massinger's topical plays see, Gardiner, *Political Elements in Massinger,* N. S. S. Trans. (1875), and J. Stocholm, *op. cit.*

† For discussion of the date, see the introduction to W. W. Greg's edition for the Malone Society, and S. A. Tannenbaum's *The Booke of Sir Thomas Moore,* (New York, 1927), p. 17ff.

and sound sense, the insurrection of the citizens against the foreign residents, on the "ill May day" of 1517; then as Lord Chancellor, entertaining at his house the Lord Mayor and the Aldermen; later as refusing to subscribe to the "articles" sent him by the King; imprisoned in the Tower; and finally on his way to execution. . . . As for the insurrection against foreigners, though there are many sound speeches against rioting and sedition, and concerning obedience due to the King, the sympathy of the writer or writers is clearly with the citizens in their protests against the encroachments and outrages of foreigners.

I subjoin the following account of the play and Tilney's dealing with it from Dr. Samuel Tannenbaum's *The Booke of Sir Thomas Moore* (pp. 98-100):

It is not to be wondered at that at such a time as this, when Englishmen's bloods were stirring, and when the prevalence of the plague augmented the sufferings of the disaffected citizenry, Sir Edmund Tyllney objected to a play which contained such lines as these: "It is hard when Englishmens pacience must be thus ietted on by straungers and they dare not to reuendge their owne wrongs" (I, i, 32-34); . . . "if mens milkie harts dare not strike a straunger, yet women shall beate them downe" (72-73); "I am ashamed that freeborne Englishmen, hauing beatten straungers within their owne homes should thus be brau'de and abused by them at home" (92-96); "Aliens and straungers eate the breade from the fatherlesse children, and take the liuing from all the Artificers, and the entercourse from all Merchants whereby pouertie is so much encreased" (143-47); . . .

"But if the Englishe blood be once but up,
As I perceive theire harts alreadie full,
I feare me much, before their spleenes be coolde,
Some of these saucie Aliens for their pride,
Will pay for't soundly," (I, iii, 57-61);

"Come gallant bloods, you, whose free soules doo scorne
To beare th'enforced wrongs of Aliens.
Add rage to resolution, fire the houses, of these audacious straungers" (II, ii, 23-26);

"Shall these (outlandishe fugetiues) enjoy more priueledge then we in our owne countrie? lets then become their slaues.
Since iustice keeps not them in greater awe weele be our selves rough ministers at lawe" (31-34);

and many other passages expressing the discontent of the citizens and their determination to put an end to the "vilde enormities" of the aliens and their own "extreame pouertie," at any cost.

It is not insignificant in this connection that in the play (I, iii) the English nobility, the Earl of Shrewsbury, the Earl of Surrey (the distinguished poet), Sir Thomas Palmer, and Sir Roger Chomely, are in sympathy with the "wronged citizens" and denounce the "high-creasted insolence" of the "hott ffrenche-men" * and the other aliens "that fatned with the trafficque of our country." Dr. Tannenbaum continues:

> It must be noted that a lofty patriotic strain runs throughout the original version of the play, the version damned by Tyllney, and that it is only in the alleged Shakesperian portion (the revised insurrection scene, II, 4) that the outraged citizens, even Lincoln, are made to talk and act like fools. Even brave John Lincoln makes no reference to the insults they have to submit to or to their just grievances, and can charge the foreigners only with being great eaters and with having brought into the country strange roots, parsnyp and pumpions, which 'breed sore eyes' and infect the city with the Palsy. If Shakespeare wrote that, he must have done so only because he thought that in no other way could the play be saved.

Tilney's attitude toward this play is very similar to Herbert's position in the case of *Believe As You List.* Both at once recognized the application to the current situation and both were content to reform rather than to forbid the plays, though in the case of *Sir Thomas Moore* there is no proof that the play was ever actually staged. The feud between the aliens and the citizens had been smouldering in London ever since the outburst in 1586, and the parallel between these riots and the famous one of "ill May Day" 1517 was well recognized. In September 1586, Recorder Fleetwood wrote to Burleigh that the apprentices had conspired an insurrection against the French and the Dutch, but especially the French "all things as like unto ill May day as could be devised, in all manner of circumstances, *mutatis mutandis.*" (Gildersleeve, *op. cit.,* p. 94.) It is not known whether the play of *Sir Thomas Moore* refers to the 1586

* There is an interesting similarity between the orthography of parts of the MS and the Egerton MS *Richard II.*

riots, or to those of 1595, or to the discontent that was seething in the city between the two outbursts, during which interim Kyd was arrested for his supposed authorship of certain libels against the foreigners; but it is obvious that Tilney would be ready to pick up any allusion to the situation and to condemn any scenes or lines which might serve to fan this popular feeling, or in any way to stir up further rioting. Again to quote Dr. Gildersleeve *(ibid.,* p. 94):

From Tilney's "reformations" it appears that he was willing to have More's character portrayed, but felt some uneasiness at seeing such a popular and admirable person represented as disobedient to the royal authority. At the point where the Chancellor refuses to accede to the King's demand, the action is set forth without any seditious or disrespectful language whatsoever, and the content of the "articles" is tactfully left unspecified. Nevertheless Tilney drew his pen through all the concluding portion of the scene, where More's refusal is represented and wrote in the margin "all altered."

He appears to have been even more afraid of anything tending to arouse, or even to suggest, popular discontent or rebellion. Opposite the following speech by Shrewsbury he had written "Mend yt":

"My Lord of Surrey and Sir Thomas Palmer,
Might I with patience tempte your graue aduise,
I tell ye true, that in these daungerous times
I do not like this frowning vulgare brow;
My searching eye did neuer entertaine
A more distracted countenaunce of greefe
Than I haue late obseru'de
In the displeased commons of the cittie."

On the margin, at the commencement of the play, he wrote: "Leave out ye insurrection wholy, and the cause thereoff, and begin with Sir Tho. Moore at ye mayors sessions, with a reportt afterwardes of his good service done, being shrive off London, uppon a meeting agaynst ye Lumbardes only by a shortt reportt, and nott otherwise, att your own perrilles. E. Tilney." That is, he desired to have the players omit all the scenes where the citizens are abused by the foreigners and finally rise against their oppressors, and merely have a brief report of More's suppression of the rioting. He was particularly anxious to avoid anything tending to stir up the people against the French, and altered several lines to this end. For example, when Shrewsbury tells of insults offered by foreigners to the citizens, Tilney substitutes "Lombard" for "Frenchman"; and in the account of the Frenchman Bard's impudent assertion that

> ". . . if he had the Maior of Londons wife
> He would keep her in despight of any Englishe,"

Tilney crosses out "Englishe" and writes merely "man."

But even with these alterations it is not likely that the play was ever staged. Dr. Tannenbaum says (*op. cit.*, p. 101):

> There is not a particle of evidence extant to show that the play was ever put on the stage. From the fact that the revised portions bear no trace of Tyllney's pen, not even opposite highly objectionable utterances, it is reasonably certain that the revised manuscript was not submitted to him, even though the producer had gone so far as to plan the casting of the play. When we ask ourselves what the reason was for the play's not being completed, not being resubmitted to the Master of the Revels and its not being acted, the obvious answer is: Tomas Kyd's arrest on a charge of being involved in the publication of seditious libels, which threatened to involve the capital in rebellion and the nation in international difficulties. With that the play was doomed.

As in all the other cases noted thus far, the trouble arose not from the mere presence of topical allusion, but from the supposedly seditious nature of the allusions; so we are beginning to suspect, therefore, that the policy of the Censor was to ignore all but the most obvious and most flagrant cases of implied criticism of the government. One point, perhaps, needs emphasis, namely, the fact that of all the plays so far mentioned as containing, unquestionably, serious political matter, only one—*Sir Thomas Moore*—was actually "stayed" by the office of the censor, though the disguise in the other cases was the very thinnest.

The play I shall discuss next, Jonson's and Nashe's *Isle of Dogs*, did not come off so well in the skirmish with the authorities. Inasmuch as the play is lost, we can only conjecture the nature of the offense for which it was suppressed, the authors imprisoned, and the players temporarily "restrayned" from playing. It should be noted that the offensive matter was not detected by the censor before the play was acted.

The following possible interpretation of the play has been

offered by Sir Edmund Chambers *(Elizabethan Stage,* III, p. 454):

> By dogs we may take it that Nashe meant men. The idea was not new to him. In *Summer's Last Will and Testament* he makes Orion draw an elaborate parallel between dogs and men, at the end of which Will Summer says that he had not thought 'the ship of fooles would have stayde to take in fresh water at the Ile of dogges' (1. 797).

It should be noted that the title does not necessarily indicate allegory, for the Isle of Dogs is a district of London on the north bank of the Thames, opposite Greenwich, and may be simply the scene of the play. The contemporary comments on the play, however, make this unlikely.

A reference to the affair by Dekker in *Satiromastix* (1.1513) confirms this guess of Sir Edmund's and others. Here Dekker makes Tucca declare that "when the Stagerites banished thee (Horace) [Jonson] into the Ile of Dogs, thou turn'dst Bandog (villanous Guy) & ever since bitest." Another possible sidelight may be gained from a passage in Meres's *Palladis Tamia* (1598):

> As *Actaeon* was wooried of his owne hounds: so is *Tom Nash* of his *Isle of Dogs.* Dogges were the death of *Euripides,* but bee not disconsolate gallant young *Iuuenall, Linus,* the sonne of *Apollo* died the same death. Yet God forbid that so brave a witte should so basely perish, thine are but paper dogges, neither is thy banishment like Ouids eternally to conuerse with the Barbarous Gates. Therefore comfort thy selfe sweete *Tom,* with *Ciceros* glorious return to Rome, & with the counsel *Aeneas* giues to his seabeaten soldiers.

As I have observed, it is not now possible to say how seditious or libellous the play was, but it is known that Nashe suffered much under the imputation that it was local allegory. My own guess is that Nashe was calling England an Isle of Dogs because of the cruelty with which the enemies of Essex were attempting to tear to pieces the good name of the Queen's favourite. Such a symbolism would not necessarily be inconsistent with the tone of comedy which, Nashe declared, the *Isle of Dogs* was meant to be; at the same time, it may also have suggested the tragic possibilities which Jonson later developed in *Cynthia's Revels.* Whereas the dogs in Nashe's play may have represented the cruelty of Essex's enemies, in Jonson's play they represented a divine retribution visited upon the bold young lover for his intolerable presumption. Such an interpretation of *Cynthia's Revels* has been somewhat generally accepted, though scholars are not agreed as to the precise episode to which Jonson was referring.* The relevant passages are, for the most part, to be found in the folio version only. The reader will remember that the play is laid in the Vale of Gargaphie, which Jonson himself declares is a fustian country. Here, Cupid tells us (Act I, sc. i):

> The huntress and queen of these groves, Diana, in regard of some black and envious slanders hourly breathed against her, for her justice on Acteon, as she pretends, hath here in the vale of Gargaphie, proclaim'd a solemn revels, which (her godhead put off) she will descend to grace, with the full and royal expense of one of her clearest moons: in which time it shall be lawful for all sorts of ingenious persons to visit her palace, to court her nymphs, to exercise all variety of generous and noble pastimes; as well to intimate how far she treads such malicious imputations beneath her, as also to show how clear her beauties are from the least wrinkle of austerity they may be charged with.

As the Revels draw to a close, Cynthia thanks the authors and devisors (Act V, sc. iii):

> And if you judge it any recompence
> For your fair pains, t' have earn'd Diana's thanks,
> Diana grants them, and bestows their crown
> To gratify your acceptable zeal.
> For you are they, that not, as some have done,
> Do censure us, as too severe and sour,
> But as, more rightly, Gracious to the good;
> Although we not deny, unto the proud,
> Or the profane, perhaps indeed austere:
> For so Acteon, by presuming far,
> Did, to our grief, incur a fatal doom;
> And so, swoln Niobe, comparing more
> Than he presumed, was trophǣed into stone.
> But are we therefore judged too extreme?
> Seems it no crime to enter sacred bowers,
> And hallow'd places, with impure aspect,

* See, E. K. Chambers (*Elizabethan Stage*, III, p. 364), for summary of the discussion.

Most lewdly to pollute? Seems it no crime
To brave a deity? Let mortals learn
To make religion of offending heaven,
And not at all to censure powers divine.
To men this argument should stand for firm,
A goddess did it, therefore it was good:
We are not cruel, not delight in blood.
But what have serious repetitions
To do with revels, and the sports of court?
We not intend to sour your late delights
With harsh expostulation. Let it suffice
That we take notice, and can take revenge
Of these calumnious and lewd blasphemies.
For we are no less Cynthia than we were.
Nor is our power, but as ourself, the same:
Though we have now put on no tire of shine,
But mortal eyes undazzled may endure.
Years are beneath the spheres, and time makes weak
Things under heaven, not powers which govern heaven.
And though ourself be in ourself secure,
Yet let no mortals challenge to themselves
Immunity from thence. Lo, this is all.

If this interpretation of *Cynthia's Revels* is correct, it explains Tucca's sneer (*Satiromastix,* 1.1513): In effect, Dekker is saying: "The Stagerites, or thinking people, despising the cruelty of the judgment expressed in *Cynthia's Revels,* have banished thee, Horace-Jonson, to the Isle of Dogs, to run with the pack that brought Essex down." *The Isle of Dogs* then may have presented the opposite view, the view of the Stagerites, which would, of course, be severely critical of Essex's enemies, though we must be careful to note that the *Isle of Dogs* could not have referred to the entrance of Essex into the Queen's chamber in 1599. It was not because the play was topical, but because it was topical and hostile to authority, that Nashe was in trouble. He tried again and again to clear himself, first by declaring that he had not written the offensive part of the play at all, but only the induction and the first act, and by inveighing mightily against lawyers who insist on finding "a deep politique state meaning" out of what was quite innocent entertainment. "Talk I of a beare," he says in *Lenten Stuffe* (McKerrow's edition of

Nashe, III, p. 153), "O, it is such a man that emblazons him in his armes, or of a woolfe, a fox, or a camelion, any lording whom they do not affect it is meant by." This sounds as if he had been accused of satirizing some nobleman; but this was not all. He continues, "Out steps me an infant squibb of the Inns of Court . . . and he, to approve himself an extravagant statesman, catcheth hold of a rush, and absolutely concludeth it is meant of the Emperor of Russia, and that it will utterly marre the traffic into that country if all the Pamphlets bee not called in and suppressed, wherein the libelling word is mentioned."

The things about this play of which we may be sure are: first, that although it was regarded officially as a seditious allegory, the fact was not discovered by the censor, but by Topcliffe (Gildersleeve, *op. cit.,* p. 97); and second, that it was the Lord Chamberlain himself who secured the release of the players who had been imprisoned and "restrayned" from acting—an indication that the Lord Chamberlain was on their side. Another inference that may be drawn from this case is that often the fustian was not only subtle enough to elude the censor, but even to defy correct analysis when suspected. The history of Hayward's *Henry IV* is another case in point. When the Queen had been led to suspect treason in the application of the abuses of Richard II to her own policies, she asked Bacon to read it and report to her any possible treason. Bacon's report was that as far as treason was concerned he found no ground for the accusation, but at Essex's trial he reversed his judgment and regarded the implied parallel as the strongest evidence of treason. The full discussion of *Richard II* is, however, reserved for a later chapter. (See pp. 126ff.)

The Hog Hath Lost His Pearl is another play that was incorrectly glossed when the presence of fustian was suspected. The title would lead us to expect another animal allegory, but the characters are ordinary men and women. Our earliest reference to it is contained in a letter written by Sir Henry Wotton to Sir Edmund Bacon early in 1613 (*Reliquiae Wottonianae,* [1672], pp. 402-3):

On Sunday last at night, and no longer, some sixteen Apprentices (of what sort you shall guess by the rest of the story) having secretly learnt a new Play without Book, entituled *The Hog hath lost his Pearl;* took up the *White Fryers* for their Theatre: and having invited thither (as it should seem) rather their Mistresses than their Masters; who were all to enter *per buletini* for a note of distinction from ordinary Comedians. Towards the end of the Play, the Sheriffs (who by chance had heard of it) came in (as they say) and carried some six or seven of them to perform the last Act at Bridewel; the rest are fled. Now it is strange how sharp witted the City is, for they will needs have Sir *John Swinerton* the Lord *Maior* be meant by the *Hog,* and the late Lord Treasurer [Salisbury] by the *Pearl.*

It is curious that Wotton's statement has been so inadequately investigated. The fact is that it is difficult to know how seriously to take it, the vein of ironical amusement being so apparent throughout. Does he think "the City" stupid to have suspected satire where there was none, or is he jeering at them for the absurdity of their interpretation? Finally, were these players really apprentices, or professional actors, or men of the court in disguise? At all events, it is pretty certain that the City *was* wrong and that the Apprentices were at least not the ordinary kind: that is, they had unusual backing. The title page states that the play was "divers times publickly acted by certain London Prentices." There are, indeed, many reasons for discounting the City sages even though their guess has been somewhat bolstered by the opinion of Sir Edmund Chambers.* The main difficulties attendant upon any attempt to identify "the Pearl" as Lord Salisbury are: First, there is no such character as *Pearl* or *the pearl* in the play! True, Hog has a daughter Rebecca, whom he loses temporarily, along with his wealth; but he regains both through a most edifying reconciliation, and there is a notable conversion from avarice to charity. As Haddit, the thief who has eloped with Rebecca, says:

> Yet all, I trust, are pleased; and will our ills requite,
> Since it hath saved a soul was hell's by right.

Aside from the obvious awkwardness of identifying Hog's marriageable daughter with Lord Salisbury, in no place what-

* Sir Edmund says (*Elizabethan Stage,* III, p. 496), "A passage in Act III (Dodsley, p. 465) bears out the suggestion of a satire on the House of Cecil." Note that in the edition of Dodsley here referred to, the position of the names in this letter has been reversed by Collier, for reasons best known to himself.

ever does Hog refer to his daughter as his Pearl, in spite of the strong precedent for doing so. Whatever may be underlying the fustian in this play, I can find no explanation for the title other than the obviously symbolic one, e.g., The Hog hath lost his Treasure, including his daughter.

When the play was finally published in 1614, it contained a Prologue referring to the difficulties of the producers. The play had been "tossed from one house to another." There had been attempts to "prevent" it; but "it hath a Knight's license" and may "range at pleasure." The Prologue expressly disclaims any "grunting at state affairs" and "invecting at city vices," but as in the Prologue to *Damon and Pythias* (see p. 45), it would seem that the players "do too much protest" their innocence. The Knight, as Sir Edmund Chambers points out, was doubtless Sir George Buck. Again, the things to note are: first, that although objectionable matter was suspected, the play had no difficulty with the censor; and second, that the fustian, if there was any, was sufficiently subtle to defy popular analysis, at least by any but the esoteric group for whose amusement it was designed.

CHAPTER FOUR

The Authors' Protest

THE DRAMATISTS THEMSELVES, in many prologues, inductions, epistles, and epilogues which accompany the first printed texts, bear eloquent testimony to their resentment at such popular analysis, and to their hatred of informers who reported their conjectured interpretations to the authorities. We have already seen how Nashe scored the practice in the Induction to *The Isle of Dogs* and in *Lenten Stuffe,* but this is only one of many such protests. Gervase Markham, in the Epistle to *The Dumb Knight,* says that "Rumour hath made strange constructions on this Dumb Knight."

John Day (*Isle of Gulls,* IV, 4; Bullen, p. 91) refers to the "libelling" ascribed to poets by "false informers," while Jonson declares that it is the informers themselves who are the libellers; and he claims in the Prologue to *Epicoene* [italics inserted]:

If any yet will, with particular sleight
Of application, wrest what he doth write,
And that he meant, or him, or her, will say
They make a a libel which *he* made a play.

The Induction to *Mucedorus* offers a more elaborate example.* Here the case is presented in the form of a dialogue between two abstract characters, *Comedie* and *Envy*. Envy boasts that he can overthrow Comedie utterly by inducing a poet to write a play

Wherein shall be compos'd darke sentences,
Pleasing to facetious braines:
And euery other where, place me a Iest,
Whose high abuse shall more torment than blowes:
Then I my selfe (quicker then Lightning)
Will flie me to a puisant Magistrate,
And waighting with a Trencher at his backe,

* Sir Edmund Chambers says (*Elizabethan Stage,* IV, p. 35): "The induction is altered to compliment James instead of Elizabeth."

In midst of iollitie, rehearse these gaules,
(With some additions)
So lately vented in your Theator.
He, upon this, cannot but make complaint,
To your great danger, or at least restraint.

To be sure, Comedie could afford to laugh at this threat, calling it a "trap for boys," for, indeed, drama throve on the sauce of esoteric allusion; still, the poets who wrote the plays were often both in "danger" and "in restraint" because of their share in the practice. Jonson, who had been in both situations, wrote bitterly, in the Epistle to *Epicoene,* "When you shall consider, through the certain hatred of some, how much a man's innocency may bee endangered by an uncertain accusation; you will, I doubt not, so begin to hate the iniquitie of such natures, as I shall love the contumely done me, whose end was so honourable as to be wiped off by your sentence." The last allusion is probably to the efforts of Sir Francis Stuart to extricate Jonson from trouble over this very play; but of this, more later. In the Induction to *Bartholomew Fair,* Jonson is even more severe in calling them "politic pick locks." He lays upon the "hearers and spectators" the following obligations:

That they neither in themselves conceal, nor suffer by them to be concealed, any state-decypherer, or politic pick-lock of the scene so solemnly ridiculous, as to search out, who was meant by the gingerbread woman, who by the hobby-horse man, who by the costard-monger, nay, who by their wares. Or that will pretend to affirm on his own inspired ignorance, what Mirror of Magistrates is meant by the justice, what great lady by the pig-woman, what concealed statesman by the seller of mouse-traps, and so of the rest.

Finally he asks that "such person, or persons, so found, be left discovered to the mercy of the author, as a forfeiture to the stage, and your laughter aforesaid."

The Induction to *Cynthia's Revels* further inveighs against the stupid critic who "miscalls all by the name of fustian, that his grounded capacity cannot aspire to." Indeed, the satirists, dramatic and non-dramatic, ply this bluff until it becomes wearisome. In his *Epistle to the Reader Whatsoever* attached to *A Fig for Momus,* Lodge, like Jonson, brazenly defies the censor who condemns a satire without understanding it. Explaining his "so peremptory a title," he says:

> I entitle my book [*A Fig for Momus*] not in contempt of the learned, for I honour them; not in disdaine of the wel-minded, because they cherish science; but in despight of the detractor who having no learning to iudge, wanteth no libertie to reproue.

It is not certain that Lodge intended Momus to represent the official censor, in this case, Sir Edmund Tilney; he may have been thrusting at an unofficial decipherer, such as Dr. John Rainolds, the Oxonian critic, who had attacked both the stage plays and the players. (See below, pp. 205ff.) In Epistle 5 to Master Michael Drayton, he speaks of the "rayling and detraction" which is "proper to Momus and his hateful faction," and in his appeal to Lord Hunsdon for a patron's protection for *Rosalynde,* the defiance seems to be too deliberate to be general. With full expectation that resentment will follow the publication of this seemingly harmless romance, Lodge says:

> If *Momus* or anie squint-eied asse that hath mightie eares to conceive with *Midas,* and yet little reason to judge; if hee come aboard our Barke to find fault with the tackling, when he knows not the shrowdes, Ile downe into the hold, and fetch out a rustie pollax, and either well be bast him, or heaue the cockscombe ouer boord to feed cods.

If by Momus Lodge did mean the official censor, he was indeed a bold, not to say a rash man.

But apparently these protestations of innocence and bravado fooled no one, and indeed, the dramatists themselves admit again and again that the plays without such hidden meanings are "mere toys" and totally out of fashion. Chapman, for instance, in the Prologue to *All Fools* speaks of merely comical and harmless jests which, he says "though ne'er so witty, be esteemed but toys if void of th'other satirism's sauce," and he admits frankly that "The ancient comic vein of Eupolis and Cratinus" are now "revived, *subject to personal application.*" [Italics inserted.] In this admission he was following the example of earlier topical writers, such as Richard Edwardes and George Gascoigne, who definitely announced their abandonment of the drama of mere delight as pastimes suitable only to "young desires." The Prologue to *Damon and Pythias* states that the author's muse used to "maske in delight"; now, however, it leaves such sports, and writes henceforward with didactic intent. Similarly Gascoigne, in the Prologue to his *Glass of Government,* jeers at the theatre-goers who seek mere entertainment:

> What man hath minde to heare a worthie Jest
> Or seekes to feed his eyes with vayne delight
> That man is much unmeete to be a guest
> At such a feaste as I prepare this night.
> Who list laye out some pence in such a marte,
> Bellsavage fayre were fittest for his purse.

To be sure, whenever the authors got into trouble, they promptly and stoutly claimed that they meant no such application. "Application," says Jonson in the Dedication to *Volpone,* "is now grown a trade with many; and there are that profess to have a key for the decyphering of everything: but let wise and noble persons take heed how they be too credulous, or give leave to these invading interpreters to be over-familiar with their fames, who cunningly and often, utter their own virulent malice under other men's simplest meanings." Either they claim that their satire is directed against vices, not persons, or that they are showing up only such faults in persons as deserve to be taxed. *Epicoene* and *Bartholomew Fair* illustrate the former kind of apology, *Volpone, Philotas* and *The Malcontent,* the second. The second Prologue to *Epicoene* says:

> The ends of all, who for the scene do write,
> Are, or should be, to profit and delight.
> And still't hath been the praise of all best times
> So persons were not touched, to tax their crimes.

He warns particularly against the incriminating evidence supplied by a recognition of the coat that fits. The Epilogue to *Bartholomew Fair* shows clearly, (even if Aubrey had not told us that "King James made him write against the Puritans who began to be troublesome at this time"), that Jonson had been given leave to criticize the Puritans as a class, but not to draw literary portraits of any particular Puritan. It seems, however, that in spite of his protestation of innocence and discretion, this play, like all of Jonson's, does abound in such portraits.

(See below, *passim.)* In fact, he became so adept in the art of fustian, that, as he says in the Prologue to the *Alchemist,* he was able to show up follies so naturally "as even the doers may see, and yet not own." Similarly Marston, in the Epistle to the Reader in *The Malcontent,* protests: "It was my care to write so far from reasonable offence, that even strangers, in whose state I laid my scene, should not from thence draw any disgrace to any, dead or living." Yet again and again the satirized did "see and own." In this same Epistle, Marston states, "Yet, in despite of my endeavours, I understand some have been most unadvisedly over-cunning in misinterpreting me, and with subtlety (as deep as hell) have maliciously spread ill rumours, which springing from themselves have heavily returned."

Sometimes these protestations of innocence are palpably facetious. In the Apologetical Dialogue to *The Poetaster,* Jonson denies that he "taxed/ The Law and Lawyers; Captaines, and the Players/ By their particular names"; but who ever of his accusers in this case thought that Tucca and Lupus were the proper names of the Soldiers and Lawyers whom he was ridiculing? So Richard Edwardes, in the Prologue to *Damon and Pythias,* after having admitted that he was writing a "tragical comedy" in which "mirth is mixed with care," concludes:

> Wherein, talking of courtly toys, we do protest this flat,
> We talk of Dionysius court, we mean no court but that.

So claimed Lyly in, perhaps, the most daring of all his courtly fustians, *Endymion*:

> Most high and happy Princesse, we must tell you a tale of the Man in the Moone, which if it seeme ridiculous for the method, or superfluous for the matter, or for the means incredible, for three faultes wee can make but one excuse. It is a tale of the Man in the Moone.
>
> It is forbidden in olde time to dispute of Chymera, because it was a fiction; we hope in our times none will apply pastimes, because they are fancies; for there liues none vnder the Sunne, that knowes what to make of the Man in the Moone. We present neither Comedie, nor Tragedie, nor storie, nor anie thing, but that whosoeuer heareth may say this, Why heere is a tale of the Man in the Moone.

So he claims also for Pandora in the Prologue to *The Woman in the Moone.* "Remember," he says, "all is but a Poet's dream." So claimed the greatest of his followers:

> If we shadows have offended,
> Think but this, and all is mended,
> That you have but slumbered here,
> While these visions did appear.
> And this weak and idle theme,
> No more yielding but a dream.

And so with many another brazen offender, and sometimes the ruse was successful. The author of *Two Wise Men and All the Rest Fools* gives (V, iv) an amusing representation of such a piece of literary strategy. The scene shows Proberio inducing his master Noverindo, a usurer, to accept a perfectly fatuous interpretation of a piece of "mystery":

(Enter Proberio, bringing a cloth wherein is pictured an Usurer bareheaded with a purse in his left hand, on the outside of which purse is set this inscription "30 p. pro 100." And behind him the picture of the Devil, with his arms stripped up, and white half-way, like the hangman's shirt sleeves, putting a halter about the Usurer's neck: and shewing it to the people, saith):

Now, could I meet my merchant Noverindo, I have here a whole library for his learning. Here he may study while he spend his heart-blood with struggling, yet never reach the depth with his pettitoes.

(He rolls it up again.)

Enter Noverindo.

Nov. How long I think until I meet Proberio.
All is ready at our office, but the blazonry of our coat of arms to be set up.

He discovers Proberio and demands of him the device, but the clever rogue makes his master pay in advance before he will show him the scroll. When the "two pieces" have been paid, Proberio says:

Now you shall see it. *(Then he sets it up with some device upon a staff that with turning it all the spectators may view it.)*

Nov. (Looks earnestly upon it a long time, and then fetching a great sigh, saith): What Tyburnist is this? And what's the mystery of all this picture?

Pro. Sir, this Tyburnist or hangman is the devil. And this fellow that hath the purse is Judas, the figure of 30 with p. joined to it signifies 30 pence, for which he sold his master. That which followeth is meant of Christ, worth a hundred worlds; for which fact the Devil put a halter about his neck and hanged him. So shortly this is the sum of all:

> Judas who for 30d. sold Christ infinitely greatest
> Was hanged by the Devil's help, and reputed with the basest.
> Before you saw the history,
> Now you hear the mystery.

Nov. 'Tis a good exposition. But I would I had my two pieces again. I do not like it very well, for many ignorant people will take it far otherwise; as thus, 30 p. 30 for a hundred. And he that taketh 30 for the 100 is to be hanged by the devil.

Pro. 'Tis true, many may think so, but your clerks must inform them in the sense. No man can put a secret in figures but it may be diversely interpreted. And so be all oracles taken in sundry senses.

Nov. But I wish it were made plainer to the understanding: for the more part will take it as I did at first sight.

Pro. Why should you think so?

Nov. Because I cannot imagine any other meaning so proper to those figures as that I conceived.

Pro. That's because you are parcel guilty. But I will gather two other conceits as proper as that of yours.

Nov. If you can do so I am satisfied.

Pro. Thus 30 p. pro 100, that is, he that gives 30 in the 100 is worthy to be hanged.

Nov. That judgement is very prejudicial for us, and may force from us many clients.

Pro. I do but guess this as for variety sake. And then another is this: 30 p. in the 100; he that will not give 30 in the 100 is worthy to be hanged.

Nov. O this, none like to this! Now I like this riddle excellent well, that yields so many and so witty constructions.

Pro. Nay here one more comes flowing in. I tell you 'tis a very copious theme. I could keep you here this hour with voluntary variety. I remember them as fast as they come into my brains by huddles. 30 in the 100, and the hangman by; that is, he that will not give 30 in the 100 shall be hanged before he get any money there.

Nov. And so he shall, I warrant him. This is as good or rather better than the other. I commend thee, Proberio, either of these will serve our turn. Here, thou shalt have one piece more. I'll be bigger to thee than my word. Thou wilt make all our worship's hearts merry with this device.

Pro. I thank you, Sir. And if you knew with what alacrity and willingness I went about it, you would think it well bestowed.

[*exit* NOVER.]

Let him go; he carries his own rod. No man that hath his senses will conjecture otherwise than himself did at first, *videlicet*

He that takes 30 in the 100, and not a penny under,
Is worthy to be pendent till the hemp crack asunder.

Nothing could show up more clearly the dangerous but intriguing game of fustian. The more stringent was the watch upon free discussion of current issues and outstanding political personalities, the more ingenious the poets had to be in order to protect themselves. In a possible ambiguity such as that exploited by Proberio, lay their greatest safety. The Nathans who undertook to rebuke the Tudor sovereigns had need of a deeper subtlety than that offered by mere allegory; the allegory itself had to be sufficiently obscured to allow of more than one interpretation. Nashe, in *Have With You to Saffron Walden,* (ed. Grosart, III, p. 174), makes an interesting comment upon the nature of Elizabethan satire. Speaking of its moral, personal, religious, and political significance, he says, "Neither are these parts severally distinguished in order of handling, but like a Dutch stewd-pot jumbled together and linsey-wolsey woven, one with another." All the dramatists who undertook to handle the "dangerous arcana" of current issues, took full advantage of the obliquity involved in fables, parables, and even in historical parallels; but perhaps of all the poets, Chapman has written most clearly in defense of this practice of deliberate double entendre. In his attempt to explain the allegory of *Andromeda Liberata,* dealing with the nuptials of the Countess of Essex and the Earl of Somerset, which had caused such "violent hubbub," he says, in his "A free and offenseless Justification of a Lately publisht and most maliciously interpreted drama, Andrómeda Liberata," declaring (Swinburne, *Works of Chapman: Poems,* p. 195):

As learning hath delight from the cradle to hide herself from the base and profane Vulgar, her ancient Enemy, under divers veils of Hieroglyphics, Fables and the like, so hath she pleased herself with no disguise more than in Mysteries and allegorical Fictions of Poesy . . . ever, I say, enclosing within the rind some fruit of knowledge, howsoever darkened; and by reason of the obscurity, of ambiguous and different constructions. *Est enim ipsa Natura universa Poesis aenigmatum plena, nec quivis eam dignoscit.* This ambiguity in the sense hath given scope to the variety of expositions.

So Cordatus in *Everyman Out of His Humour* (II, ii) insists that to construe a condemnation of Nero as a condemnation of all emperors, or an indictment of Machiavel as a censure of all statesmen, etc., is "absurd and malicious"; but he admits that such an inference is almost sure to be made of his play by certain critics who will come to the theatre with their note-books to jot down the offensive passages. Cordatus defies these "narrow-eyed decypherers . . . that will extort strange and abstruse meanings out of any subject, be it never so innocently delivered." But to all such "wherever they sit concealed" the author hurls defiance—"to them and their writing-tables."

This is precisely what Proberio claimed in *Two Wise Men.* Swinburne says ironically of Chapman's defense *(ibid.,* p. lix):

> Such is the perversity of man, that on perusing this most apt and judicious allegory "the base, ignoble, barbarous, giddy multitude" of readers actually thought fit to enquire from what "barren rock" the new Perseus might be said to have unbound his fettered virgin, and in answer to this not unnatural enquiry Chapman had the audacious innocence to affirm—and I doubt not in all truth and simplicity—that the inevitable application of this happy and appropriate symbol had never so much as crossed his mind.

This is the old story of "unwilling error" repeated for the nth time in the Epilogue to *Mucedorus.* Such and such an application was never intended at all; dear me! no! But what can I do if ignorant or malicious persons will construe so badly? So Massinger, in the Prologue to *The Emperor of the East,* opines:

> He cannot 'scape their censures who delight
> To misapply whatever he shall write.

So Robert Daborne, in the Epistle of *A Christian Turned Turk,* claims that "it is to publish mine innocence concerning the wrong of worthy personages, together with doing some right to the much-suffering Actors, that hath caused my name to cast it selfe on the common rack of censure." Obviously, the authorities had found this play offensive and had, in their ignorance of the author, laid some punishment upon the actors, who were really not guilty at all. However, before Daborne could get it into print, he was obliged to make such concessions to the censor that he described the text as "this oppressed and much martired Tragedy."

The Prologue to *Campaspe* shows the author in a more frisky, but no less impudent mood:

> Whatsoeuer we present, we wish it may be thought the daunsing of *Agrippa* his shadowes, who in the moment they were seene, were of any shape one woulde conceiue: or Lynces, who hauing a quicke sight to discerne, haue a short memory to forget. With vs, it is like to fare, as with those torches, which giuing light to others, consume themselues: and wee shewing delight to others, shame our selues.

It is clear from the Epilogue that Lyly is in this case capering about these slippery paths with unusual *sang froid* because of his assurance of royal protection. In the Epilogue he expresses the hope that

> being shielded with your highnesse countenaunce, wee shall, though hear the neighing, yet not feele the kicking of those iades, and receiue, though no praise (which we cannot deserue) yet a pardon, which in all humilytie we desire. . . . For ourselues againe, we are those torches waxe, of whiche being in your hignesse handes, you may make Doues or Vultures, Roses or Nettles, Lawrell for a garland, or elder for a disgrace.

In other words, your Majesty is free to construe this play in any way you like, let who will object.

Often the poets tried the other dodge of claiming that they satirized only general vices, or at most, only those particular vices of particular men that were a danger to the state. Thus Jonson in the dedication of *Volpone*:

> Howsoever I cannot escape from some the imputation of sharpness, but that they will say, I have taken a pride or lust to be bitter, and not my youngest infant but hath come into the world with all his teeth; I would ask of these supercilious politics, what nation,

society, or general order or state, I have provoked? What public person? Whether I have not in all these preserved their dignity, as mine own person, safe? My works are read, allowed (I speak of those that are intirely mine), look into them, what broad reproofs have I used? Where have I been particular? Where personal? except to a mimic, cheater, bawd, or buffoon, creatures for their insolencies, worthy to be taxed? yet to which of these so pointingly, as he might not either ingenuously have confest, or wisely dissembled his disease? But it is not rumour that can make men guilty, much less entitle me to other men's crimes. I know, that nothing can be so innocently writ or carried, but may be made obnoxious to construction.

Yet Aubrey tells us that *Volpone* was a satire on Sutton, the founder of the Charter House: " 'Twas from him that B. Jonson took his hint for the fox and by Signeur Volpone is meant Sutton."

A smilar parallel is afforded by Dekker in the Epistle to the World, prefixed to *Satiromastix*:

Thus much I protest (and sweare by the diuinest part of true Poesie) and (howsoeuer the limmes of my naked lines may bee and I know haue bin, tortured on the racke) they are free from conspiring the least disgrace to any man, but only to our new Horace; neyther should this ghost of Tucca, haue walkt vp and downe Poules Churchyard, but that hee was raiz'd vp (in print) by newe Exorcismes.

That is, he denies all intention of offence to any but to those who deserve it. Similarly Marston, in answering the charge of personal satire, protests in the Prologue to *The Malcontent:*

. . . with my free understanding, I have not glanced at disgrace of any but of those whose unquiet studies labor innovation, contempt of holy policy, reverend, comely superiority, and established verity.

But this, like the apology of Jonson, admits all; so does Daniel admit all in his Apology to *Philotas,* written to protest against "the wrong application and misconstruing" of it. He says:

For any resemblance that through the ignorance of the history may be applied to the Late Earl of Essex, it can hold in no proportion, but only in his weaknesses, which I would wish all that love his memory not to revive. And for mine own part, having been particularly beholding to his bounty, I would to God his error and disobedience to his Sovereign might be so deepe buried underneath the earth, and in so low a tombe from his other parts, that hee might never be remembered among the examples of disloyalty in this Kingdome, or paralleled with Forreine Conspirators.

Students of the period need not be reminded of the imprisonment and threatened punishment which lay behind this pious but insincere repudiation of Essex partisanship. (See pp. 116ff.) The Prologue to Beaumont's *Woman Hater* shows the author in a similar intimidated state. He assures the reader of his discretion and expresses his intention not to lose his ears. As Sir Edmund Chambers has pointed out, this last is possibly an allusion to Jonson's and Chapman's peril after *Eastward Ho!* Again, the Prologue to *Gallathea* shows Lyly in a similarly cautious mood. He assures the Queen that he "has endeuoured with all care, that what wee present your Highnesse, should neyther offend in Scaene nor sillable." In discussing the stage-history of this play, which was performed before the Queen at Greenwich "on Newyeeres day at Night," (entered in the S. R. in 1585, but no Quarto till 1592), Sir Edmund Chambers says:

> The stay of publication may have been due, not to renewed opportunity of performance, but to the presence in the piece of matter in some way objectionable which was removed by Lyly, or "reformed and altered" by the Master of the Revels before the subsequent Court-performance.

CHAPTER FIVE

Personal Satires

OCCASIONALLY A VICTIM might prevent the continuance of a satire on the stage. Inigo Jones, for instance, made a successful protest against the representation of himself as Vitruvius Hoop in Jonson's *Tale of a Tub*. (Gildersleeve, *op. cit.,* p. 124.) Later, one Mr. Sewster complained that he had been offensively satirized in *The City Shuffler*: Whereupon Herbert "stayed the play, till the Company have given him satisfaction." *(Ibid.,* p. 125.) My readers are, of course, aware of the doubtfully successful protest of the Cobhams against the satire in Oldcastle.

In these cases the protest forced a change in the play, but brought no punishment to the author. It was quite otherwise, however, if the company acting a libellous play was so unfortunate as to lack a powerful patron, particularly if the action were direct, i.e., not under a fustian. The fate of the actors who performed a play against the Earl of Lincoln at the house of Sir Edward Dymock in 1610, should have been a sufficient warning against the practice of stage libel. The play, we are told in a report of the Star Chamber trial *(ibid.,* p. 108), was acted "on a May-pole green near Sir Edward Dymock's house," and it contained "scurrelous and slanderous matter against the said Earl by name." After the play was ended, one of the actors, "attired like a minister, went up into the pulpit attached to the Maypole with a book in his hands, and did most profanely, in derision of the holy exercise of preaching, pronounce vain and scurrilous matter and afterward affixed to the Maypole an infamous libel against the said Earl." For this offense the punishment was extraordinarily severe: the three principal actors were sentenced to be pilloried and whipped at Westminster Hall, and then to be taken into Lincolnshire and suffer the same punishment again. Here they were also to "acknowledge their offences and to ask God and the Earl forgiveness," and to pay a fine of £300 apiece. Sir Edward Dymock, as privy and consenting to the performance, was to be committed to the Fleet during the King's pleasure, and to be fined £1,000. (*Ibid.*, p. 108.) Miss Gildersleeve adds, "The severity of the punishments ordered shows what fate might befall players who were, as these seem to have been, without patent or powerful patron."

More often, however, the objector was obliged to "grin and bear" as in the case described by Sir John Harington, in the Preface of *Orlando Furioso* (1591):

> To speak of a London Comedie, how much good matter, yea and matter of state, is there in that Comedie called the play of the Cards, in which it is showed how four Parasitical knaves robbe the foure principall vocations of the Realme; videl, the vocation of Souldiers, Schollers, Merchants, and Husbandmen? Of which Comedie I cannot forget the saying of a notable wise counsellor that is now dead, who when some (to sing Placebo) advised that it should be forbidden, because it was somewhat too plaine, and indeed as the old saying is, *sooth boord is no boord,* yet he would have it allowed adding, that it was fit that *They which doe that they should not should hear that they would not.*

Sir Edmund Chambers observes (*Elizabethan Stage,* I, p. 324):

> Tarlton, although a *persona grata* at the court, got into trouble for his hits at Leicester and Raleigh, possibly in the very play on the pack of cards already mentioned.

That is, Sir Edmund surmises that Ralegh is the person attacked for his activities as scholar, soldier, merchant, and husbandman. The Elizabethan student will not need to be reminded of Tarlton's famous jest about Ralegh, wherein the "fool" exclaimed, "See the knave commands the Queen."

The Acts of the Privy Council for 16 May, 1601, describe another case of fairly ineffectual protest. They sent an order to the Middlesex Justices to examine and, if need be, suppress a play at the Curtain in which were represented, they declare, "the persons of some gentlemen of good desert and quality that are yet alive, under obscure manner, but yet in such sort as all the hearers may take notice both of the matter and of the persons that are meant thereby, this being a thinge very unfitte and offensive." The Council therefore orders the Justices to investigate the play, and if they find it "so odious and inconvenient as is informed" they are required to "take bond" of the chief players "to answere their rashe and undiscreet dealing before us." Whatsoever the finding of the Justices, the records show that the Council took no further notice of it.

Oftener than not the Council were apparently unwilling to act against the players, probably because of some powerful but unseen protector-patron in the background. Such would seem to have been the case in several University plays which dramatized certain aspects of town-and-gown warfare. One of the most interesting of these is the play called *Club Law,* performed at Clare Hall, Cambridge, sometime during the academic year 1599-1600. The play is described in a MS annals of Cambridge, probably by Fuller, as follows (*ibid.,* iv, p. 6): "Aula Clarensis, Club Law, fabula festivissima data multum ridentibus Academicis, frustra Oppidanis dolentibus." Sir Edmund says:

> The play is a satire on the townsmen, and especially the anti-gown mayor of 1599-1600, John Yaxley. Fuller says that the townsmen were invited to the performance and made to sit it through, and that they complained to the Privy Council, who first 'sent some slight and private check to the principall Actors therein' and then, when pressed, said that they would come to Cambridge, and see the comedy acted over again in the presence of the townsmen.

There is no record of these letters in the extant register of the Council, so that we are left to our own guesses concerning this obviously prejudiced jury, who not only refused to punish the offenders but actually suggested for itself the treat of watching the baiting of the townsmen by the impudent undergraduates.

It is possible that this play is by the same author as the later Clare Hall play by George Ruggle, namely, *Ignoramus,* played before James, to his apparent delight, on 8 March, 1615. Of this play Chamberlain wrote to Carleton (*ibid.,* III, pp. 475-76):

> The second night (8 March) was a comedy of Clare Hall, with the help of two or three good actors from other houses, wherein David Drummond, on a hobbyhorse, and Brakin, the recorder of the town,

under the name of Ignoramus, a common lawyer, bore great parts. The thing was full of mirth and variety, with many excellent actors: among whom the Lord Compton's son, though least, yet was not worst, but more than half marred by extreme length.

Miss Aikin (*Memoirs of the Court of King James the First,* II, p. 3), describes this play as follows:

This piece was the Latin comedy of *Ignoramus,* which, contrary to the common fate of occasional pieces, has held an enduring place in literature, and, besides being several times reprinted, was twice within the last century selected for performance by the Westminster scholars. It is doubtless a very amusing drama, full of bustle and incident, and abounding with laughable situations and grotesque characters; but its comic merits were not its only or principal recommendation to the favor of James. The hero of the piece is a practitioner of the common law, so much decried by the courtiers of the day; and the ridicule attached to his cunning, his pedantry, and the barbarous jargon of technical terms and latinized English of which his discourse is compounded, was no less agreeable to the monarch than it proved offensive to the profession of which Ambidexter Ignoramus is the representative. Those other distinguished objects of his majesty's contempt or aversion—the pope, the jesuits, with their doctrine of equivocation, Garnet's straw, and the puritans, all came in for a share of the lashing dealt around by the courtly satirist, and on the repetition of the piece, a new prologue added to the gratification of the royal auditor. The author was George Ruggle of Clarehall; a person not otherwise distinguished.

Notwithstanding the boasted scholarship of James, the Latinity of the speech addressed by him to the university is said to have been very indifferent, and much inferior to that of Queen Elizabeth's harangue on a similar occasion. That of Nethersole, the university orator, was also much criticized, on account of his addressing the prince as "Jacobissime Carole." This absurdity, among others, was ridiculed in a ludicrous ballad composed on the occasion by Richard Corbet of facetious memory, an Oxonian, and afterwards bishop of Norwich.

On 31 March Chamberlain told Carleton of the Oxford satires on the play and of a possible second visit by the King, unless he could persuade the actors to visit London. Apparently the King was unable to persuade them, for on 20 May Chamberlain wrote:

On Saturday last (13 May) the King went again to Cambridge to see the play "Ignoramus" which has so nettled the lawyers, that they are almost out of all patience.

Obviously, no Privy Council would move to punish actors who had contributed so highly to the merriment of his Majesty. Chamberlain adds what is for us an important bit of information, namely, that rhymes and ballads had been written by the lawyers and answered. This is an instance of what Lyly calls "having a bout with a ballater."

Sir Edmund Chambers says (*Elizabethan Stage,* III, p. 476): "Fuller (*Church History* [1655], X, 70) reports a story that the irritation caused to the lawyers also led to John Selden's demonstrations of the secular origin of tithes."

Ignoramus is especially interesting as an illustration of the Gonsago device, i.e., of a plot, extant and in print, into which was foisted a topical addition. Sir Edmund Chambers says (*ibid.*), "*Ignoramus* was largely based on the *Trappolaria* (1596) of Giambattista Porta into which Ruggle introduced his satire of the Cambridge Recorder, Francis Brackyn, who had already been the butt of 3 *Parnassus.*" Of this play, one of the most complex and baffling of the indubitably topical plays, something must be said when we come to the discussion of the *Poetomachia.* (See pp. 199ff.) Here it is sufficient to point out that, like the two former Cambridge plays, it abounds in personal satire.

There are many records of the employment of this device by the theatrical people. Dekker's *Satiromastix* is a case in point. Of this play Sir Edmund Chambers says *(op. cit.,* III, p. 293):

Jonson is satirized as Horace. Asinius Bubo is some unknown satellite of his, probably the same who appears as Simplicius Faber in Marston's *What You Will.* Crispinus, Demetrius, and Tucca are taken over from Jonson's *Poetaster.* The satirical matter is engrafted on to a play with a tragic plot and comic sub-plot, both wholly unconcerned with the Poetomachia.

Often a play seems to start out as a general satire and, perhaps, remains such for the most part. Usually, however, when the play is satirical at all, it includes at least one or two personal gibes.

The history of the Martin Marprelate plays, because of their particular connections with Marlowe and Ralegh, has been deferred to a later chapter. It will, however, not be out of place here, to notice the evidence supplied in various references to these plays concerning this very phenomenon, namely, the frequent presence of personal satire in a piece of general propaganda. The anti-Puritan propaganda in the Marprelate plays has, of course, always been conceded. Even the satires on Penry are too well authenticated to doubt, but an aspect of Martinism which has not been so generally realised is its degeneration into a war of personalities. What began as a controversy between Puritanism and Ecclesiasticism ended as a series of personal libels in which Martinism, or Barrowism, or Greenwoodism, (generally lumped together as Atheism), sank into the background, leaving the scene to the more spectacular, but even less attractive private quarrel between Lyly, Nashe, and Greene, on the one hand, and the Brothers Harvey, on the other. As Bond observes *(Works of Lyly,* I, 60), "The strong Puritan feeling was smothered for the time" and the "quarrel was transferred from the sphere of religious polemics to that of private personalities." It came about in this way; in Lyly's first anti-Martin pamphlet, *Pappe with a Hatchet (ibid.,* I, 30, n. 2), he girded at Harvey for slipping a personal satire into an impersonal scientific discussion. He declared he had written "a familiar Epistle about the natural causes of an earthquake and fell into the bowels of libelling, which made his ears quake for fear of clipping." We have already alluded to this quarrel, which started with Lyly's informing Oxford that Tuscanismo was a satire on his Italianate fashions. In the following extract, Harvey is accusing Lyly of doing precisely that of which Lyly had accused Harvey. From the latter's retort, it is obvious that Lyly had included, or had threatened to include a lampoon on Harvey in one of the anti-Martinist plays. Harvey declared *(ibid.,* I, p. 54):

I am threatened with a Bable, and Martin menaced with a Comedy; a fit motion for a jester, and a player to try what may be done by the employment of his faculty. Bables and Comedies are parlous fellows to decypher and discourage men, (that is the point), with their witty flouts and learned jerks, enough to lash any man out of countenance. Nay if you shake the painted scabbard at me, I have done: and all you, that tender the preservation of your good names, were best to please Paphatchet, and fee Euphues betimes, for fear lest he be moved, or some one of his apes hired, to make a play of you [*cf.* the opening of Bk. iii: 'Nashe the ape of Greene, Greene the ape of Euphues, Euphues the ape of Envy, the three famous mammets of the press, and my three notorious feudists, draw all in a yoke'] and then is your credit quite undone for ever and ever. Such is the public reputation of their plays. He must needs be discouraged, whom they decypher. Better anger an hundred other than two such, that have the stage at commandment, and can furnish out vices and devils at their pleasure.

Jonson's *Bartholomew Fair* may be another case in point. Aubrey tells us (ii, 14) that Jonson had been commanded by the King to write something against the Puritans, and there is no doubt that Jonson understood the tastes of his royal commissioner when he represented the Puritans, Purecraft and Zeal-of-the-land Busy, as guilty of every nameable and unnameable vice, from hypocrisy to unparalleled obscenity. But there are, in the play, elements which are obviously unconnected with the general satire on the Puritans; but these scenes are cryptic and difficult to interpret. In fact, without a gloss, the whole episode of the puppet-show in Act V is all but unintelligible. Many suggestions for such a gloss have been made, but so far little in the way of proof has been offered. Sir Edmund Chambers, however, is inclined to accept one suggestion of Fleay's and he offers one of his own to go with it. He says *(Elizabethan Stage,* III, p. 373): "I see no reason to accept Fleay's identification of Littlewit with Daniel; that of Lanthorn Leatherhead with Inigo Jones is more plausible"; and he ventures the further identification between Beaumont and Fletcher, and the Damon and Pythias of the puppets. He cites (*ibid.,* III, p. 217) "the gossip of Aubrey (i, 96) who learnt from Sir James Hales and others that Beaumont and Fletcher 'lived together on the Banke Side, not far from the Play-house, both batchelors; lay together; had one wench in the house between them, which they did so admire; the same cloathes and cloake, &c between them.'" He notes also the speech of Oldwit in Shadwell's *Bury-Fair* (1689) *(ibid.,* III, p. 314): "I knew Fletcher, my friend Fletcher, and his maid Joan; well, I shall never forget him: I have supped with him at his house on the Bank-side; he loved a fat loin of pork of all things in the world; and Joan his maid had her beer-glass of sack and wee all kissed her, i' faith, and were as merry as passed"; and he adds, "I have sometimes wondered whether Jonson is chaffing Beaumont and Fletcher in *Bartholomew Fair* (1614) V, iii, iv, as Damon and Pythias, 'two faithful friends o' the Bankside,' that 'have both but one drabbe,' and enter with a gammon of bacon under their cloakes." According to these suggestions then, the puppet play would present Inigo Jones as Lanthorn Leatherhead, presenting a satire on Beaumont and Fletcher as Damon and Pythias. Leatherhead explains that though the play is called "The ancient modern history of Hero and Leander, otherwise called the Touchstone of true Love, with as true a trial of friendship between Damon and Pythias, two faithful friends o' the Bankside," it really is no such learned device at all, but a plain piece of fustian *(Batholomew Fair,* Act V, sc. iii):

(Leatherhead explains:)

That [the Book of Hero and Leander] is too learned and poetical for our audience: what do they know what *Hellespont* is, *guilty of true love's blood?* or what *Abydos* is? or *the other, Sestos hight?*

(Cokes replies:)

Thou art in the right; I do not know myself.

Leatherhead: No, I have entreated master Littlewit to take a little paines to reduce it to a more familiar strain for our people.

Cokes: How I pray thee, good master Littlewit?

Littlewit: It pleases him to make a matter of it, sir; but there is no such matter, I assure you: I have only made it a little easy, and modern for the times, sir, that's all. As for the Hellespont, I imagine our Thames here; and then Leander I make a dyer's son about Puddlewharf: and Hero a wench o' the Bank-side, who going over one morning to Old Fish-street, Leander spies her land at Trig-stairs, and falls in love with her. Now do I introduce Cupid, having metamorphosed himself into a drawer, and he strikes Hero in love with a pint of sherry; and other pretty passages there are of the friendship, that will delight you, sir, and please you of judgment.

If Sir Edmund is right in his suggested gloss, then this play offers a good illustration of the phenomenon under discussion.

Before dismissing these plays on the Puritans, into which it seems likely that personal satire has been introduced, we ought at least to mention another on the same subject, which likewise contains a certain amount of personal allusion. I refer to the anonymous *Puritan of* 1606, which, Sir Edmund believes, foreshadows Jonson's play. "In this play," he declares (*Elizabethan Stage,* IV, p. 42), "the character George Pyboard is clearly meant for Peele, and the play uses episodes which appear in *The Merrie Conceited Jests of George Peele, Gent.*"

As in the case of *Gallathea,* or *The Hog Hath Lost His Pearl,* the clue to the fustian in many of these plays has been lost, or, at least, has not yet been fully deciphered; but the reasons for believing in their topicality are none the less valid. Tell-tale accompaniments, epistles, prologues, epilogues, inductions, or external contemporary reference, or a confused stage or text history, often give us the hint, sometimes even the assurance of topical intention on the part of the author; but it remains for students of the drama to unravel the clues and thus to establish the relation between the play and its original audience. This task involves not only the careful excavation of political and social data, but a kind of literary instinct as well; for, after all, the purpose of such research is to bring us to a better understanding of the artistry of the period under consideration. However impressive the mass of historical material may be, unless the attempted reconstruction makes artistic as well as scientific sense, literary critics are bound to be sceptical of the interpretation. Our aesthetic judgment must be satisfied, as well as our reason. The would-be archaeologists of the drama—if one may use such a term—have too often failed in one or another of these obligations. The equating of James I with Ariel, for instance, seems to many an astute critic to be even less intelligible than *The Tempest.* On the other hand, a refusal to entertain *any* attempted solution to a mysterious text, however plausible, argues, perhaps, more discretion than candour. The fact is that many such interpretations have been worked out and presented by the very best of Elizabethan scholars. It would obviously be impossible, in the scope of a chapter, to give a complete account of the work that has been done and that is constantly being done in this line. Some notion of it, however, is essential to our argument.

CHAPTER SIX

Anti-Spanish Plays

WE HAVE ALREADY ALLUDED to the long list of plays dealing with the Anglican schism and the growth of extreme Protestantism. We shall see later how both these subjects developed and how the changes were represented on the stage. I should like first, however, to notice the presence in the drama of political issues other than religion. Among the most convincing cases in the early years of Elizabeth's reign are those concerning the growing hostility to Spain. In the subsequent discussion of Ralegh's attitude on this question, we shall have occasion to describe this controversy in some detail. Here it must suffice to mention only the earlier cases, which form a background for Ralegh's fierce campaign. Many, indeed, most of these anti-Spanish plays are lost. Some we know only by title, for instance, Hathaway's *Conquest of Spain,* Haughton's *Conquest of the West Indies* (in collaboration with Day and Smith), Day's *Spanish Moor's Tragedy* (in collaboration with Dekker and Haughton), Chettle's *King Sebastian of Portugal.* We have already noted several of the later ones—*Believe As You List, Game at Chess,* and in our discussion of Ralegh's anti-Spanish activity we shall notice *Lust's Dominion,* Massinger's *Spanish Viceroy,* and others. Since some of these plays are lost, it is impossible to say with assurance that they were hostile to Spain, but in the light of the outrageously violent character of those that are extant, and in view of the similar violence displayed in the welter of pamphlets on the subject, the inference does not seem a bold one. Other anti-Spanish plays are referred to in contemporary letters, but, alas! without even the titles. Thus on 29 April, 1559, Feria wrote to Philip: *

She (Elizabeth) was very emphatic in saying that she wished to

* *Spanish State Papers,* I, p. 62. All these notices from the *Spanish State Papers* were gathered for me by Miss Helen Pascoe, a member of my seminar in Elizabethan Drama, Bryn Mawr, 1930.

punish severely certain persons who had represented some comedies in which your Majesty was taken off. I passed it by and said that these were matters of less importance than the other, although both in jest and earnest more respect ought to be paid to so great a prince as your Majesty, and I know that a member of her Council had given the arguments to construct these comedies, which is true, for Cecil gave them, as indeed she partly admitted to me.

Quite clearly, however, the Queen had no intention of punishing the presenters of such comedies, for they continued to be played at court throughout her reign. On July 20, 1586, the Venetian ambassador in Spain reported Philip's resentment at "the masquerades and comedies which the Queen of England orders to be acted at his expense. His Majesty has received a summary of one of these which was lately represented in which all sorts of evil is spoken of the Pope, the Catholic religion, and the King." *(Calendar of Venetian State Papers,* VIII, p. 182.)

The same "scandalous" procedure is alluded to in a pamphlet printed abroad in 1592, entitled *A Declaration of the true causes of the Great Troubles supposed to be intended against the Realm of England."* The following is quoted from Collier's *History of Dramatic Poetry* (i, p. 277):

And therefore as an introduction hereunto to make him [the King of Spain] odious unto the people, certain players were suffered to scoffe and jest at him upon the Common stages; and the like was used in the contempt of his Religion, first by making it no better than Turkish, by annexing unto the Psalms of David . . . this ensuing matter.

This last statement is elucidated by Miss Strickland *(op. cit.,* p. 286), in her citation of Robin Wisdom's paraphrases, such as the following:

Defend us, Lord! by thy dear word;
From Pope and Turk defend us, Lord.

It is not now possible to identify the pre-Armada plays on the subject, but Lyly's *Midas* will furnish an illustration which, as far as temper goes, is probably typical of the whole group. The account which follows is taken from Professor R. Warwick Bond's Introduction to the play. (*Works of Lyly,* III, pp. 107-111.) The Argument is thus summarized:

Bacchus, in return for the hospitality of Midas, king of Phrygia, offers to grant him anything he may desire. Eristus advises him to ask his Mistress; Martius, the sovereignty of the world; but Midas prefers the advice of a third councillor Mallacrites, and asks that his touch may turn everything to gold. A brief exercise of this power, which operates on his food, wine and raiment, reduces him to beg to be released from it. By the god's advice he bathes in the Pactolus, and transfers to its waters the fatal gift. A mood of sullen discontent follows (iv. 1, p. 141; v. 3, p. 159). As he is hunting in a wood on Mount Tmolus, he comes upon the gods Pan and Apollo about to engage in a musical competition, of which the Nymphs are to be umpires. Associated with them in this function, Midas decides for Pan, and his crass judgment is punished by Apollo with asses' ears. For a time he contrives to conceal them beneath a tiara; but the Nymphs have spread the news of his disgrace, and the words 'Midas the king hath asses ears,' spoken by shepherds, are reproduced by some reeds as they wave in the wind. This prodigy is reported to the king by his discreet and affectionate daughter Sophronia, by whose advice he seeks Apollo's oracle at Delphi. There on his acknowledgement of folly and profession of repentance the curse is removed, and he returns to Phrygia vowing to relinquish those designs of conquest, especially against the heroic islanders of Lesbos, his ill-success in which has supplied the undercurrent of his thoughts throughout the play.

Comic relief is sought in the relations between some Court-pages and the royal barber Motto, who, robbed by them of the golden beard he has cut from Midas' chin, recovers it by curing Petulus' toothache; but is afterwards entrapped into treasonable utterances of the secret of the asses' ears, and compelled to surrender the beard as the price of their silence.

Describing Lyly's changes in source material, Professor Bond says:

There remains as Lyly's sole source Ovid's *Metamorphoses,* xi, 85-193, which he closely follows. The only differences are that in Ovid Bacchus is under obligation for a service rendered to Silenus rather than to himself: that in Ovid no motive for Midas' desire of gold is suggested, while Lyly (as Hense suggests) supplies one in the thirst for conquest; that after ridding himself of the fatal gift Midas betakes himself to a rural life, represented in Lyly by his hunting expedition; that in the contest between Pan and Apollo, though Nymphs are present, it is Tmolus, the Genius of the mountain, who acts as umpire and whose decision is gratuitously contravened by Midas; that it is Midas' barber, alone cognizant of the ears, who whispers the secret into a hole he digs in the ground, afterwards filling in the soil, above which reeds spring up to repeat his words when stirred by the wind; and finally that Ovid mentions no expedition of Midas to Delphi, and no remission of the punishment; nor is any such recorded by Hyginus, whose 191st Fable relates both incidents, with the omission of the barber and the reeds.—A few words in iv. 2, p. 145 seem indebted to a chapter about Midas in *The Diall of Princes.*

Lyly, then, has added the comic elements of the Pages and Pipenetta and the Huntsman, and the contest between the former and the barber for the possession of the golden beard. He has added, too, the characters of Midas' daughter and her ladies, and of Midas' three councillors; and has credited Midas with ambitious designs on the territories of his neighbors, particularly on the island of Lesbos. Dilke (1814) was the first to observe that in this respect the play is intended as a satire on Philip II of Spain, representing "the produce of his mines in S. America by his desire to turn everything about him into gold; and the defeat of the Armada by the fruitless attempts of Midas to subdue the Island of Lesbos." Halpin in *Oberon's Vision* (Shakespeare Society [1843], p. 104) offers the following conjectural key:

Midas, king of Phrygia = Philip of Spain.
Isles north of Phrygia = British Isles. Lesbos = England.
Getulia, Lycaonia, Sola, etc. = Portugal, the Netherlands, and other countries cruelly tyrannized over by Philip.
Bacchus (the presiding deity of India) = The Genius of the Indies.
The golden gift = the influx of precious metals into Spain.
Pactolus (with golden sands) = the Tagus.
The contest in music = the controversy of the Reformation.
Tmolus = (probably) Trent.
Pan ('all'-Catholic) = Papal Supremacy.
Apollo (the antagonist principle) = Protestant Sovereignty.
Syrinx = the Roman Catholic Faith.
Daphne = the Protestant Faith.
Motto (who betrays the ears of Midas) = Anthonio Perez, Philip's secretary, banished for betraying secrets.
Sophronia (daughter and successor of Midas) = Isabella, Philip's daughter, to whom, on her marrying the Archduke Albert, he resigned the sovereignty of the Netherlands.

Martius, Mellicrates = The Dukes of Medina Sidonia and d'Alva.
Eristus (probably) = Ruy Gomez de Libra.
The golden beard perhaps alludes to the order of the Golden Fleece.

Subsequent scholars have made many minor changes in Halpin's tentative equation. Professor Bond notes several points in which the parallels suggested could have no application, and to his exceptions I should like to add a protest against the last item on the list. Surely the golden beard which has been cut from Midas' chin is a continuation of the famous jest which described the English depredations upon Spanish shipping as "the singeing of the King of Spain's beard." Professor Bond has further pointed to the obvious parallel between "the chaste Celia" and Elizabeth, and reminds us of the similarity between Midas' unsuccessful suit to Celia and Philip's to the English Queen in 1559. He concludes:

> There can be little doubt about the identification of Martius, whose 'councell hath shed as much bloud as would make another sea,' (v. 3, iii) with the pitiless Alva; and the play abounds in allusions to Philip's covetousness, treachery, and to current events such as the bloodshed in the Netherlands, the defeat of the Armada, the expedition of Drake and Norreys, iv. 4, 12, and other points.

It is difficult to understand why this stridently orthodox argument should have been objected to by authority; but an allusion in Nashe's *An Almond for a Parrot* clearly indicates that it brought Lyly into official "displeasure." Nashe says, "Now a days, a man can not haue a bout with a Ballatter or write *Midas habet aures asininas* in great Romaine letters, but hee shall bee in daunger of a further displeasure." It is possible, of course, that the play was incorrectly glossed and hence objected to on false grounds. Act IV, sc. iii has, incidentally, an amusing comment not only upon the danger of "calling a dog, a dog," * but also the difficulty of deciphering the fustian terms. Licio and Petulus, pages of the court, are trying to instruct Minutius in the esoteric language of the hunt. When Minutius declares that he cannot understand it, Petulus exclaims: " 'Tis the best Calamance in the world, as easilie deciphered, as the Characters

* The title page of *Pappe with a Hatchet* declares it to have been "written by one that dares to call a dog, a dog."

in a nutmeg." The reader may be glad to know that Calamance was another sort of Dutch fustian. It is described in the N. E. D. as "a Flanders woollen stuff of glossy surface, woven with a satin twill and checkered in the warp so that the checks are seen on one side only." As Bond points out, the "glossy surface and invisibility of the pattern" no doubt suggested the figurative use of the word to signify a device for obscuring the meaning. The Huntsman in the scene declares that Petulus' remarks are "worse than fustian." The modern reader no doubt thinks the same of the entire play. On the whole, however, scholars have accepted the interpretation suggested by Dilke, Halpin, Bond, and others. Sir Edmund Chambers expresses the orthodox view concerning this whole group of plays when he concedes that "you could beat the patriotic drum against the Spaniard, of course."

CHAPTER SEVEN

Marriage Plays

Concerning the prevalence on the stage of the next issue, there may be less agreement among scholars. I allude to the topic of the Queen's marriage. There are scholars who feel that it would have been all but impossible to discuss this subject with impunity. It is well to remind ourselves, however, of the long line of bold efforts made by the nobility and the commons to force the Queen to a decision. Describing the Parliament of 1566, Camden says (ed. 1688, p. 83):

> As soon as she returned to *London,* the Estates of the Realm assembled themselves in great number the first of *November,* being the day appointed by Summons: and after they had passed a bill or two, they began to debate roundly about the Succession, for that the Queen, as if she had vowed Virginity, had now in full 8 years of time thought nothing seriously of a Husband: and on the one side the Papists propounded unto themselves the Queen of *Scots,* which had newly brought forth a Son; on the other the Protestants, with different Affections, propounded to themselves, some one man, and some another; and every of them having respect to his own Security, and Religion, presaged the Storms of a most lamentable time, if she should die without a certain Successour. And so far brake forth their sharp and hot spirits, that they taxed the Queen as if she neglected her Countrey and Posterity; defamed *Cecyl* with Slanders and scandalous Books, as a corrupt Counsellour in this matter; and cursed Huic, the Queen's Physician, as a Disswader of her Marriage for I know not what womanish Impotency. The Earls also of *Pembroke* and *Leicester* and others openly, and the *Duke of Norfolk* more closely, thought that an Husband was to be imposed upon the Queen, or a Successour to be publickly designed by a Act of Parliament, even against the Queen's will. Whereupon they were excluded out of the Presence-Chamber, and prohibited Access to the Queen. But they soon submitted themselves to the Queen, and obtained Pardon.

All the same, they continued to "beseech the Queen with all earnestness, by the mouth of Bacon, Lord Keeper, their Speaker," to the effect that she presently marry, and "withall design a Successour."

Moreover they set before her how great a Storm of Calamities would threaten *England,* if she should depart this life without designing a certain Successour: that Seditions and Civil wars would break forth, wherein the Victory it self were most miserable: that Religion would be abolished, Justice smothered, the Laws troden underfeet, when there should be no certain Prince, which is the Soul of the Law; and that the Kingdom would fall as a Prey to Foreigners. And other Calamities of that sort they reckon up and aggravate wherein all men would be involved if she should die without issue. Out of the Sacred Scriptures also they modestly joyn hereunto Precepts, Counsels and Examples.

So far the Lords proceeded, even in the face of discipline; but the Commons spoke without any fear at all, and in a language which is really astonishing. Camden tells us *(ibid.,* p. 84):

But in the Lower House some there were which handled things more tumultuously, namely, *Bell* and *Monson,* great lawyers, *Dutton, Paul Wentworth,* and others, which twitted the Authority of the Queen's Majesty too much, and amongst other things maintained, "That Kings are bound to design a Successour: that the love of the Subjects is the strongest, yea the impregnable, Fort of Princes, and their onely Prop and Pillar. But this Love Princes cannot get, unless they provide that it may go well with their Subjects, and not onely whilst they live themselves, but after their death also. And this can by no means be effected, unless there be a Successour certainly known. That the Queen, by not designing a Successour, doth both provoke the Wrath of God, and alienate the Hearts of her People. But, that she may have God favourable towards her, and her People most loving and fast tied unto her, and that she may set up Monuments for herself in men's minds which shall never decay, let her design a Successour. If not, she may be reckoned of, not as a Nurse, not as a Mother of her Country, but as a Step-mother, nay, as a Parricide of her Countrey, which had rather that England, which now breathed with her breath, should expire altogether with her than survive her. That no Princes but Cowards, and such as are hated of their own People, and timorous Women, have ever stood in fear of their Successours; and the dangers of a designed Successour are not to be feared of that Prince which is fortified with the Love of his People."

Compared with this address, the boldness of the dramatists seems nothing incredible. Yet Camden informs us that "All this Queen Elizabeth heard with much Discontentment, yet for a while she either contemned it, or concealed it within her Breast" (that is, she concealed it from the petitioners); but to Cecil she wrote: "If these fellows were well answered and paid with lawful coin, there would be no fewer counterfeits among them"—which certainly indicates her temper if not her precise meaning. Miss Strickland says, "We fear she meant the members of the House of Commons."

Meanwhile there is abundant contemporary witness to the fact that the "Ballaters" and the dramatists did present the matter again and again, and from almost every conceivable angle. In spite of the delicate nature of the question and with full knowledge of the grave danger incurred should the royal wrath be stirred, the subject was presented at court, not only once or twice, but—if we may believe the Spanish Ambassador who saw the plays in the Queen's company—continually and habitually. Every aspect of the question was dramatized and every point of view urged. Some, like *Gorboduc,* represented the evils attendant upon failure to provide an heir; others, like *Hemetes the Hermit,* urged the Queen to accept a certain suitor; some even went so far as to condemn certain royal wooers in the very presence of their own ambassadors. Contemporary letters are strewn with references to the practice. On 10 July, 1564, Silva wrote to Philip *(Spanish State Papers,* I, pp. 367-68):

> The Queen came out to the hall, which was lit with many torches, where the comedy was represented. I should not have understood much of it if the Queen had not interpreted as she told me she would do. They generally deal with marriage in the comedies and she turned to me and asked again about your Majesty, and whether the Prince (Don Carlos) had grown. . . . The comedy ended and then there was a masque of certain gentlemen dressed in black and white, which the Queen told me were her colours, and after dancing a while, one of them approached and handed the Queen a sonnet in English, praising her.

Some months later he wrote again describing a new comedy. The plot centered about a discussion between Juno and Diana on the vexed question, Juno advocating marriage, Diana chastity. Jupiter gave the verdict in favour of matrimony. Silva says *(ibid.,* I, p. 404), "The Queen turned to me and said, 'This is all against me.' "

Sometimes, however, she seemed to be in connivance if not in actual co-operation with the Court comedians. On 13 July, 1559, the Bishop of Equila wrote to Philip *(ibid.,* I, p. 91):

> The King of Sweden's ambassadors who have arrived are being treated by the Queen in a manner that does away with any doubt about her marrying their master, for they are being made fun of in masques in their own presence.

Cecilia, the Swedish King's sister, who spent the year 1565-6 in London,* wrote to her brother of how "another time she, being bidden to see a comedy played, there was a black man brought in, and as he was of an evil favoured countenance, so was he like manner full of lewd, spiteful, and scornful words, which, she said, represented the Marquis, her husband." *(Calendar of State Papers, Foreign,* XI, [1569-1571], no. 2149, p. 567.) It is astonishing how few are the records of prosecution where the records of offense are so plentiful. On one occasion, a play was actually interrupted by the Queen, but we do not even know the name of the play, or the author, much less the details of his punishment—if, indeed, he was ever punished at all. The account is given by Miss Strickland *(op. cit.,* p. 136):

> On the last day of the merry year 1559, a play was acted in the court before the queen; but we learn that the license usually allowed on such occasions being abused in this instance, they acted something so distasteful to her majesty that they were commanded to break off, and were superseded by a masque and dancing.

Again, we shall find in Lyly's comedies of the Court the fullest illustrations of the plays in this group. We may remind ourselves of Lyly's special opportunities for gleaning inside information, if not indeed for fulfilling actual literary and theatrical commissions. From his undergraduate days he had en-

* For a most interesting discussion of this visit, see, Miss Ethel Seaton's *Queen Elizabeth and a Swedish Princess* (London, 1926).

joyed the protection and patronage of Burleigh, and during the decade of Oxford's favour at Court (approximately 1580-1590) he acted as private secretary to the Earl, who was himself a writer of plays and sponsor of a company of actors "probably made up of boys from the Chapel and St. Paul's choirs." (Chambers, *Elizabethan Stage,* III, p. 412.) Lyly was in some sort a master of these boys, being responsible for their theatrical as well as musical training, and he took them to court in 1584 where they performed, before the queen, *The History of Agamemnon and Ulisses.* Harvey calls him the "Vicemaster of Paules and the Foolmaster of the Theatre." He may be alluding to the Martinist plays at The Theatre.

Incidentally, the quarrel between Harvey and Lyly was occasioned by Lyly's playing the fustian interpreter of Harvey's *Speculum Tuscanismi* in *Three Proper and Wittie familiar Letters.* (Bond, *Works of John Lyly,* I, p. 30.) In satirical hexameters, Harvey had described the fopperies of an Italianate Englishman, and Lyly had informed the Earl of Oxford that he himself was the prototype of this ridiculous figure. Naturally, Harvey resented this piece of service on Lyly's part, promptly accused him of being Oxford's "minion secretary" and, of course, vigorously denied the charges. He wrote bitterly of him as one who

> . . . would needs forsooth verye courtly perswade the Earle of Oxford, that something in those Letters, and namely, the Mirror of Tuscanismo, was palpably intended against him; whose noble Lordship I protest I neuer meante to dishonour with the least prejudicial word of my Tongue, or pen, but euer kept a minde full of reckoning of many bounded duties toward the same.

Harvey was summoned before the Privy Council (Nashe even suggests that he was imprisoned in the Fleet), but he was saved by the above denial and apology. A man might write Athens when he meant the University of Oxford, as Lyly actually did in *Euphues,* or Gonsago when he meant Claudius, as Hamlet did; or, as we have noted, as many others did upon various occasions; but who can *prove* that he meant more than he wrote? The fustian "dodges" are legion: he may protest flat that he talks of Dionysius' court and of no court but that; or that it is extant, writ in choice Italian; or that he speaks of vices, not persons, etc., etc.

This note on the Lyly-Harvey quarrel, though not a war of the theatre, is nevertheless, not a digression from the subject in hand, as it gives a view from another angle, of the literary habits of the man and the times.

I have already noted that no detailed interpretation of *Gallathea* has ever, so far as I know, been presented. Nevertheless there are, as Professor Bond observes *(ibid.,* I, p. 45),

> . . . fairly strong reasons for connecting *Sapho, Gallathea, Love's Metamorphosis,* and *Endymion* as links of a continuous chain. . . . All four may perhaps be regarded as reflective of Elizabeth's changing attitude towards love and marriage, or at least of what a courtier might deem to be such. *Sapho* ends with the defeat of Venus, and the assertion of the Queen's independence. Diana in *Gallathea* develops this attitude into one of active hostility, a composition with Venus and her rascally son being with difficulty effected at the close. Ceres in *Loves Metamorphosis* exhibits a new reverence for the power of the god and an anxiety to save her wilful nymphs from the consequences of contemning it. Cynthia, in *Endymion,* has a similar tenderness for love and lovers, condescends to minister by a kiss to the restoration of the hero, and accepts his faithful devotion.

Professor Bond omits all discussion of the possible allegorical interpretation of *Campaspe,* but the nearness of its date to *Sapho,* and the connection between the Appelles and Pygmalion stories, together with the relation between Appelles and *Euphues* legends, all seem to me to demand at least a note. In his discussion of the sources of *Campaspe,* Bond mentions the appearance in the Stationers' Register of several "balletts" connected with Appelles. One of these, "a ballett entituled an history of Alexander, Campaspe and Appelles, and of the faythfull fryndeshippe between them," was printed for Colewell in 1565. Another, not noted by Bond, by Bernard Garter, was entitled "A Strife between Appelles and Pigmalion"—probably the ballad referred to in the *Register* as "a ballet of Appelles and Pygmalyne to the tune of the first Appelles." This ballad has been printed by Mr. Joseph Lilly, in *A Collection of Seventy-Nine Black-Letter Ballads and Broadsides, printed in the reign of Queen Elizabeth, between the years 1559 and 1597,* from a collection in the library of Henry Huth. In this ballad-story, the editor tells us, the author, "a not unknown writer of that age feigns a contest between the two artists, Appelles and Pygmalion, for superiority, the result of which was a statue by the latter of a woman of such surpassing beauty as had never been seen before, and Dame Nature took it away, gave life to it, and restored it to earth in the person of Queen Elizabeth." The commentators add, "The pious Englishman of that day imagined in his devotion, that no beauty could surpass that of the great champion of Protestantism." The ballad is, undoubtedly, a part of the propaganda to induce the Queen to decide on a "mate," but without more precise knowledge, it would be hazardous to suggest an identification for "the highest man of the state" on whom Dame Nature bestows the enlivened beauty. The ballad is sufficiently rare to justify its inclusion here:

A Strife Betwene Appelles and Pigmalion.

When that Appelles liued in Grece,
Pigmalion also raigned than:
These two did striue to frame a pece,
Which should amaze the sight of man,
Whereby they might win such a name,
As should deserue immortall fame.

Appelles then strayed euerie where,
To marke and view ech courtlie dame,
And when he heard where any were
Did well deserue the prayse and fame,
He thither rode, with willying harte,
Of her to take the cumliest parte.

And when he had, with trauaile great,
A thousand wights knit vp in one,
He found therewith to wurke his feat,
A paterne such as earst was none;
And then with ioye retourned backe,
For to those limmes but lyfe did lacke.

Pigmalion eke, to shew his arte,
Did then conclude in iuorie white
To forme and frame in euerie parte
A woman fayre to his delighte,

Wherein was euerie limme so coucht,
As not a vayne he lefte vntoucht.

When their two cunnings ioyned were,
A worlde it was to see their wurke;
But yet it may greue euerie eare,
To heare the chaunce therein lurke;
For through the pece they framed had,
For loue Pigmalion did run mad.

Which seene, Appelles shut his booke,
And durst no longer viewe that sight;
For why? her comelie limmes and looke
In one did passe ech other wight;
And while Appelles wiped his eye,
The pece did mount vnto the skye.

Whereas Dame Nature toke it straight,
And wrapt it vp in linnen folde,
Esteeming it more then the waight
Had ten times ben of glistryng golde;
Shee lockt it vp fast in a chest,
To pleasure him that shee loued best.

Appelles then, dismayed much,
Did throw his booke into the fire;
He feared lest the gods did grutch
That wurkmen should so high aspire;
Yet once agayne he trauailed Grece
With lesse effect, and made a pece,

Which long time did hold great renowne,
For Venus all men did it call,—
Tyll in our dayes gan Nature frowne,
And gaue the workemannes worke a fall;
For from her chest, t'auoyde all stryfe;
Shee tooke the pece, and gaue it lyfe;

And for a token gaue the same
Vnto the highest man of state,
And said, Since thou art crownd by Fame,
Take to thee here this worthie mate,—
The same which kyld the caruers strife,
Before that Nature gaue it life.

Lorde! yf Appelles now did know,
Or yf Pigmalion once should heare,
Of this their worke the worthie show,
Since Nature gaue it life to beare;
No doubt at all her worthie prayse
Those selie Grekes from death wold rayse.

Then those that daylie see her grace,
Whose vertue passeth euerie wight,—
Her comelie corps, her christall face,—
They ought to pray, both day and night,
That God may graunt most happie state
Vnto that Princesse and her mate.

Finis. Ber. Gar.

Imprinted at London, without Aldersgate, in Little Britaine, by A. Lacy.

With such a background it is difficult to understand Professor Bond's reserve concerning *Campaspe.* Euphues declares (Part II) that "Appelles (loved) the counterfeit of Campaspe," but Bond declares this fact to be "a circumstance that cannot be said to form part of Pliny's brief account, but only of Lyly's play." Surely, it could have referred to the above ballad as well as the play, and if so, it is impossible not to regard the play as somewhat allegorical too. In 1579, while Lyly was writing *Campaspe,* he was proceeding very cautiously. As he says in his dedication of *Euphues and his England* to Oxford, "I being a naughtie painter, have gotten a most noble patron: being of Vlysses minde, who thought himself safe vnder the shield of Ajax." He declares that it suffices him "to grind colours for Appelles, though I cannot garnish, so I be of the same shop." He declares that he had been delayed "many a month in Italy viewing the Ladyes in Painters shop,"—i.e., like Appelles, he had been gathering materials for his new "pece" which I believe to be the portrait of Campaspe. In this I concur with Professor Bond, who says, anent this passage, "I am inclined to believe that the first half of 1579 was occupied, not so much with *Euphues and his England,* as with his first dramatic venture *Campaspe.*" In my opinion *Campaspe* intervened between Parts I and II of *Euphues* and the allegory of all three had to be restricted and left incomplete, for two reasons: first, for fear of making a wrong guess as to the outcome of the contemplated marriage negotiations. In the Prologue to the Ladies, he says (*op. cit.*, II, p. 8):

When *Venus* is paynted, we can-not see hir back but hir face, so that all other thinges that are to be recounted in loue, *Euphues* thinketh them to hang at *Venus* back in a budget, which bicause hee can-not see hee will not set downe;

and second, because of the powerful resentment of those satirized. In the Epistle to Oxford, Lyly declares (*ibid.*, p. 6), "Appeles dyed not before he *could* finish *Venus,* but before he *durst*: [Italics inserted.] Nichomachus left Tindarides rawly, for feare of anger, not for want of Art; Timomachus broke off Medea scarce halfe coloured, not that he was not willing to end it, but that he was threatened." My view is that although Lyly was planning Part II of *Euphues,* after he was threatened for Part I, he undertook to write an interlude in which the allegory would be both general and inoffensive, so as to throw the pursuers off the trail. *Campaspe* was, I believe, that interlude. He says in the Dedication to *Euphues and His England (ibid.*, p. 4) that he had undertaken some such blind which would mislead the sleuths from the scent of the true interpretation of Part II:

I resemble the Lappwing, who fearing hir young ones to be destroyed by passengers, flyeth with a false cry farre from their nestes, making those that look for them seeke where they are not: So I suspecting that Euphues would be carped at by some curious Reader, thought by some false shewe to bringe them in hope of that which then I meant not.

He further declares (*ibid.*, p. 6):

I haue not made Euphues to stand without legges for that I want matter to make them, but might to maintein thẽ: . . . For he that vieweth Euphues wil say [as Dryden did of Absolom] that he is drawen but to the wast, that he peepeth, as it were behinde some screene.

To the Gentlemen Readers, he admits (*ibid.*, p. 12):

My discourses shall be regarded, some for the smell, some for the smart, all for a kinde of a louing smacke.

He concludes the Dedication by assuring himself (*ibid.,* p. 7)

. . . that the little Cock boat is safe, whẽ it is hoised into a tall ship, that the Cat dare not fetch the mouse out of the Lion's den.

But first he produces *Campaspe* as a blind. The Prologues, both at court and at the Blackfriars, are full of strategic skirmishing, all to this effect (*ibid.,* p. 315):

They that feare the stinging of waspes make fannes of peacockes tailes, whose spots are like eyes.

That is, *Campaspe* is like a fan through which he can peep to see how the ball is progressing.

We which stand in awe of report, are compelled to sette beefore our owne *Pallas* shield, thinking by her virtue to couer the others deformitie.

That is, by the inoffensiveness of *Campaspe* he hopes to gain so strong a place in the royal favour that he may be protected from the resentment of those "touched" in *Euphues.* He realizes that *Campaspe,* by being "less curious than you look for," will disappoint those lively ladies of the court who are thirsting for some big excitement, but he begs they will be

. . . as Theseus, being promised to be brought to an Eagles neast, and trauailing al the day, found but a wrenne in a hedg, yet said, this is a bird: so we hope, if the shower of our swelling mountaine seeme to bring foorth some Eliphant, perfourme but a mouse, you will gently say, this is a beast.

That is, if you are expecting the allegory in this play to be of elephantine proportions, I hope you will not be too disgusted at finding it only the size of a mouse. Even so, he says,

Wee feare that our labours slylye glaunced on, will breede some content, but examined to the proofe, small commendation . . . [for] we haue mixed mirth with counsell, and discipline with delight, thinking it not amisse in the same garden to sowe pothearbes, that we set flowers.

In conclusion, he warns them that

Basill softly touched, yeeldeth a sweete sent,
but chafed in the hand, a ranke sauour.

Precisely what lay behind the story of Appelles' love for the "counterfeit of Campaspe" or the dotage of Pygmalion upon the image of Gallathea, or who was suggested by these "fond artists" (Leicester and Oxford?), or who by Alexander (Alençon?), or who by "the highest man of state," I do not presume to decide. It is worth noting, however, that Marston's satire on this subject was among those condemned for their offensiveness to be burned in 1599.

As in the case of *Midas,* Bond, following Fleay, gives for *Sapho* a fairly complete interpretative analysis. The Argument is as follows *(ibid.,* p. 363):

> Venus, travelling to Syracuse to reduce the pride of queen Sapho, dowers the ferryman Phao with preternatural beauty, which while filling his heart with vague desires makes him scornful of all women, until a chance meeting kindles a mutual passion between Sapho and himself. The lovesick queen, torn with the conflict between pride and affection, prays Venus' aid and meanwhile sends for Phao to cure with his simples the fever she feigns before her ladies. Venus meets Phao in the palace; and herself falls a victim to the beauty she has created. Jealous of Sapho, she cajoles Vulcan to furnish Cupid with special arrows which may undo the work of his former shaft and transfer the ferryman's love to herself. But Cupid, having fulfilled part of his task by cooling Sapho's affection, is won to betray the design and to inspire Phao with loathing instead of love for Venus: nor can the goddess by threats or coaxing disengage her son from Sapho, with whom he takes up his abode, while Phao quits Sicily in despair.
>
> Variety is sought in the conjugal relations of Venus and Vulcan, in the opposition between the spirit of the Court and that of the student as represented by the two friends Trauchinus and Pandion, in the sprightly talk of Sapho's ladies, among whom Mileta is chief, in the love-precepts given to Phao by the crone Sybilla, and in the intercourse between the smith Calypho and a couple of Pages, which is made the occasion for a parody of formal logic.

Of the sources and allegory, he says *(ibid.,* p. 364):

> He avails himself of the classical legend of a passion between Sappho and Phao, which, appearing first in several lost Attic comedies, and "probably derived," says Smith, "from the story of the love of Aphrodite for Adonis, who in the Greek version of the

myth was called Phaethon or Phaon," receives beautiful development in Ovid's Epistle (*Heroid.,* xv) which formed our author's chief authority. With this he combines the fable, unconnected with Sappho, which is related in Aelian's *Varia Historia,* xii, 18, and Palaephatus' *De Fab. Narrat.* lib. i, of Venus' gift to Phao of extraordinary beauty on the occasion of his ferrying her across a straight at Mytilene in Lesbos. . . .

Combining Ovid and Aelian, Lyly makes Venus the enemy and rival of Sapho and protagonist of his plot; and amplifies her part by introducing her conjugal relations with Vulcan. A transfer of the scene from Lesbos to Sicily, where in Ovid's Epistle Sappho addresses her lover, enables him to introduce Vulcan's forge at the neighbouring Aetna, and suggests the addition of the Cyclops, not the pastoral monster of Homer, but one of the smiths of Virgil's *Fourth Georgic,* ll. 170-75. . . . Further, Lyly introduces the Sibyl and her cave from Ovid, *Met.,* xiv, 104ff. . . . This medley of classical suggestion is made to serve the author's main purpose of flattering the Queen by an allegorical representation of the relations between herself and her suitor, the Duc d'Alençon. The idea of this match, first mooted by Catherine de Medici when Anjou, the elder brother, showed signs of cooling in his suit, was seriously renewed in 1578, and not wholly abandoned till 1582. Froude's *History* (vol. xi) details the long course of vacillation and chicanery by which Elizabeth used her marriage-negotiations with France, Spain, and the revolted Netherlands. On Feb. 6, 1582, Alençon finally quitted England to assume the sovereignty of the United Provinces that had been offered him by the Prince of Orange, a sovereignty never more than nominal, and soon terminated by his unsuccessful military attempt on the liberties of Antwerp (Jan., 1583). He died on June 9, 1584. It is to this underlying allegory, clearly alluded to in the Prologue at Court and the Epilogue, especially in the words about 'the necessitie of the hystorie' and the comparison of the whole inconclusive story of the mazes of a labyrinth, that the changes made in the classical myth of Sappho are chiefly due. Hence the representation of her as a queen with a Court, and the suppression, surprisingly and needlessly thorough, of her poetic fame and functions: hence the striking beauty and majesty of person with which she is dowered, whereas Ovid represents her as of dark complexion and short stature (xi, 33-6); hence the invitation of Phao to her Court, her struggle against her passion and final conquest of it: while her secure assumption at the close of the prerogatives of Venus and the person of Cupid are in the happiest vein of courtly flattery. The distress and perplexities of Phao, and his departure from Sicily at the call of other destinies, are quite in keeping with the facts of Alençon's courtship; nor need the marked ugliness of the duke disqualify him for the part. Elizabeth had declared in 1579 that "she had never seen a man who pleased her so well, never one whom she could so willingly make her husband" (Froude, xi, p. 155); and the courtly poet saw and seized his opportunity in the tale that Love herself had made Phao beautiful.

I do not know that it is necessary to find originals for any of the other characters; but Mr. Fleay (*Biograph. Chron.*, vol. ii, p. 40) identifies Pandion, the university student newly arrived at court with Lyly himself, the Sibyl might stand for Catherine de Medici; and the clear personality of the witty Mileta, with her obvious attempt on Phao in iii, 4, suggests that an original might also be found for her, if our knowledge of the Court history were fuller.

To his interpretation of the general allegory, Bond adds his interpretation of Sapho's dream in IV, ii *(ibid.,* p. 405):

Sapho: What dreames are these Mileta? and can there be no trueth in dreams? yea, dreams haue their trueth. Me thought I saw a Stockdoue or woodquist, I knowe not how to tearm it, that brought short strawes to build his neast in a tall Cædar, where, whiles with his bill hee was framing his buylding, he lost as many fethers from his wings, as he laid strawes in his neast: yet scrambling to catch hold to harbor in the house he had made, he sodenly fell from the bough where he stoode, And thẽ pitifully casting vp his eies, he cried in such tearmes (as I imagined) as might either cõdemne the nature of such a tree, or the daring of such a minde. Whilest he lay quaking vpõ the ground, & I gazing one the Caeder, I might perceiue Antes to breede in the rinde, coueting only to hoord, & caterpillers to cleaue to the leaues, labouring only to suck, which caused mo leaues to fall frõ the tree, thẽ there did feathers before frõ the doue. Me thought Mileta I sighed in my sleepe, pittying both the fortune of the bird, & the misfortun of the tree: but in this time quils began to bud againe in the bird, which made him looke as though he would flie vp, and then wished I that the body of the tree woulde bowe, that hee might creepe vp the tree; then—and so—Hey ho!

Mileta: And so what?

Sapho: Nothing Mileta: but, and so I waked. . . .

Professor Bond interprets as follows (*ibid.*, p. 562):

In this dream of Sapho's, which is of course allegorical, the lofty cedar represents Elizabeth herself; the ants those who would enrich themselves at her expense; and the caterpillars probably the Jesuits and seminary priests with designs against Elizabeth's government, a proclamation against whom was issued in June, 1580. In the stock-dove who strove to build his nest in the cedar, who fell from the bough, but whose quills began to bud again, I think we are to recognize not Alençon, who is represented by Phao, but Leicester, his favour with the Queen, his disgrace in 1579-1580, and his reviving credit with her, which was no doubt one of the reasons for her recent rejection of Alençon. Notice that the dream is not introduced till after the new scheme, which is to divert Sapho's affections from Phao, has been set in motion. Compare the allegorical dream of Endimion (v. i. pp. 66-7).

Whether or not Professor Bond is correct in his analysis, it is obvious that the dream was allegorical, and it is fairly certain that the audience so regarded it.

As already indicated, all four plays, *Sapho, Gallathea, Love's Metamorphosis,* and *Endimion,* probably deal with the queen's views on this matter, but I subjoin an account only of the last, partly because this play has received the fullest analysis; partly, too, because the interpretation offered by Bond, following Halpin, is so interestingly supplemented by Chapman's *Hymn to Cynthia.* Again I quote Bond's analysis (*ibid.*, III, p. 9):

In Lucian's short dialogue (Decorum Dial. 11) Selene draws for Venus a pretty picture of Endymion lying asleep on his cloak, after hunting, upon the mountain of Latmos, his darts slipping from his left hand while his right is thrown back round his head, and of herself advancing on tiptoe so as not to awaken him, and—"but you know the rest"—she breaks off, "and I needen't tell you more, except that I am terribly in love with him." Brief allusions are also found in Pausanias, v. i, §§ 2-4; Hyginus, *Fab.* 271; Ovid, *Art. Am.*, iii, 83; etc. But it is obvious that the materials afforded by the classical myth, the perpetual sleep and the kiss of Cynthia, were insufficient for a play; and what Lyly has done is to weave around this beautiful picture an allegorical drama of Court-life whose action has no place nor counterpart at all in the myth. The Moon-Goddess becomes a queen surrounded by her Court; the Greek shepherd, her favourite courtier. As the double subject of this

Court-allegory, Lyly takes the two most salient features in the domestic history of the reign: (1) the rivalry between Elizabeth (Cynthia) and Mary of Scotland (Tellus); (2) the Queen's perennial affection for, and temporary displeasure (in 1579) with, Robert Dudley, Earl of Leicester (Endymion); a sufficient warrant for the dramatic connection of the two being supplied in the match actually contemplated between Mary and Leicester in 1563-1565. This double subject is supplemented by two subordinate and connected subjects: (1) the quarrel between the Earl and Countess of Shrewsbury (Geron and Dipsas); (2) the relations of Sir Philip Sidney (Eumenides) with his uncle Leicester, and his love for Penelope Rich, née Devereux (Semele); while several other personages more or less prominent are introduced. With this Court-allegory Lyly attempts, without much success, to combine a physical allegory of the Moon and the Earth as heavenly bodies.

This elaborate method of combining literary sources with allegories of Nature and Politics is, of course, familiar to us through Spenser, and, as we have seen, through Chapman; but in these plays Lyly has introduced the fashion into the drama. The boldness of the allusions is, perhaps, the less incredible if we realize the amazing publicity which the whole affair of Leicester's proposed marriage to Mary received, both at home and abroad. As early as 1559, Sir Thomas Challoner, the Queen's representative at the Spanish court, described his embarrassment at hearing the matter so frankly and contemptuously "discanted upon lewd tongues." (Strickland, *op. cit.*, p. 134.) In a private postscript to one of his dispatches to Burleigh, printed in the *Burleigh Papers,* he observed:

> I assure you, sir, these folk are broad-mouthed, where I spoke of one too much in favour as they esteem, I thinke ye guess whom they named. [Leicester] . . . As I count the slander most false, so a young princess cannot be too wary what countenance or familiar demonstration she maketh more to one than another.

At the French court, the English Ambassador, Nicholas Throgmorton, was suffering similar vexations and humiliations, so much so that he took the bold step of sending his secretary Jones on a special mission to inform Her Majesty how the affair was being treated in France.

When Leicester was actually offered to Mary, that proud

princess replied, with more wit than discretion, "that she looked on the offer of a person so dear to Elizabeth as a proof of good will rather than good meaning." Mary afterward denied that she had ever made such a jest; but, as Miss Strickland observed (*op. cit.*, p. 167), "If Mary forebore from mockery at this offer, no one else did, for it was a theme of public satire and mirth in England, Scotland, and France." Certainly, the reports that Sir James Melville sent home about the Queen's fondness for Dudley, were not such as to induce a lady of Mary's breeding to take the offer seriously. In describing the investiture of Dudley as Earl of Leicester and Baron of Denbigh, Melville says that the Queen herself helped to put on his robes, "he sitting on his knees before her, and keeping a great gravity and discreet behaviour; but as for the Queen, she could not refrain from putting her hand in his neck to tickle him, smilingly, the French ambassador and I standing beside her."

On all hands, the reports of such unregal, if not disrespectable familiarity tended to embarrass her ambassadors who were trying to carry through the farce of her various marital negotiations. On one occasion the Queen herself not only discussed the whole delicate subject with Quadra, the Spanish ambassador, but, says Miss Strickland (*op. cit.*, p. 178), she actually "forgot the dignity of a gentlewoman and a sovereign as far as to demonstrate the improbability of what had been said, by showing him the situation of her sleeping apartment and that of her favourite. Subsequently, however, she found that her favourite's health was likely to be impaired by the dampness of the room he occupied in the lower part of the palace, and assigned him a chamber contiguous to her own."

When in 1566 it began to look as though she would actually marry her "Robin," Cecil drew up six important objections to the marriage, one of which was that this marriage with his sovereign would be taken as a confirmation of all the scandalous reports that had so long and so confidently circulated both at home and abroad.

It may be seen from these several quotations that the scandal—or libel—had become so notorious that it was no longer possible to treat it with diplomatic reserve or decorum. Again and again the Court witnessed "high scenes" between Her Majesty and foreign ambassadors—scenes which certainly were no credit to the Queen and mortifying to the ambassadors, and which must have struck the attendant courtiers as intensely diverting. Lord North, whom Elizabeth had sent as special ambassador to congratulate Henry III on his accession to the throne of France, sent home a series of reports concerning the shocking dramatic satires in which the Queen's morals and manners were mercilessly lampooned, at the direct instigation of the Duke of Guise and the Queen-Mother. North declared that they had dressed up a buffoon in the English fashion and called him in derision a "milor' of the north." Elizabeth was so enraged at these stories that, we are told (Strickland, *op. cit.*, p. 295), she charged the French Ambassador with the matter before the whole Court, to his great consternation. He related how "she raised her voice in great choler" and spoke so loudly "that all her ladies and officers could hear her discourse." The capable ambassador assured the irate lady "he would maintain to his last sigh" that the Queen-Mother was far too polite a princess, and the Duke of Guise too finished a chevalier to say, or cause to be said, anything which reflected on the Queen of England, the dignity of her crown, or the honour of the late King Henry, her father; that *milor'* North had misunderstood the whole, and was consequently a bad negotiator between princes." (*Dépêches de La Mott Fénélon,* VI, p. 331.) It was, however, impossible to mistake the intention of the buffoonery in the French court. Lord North had related how "two female dwarfs had been dressed up in the chamber of Catherine de Medici, and that the queen and her maids had excited them to mimic her [Queen Elizabeth] and ever and anon throwing in injurious words to prompt the vile little buffoons to a vein of greater derision and mockery." As La Motte observed: "It was not the mockery of her father first mentioned, but of herself which had really lain boiling and swelling at the bottom of her heart."

My belief is that Chapman's *Hymnus in Cynthiam* is a direct reply to these scandalous rumours. Under cover of the Endymion myth, or by *prosopopoiea,* as Chapman himself learnedly describes the process in the gloss, he rebukes these detractors of the Queen and her favourite, maintaining that the relation between them was purely platonic:

> This beauty [glossed as *Beauty of the Mind*]
> hath a fire upon her brow
> That dims the sun of base desires in you [Cynthia],
> And as the cloudy bosom of the tree
> Whose branches will not let the summer see
> His solemn shadows; but do entertain
> Eternal winter, so thy sacred train,
> Thrice mighty Cynthia, should be frozen dead
> To all the lawless flames of Cupid's godhead.
> To this end let thy beam's divinities
> Forever shine upon their sparkling eyes,
> And be as quench to those pestiferent fires
> That through their eyes impoison their desires.
> Thou never yet wouldst stoop to base assault;
> Therefore those poets did most highly fault
> That feigned thee fifty children by Endymion,
> And they that write thou hadst but three alone.
> Thou never any hadst, but didst affect
> Endymion for his studious intellect.
> Thy soul-chaste kisses were for virtue's sake;
> And since his eyes were evermore awake
> To search for knowledge of thy excellence—
> And all for astrology—no negligence
> Of female softness fed his learned trance,
> Nor was thy veil once touch'd with dalliance.

It is possible that many plays, poems, ballads and emblems reflecting both the courtly and the popular attitude toward this favourite have either been lost or not yet deciphered; but many are still extant. The wealth of Dutch medals both hostile and friendly to him is, perhaps, an indication of the extent of the propaganda concerning him. A glance at some of these non-dramatic allegories upon the Queen and her affairs will reveal, I believe, an important aspect of sixteenth century satire.

CHAPTER EIGHT

Non-dramatic Satire

THE GENERAL SUBJECT of the relation between the stage and the audience has often been discussed, but, as far as I know, no thorough attempt has been made to relate the temper of theatrical audiences to the mental habits and temper of the sixteenth-century readers of novels, pamphlets, letters, and even broadsides, though, as Professor G. B. Harrison has pointed out in the preface to his edition of Marston's *Scourge of Villanie* (p. v), without such a study, a complete understanding of the plays is impossible. In spite of this truth, however, all too often critics have set up and fostered a distinctly artificial separation between the theatrical and other literary activities of Elizabethan authors. If known, it is at least not generally recognized, that most of the dramatists were not only pamphleteers, or novelists, or satirists as well, but more often than not, they were actually government agents of one kind or another, or in residential service to a man of political or social importance, so that their literary works were often definite commissions of political propaganda or social satire. Lodge, Lyly, Nashe, Gascoigne, Whetstone, Watson, Chapman, Drayton, Daniel, Dekker, Heywood, Marlowe, Massinger, Munday, Tourneur, and scores of less well known men, were so engaged and were, as a result, involved in constant social or political controversies that found expression in current prose pamphlets, satire in prose and verse, the latter in all forms, from the crudest broadsides to formal narrative and lyric poetry. Here even the most ardent of the anti-topicalists would admit that allegory was the order of the day. None seriously doubts that Luxurio, Torquato, & Co., from the *Scourge of Villanie* had contemporary prototypes, or that Mavortio paralleled Essex in *The Transformed Metamorphosis,* or that Martin was Penry, or that Epistle and Epitome were libels on Whitgift and Aylmer, or that the Phyllis of *Colin Clout* was Anne Spencer, or that Theana of the same poem was Anne Russel, or that the Ape and the designing Fox of *Mother Hubbard's Tale* represented Simier and Alençon, or that Timias suggested Ralegh, or that Meliboe in the *Ruines of Time* was Walsingham, or that the Gnat stood for Spenser and the Sleeping Shepherd for Leicester, or that the Frog of *Mother Goose,* who "would a-wooing go," was a gibe at Alençon, or that Egdon is Burleigh in the Second Eclogue of *A Fig for Momus,* or that Hepar is Tom Stuckley in the Fifth Satire *(ibid.),* or that Phrigio is Lodge in the *Scourge of Villanie,* or that Cosmosophos is Walsingham, Philoplutos is Burleigh, and Diogenes is Lodge in *Catharos: Diogenes in his Singularitie,** etc., etc., *ad infinitum.*

Indeed, the Elizabethan fad for nicknames was part and parcel of the same device. Almost every notable person appears in contemporary letters under the guise of a nickname. Catherine de Medici was constantly referred to as "Madame le Serpent"; Mary Stuart is called by Walsingham "the Bosom Serpent"; the Lord-Keeper Egerton was called by Lord Henry Howard, in a letter to Essex, "The Dromedary, that would have won the Queen of Sheba's favour by bringing pearls" [referring to a gift of pearls made by Egerton to Elizabeth]; Parsons said that Ralegh was a courtier too high in the regard of "the English Cleopatra"; both Drayton and Spencer called him "the Summer's nightingale"; Burleigh and Cecil were designated as "old Leviathan and his cub"; the Earl of Westmoreland was "the bull," and Northumberland "the moon" (this was the "cow that jumped over the moon" in the "hey diddle diddle" rhyme); the Queen called Leicester her "lapdog" and her "robin," Simier her "little ape," Alençon her "frog," Hatton her "belwether," and her "mutton," and her "pecora campi," Ralegh her

* This satire is described on the title-page as follows: "Catharos: Diogenes in his Singularitie. Wherein is comprehended his merrie baighting fit for all mens benefits: Christened by him, A Nettle for Nice Noses."

Of this satire, Dr. Edward Tenney says (*Thomas Lodge,* Cornell Univ. Press, 1935, p. 108), "Its interest for the Londoner probably lay more in the satire directed at Sir Francis Walsingham and Lord Burghley than in the heavy moralizing of the latter part of the book. In opening, Diogenes (Lodge) lectures Cosmosophos (Walsingham) and Philoplutos (Burghley) on their defects as citizens and statesmen." The identification of these characters is Miss Alice Walker's. See, *The Reading of an Elizabethan,* R. E. S. viii, p. 266.

"water," and her "fish." She actually wore upon her person jewels cut in these shapes as mementos of her lovers. The one of Alençon was in the shape of a frog with the Duke's face cut thereon! The Jesuits were called "caterpillars," the Covenanters "ravens," the Protestants "sheep," the Catholic Church "the wolf." Leicester's enemies called him "the gypsy" and "the bear." Naunton tells us (*Frag. Reg.*) that on his deathbed, Sussex said to his friends and dependents, "I am now passing into another world and I must leave you to your fortunes and the queen's grace and goodness. But beware the gipsy [Leicester] or he will be too hard for you; you know not the nature of the beast as I do." Lady Douglas Sheffield and her rival, the Countess of Essex, were called Leicester's "Old and New Testament." There was an elaborate correspondence carried on between the "king of Scots" and Lord and Lady Rich "under the feigned names of Ricardo and Rialta." James they called Victor. Their letters were written in cipher, and they had nicknames for all the court. Thomas Fowler, Burleigh's spy in Scotland, gave information of this correspondence to his employer, with these particulars: "That Queen Elizabeth herself was called Venus, and the earl of Essex 'the weary knight,' because he was exceeding weary of his office, and accounted his attendance 'a thrall that he lived in, and hoped for a change, which was, that the queen would die in a year or so.' " (Strickland, *op. cit.*, p. 515.) Mrs. Charlotte Carmichael Stopes *(The Third Earl of Southampton* [1922], p. 94) quotes a letter, dated 9 July, 1595, from Sir Thomas Cecil to his brother Robert:

> I left the moon in the wane at my last being at the Court; I hear now it is half moon again, yet I think it will never be at the full, though I hope it will never be eclipsed, you know whom I mean.

Would that *we* did! Could it have been Northumberland? We should also like to know to whom Birch refers when he tells us (II, p. 489) that Essex "had against one man, Henry, Lord Cobham, for sworne patience, calling him *The Sycophant* even to the queen herself, tho' that lord was of no small insinuation with her; and he had a great aversion to one lady whom he used to term the spider of the court."

The use of animal names for sobriquets had two general sources: (1) puns on a person's name, as "water" for Walter, "robin" for Robert, "bush" for Bushey, etc.; and (2) crests from a person's coat-of-arms, such as "the moon" for the Percies, "the bull" for Westmoreland, "the steed" for Arundel, etc. The following stanzas taken from a MS ballad dated 1399, printed by Thomas Wright in the first volume of his *Political Poems and Songs* (London, 1859, p. 363), illustrate both classes of symbol-names:

Ther is a busch [Sir John Bushey] that is forgrowe;
Crop hit welle, and hold hit lowe, or elles hit wolle be wilde.
The long gras that is so grene [Sir Henry Greene]
Hit most be mowe, and raked clene; forgrowen hit hath the fellde.

The grete bagge [Sir William Bagot] that is so mykille,
Hit schal be kettered, and maked litelle; the bothom is ny ought.
Hit is so roton on ych a side,
Ther nul no stych with odur abyde, to set thereon a clout.

Thorw the busch a swan [Thomas of Woodstock] was sclayn;
Of that sclawter fewe wer fayne; alas! that hit betydde!
Hit was a eyrer good and able,
To his lord ryght profitable; hit was a gentel bryde.

The grene gras that was so long,
Hit hath sclayn a stede [Arundel] strong, that worthy was and syth.
Wat kyng had that stede on holde,
To juste on hym he might be bold, als schulde he go to fyth.

. . . . .

No literary student of the period needs to be reminded of the myriad of fanciful names under which the poets and courtiers were fain to present their absurd gifts and flatteries to the Queen. In the Prologue to *Old Fortunatus,* the Pilgrim, addressing "Eliza" as "Dread Queen of the Fairies," declares (Dekker, *Pearson Reprints,* I, p. 83):

Some call her Pandora, some Gloriana; some Cynthia; some Belphoebe; some Astraea: yet all by severall names to express severall loues. Yet all those names make but one celestiall body, as all those loues meete to create but one soule.

As we know, he might have added Britomart (as in the *Faerie Queene*), Urania (as in the *Arcadia*), Sidanen (as in *John a Kent*), Titania (as in the *Eltham Pageant*), Dido (as in Ashe's *Elizabeth's Farewell to the Army)*, Judith (as in the *Mask of the League)*—not to mention the whole galaxy from Lyly—Diana, Sappho, Gallathea, Ceres, etc. These, of course, belonged to the language of Presentations. Behind her back, however, in private letters and in the popular jingles of contemporary *Satura,* she appears under far less dignified appellations. The affair of Amy Robsart brought many such uncomplimentary allusions. Dame Dudley—as she was then called—had been living cosily with her husband in their retired little nest in the country, even while he shamelessly wooed the Queen. When the inconvenient wife was found dead at the foot of a staircase in Cumnor Place, some impudent satirist, suspecting treachery, summed up his view of the situation as follows:

> Elizabeth, Lizzie, Betsy, and Bess
> They all went together to seek a bird's nest.
> They found the bird's nest with two eggs in it;
> They took one and left one in it.

For a worse stave than this, celebrating Anne's triumph over the electress Sophie, that royal lady bestowed on Tom D'Urfey a fee of forty pounds! *

Miss Strickland tells us that at dinner D'Urfey used to stand by the sideboard during dessert and repeat just such political gibes and doggerel ballads; and she suggests that Tarlton fulfilled a like office to Elizabeth. Whether or not these particular doggerel verses refer to Leicester and the Queen, it is quite certain that contemporary satirists did not fail to capitalize the death of Lady Dudley. The author of *Leicester's Commonwealth* takes the following view of the subject:

* The rhyme is given by Miss Thomas (*op. cit.*, p. 315):

> The crown's far too weighty
> For shoulders of eighty
> She could not sustain such a trophy;
> Her hand, too, already
> Has grown so unsteady
> She can't hold a sceptre;
> So Providence kept her
> Away, poor old Dowager Sophy.

For, first, his lordship hath a speciall fortune, that, when he desireth any woman's favour, then what person soever standeth in his way, hath the luck to die quickly for the finishing of his desire. As for example, when his lordship was in full hope to marry her majesty, and his own wife stood in his light, as he supposed, he did but send her aside to the house of his servant, Forster of Cumnor, by Oxford, where, shortly after, she had the chance to fall from a paire of staires, and so to break her neck; but yet without hurting of her hood that stood upon her head. But Sir Richard Varney, who, by her commandment, remained with her all that day alone, with one man only, and had sent away, per force, all her servants from her to a market, two miles off; he (I say) with his man, can tell how she died: which man, being taken afterward for a fellony, in the marches of Wales, and offering to publish the manner of the said murder, was made away privily in the prison: and Sir Richard himself dying about the same time in London, cried pitiously, and blasphemed God: and said to a gentleman of worship of mine acquaintance, not long before his death, that all the devils in hell did teare him in pieces. The wife also of the Bald Butler, kinsman to my lord, gave out the whole fact a little before her death. But to return unto my purpose, this was my lord's good fortune to have his wife dye at that time when it was like to turne most to his profit.

The editor of the *Traditional Memoirs* appends the following note:

The fate of this unfortunate lady is often alluded to in the plays and satires of the time. The author of the *Yorkshire Tragedy,* imputed to Shakespeare, thus hints at it:

> The surest way to charm a woman's tongue,
> Is, break her neck, O a politician did it.

At her funeral sermon, preached at Oxford, Leicester's chaplain, meaning to say, "This poor lady, so pitifully killed," stumbled on the unhappy phrase, "so pitifully *murdered,*" which made a strange impression on the hearers.

Marston, who was perhaps as complete an artist in fustian as any, railed at this inelegant popular balladry (Prologue to *The Scourge,* p. 9) which affected "too much obscurity & harshness," and noted "vices so that no man can understand them," and which were "so palpable dark and so rough writ, that the hearing them reade would set a man's teeth on edge." In the *Fifth Satire,* he girds at such again:

> Yon's one hath yean'd a fearfull prodijie,
> Some monstrous mishapen Balladry.
> His guts are in his braine, huge Jobbernoule,
> Right Gurnets-head, the rest without all soule.

It is true that many of these political jingles are so "palpable dark" that it is exceedingly difficult at this date to make an incontrovertible analysis. Indeed, a prime desideratum in this whole field of Elizabethan satire is a good book on sixteenth- and seventeenth-century broadsides and chapbooks. Scholars have long vaguely realized this gap in our historical knowledge of this period, but little has been done to remedy the situation. As early as 1842, James Orchard Halliwell made a beginning attack on the problem by his publication for the Percy Society of *The Nursery Rhymes of England,* which, he states, were "collected principally from Oral Tradition." The fourth edition of this book is described by the author as a "vernacular anthology." A subsequent essay by Halliwell, entitled *Popular English Rhymes,* was followed by a study by J. Bellender Kerr, entitled *Popular English Phrases and Rhymes.* In 1866 the London Society of Antiquaries published a catalogue of their *Collection of Printed Broadsides,* and in 1867 Mr. Joseph Lilly published his admirably annotated *Collection of Seventy-Nine Black-Letter Ballads and Broadsides, printed in the reign of Queen Elizabeth between the years 1559 and 1597.* Besides the early editions of *Mother Goose's Melody,* and the excellent *Collection of Rump Ballads,* printed in 1662 for Henry Brome, there were the *Chap-Books* of John Marshall of Aldemary Churchyear, Bow Lane, London, dated 1817. None of these collections, however, was deemed of sufficient importance by Dr. Thomas Wright to be noticed by him in his complaint on the lack of any public collection of informal satire. In the preface to his *Caricature History of the Georges,* 1867, Dr. Wright says (p. vii):

> No public collections of caricatures, or political tracts, or papers, exist. The poverty of our first national establishment, the British Museum, in works of this class is deplorable. As far as regards

caricatures, I had fortunately obtained access to several very extensive private collections. Unfortunately, no one, as far as I have been able to discover, has made any considerable collection of political songs, satires, and other such tracts, published during the last century and the present. This is a circumstance much to be regretted, for it is a class of popular literature which is rapidly perishing, although the time is not yet past when such a collection might be made with considerable success.

Dr. Wright is correct in saying that there exist no "public collections" of popular English *satura,* whether of tales, or ditties, or both in mixture, and there are almost no modern scholarly commentaries on this class of literature worth speaking of. It is, however, not quite correct to assume that there have been no collections whatever. Miss Katherine Elwes Thomas, in her delightful popular book on this subject, *The Real Personages of Mother Goose,* (Boston, 1930, p. 25), alludes vaguely to descriptions made by the librarians of the Bodleian and the British Museum of an "edition" as early as 1620 of *The Rhymes and Jingles of England.* Whether or not there was such a collection at this date, it is certain that many and various highly eclectic collections have appeared at intervals ever since that time.

This is not the place to give a careful account of these many satirical collections or "garlands," or "gallimaufrys," or "Old Wives' Tales" that have appeared both in English and in French under the sponsorship of a variety of literary "mothers"—Mother Goose, Mother Hubbard, Mother Bombie, Mother Bunch, Mother (or Gamer) Gurton, etc. Such an account will undoubtedly form the subject of a separate volume on sixteenth- and seventeenth-century social and political history. Suffice it to observe here that such satires, both in verse and prose, were turned out during this period in quantities which might almost be described as "mass production." Every tavern, every buttery-bar, every booth at a fair became a "ballad factory"; and not only every petty poetaster and rhymester who could spin out a song "extempore," or "yark up a pamphlet" over night, but indeed almost any rover or rogue who could learn rhymes at a game of crambo was sure of a formula "to keep a drink in his purse."

The early drama abounds in allusions to these irresponsible balladists and their wares—"chocolate-house lampoons," Congreve later calls them. From these allusions we learn not only how prevalent and how offensive such balladry was, but how feared and detested were the popular "ballaters." When Helena in *All's Well* is trying to convince the King of her reliability, she offers to submit to "the vilest torture," which includes the absolute humiliation of being "traduced by odious ballads." When Falstaff is threatening the worst possible revenge against his colleagues, he swears he will have "ballads made on them all and sung to filthy tunes." (*I Henry IV,* II, ii.) Jonson assured Drummond that "a poet should detest a ballet maker," and in *Neptune's Triumph* he raged because the poet's Masque was held up in the performance till they had done with "the abortive and extemporal din of balladry." Indeed, almost every dramatist, at one time or another, was engaged in what Nashe called "a bout with a Ballater." In his introduction to the *Collection* already referred to, Lilly discusses many of these famous controversies in popular verse. The fall of Thomas, Lord Cromwell, the Rising in the North, the Bartholomew Massacre, the Babington Conspiracy, the Succession episodes, the death of Essex, the Overbury murder, the hanging of Sir Thomas Plumtree, the mutilation of a Priest "that lost his nose/for saying of Mass as I suppose"—all these events and many others not mentioned by Lilly brought forth scores of satires from every faction.

Of course, the broadsides were not always intentionally satirical. Sometimes they were sentimental or "woeful"; sometimes they were just newsy or "curious"; sometimes they were personal or political boomers. There were ballads for and against Leicester and Ralegh and Essex and Cecil and D'Alençon and Mary Stuart and Philip of Spain. Indeed, every subject of popular interest introduced new scores in this "din of balladry." The ballad makers and ballad hawkers haunted every public or semi-public gathering. They were at once the tool and the bane of every faction of contemporary agitation. Lilly declares that almost immediately after the invention of printing, the popular press became the most powerful of all agents in social agitation.

Motley, in his *Rise of the Dutch Republic* (I, p. 347), describes the similar development of this "tavern literature" in the Netherlands: there the balladeers described their rendezvous as "Rhetoric Chambers." Of these Motley says:

> These popular clubs for the manufacture of homespun poetry and street farces out of the raw material of public sentiment, occupied the place which has been more effectively filled in succeeding ages and in free countries by the daily press. . . . The authors and the actors of these comedies, poems, and pasquils were mostly artisans or tradesmen.

Naturally "authority" frowned upon such irresponsible handling of controversial matters. We have already noted Wolsey's fight with the balladists. (See p. 13.) Bishop Bancroft, plagued by the dissemination of Essex ballads, wrote (*Cecil Papers,* lxxxviii): "A fellow goeth about the streets selling the Ballads whereof here is a copy enclosed. He giveth it out that the Countess of Essex made it, which induced many to buy. I am told the ballad was ready half a year ago, upon some other occasion. I have sent for the Wardens of the Stationers. These villainous printers trouble me more than I write of." From the Continent, Cardinal Granvelle wrote to Philip, "These rhetoricians who make farces and street plays are particularly angry with me, because two years ago I prevented them from ridiculing the holy Scriptures." (Motley, *op. cit.,* p. 349.) Similarly Richard Clough wrote to Sir Thomas Gresham, "Such plays [of rhetoric] . . . have cost many a thousand man's lives, for in these plays was the word of God first opened in this country, which plays were and are forbidden much more strictly than any of the books of Martin Luther." Motley refers to "the uncouth gambols," the "awkward but stunning blows" meted out by these literary artisans in "an endless succession of rhymes and rebuses, epigrams, caricatures, and extravaganzas." On the Continent, as in England, "poems were pasted upon the walls of every house and passed from hand to hand, and farces were enacted in every street." Even so staid a person as Isaac Pennington was guilty of pinning a hostile limerick of his own devising on the door of St. Paul's Church. The sixteenth century was, in fact, the heyday of political tracts, chapbooks, and broadsides. These latter, by the very nature of the case—that is, because they were printed on single, unattached sheets—were exceedingly ephemeral. The German name for them, "fliegender Blätter," indicates at once the reason for their vast influence and their perishability. They were so cheap that they could be scattered abroad wholesale, like modern handbills, and, like these latter, they were rarely preserved. The sixteenth-century equivalent for our current phrase "not worth cigarette paper," was "not worth a ballad sheet." Indeed, they were often used for pipe-lighters. In Chapman's *All Fools,* the knight declares: "My boy once lighted a pipe of cane-tobacco with a piece, a vile ballad, and I'll swear I had a singing in my head a whole week after."

As can be gathered from these various contemporary allusions, the word "ballad" in sixteenth-century usage, covered all types of popular verse, from limerick to elegy, and the same subject would be treated in a dozen different ways. The tragical debacle of the Rising in the North could be ticked off in a nameless ditty of Mother Goose's with a flaunting reference to "the cow that jumped over the moon," (alluding to the escape of Westmoreland, whose crest was a bull, and the capture of Northumberland, whose crest was a moon); or it could be more pompously set forth by one John Barker in a fifteen-stanza effusion, known as *The Plagues of Northumberland* "to the tune of Appelles"; or the even more elaborate version of the tragedy by W. Kyrkh, who sang of the "Westmereland Bull and the Man in the Moon," and "the bear that brought their bravery down." Both these ballads are in Lilly's collection. It is fairly safe to say that the longer the poem, the better its chance of preservation in contemporary typography. So far as I know, there exists no sixteenth-century copy of the "Hey, diddle diddle" limerick, but Lilly refers to at least five extant versions of longer ballads on the subject. The original of the Barker ballad furnishes an illustration of the style of the typical broadside. At the top of the poem there is a row of five woodcuts. Such an accompanying illustration was the usual thing, and it supplied, as do our modern cartoons, the key to the mystery of that "palpable darkness" against which even a contemporary might sometimes complain. Such an illustrated ballad is described by Falstaff when he threatens to memorialize his "capture" of Sir John Coleville in a ballad, if Prince John will not promise to have the deed officially recorded (*II Henry IV*, IV, iii):

I beseech your Grace, let it be booked with the rest of this day's deeds; or by the Lord, I will have it in a particular ballad else, with mine own picture on the top of it, Coleville kissing my foot.

The significance of a portrait of a fat knight offering his foot to be kissed would, of course, he recognized by anyone who saw in the features of the cartoon a resemblance to some contemporary historical figure. I have, unfortunately, been unable to procure for this volume a reproduction of a sixteenth-century ballad or cartoon. Believing, however, that such an illustration would be valuable in helping the reader to sense the dynamism in this popular fustian device, I have ventured to include one or two samples of a later date. The first one has to do with a series of Whig lampoons directed against the Pretender and his party, the so-called "High Church," or "Catholic" party. Dr. Wright observes (*op. cit.*, p. 4), "The Whig pamphlets and songs pictured in broad colours the unsanctified lives of many of the Church clergy, their venality and greediness; and one song ends with the taunt, that

They swallow all up
Without e'en a gulp;
There's nought chokes a priest but a halter."

On one of the Tory ballads Dr. Wright continues (*ibid.*, p. 20):

It was by songs of this character that the minds of the lower classes in England were to have been prepared, it was hoped, to join in a general rising in favour of the exiled house of Stuart. The Jacobite minstrelsy of Scotland had, no doubt, its counterpart in this country; but its effects were much less considerable, and it was soon forgotten, with the exception of scattered scraps. The name of the Pretender was sometimes uttered by the disorderly rabble amid the election riots at the beginning of the year; but after the flight of Bolingbroke and Ormond, it was heard much more frequently, and songs and satires against the Hanoverian family were sought and listened to with avidity. The Whigs replied to these with a shoal of pamphlets and papers, reproducing all the old tales of the Revolution, and casting ridicule and contempt upon the son of James II, whom they insisted on looking upon as a mere impostor. The common story was, that the Pretender was the child of a miller, and that, when newly born, he had been conveyed into the Queen's bed by means of a warming-pan; and this contrivance having been ascribed to the ingenuity of Father Petre, the Whigs always spoke of the Pretender by the name of *Perkin,* or little Peter. The *warming-pan* figures repeatedly in the satirical literature of the day.

In the light of this background it will readily be seen that the following ballads were *not* "nonsense verses," but pungent, if somewhat "rough writ," current satire:

'T was when the seas were roaring
With blasts of northern wind,
Young Perkin lay deploring
On warming-pan reclined:
Wide o'er the roaring billows
He cast a dismal look,
And shivered like the willows
That tremble o'er the brook.

Similarly when Sir Constantine Phipps, the Jacobite ex-Chancellor of Ireland, who had been Sacheverell's * advocate at his trial, was granted a degree by the University of Oxford, the balladeers sang:

The impudent P—pps
Must come in for snips,
Who at Oxford so lately was dubbed;
Though instead of degree,
Such a bawler as he
Deserved to be heartily drubbed

Young Perkin, poor elf,
May promise himself
Two things from the face of that man;
There's brass within reach
To furnish a speech
And the lid of a warming-pan.

* Sacheverell was "the man who jumped into a bramble bush and scratched out both his eyes."

Dr. Wright does not publish a cartoon of either of these ballads, but he does print one, satirizing this story of the Pretender's birth, stating, incidentally, that many of these were printed abroad.

Here the Queen is sitting by the cradle while her Jesuit adviser, with his arm around her neck, whispers in her ear. The infant has a child's windmill on his bed to mark the trade of his real parents. It is labeled "The Catholic Family." Obviously all, or mostly all, of these details would be quite lost on a modern observer, unless the key were supplied. And so it is with all such satire. The contemporary of Napoleon did not need to be told who was "Bloody Boney, the carcass butcher who retired to Scarecrow Island," and no more did an English contemporary of Philip II of Spain need to be told who was the terrible ogre, or "giant," who was hogging all the "golden eggs" and "money bags," while he listened to the melodious "harp-strains" of Irish Catholic rebellion at the top of his great "bean stalk," always threatening brave little "Englishmen," like "Jack," who ventured to invade his "plantation" and help himself to a bit of colonial gold. Elizabethan children were literally sung to sleep by such anti-Spanish "lullabies," or "lullibuleroes," as,

> Fee, fie, fo, fum,
> I smell the blood of an Englishman.
> Whate'er he be, alive or dead,
> I'll grind his bones to make my bread.

or,

Rain, rain, go to Spain, . . .

and so on, *ad infinitum*. The early editions of political jingles were, in fact, issued under the caption of *Lullabies*.

It is to be regretted that Miss Thomas' very valuable, though popular book on *The Real Personages of Mother Goose* is so informally documented that, without further contemporary analogues, it is not always quite safe to accept her identifications; though, on the whole, she has presented very good grounds for her parallels, which include (beside many others): Richard III, the hunchback, with "Humpty-Dumpty," who "had a great fall" on Bosworth Field, so that "all the King's horses and all the King's men" could not put him together again; Henry VIII with a long line of "big-bellied Bens," including "big Tom Stout," who pulled Elizabeth, "the pussy-cat," out of the well, and "Robin the bobbin, the big-bellied Ben," who in his despoiling of the monasteries "ate the church and ate the steeple, and ate the priests and all the people," who gloated over the various "Christmas pies" and "dainty dishes" that were presented to him stuffed full of the title-deeds of abbey lands, while he sat in his "counting-house counting out his money." His poor queen, Catherine of Aragon, was, of course, cooped up "in the parlour, eating bread and honey," while the new favourite "maid"-in-waiting, Anne Boleyn, was out in the garden of the royal palace, showing off "the clothes" from her exquisite French wardrobe, with which she had just returned from Paris in the train of the King's sister, until "along came the blackbird," Wolsey, "who snipped off her saucy nose," by sending her home. Wolsey, who, because he finished his baccalaureate studies at the astonishing age of fifteen, was commonly called the "Boy Bachelor," appears as "Little Boy Blue"; he is also "Little Tommy Tucker," and later, poor "Jack," who with Bishop Tarbes as his playmate "Jill," failed in the mission entrusted to them of arranging a marriage for Mary Tudor, and consequently "fell down the hill" into the King's displeasure and so "broke his crown," while "Jill came tumbling after." Wolsey is also the "Poor dog" for whom Mother Church, as "Old Mother Hubbard," went to her Papal treasury, or "cupboard," to fetch him a bone.

Robin The Bobbin,

the big bellied Ben
He ate more meat
than threescore men
He ate the Church,
he ate the steeple
He ate the Priests
and all the people.
And yet he complained
his belly was n't full.

From a Unique Print of the same size

by Remigius Hogenbergh *1582.*

In the Collection of Richard Bull, Esqr.

Publish'd by J. Thane. *Octr. 1st 1791.*

Philip II of Spain, because of his short stature was Queen Mary's "little husband no bigger than her thumb," to whom she gave "some little garters to garter up his hose," i.e., upon whom she bestowed the Order of the Garter. It was this marriage that was mocked in the Mother Goose riddle or "Recipe for a Christmas Pudding":

Flour of England, fruit of Spain
Met together in a shower of rain.
Put in a bag and tied with a string.
If you tell me this riddle
I'll give a gold ring.

The final quarrel between Philip and Mary is the subject of the story in

My little old man and I fell out,
I'll tell you what it was all about;
I had money and he had none,
And that's the way the trouble begun.

Mary herself was "the farmer's wife," who ran after the "three blind mice," Cranmer, Ridley, and Latimer, "with a carving knife." Of course, Mary Stuart comes in for her share. She is "little Miss Muffet who sat on a tuffet" until along came a "great spider," named John Knox, and "sat down beside her and frightened Miss Muffet away." She is also little "Mary, Mary, quite contrary," who with her "Pretty maidens all in a row," i.e., her famous "four Mary's," was being so tenderly reared in the lovely gardens of Linlithgow.

The most frequent sobriquet for Elizabeth in these jingles was "the cat." She is the "little pussy whose coat is so warm," and who will "do no harm," as long as she is stroked and flattered. With her sister Mary as the "little dog," she appears as Edward's "pussy-cat" in the jingle

Highty Cock O!
To London we go;
To York we ride;
And Edward his pussy-cat tied to his side;
He shall have little dog tied to the other
And then he goes trid trod to his grandmother.

Her flirtation with D'Alençon, "the frog who would a-wooing go," is glanced at in

> The rose is red, the grass is green,
> Serve Queen Bess, our noble Queen!
> Kitty the spinner
> Will sit down to dinner,
> And eat the leg of a frog.
> All good people
> Look over the steeple,
> And see the cat play with the dog.

As has already been pointed out, "the dog" was a very common nickname for Leicester. He is "the little dog" who "laughed to see such sport," while the Queen's Carver, or "Dish," Edward Seymour, ran away with her Taster, or "Spoon," Catherine Grey. Leicester and Essex both appear as "Robin," the most common nickname for Robert. Either might be the subject of

> The north wind doth blow
> And we shall have snow,
> What will poor Robin do then?
> Poor thing!
> He will sit in a barn
> To keep himself warm
> And hide his head under his wing,
> Poor thing!

The "north wind" is very often the symbol of the Queen's "ingratitude."

If within her own realm the critics of the Queen dared to speak out thus impudently, we shall not be surprised to find that her enemies in Spain and France expressed themselves even more unreservedly. That such satires were couched in fustian terms, even when there could have been no danger from the use of real names, is an important witness to the prevalence of the fashion. Camden states that D'Espes, the Spanish ambassador, had written some shameful libels upon Elizabeth, under the title of *Amadis Oreana*. The Queen told the French ambassador, La Motte Fénélon, (*Dépêches de La Motte Fénélon*) that D'Espes had "kindled a war between his master's country and hers," and she implied that he had done so by writing of her "in a different manner from what he ought, he having named her Oreana in some of his letters; at which she was so indignant, that if he had been her subject, she would have pursued him with the utmost rigour of the law."

It is worth emphasizing that much English satire had to be printed abroad, because of the danger involved. We are told that William Roy's satire against Wolsey was "a proceeding so dangerous that at that period he was afraid to print in England, but had it done in Holland by some friend whose sentiments to the Cardinal in this respect were pretty much the same as his own." We have already noted Doleman's treasonable book. On 5 November, 1595, Rowland Whyte wrote to Sidney about this book concluding with the following postscript (C. C. Stopes, *op. cit.,* p. 87): "The Book I spake of is dedicated to my lord Essex and printed beyond the sea, and is thought to be treason to have it."

The admirable *Catalogue of Satirical Prints and Drawings in the British Museum,* prepared by Mr. Frederick George Stevens (1870), describes many emblems, medals, and other illustrations of such satire, both at home and abroad. These, of course, date from much earlier times than our period, the earliest, as a matter of fact, dating about 1320. But the entire series offers a most illuminating commentary and supplement to much literary satire with which we are already familiar, from Skelton to Dryden. Reproductions of these old prints and medals should accompany any discussion of the literary propaganda of the period under consideration, for they follow exactly the changing styles of satire which we have already noted—from what Saintsbury called the "dim and dreary personages of allegory" characteristic of the fourteenth century, to the stinging personal satires of the sixteenth and seventeeth. Every type appears, from animal allegory to precise portraiture. We have noted how the stream of reforming satire, attacking both Church and State, straggling but never really interrupted, widened suddenly, after Henry's divorce, into the uncontrollable flood of Reformation propaganda; just so these pictures, which had, before 1530, been sporadic and casual, began after that date to multiply so rapidly that neither the censoring legislation nor the prosecutions could keep pace. The student of Tudor literature could hardly find a more profitable field to explore than these old prints and medals in the British Museum. Here it must suffice to mention only a few among those which best illustrate the hostile foreign propaganda of which we have been speaking. The Dutch Medal on the Relations between England and the Low Countries offers a striking illustration. It is described in Stevens' Catalogue (no. 39, p. 21) as follows:

> Obverse, an inhabitant of the Low Countries, in trying to avoid the smoke of the Spanish Inquisition, is throwing himself into the fire of English perfidy; legend, *"Fugiens Fumum Incidit in Ignem, 1587."* Reverse, a monkey squeezing its young ones to death in embraces; legend, *"Libertas ne ita chara ut simiae Catuli."*

Stevens hazarded no interpretation or identification of this monkey, but it is obvious that the whole scene is allegorical. The same may be unhesitatingly claimed for the Dutch Medal struck two years earlier, representing Queen Elizabeth and the State deputies. An engraving of this medal is published in Pinkerton's *Medalic History of England* (1790), as no. 4 in Plate VIII, and is described in Stevens' Catalogue (no. 31, p. 19) as follows:

> Obverse, the Queen sitting amid roses, holding out her hand to the deputies with legends, *"Rosa Nectare Imbuta,"* and *"Macte Animi."* Reverse, two men eating hay out of a manger with a horse and an ass; with legend *"Spreta ambrosia Vescilis Feno, 1585."*

The medals satirizing Leicester's conduct of affairs in the Netherlands are numerous. In Stevens' Catalogue, numbers 32-35 are all variants of one device which might have served as illustrations to Naunton's gibe:

> He was sent governor by the queene to the revolted states of Holland, where we read not of his wonders; for they say, he had more of Mercury than he had of Mars, and that his device might have been, without prejudice to the great Caesar, Veni, vidi, redivi.

The medal commemorating his departure from the States is described thus by Stevens (no. 34):

Obverse, a bust portrait of the Earl of Leicester, with the name and title as governor of the Low Countries, 1587. Reverse, a flock of sheep feeding in a field; the shepherd's dog, *"Invitus Desero,"* walks before the sheep, as if to leave them; legend, *"Non Gregem, sed Ingratos."*

Of course, we must not imagine that such foreign comment upon English affairs was always hostile. The engravings by Peter Miriceyns of Elizabeth as Diana, seated in judgment upon the Pope as Calisto, after her Transgression, is obviously friendly in intention. Stevens' description is as follows (pp. 6-7):

Altered from an engraving representing Calisto brought before Diana. Queen Elizabeth, naked and accompanied by female allegorical figures, is seated on our right and beneath a group of trees; each personage holds a shield, and upon these are the armorials of the Protestant allies in Europe. On the other side of the design the Pope, as Calisto, is struggling upon the ground and uncovered by Time, the ordinary allegorical figure, and Truth, a naked female. Beneath the seat of the Pope is gathered a nest of eggs at the moment of hatching; from one of these issues a cockatrice, with the word *"Inquisition"* written on its side; *"Draghon"* appears upon another egg, from which a monster also issues; the ground beneath is strewn with daggers, partisans, &c. One of the eggs is inscribed *"Baltasar sera morder vandê Prins,"* in reference to the murder of the Prince of Orange; under these words is a gallows. In the distance and beneath the wing of Time is another gallows, with a man hanging from it. In the lower right-hand corner is a Dutch inscription lauding the queen and describing the subject. Artist's monogram at foot of a tree. (10x8¼ in.)

In another metier, this furnishes a clear example of the Gonsago device—foisting a new political interpretation on to an old pattern.

It is possible that the Queen herself was somewhat responsible for the silly fashion of nicknames, though the sobriquets of *Mother Goose* are older than Richard III. Certainly, however, she contributed to it both in her letters and in a goodly number of bad rebuses. Thus, of several Nottingham knights she wrote:

Gervase the gentle, Stanhop the stout,
Markham the lion, and Sutton the lout.

She was fond of referring to her father as a "princely lion," and on one occasion declared, "She was not exactly a lioness; yet she allowed she had the temperament and was the issue of a lion, and that accordingly as the king of France behaved placably to her, so he should find her soft and tractable as he could desire; but if he were rough, she should take the trouble to be as rude and offensive as possible"! (La Motte Fénélon, *op. cit.*, VI, p. 190.)

In reply to Hatton's laboured rune about the Book, Bucket and Bodkin,* she ordered Heneage to write (Strickland, *op. cit.*, pp. 340-41) that she liked the preamble so little

. . . that she had little inclination to look on the bucket or the book; and that if princes were like gods (as they should be) they would suffer no *element* [water—Walter] so to abound as to breed confusion; and that pecora campi [Hatton] was so dear unto her, that she had bounded her banks so sure, that no 'water' nor floods should be able to overthrow them. And for better assurance unto you that you should fear no drowning, she hath sent you a bird, that, together with the rainbow, brought the good tidings that there should be no more destruction by *water*. And further, she willed me to send you word, with her commendations, that you should remember that she was a shepherd, and then you might think how dear her *sheep* was unto her.

Nevertheless, as Miss Strickland observes, "neither the gracious token of the dove from the royal spinster, nor her condescending protestations how dear her pet sheep was to her, satisfied her jealous vice-chamberlain, who, after sulking for two months, took the liberty of sending her a jewel in the form of a fish-prison, a far-fetched conceit in allusion to Ralegh's cognomen 'water.' " To this rubbish, she replied, through Heneage:

. . . that the 'water,' and the creatures therein, do content her nothing so well as you ween, her good having been ever more of flesh than of fish, and her opinion stedfast that flesh is more wholesome; and further, that if you think *pecora campi* be not more cared for of her both abroad and at home, and more contenting to her than any waterish creatures, such a beast is well worthy of being put in the pound, [i.e., in the fish prison].

* The rune meant that he swore on the Bible that if there were too much of Walter [Ralegh], he would kill himself with a bodkin.

Even if *Mother Hubbard* and the *Ruines of Time* had not been "called in" (probably because of the reference to Burleigh as "the foxe" who "crept into the whole which the badger [Leicester] swept"), or if Marston's *Satires* had not been burned along with others including Sir John Davie's *Epigrames,* or if the Marprelate tracts, even the orthodox ones, had not been condemned because they were "utterly misliked" by Mr. Tilney, or if Harington had not been forbidden the court because of the lampoons in the *Metamorphosis of Ajax,* or if Donne had not been refused permission to publish Elegies 1, 2, 10, 11, 13, and parts of the Second Satire—even if history were lacking in these positive proofs of the libellous nature of these pamphlets and verses, still contemporary annals are full of references which make the fact of fustian, and many of the identifications, as indubitable as that of Lycidas with King, or Achitophel with Shaftesbury, or Belinda with Miss Fermor. Of *Mother Hubbard,* Middleton says, in the *Black Book,* (1604), [if the *Black Book* was by Middleton], "She that was called in for selling her working bottle-ale to bookbinders, and spurting the froth upon Courtier's noses." Nashe, in *Strange Newes,* (1593), accused Harvey of having played the informer in this case. Harvey had written in a *Letter* of 1592, how "Mother Hubbard in heat of choler . . . wilfully overshot her malcontented selfe"; John Weever, in an epigram published in 1599, also refers unmistakably to the row over the *Ruines of Time:*

> Spencer is ruined, of our latter time
> The fairest ruine, Faeries foulest want.
> Then his Time-ruines, did our ruine show,
> Which by his ruine, we untimely know.

The game was difficult and dangerous, but the authorities could not suppress it. They could cut off the hand of a man like Stubbs who attacked the French match openly, without disguise; even a Sir Philip Sidney could feel the Queen's bitter displeasure for his forthright remarks upon the subject; but under cover of a fustian, Lyly escaped entirely and Spenser was let off with a temporary rustication in Ireland. Moreover, when he returned to England, he returned also to his old literary tricks. Middleton wrote puckishly of his *Father Hubbard's*

Tales: "Why I call these *Father Hubbard's Tales* is not to have them called in again." The defence mechanism for these satires is identical with that furnished in the prefaces, dedications and prologues to the plays. In fact, Lodge claimed for his fustian devices a dignity something like a duelling code. He says frankly in *A Fig for Momus:* *

> In my satyres, (under the names of certain Romans) where I reprehended vice, I purposely wrong no man but observe the lawes of that kind of poeme; If any repine thereat, I am sure he is guilty, because he bewrayeth himself.

Lodge, however, did not trust entirely to his fustian for protection. He also secured an able patron. The poems in *A Fig for Momus* were dedicated to William, Earl of Derby because, Lodge admits, they will be "subject to much prejudice, except they were graced with some noble and worthy patron." The reader will recall Lyly's use of the same combination, i.e., fustian and patronage, in many of his topical plays.

With Lodge's admission that he is using the names of certain Romans for his attacks on his contemporaries, compare Massinger's Prologue to *Believe As You List,* where he begs pardon in case it should be found that

> . . . what's Roman here,
> Grecian or Asiatic, draws too near
> A late and sad example . . .

Jonson's Apologetical Dialogue to *The Poetaster* is similar; here he admits that he

> . . . chose Augustus Caesar's times
> When wit and arts were at their height in Rome
> To show that Virgil, Horace and the rest
> Of those great master-spirits did not want
> Detractors then, or practicers against them.

"By this line, although no parallel"[!] Jonson declared he hoped he would force the guilty lawyers to "sit down and blush." In other words, he justified his attack on a certain lawyer by declaring that if he blushed, he was guilty.

It is not surprising that the satirist's victims often side-

* See p. 206 for identification of Momus with Dr. John Rainolds.

stepped such traps, preferring to ignore the attack in public, while arranging, wherever possible, some oblique revenge. So far as we know, neither Walsingham nor Burleigh ever recognized their portraits as Cosmosophos and Philoplutos in Lodge's *Catharos: . . . A Nettle for Nice Noses,* but it is safe to say that neither the Secretary nor the Lord Treasurer allowed their noses to be nettled with impunity if the nettler ever came within their proper reach. It may be that the long list of persecutions which Lodge suffered were not due solely to his Catholicism.

The scene from *The Poetaster* referred to above is illustrative of so many aspects of the question of topicality, particularly the close connection between dramatic satires with their attendant informers, and the emblemists, that we think we are justified in setting it forth in this context, despite its familiarity to literary students. The scene takes place in *An Apartment in the Palace* where Caesar, Maecenas, Gallus, Tibullus, Horace, and *Equites Romani* are enjoying a feast of poetry—that is, they are listening to Virgil's reading of his *Aeneid.* This picture of the noble, yet courtly delight in poetry is rudely interrupted by the clamours of Lupus, who claims that he comes on "no common business," but upon such "as being neglected, may concern the life of Caesar." When, upon this hint of danger, he is admitted, Caesar learns that the importunate business is only a picture:

Caesar: What is this, Asinius Lupus? I understand it not.

Lupus: Not understand it! a libel, Caesar; a dangerous, seditious libel; a libel in a picture.

Caesar: A libel!

Lupus: Ay, I found it in this Horace his study, in Maecenas his house, here; I challenge the penalty of the laws against them.

Caesar: Shew it to Horace; ask him if he know it.

Lupus: Know it! his hand is at it, Caesar.

Caesar: Then 'tis no libel.

Horace: It is the imperfect body of an emblem, Caesar, I began for Maecenas.

Lupus: An emblem! right: that's greek for a libel. Do but mark how confident he is.

Horace: A just man cannot fear, thou foolish tribune:

Not though the malice of traducing tongues,
The open vastness of a tyrant's ear,
The senseless rigour of the wrested laws,
Or the red eyes of strain'd authority,
Should, in a point, meet all to take his life:
His innocence is armour 'gainst all these.

Lupus: Innocence! O impudence! let me see, let me see! Is not here an eagle! and is not that eagle meant by Caesar, ha? Does not Caesar give the eagle? answer me; what sayest thou?

Tucca: Hast thou any evasion, stinkard?

Lupus: Now he's turned dumb. I tickle you, Satyr.

Horace: Pish: ha! ha!

Lupus: Dost thou pish me? Give me my long sword.

Horace: With reverence to great Caesar, worthy Romans,
Observe but this ridiculous commenter;
The soule to my device was in this distich:
Thus oft, the base and ravenous multitude
Survive, to share the spoils of fortitude.
Which in this body I have figured here,
A vulture—

Lupus: A vulture! Ay, now, 'tis a vulture. O abominable! Monstrous! monstrous! has not your vulture a beak? has it not legs and talons, and wings, and feathers?

Horace: And therefore must it be an eagle?

Maecenas: Respect him not, good Horace: say your device.

Horace: A vulture and a wolf—

Lupus: A wolf! good: that's I; I am the wolf: my name's Lupus; I am meant by the wolf. On, on; a vulture and a wolf—

Horace: Preying upon the carcass of an ass—

Lupus: An ass! good still: that's I too; I am the ass. You mean me by the ass.

Maecenas: Prithee, leave braying then.

Horace: If you will needs take it, I cannot with modesty give it from you.

In other words, he retires behind the Law of Satire mentioned by Lodge, to wit, "if any repine thereat, I am sure he is guilty because he bewrayeth himself." Trebatius' judgment, in the satirical dialogue appended to the play, restates the Satire's Law and claims that Horace (Jonson) shall be free of all danger of prosecution in its application:

. . . if thou thyself, being clear,
Shalt tax in person a man fit to bear
Shame and reproach, his suit shall quickly be
Dissolved in laughter, and thou thence set free.

The stage history of the *Poetaster* proves, however, that Jonson's faith in the protection afforded by the Satire's Law was not quite justified; nevertheless all the satirists continued to claim protection under it. Thus Harington in The Epilogue to the *Metamorphosis of Ajax* (Fanfolico Press, p. 103), boasts to his readers "what pettie pils" they have swallowed somewhat unwillingly as they perused the pages of *Ajax,* and "what wholesome worme wood was enclosed in these raisins of the sunne." (*Ajax,* p. 103.) He then states unequivocally that "Against malcontents, Epicures, Atheists, heritickes, and careless and dissolute Christians, and especially against pride and sensualitie, the Prologue and the first part are chiefly intended"; and he admits that while he is writing to teach "a reformation of the matter in question, so also it toucheth in sport, a reprehension of some practices too much in custome." Concerning these practices–to wit, heresy, atheism, etc., he says "Ajax when he is at the worst, yeeldes not a more offensive savour to the finest nostrils, than some of the faults I have noted doe, to God and the world." But he strictly insists, as Lodge and Marston and Jonson, *et omnes,* did habitually, that he who squealed when the shoe pinched betrayed his guilt. "For some that may seem secretly touched, and be not openly named, if they say nothing, I will saye nothing. But as my good freend Mr. Davies saide of his Epigrams that they were made like dublets in Birchen lane, for every one whom they will serve, so if any man finde in these my lines any raiment that sutes him so fit as it were made for him, let him weare it and spare not, and for my parte I would he would weare it out." He warns, however, that if "he will be angry at it . . . then he will come and take a precise measure of him [and] make him another garment of the same stuffe, in that what sheere soever he dwelleth he may be known by such a coat as long as he liveth."

If I mistake not, that is precisely what happened to Lord Cobham, when he complained of the satire implied in the frivolous old wag, Oldcastle, who clowned his way into the company of Prince Hal; the result was a further insult in the portrait of the degraded old sot of *Merry Wives.*

It is small wonder that individually the satirists were not much persecuted. As Lodge says in the Preface to the Reader of *A Fig for Momus:* "If any man reprove me, let him looke to it, I will nip him."

Any one of these fustian identifications may be wrong. It is possible that Timias is not Ralegh, or that Tuscanismo is not Oxford, or that the Sleeping Shepherd is not Leicester, or that Mavortius is not Essex, or that Sidanen is not the Queen; but the discounting of any one identification, or any several, is certainly not sufficient to outweigh the overwhelming evidence concerning the general prevalence of allegory in sixteenth-century literature. It would be absurd to doubt that Mr. Luke was Matthew Arnold in Mallock's *New Republic* because we are sceptical of any definite identification for Lady Ambrose. By the same token, we may legitimately protest against a general denial of topicality in the drama, even when the case for this or that identification may strike one as weak.

We must not forget the great number of aristocratic litterateurs who were also playing the game. There were the Cecils whom we have seen giving the arguments for Court plays; there was Sir Fulke Grevill who, after the Queen's wrath against Sidney, thought best to suppress several of his plays; there was the Queen's "saucy Godson" whose book of personalities the Queen secretly enjoyed even when it was officially condemned. Robert Markham wrote, anent the *Metamorphosis of Ajax,* which had caused such a storm that the author thought it best to betake himself to Ireland with Essex (*Ajax,* p. xixff.):

> Since your departure from hence, you haue been spoke of, and with no ill will, both by the nobles and the Queene herself. Your book is almost forgiuen, and I may say forgotten; but not for its lacke of wit or satyr. Those whome you feared moste are now bosoming themselues in the Queene's grace; and tho' her Highnesse signified displeasure in outwarde sorte, yet did she like the marrowe of your booke. Your great enemye, Sir James, did once mention the Star-chamber, but your good esteeme in better mindes outdid his endeauors, and all is silente again. The Queen is minded to take you to her fauour, but she sweareth that she belieues you will make epigrams and write Misacmos again, on her and all her court.

Harington's satire was written in epistles, purporting to be addressed by Misacmos, the hater of filth, to his friend and cousin Philostilpnos, the lover of cleanliness.

We must not fail to mention the hundreds of ladies and gentlemen to whom these fustian works were dedicated; it is highly unlikely that they were ignorant of the jest intended by the dedicator. We do not now know the plays of William Stanley, Earl of Derby, or Edward de Vere, Earl of Oxford, or those of Sir Henry Wotton, or Sir Francis Bacon; and all too little of the dramatic productions of Thomas, Lord Buckhurst, or David, Lord Barry, or of the lady dramatists like Jane, Lady Lumley, or Mary, Countess of Pembroke; but the fact that plays were being written by such persons, who would certainly not be ignorant of the prevailing fashion in court plays, is itself significant. Fustian was, in fact, so much the rule rather than the exception, that Marston claims that many a poet affected to obscure his meaning even when he had nothing to hide, merely to be in fashion. In *The Scourge of Villanie,* he says:

> . . . This affectation,
> To speake beyond mens apprehension,
> How Apish 'tis. When all in *fusten sute*
> Is cloth'd a huge *nothing,* all for repute
> Of profound knowledge, when profoundnes knowes
> There's nought containd, but only seeming showes.

Nevertheless, he knew that his satire would be regarded as fustian, and so sought to protect himself by protesting further, in the Epilogue:

> If any one (forced with his owne guilt) will turne it home and say 'Tis I,
> I cannot hinder him. Neyther doe I iniure him.

In almost the same words Tourneur protested his innocence of "application" in *The Transformed Metamorphosis:*

> Who finds him touch't, may blame himself not me
> And he will thanke me, doth himself know free.

But those who were "touched" did object, with all their might, as we shall see again and again.

CHAPTER NINE

Essex Plays

I TURN NOW TO A CONSIDERATION of a group of plays dealing with Leicester's successor, the Earl of Essex. How early and how widely the affairs of this unfortunate man were represented on the stage we do not yet know. Contemporary research is still much occupied with investigation of this question, and many of the findings are still the subject of scholarly controversy. Several cases have, however, emerged into something like credible, if not certain solutions, and I propose briefly to review some five or six of these, though many others have been suggested. One or two have already been noted under more general headings, i.e., *The Isle of Dogs* and *Cynthia's Revels*.

For many years, in fact as early as 1578, the character and government of Richard II had been used as a fustian parallel for Elizabeth and her conduct of affairs. In 1578 Sir Francis Knollys used the analogy openly in a letter to the Queen's secretary, wherein he opined that if the Queen would not hear him or take the sound advice of true men, she would thereby expose herself to all the ills of a flattering train such as ruined Richard II (Thomas Wright, *Queen Elizabeth and Her Times,* I, p. 75):

> For who woll persiste in gyvinge of safe counsayle, if her Majestie woll persiste in myslyking of safe counsayle? Nay who woll not rather shrynkingly (that I may say no worse) play the partes of King Richard the Second's men, then to enter into the odious office of crossing her Majesties' wylle?

He even hints at her immediate danger, if she persists in her folly:

> . . . then up startes the pryde and practice of the papists and downe declyneth the comforte and strengthe of her Majesties safety. And then King Richard the Second's men woll flock into courte apace, and woll show themselves in theyre true colours. From which companye the Lorde blesse her Majestie, and the thynking thereon

doth so abhorre me, that I am more fytte to dye in a pryvate lyfe, than to live a courtier.

Again in 1588, Lord Hunsdon made use of the analogy in protesting against his lack of advancement. He claimed that his failure to receive the earldom to which he felt himself entitled was due to his inability to play the minion to a tyrannical sovereign. "I never was one of Richard II's men," he declared (*PMLA,* 42, p. 691). From this date to the close of the century, there appeared an extraordinary number of plays on the subject of Richard II, or laid in his reign. Sometime before its entry in the *Stationers' Register* in 1593, appeared the anonymous *Life and Death of Jack Straw,* which deals with the topic of unjust taxation in the reign of Richard II. A much more elaborate attack was launched in the so-called *First Richard II.* (Egerton MS 1894). Even if there were not positive evidence that such plays were being commanded for court audiences, still, basing our opinions on internal evidence, we can hardly doubt that contemporary application could be made of these bold scenes. The years 1592-98 were noted for oppressive taxation. Subsidy after subsidy was granted, primarily for support of the wars against Spain and The League, but popularly believed to be consumed by the extravagance of the Queen's favourites. The *State Papers* for 1591-94 (vol. ccxl, no. 143, p. 162) describe a set of *Instructions for Enquiries to be Made* "whether they (the people) fall not into poverty by these continual wars, which causes imposts, subsidies & loans, while merchants become bankrupt through want of traffic." In 1593 Bacon incurred official displeasure by a speech in Parliament against these excessive taxes. An embarrassed treasury sought to raise money by extraordinary means, even going so far as to suggest a renewal of the ancient and much hated "blanckes" or "benevolences," termed by Holinshed "malevolences." Almost the entire first half of the Egerton play is pre-occupied with this subject—the taxing and "pylling" [stripping] of the "poor commons," with emphasis upon the iniquity of the "blanck chartes." Woodstock complains that should these Italianate extravagances of the courtiers persist, he would have to raise new rents, undo his poor tenants, turn away his servants; but if, on the contrary, the Court would ape his simple style, "they would not taxe and pyll the commons soe." He declares that in his homely hose, he'll "do the realme more good than those that pille the poore, to jett in gould," and he suggests that if the crown needs money, let it be taken from the "great carricks all ritchly laden, to satisfye those borrowed somes of coyne their pryd hath forced from the needy commons." But the King replies, "Those wealthy prisses, already are bestowed on these our ffreends."

How timely such utterances were we can guess when we read Sir John Harington's frank comment in his *Tract on the Succession,* p. 91 (quoted by Miss Albright, *PMLA,* 42, p. 704):

> If we marke what base shiftes the Queen is forced to (that perhaps she knows not of) to embase her coyne in Ireland, and borrowe coyne of hir poore subjectes in England, without purpose ever to pay it again, while the pulpitt speakes nothing but faith, and peace, and plenty in her eares. . . .

Woodstock's suggestion of the buccaneering prizes as a source of revenue is particularly applicable to the 1590's rather than the 1390's, for Drake and Frobisher and Norris and Ralegh were almost daily bringing in carracks too numerous to list. And yet the Commons were in no way relieved. As the suffering among the poor increased, riots became numerous, and all along the line "sedition raised her ougly head." In 1596 a Somerset justice, one Joseph Hext, wrote in a letter to a member of the Privy Council * complaining that:

> . . . there be [those] (and I fear me emboldened by the wandering people) that stick not to say boldly they must not starve, they will not starve. And his year there assembled eighty in a company, and took a cartload of cheese from one driving it to a fair, and dispersed it amongst them, for which some of them have endured long imprisonment and fine by the judgment of the good Lord Chief Justice (Sir John Popham) at our last Christmas sessions; which may grow dangerous by the aid of such numbers as are abroad, especially in this time of dearth; who no doubt animate them to all contempt both of noblemen and gentlemen, continually buzzing into their ears that the rich men have gotten all into their hands and will starve the poor.

* Tawney and Power, *Tudor Economic Documents,* II, pp. 341-44; A. V. Judges, *The Elizabethan Underworld* (London, 1930), p. x.

We have already noted the anti-alien riots of 1592-95 in which the dramatists were involved both directly and indirectly. The verses on the walls of the Dutch church were, however, merely a sample of the propaganda of protest which began to appear everywhere, in every form, and not least upon the stage. Plays about Jack Straw and Wat Tyler and Jack Cade and "ill May Day" abounded. Nor were such plays to be seen only in remote provincial towns.

Of the many historic scenes depicted as parallels to the ills of the time, none were more popular than those connected with Richard II, particularly among court circles. On 7 December, 1595, Sir Edward Hoby wrote to Cecil *(Salisbury MSS,* V, 487):

> Finding that you were not conveniently to be at London tomorrow night, I am bold to send to know whether Tuesday may be more in your grace to visit poor Canon Row, where, as late as it shall please you, a gate for your supper shall be open, and K. Richard present himself to your view.

Of course, we do not know certainly that this play was about Richard II. We do, however, know of Cecil's special interest in Richard II plays from a rather difficult letter written by Ralegh to Cecil soon after they had dined with Essex. The letter is dated 6 July, 1597. The following excerpt is modernized in spelling and punctuation. (*State Papers Elizabethan, Domestic,* 1595-7, Vol. cclxiv, art. 10.)

> I acquainted my Lord Generall [Essex] with your letter to me, and your kind acceptance of your entertainment. He was also wonderful merry at your conceit of Richard II. I hope it shall never alter, and whereof I shall be most glad of, as the trew way to all our good, quiet, and advancement, and most of all for her sake whose affairs shall thereby find better progression. Sir, I will ever be yours; it is all I can say and I will perform it with my life and with my fortune.

Here again, it is impossible to say what the "conceit of Richard II" was.

About the intended parallel of the Egerton *Richard II,* however, there can be no reasonable doubt. It is a dramatization of popular protest against the extravagances of the court which, the author would lead us to believe, are directly responsible for the woes of the people, particularly the hated form of taxation by blank chartes. As the men of the 90's posted lampoons on the walls and church doors, yea, on the very palace gates, so in this play Woodstock warns the King:

> . . . whilst thou livest at ease
> Luling thy self in nice securytye
> Thy wronged kingdom's in a mutiny
> From every providence are the people come
> With open mouths exclaymeing on the wrongs
> Thou and these upstarts have imposed on them.
> Shame is desciphered on thy pallace gate,
> Confusion hangeth ore thy wretched head.

Not only was shame to be deciphered on the palace gate, but every schoolboy was taught to sing his protest in doggerel rhyme, and the plowman whistled the tune as he went searching for his lost calves. The Egerton play shows the "Intelligencers" at work apprehending such insidious spreaders of sedition [spelling and punctuation modernized]:

Enter a schoolmaster and a servingman (the spies "standing close").

Servingman: Nay, sweet master schoolmaster, let's hear it again, I beseech you.

Schoolmaster: *Patientia!* You are a serving-man; I am a scholar. I have shown art and learning in these verses, I assure you; and *yet, if they were well searched, they are littel better than Libels. But the carriage of a thing is all, sir. I've covered them rarely*. [Italics inserted.]

Servingman: Foot! the country's so full of intelligencers that two men can scarce walk together, but they are attached for whispers.

Schoolmaster: The paper shall wipe their noses, and they shall not go to a goose for it; for I'll have these verses sung to their faces by one of my school boys, wherein I'll tickle them all, i' faith. Shall you hear else? but first let's look there be no pitchers with ears, nor needles with eyes about us.

Servingman: Come, come, all's safe, I warrant ye.

Schoolmaster: Mark then! Here I come over them for their blank charters. Wilt hear else?

> Will ye buy an parchment knives?
> We sell for little gain.
> Who are weary of their lives,
> They'll rid them of their pain.

Blank charters they are called.
A vengeance on the villain;
I would he were both flayed and bald!
God bless my Lord Tressillian.

Is it not rare?

Nimble: Oh rascals! They are damned 300 fathom deep already.

Schoolmaster: Nay, looke ye, sir, there can be no exceptions taken, for this last line helps all, wherein, with a kind of equivocation, I say, "God bless my lord Tressillian." Do ye mark, sir? Now here in the next verse I run o'er all the flatterers in the Court by name. Ye shall see else:

A poison may be green,
But Bushey can be no faggot.
God mend the king and bless the queen,
And 'tis no matter for Baggot.
Nor Scroop, he does no good,
But if you'll know the villain,
His name is now to be understood,
God bless my lord Tressillian.*

How like ye this, sir?

Servingman: Most excellent, i' faith, sir.

Nimble: Oh traitors! Master Bailie, do your authority!

Bailie: Two most pestiferous traitors! Lay hold of them, I charge ye.

Servingman: What mean ye, sir?

Nimble: Nay, talk not, for if ye had a hundred lives, they were all hanged. Ye have spoken treasons in the ninth degree.

Schoolmaster: Treason! *Patientia!* good sir, we spoke not a word.

Bailie: Be not so pestiferous! Mine ears have heard your examinations wherein you uttered most shameful treasons; for ye said, "God bless my lord Tressillian."

Schoolmaster: I hope there is no treason in that, sir.

Nimble: That shall be tried. Come, Master Bailie, their hands shall be bound under a horse's belly, and sent up to him presently. They'll both be hanged, I warrant them.

Servingman: Well, sir, if we be, we'll speak more ere we be hanged in spite of ye. *(Exeunt the schoolmaster and the servingman.)*

Nimble: Aye, when ye are hanged, speak what you will. We care

* This sixteenth-century jingle is in obvious imitation of the fourteenth-century ballad already referred to on page 91.

not. Away with them! Ye see, Master Bailie, what knaves are abroad. Now you are here, 'tis time to look about ye. See?

Bailie: I see there are knaves abroad, indeed, sir. I speak for mine own part. I will do my best to reform the pestiferousness of the times; and as for example, I have set my mark to the charters; so will set mine eyes to observe these dangerous cases.

(Enter one whistling.)

Nimble: Close, again, Master Bailie. Here comes another whisperer. I see by his look of villainy he whistles treason. I'll lay hold of him.

Whistler: Whistled treason! Alas, sir, how can that be?

Nimble: That's all one; if any man whistles treason, 'tis as ill as speaking it. Mark me, Master Bailie. The bird whistles that cannot speak, and there be birds in a manner that can speak too: your raven will your crow call, "ye knave," Master Bailie; ergo, he that can whistle can speak, and therefore this fellow hath both spoke and whistled of treason. How say you, Master Bailie Ignorance?

Bailie: Ye have argued well, sir, but ye shall hear me first, for I do not think but there are great knaves [?] and therefore, my good fellow, be not pestiferous, but say and tell the truth: who did set you a-work? or who was the cause of your whistlings? or did any man say to you, "Go whistle"?

Whistler: Not any man, woman, or child, truly, sir.

Bailie: No? How durst you whistle then: or what cause had ye to do so?

Whistler: The truth is, sir, I had lost two calves out of my pasture, and being in search for them, from the top of the hill I might spy you two at the bottom here and took ye for my calves, sir; and that made me come whistling down for joy in hope I had found them.

Nimble: More treason yet! He take a courtier and a bailie for two calves! To limbo with him! He shall be quartered and then hanged.

Whistler: Good Master Bailie, be pitiful!

Bailie: Why, law, sir! He makes a pitiful fellow of a bailie too. Away with him!

A contemporary lampoon by some member of the Essex circle against the chief personages of the rival group offers an extraordinarily interesting parallel to this song against the favourites of Richard II. This ballad, if it may be called such, is described by Mrs. Stopes as follows (*op. cit.*, p. 235):

A remarkable metrical effusion without title or date is preserved in the special volume of *State Papers* which contains the records of the conspiracy and trial. The only allusion to authorship lies in the words "*our* men lost the day," so that it must have been written by a sympathiser with Essex who had managed to escape capture. It is not of a nature to have been safely reprinted then, but it is probable that many MS copies spread. There have been preserved two copies at least among the *State Papers,* and I have discovered another among the Harleian MSS in a volume which the *Calendar* seems to have entered as collected by the third Randle Holmes as a book of "Songs and Sonnets." These were considered to be too inferior to be worth fuller description than "Epitaphs, Lampoons and Satires." This recension contains some variant readings, so I shall distinguish the three copies by A, B, and C, and number the verses, to make clear my elucidation of their meanings. This 'lampoon' was copied many years ago for Dr. Brandl, and it appeared in the volume of the *Shakespeare Jahrbuch* for 1910.

It is probably, in all three cases, incomplete, as certain names are omitted which would naturally have been included in one or other of the groups.

Inasmuch as the whole long poem is printed by Mrs. Stopes, it will not be necessary to quote here more than two or three of the stanzas illustrating the parallel. The whole poem, like that of the Schoolmaster in the Egerton play, "runs ore all the flatterers in the court by name." The following are stanzas 1, 3, and 7:

Chamberlin, Chamberlin [Sir George Carey]
hees of hir graces kinne
foole hath he euer bin
with his Joane silverpin
She makes his cockescombe thin
and *quake* in euerie limme
quicksilver is in his head
but his wit's dull as lead
Lord for thy pittie.

litell Cecill tripps up and downe
he rules both court & croune
with his brother Burlie clowne
in his great fox-furred gowne
with the long proclamation
he *swore* hee sav'd the towne
is it not likelie?

Rawleigh doth time bestride
he *sits* twixt winde and tide
yet uppe hill hee cannot ride,
for all his bloodie pride.
hee seeks taxes in the tinne
hee *powles* the poor to the skinne
yet hee sweares tis no sinne
Lord for thy pittie.

The particular trick illustrated in the Egerton play of combining stage representation with lyrical lampoons is, at least partially, what the framers of the early statutes for censorship had in mind when they condemned the "playing of enterludes and false, fond ballads." The works of the earlier satirists, like Skelton, or John Roe, or "Bilious Bale," or a little later, Nicholas Udall, or Thomas Churchyard, or George Gascoigne, or Bishop Still, offer countless illustrations of the practice.

The history of Hayward's *Life of Henry IV* furnishes an example of such a hunting down and punishing of sedition mongers. It is not now known what is the precise relationship between the various Richard II plays and Hayward's *History,* or when each was written. Without pretending to decide the matter of the chronology, therefore, I present herewith a statement of known facts concerning this complicated issue.

In the autumn of 1595, "R. Dolemans" dedicated to Essex a book entitled *A Conference about succession to the Crown of England,* putting forward the claims of the Infanta Isabella. The book and the dedication caused Essex a world of trouble. On 5 November, 1595, Rowland Whyte wrote to Sidney *(Sidney Papers,* I, pp. 357-59, 369):

Upon Monday last the Queen showed the Earl of Essex a printed book in which there is I hear dangerous praises of his valour and worthiness, which doth hym harm here. At his coming from courte, he was observed to look wan and pale, being exceedinglie troubled at this great piece of villainie donne unto him. He is sick and continues very ill. 5th November, 1595. P. S. The Book I spoke of is dedicated to my Lord Essex, and printed beyond the sea, and 'tis thought to be treason to have it. To write of these things are dangerous in so perillous a tyme but I hope it wilbe no offense to impart unto you thactions of this place.

Letters on the 7th and 12th describe his annoyance further. Clearly, the years, 1595-97 were "perillous tymes" for the unwary, particularly if he were the least ambitious.*

Essex's biographer states that the book was so dedicated to bring him into disrepute, "more especially as his own claims as a descendent of Thomas of Woodstock, Duke of Gloucester, sixth son of Edward III, had been brought forward by some persons not long before." (W. B. Devereux, *Lives and Letters of the Devereux,* I, p. 313.) Be that as it may, when Shakspere's play was published in 1597, it is clear that it had fallen foul of the censor, for it was printed without the deposition scene, the cut having been made so crudely that the lines following the gap are meaningless. The statement in IV, i, 321, "A woeful pageant have we here beheld," is intelligible only when following the act of deposition in the Parliament scene.

How touchy the authorities were on this subject of deposition may be judged by Harington's reply to "Doleman's" book, from which the following *(Tracts of the Succession,* 76, 91; Albright, *op. cit.,* p. 704):

> You harp on a seditious string of deposing of Princes for disabilitie and weakness, and that in such a tyme when malcontents so abound in citie and countrye, when in the Court the common phrase of old servantes is that their is no commiseration of any man's distressed estate, that a few favourites gett all, that the nobilitie is depressed, the Clergy pilled and contemned, forraine invasions expected, the treasure at home exhausted, the coyne in Ireland

* Though perhaps not immediately relevant, it may be well here to notice another Succession tract which has been vaguely connected with Essex through Southampton. There is, in the *Salisbury Papers* (V, 233), a "Memorandum" which states that Heneage had just handed over to Burleigh "the book about the pretended marriage of the Earl of Hertford and the Lady Katherine, deceased, daughter of the late Duke of Suffolk." This note is dated 10 July, 1595, and on the following day Heneage wrote to Cecil (*ibid.,* 273) complaining that he was "troubled greatly by an unkind and injurious son-in-law." In view of Miss Edith Rickert's study of *A Midsummer Night's Dream,* as Shakspere's plea for Hertford, this note may be of more than casual interest. Mrs. Stopes believes that *A. M. S. D.* was given at the wedding festivities of Sir Thomas Heneage and the Countess of Southampton. (Stopes, *op. cit.,* p. 75.) If Miss Rickert is right about the fustian of *Midsummer,* and if Miss Winstanley is right about Shakspere's interest in the Seymour cause in *Cymbeline,* there arises a "pretty pattern" in the biography of Shakspere.

embased, the gold of England transported, exactions doubled and trebled, and all honest hearts . . . troubled.

In subject, if not in chronology, Shakspere's *Richard II* is, whether consciously or not, a sequel to the Egerton play, its chief additions being an expansion of the injuries done to Hereford, Duke of Lancaster, through whom Essex's meagre claim to the throne must be traced, and the consequent courses pursued by the outraged barons, culminating in the deposition of the King. The woes of Hereford do certainly constitute an apt parallel to Essex's troubles between the years 1595-97. The years immediately preceding (1592-95), during which the ablest of Essex's rivals had been rusticated for his marriage to Elizabeth Throgmorton, had marked the peak of his popularity. From the date of Ralegh's return to his old post as Captain of the Guard, the Cecil faction rose in favour at Court, and the fortunes of Essex and his retainers declined. The annals of the next few years are filled with Essex's unsuccessful suits. His nominees were almost invariably passed over for those of Ralegh and Cecil. His efforts in behalf of Bacon are, of course, notorious. Though Essex had striven both for the post of Attorney-General and then for that of Solicitor-General, both prizes were bestowed elsewhere —the former to Coke, the latter to Sergeant Thomas Fleming. Essex was so galled at the latter failure in 1595 that by way of compensation, he gave Bacon "a peece of land," to wit, the goodly estate of Twickenham, which Bacon later sold for £1,800 and thought it worth more. Again, in 1595 the Secretaryship was granted to Sir Robert Cecil instead of to Essex's candidate, Sir Thomas Bodley. An even bitterer blow was the appointment of his two chief enemies to succeed to the two important offices left vacant by the death of Lord Cobham. The Chamberlainship went to Sir George Carey, Lord Hunsdon, and the Wardenship of the Cinque Ports to Henry, the young Lord Cobham, Ralegh's great friend, instead of to Sir Robert Sidney, Essex's choice. Even the meaner preferments of men like Mr. Standen, and Dr. Morison, and Antonio Perez, Essex was unable to achieve. When Mr. Standen reported to Essex his disappointed hopes, "his Lordship (Essex) laughing at the matter, said, that he found no good was to be done with the Queen touching Mr.

Standen's maintenance, and all by reason of these two hinderers of him." (Birch, II, 144.) And so with case after case, culminating in Essex's own defeat in favour of Cecil for the Chancellorship of the Duchy of Lancaster, which, considering his descent and title, he had every reason to expect. The bestowal of this concession to anyone but Viscount Hereford could hardly fail to strike his friends as a parallel to the seizure of Hereford's rights by Richard. So in Shakspere's play, York bursts out in passionate protest (II, i.):

How long shall I be patient? Ah how long
Shall tender duty make me suffer wrong?
Not Gloster's death, nor Hereford's banishment,
Nor Gaunt's rebukes, nor England's private wrongs,
Nor the prevention of poor Bolingbroke
About his marriage, not my own disgrace,
Have ever made me sour my patient cheek,
Or bend one wrinkle on my sovereign's face.

But he pleads:

Seek you to seize, and gripe unto your hands,
The royalties and rights of banisht Hereford?
Is not Gaunt dead? and doth not Hereford live?
Was not Gaunt just? and is not Harry true?
Did not the one deserve to have an heir?
Is not the heir a well-deserving son?
Take Hereford's rights away, and take from Time
His charters and his customary rights;
Let not to-morrow, then, ensue to-day;
Be not thyself—for how art thou a king
But by fair sequence and succession?
Now, afore God—God forbid I say true!—
If you do wrongfully seize Hereford's rights,
Call in the letters-patent that he hath
By his attorneys-general to sue
His livery, and deny his offer'd homage,
You pluck a thousand dangers on your head,
You lose a thousand well-disposed hearts,
And prick my tender patience to those thoughts
Which honour and allegiance cannot think.

In spite of these possible parallels, however, there is no record of prosecution of the author or the company who performed the play before its publication. Two circumstances, however, brought the whole matter forward again in 1599, and this time the intelligencers meant business. After Essex's disgrace and banishment from court, Camden tells us that the Essex faction launched an elaborate propaganda of criticism: *Homines male feriati Essexium ubique per circulos, et ministri quidam etiam e suggestu, immodicis laudibus extulerunt. (Annales* [1627], ii, p. 185. See, Bruce edition of Hayward's *Annals* for the Camden Society, p. x.)

Bruce says:

Whilst in custody, preparatory to an investigation into his conduct, his numerous friends endeavoured to excite and maintain the popular feeling on his behalf. The conduct of the Queen's advisors, and, through them that of the Queen herself, was made the subject of unsparing condemnation; defamatory libels against them were spread abroad on every side; whilst "loose idlers," remarks Camden, "wherever they came together, and even some clergymen in their pulpits, lauded Essex with most immoderate praise."

It is possible that the "certain songs" which were delivered to Sir Thomas Edmondes by Southhampton to be conveyed to Sir Robert Sidney on 15 July, 1598, (Stopes, *op. cit.,* p. 118), were part of this literary propaganda, as also Thomas Churchyard's *The Welcome Home of the Earl of Essex,* 1599. *(Ibid.,* p. 156). This is, of course, a mere guess, but the "certain songs" were clearly more important than lyrical statements of a Heynonino character. As Miss Albright notes *(op. cit.,* p. 718), "It is of some interest to observe that Daniel's *Civil Wars* (dedicated to Charles Blount, Lord Mountjoy, of the Essex conspirators, and praising both him and Essex) came out in three issues in 1595, 1599, and 1601—years critical for the inception of the Richard II analogy, the reference to the returning General Essex in *Henry V,* and the use of the play of *Richard II* by the conspirators." Whether or not Hayward's *Life of Henry IV* was undertaken earlier or at this very time, certainly its publication in 1599 was a definite contribution to this campaign. It was dedicated to Essex in a style of regal flattery: *"Serenissimae Domino Reginae a sanctioribus Consiliis."* The critical nature of the pamphlet was at once suspected, though not immediately proved. On 1 March, 1599, Chamberlain wrote concerning "the treatise of Henry IV" saying there was

. . . much descanting about it, why such a story should come out at this time—many exceptions being taken to the epistle, which is a short thing in Latin dedicated to the Earl of Essex, and objected to by him in great earnest; where on it was ordered to be cut out. I have got you a transcript that you may pick out the offence if you can; for my part, I can pick out no such bugges words, but that everything is as it is taken.

This is exactly the claim of the Schoolmaster in the Egerton *Richard II,* "the carriage of a thing is all, sir; I have covered it rarely."

No one, apparently, descanted more furiously than the Queen. In his *Apology concerning the Earl of Essex,* Bacon declared that

. . . her Majesty being mightily incensed with that book which was dedicated to my Lord of Essex, being a story of the first year of King Henry the fourth, thinking it a seditious prelude to put into the people's heads boldness and faction, said she had a good opinion that there was treason in it, and asked me if I could not find any places in it that might be drawn within the case of treason: whereto I answered; for treason surely I find none, but for felony very many. And when her Majesty hastily asked me wherein, I told her the author had committed very apparent theft, for he had taken most of the sentences of Cornelius Tacitus and translated them into English and put them into his text.

But the Queen was not convinced. On 26 July, 1600, Carleton wrote to Chamberlain: "The Queen had given him (Essex) liberty, but recalled it upon the taking of Dr. Hayward who for writing *Henry IV* is committed to the Tower." As we shall see presently, Bacon, too, was soon after convinced that the book was a "seditious pamphlet." The Archbishop of Canterbury ordered the dedicatory epistle to be cut out, but, according to the publisher, John Wolf, "500 or 600 copies were sold before such order was received." Moreover, the first edition was exhausted almost immediately. Wolf stated that "the people calling for it exceedingly about Easter, obtained a new edition of the doctor, where in many things were altered from the former, and yet the volume increased." But the new edition, of which 1,500 copies were printed, was confiscated by the Bishop of London, and all late editions burned. Hayward was imprisoned, and every effort made to induce him to implicate those who had commissioned him to write the book. Bacon tells us (Bacon's *Works,* Montague's ed., VI, p. 259; Bruce, *op. cit.,* p. xiv):

. . . when the Queen would not be persuaded it was his writing whose name was to it, but that it had some more mischievous author; and said, with great indignation, that she would have him racked to produce the author: I replied, Nay, Madam, he is a doctor, never rack his person, but rack his style; let him have pen, ink, and paper, and help of books, and be injoined to continue the story where it breaketh off, and I will undertake by collating the styles to judge whether he were the author or no.

Bruce adds: "Although thus kindly sheltered from personal outrage, he suffered a long imprisonment—how long does not appear. Beyond doubt he was confined until some time after the death of his earliest patron in 1601 and probably until the death of the Queen." In spite of this stir, however, Essex apparently continued to exploit the seditious parallel. On the eve of his rebellion, according to the testimony of Augustine Phillips:

Sir Chas Percy, Sir Joseline Percy and Lord Monteagle and several others spoke to some of the players to play the deposing and killing of King Richard II and promised to give them 40/-s more than their ordinary to do so. Examinate and his fellows had determined to play some other play, holding that of King Richard as being so old and so long out of use that they should have a small company at it, but at this request they were content to play it.

This report is confirmed by Sir Gilly Merrick, who admitted that

. . . on the motion of Sir Chas Percy, they went all together to the Globe over the water, where the Lord Chamberlain's men used to play, and were there somewhat before the play began, Sir Charles telling them that the play would be of Harry the Fourth. . . . The play was of King Henry the Fourth and of the killing of Richard the Second.

At the trial of Essex it was pointed out, first, "that Essex had fostered the book written on Henry IV, making this time seem like that of Richard II to be reframed by him as by Henry IV," even though it had been "plainly deciphered not only by the matter, but the epistle itself, for what end and for whose behalf it was made"; also that the Earl had been "often present at the playing thereof, and with great applause giving countenance to it." Coke's notes from Hayward's book (Albright, *op. cit.,* p. 699) show that

> . . . the Doctor selected a story 200 years old, and published it last year, intending the application of it to this time, the plot being that of a King who is taxed for misgovernment, and his council for corrupt and covetous dealing for private ends; the King is censured for conferring benefits on hated favourites, the nobles become discontented, and the commons groan under continual taxation, whereupon the King is deposed, and in the end murdered.

It is further stated that

> . . . all the complaints and slanders, which have been given out by seditious traitors against the Government both in England and Ireland, are set down, and falsely attributed to those times, thereby cunningly insinuating that the same abuses being now in this realm that were in the days of Richard II, the like course might be taken for redress.

As Miss Lily Campbell states in her very valuable essay, "The Use of Historical Patterns in the Reign of Elizabeth" *(Huntington Library Quarterly,* Jan. 1938, p. 150): "The evidence upon which he [Essex] was tried for his life, centered to a great extent about the intention back of the use of historical precedent on his behalf."

After Essex's death, the Queen, in converse with one William Lombarde, "fell upon the reign of King Richard II saying, 'I am Richard II, know ye not that?' " To this outburst, the obsequious Lombarde replied, "Such a wicked imagination was determined and attempted by a most unkind *Gent,* the most adorned creature that ever your Majesty made." Her Majesty replied, "He that will forget God will also forget his benefactors; this tragedy was played 40 times in open streets and houses."

In her very able discussion of this whole subject *(PMLA*, 43, pp. 772ff.), Miss Albright has shown conclusively, I think, that Shakspere's play and Hayward's history are perfect parallels, and as such were motived by the same spirit of criticism. The one aspect of the whole episode that is difficult to understand, is the complete exemption of the players from punishment. The Chamberlain's men actually played before the Queen on the night of Essex's execution.

With the account of the stage history of *Richard II* so clearly in mind, it will perhaps be easier for us to accept Miss Albright's version of the textual history of *Henry V* than for those who are not familiar with the background we have just sketched in. Without repeating all the detailed discussion of this play as presented by Miss Albright, I shall give here merely the gist of her argument. She notes, first, the statement in the chorus before Act V in the Folio, which first compares Henry V to "conquering Caesar"; then

> As by a lower, but by loving likelihood
> Were now the Generall of our gracious Empresse,
> As in good time he may, from Ireland coming,
> Bringing Rebellion broached upon his sword,
> How many would the peacefull Citie quit
> To welcome him?

She then notes the differences between the Folio and Quarto versions which, she believes, establish the priority of the Folio text. Her summary is as follows:

> Logic, grammar, meter, diction and other considerations indicate clearly the priority of the Folio reading in many passages where this Quarto shows omission or condensation. In some cases passages may have been cut or abridged for no other reason than to shorten the performance. And it is to be noticed that certain types of subject matter are regularly reduced or omitted in the Quarto, even at the sacrifice of substance and form.
>
> The loss of this matter, together with the loss of the epic form, the prologues, and the choruses, accounts in some measure for the utter flatness of the Quartos, as compared with the Folio. One misses in the Quartos a strain of patriotism and high inspiration, and the sense of excitement and tension over problems of high import. Nor is this surprising when we observe what are the topics regularly cut

down or omitted. They are subjects which would be thought "unsafe" but fascinating for discussion in a play in 1599-1600: the problem of succession to the English throne; a genealogical argument, which, if good, would support the claim of a contemporary candidate, Essex; the nature of the kingly office: the duty of king to subject; the traits of one democratic king who did not believe in the "divine right"—a monarch highly idealized by Shakespeare through three plays and now, at the summit of the trilogy, the chorus before the last act of *Henry V,* deliberately *likened* to Essex; the dread of partition of England to the Scotch; the putting down of too great ambition and vanity on the part of the French in their claims to precedence, but at the same time the idea of a friendly league with France, in which England should be at the head. Removal or great curtailment of such topics would naturally carry with it the disposal of prologues and choruses, as these (in accordance with a common practice in plays of special meaning) contain the hints to look for contemporary application.

Whether Miss Albright is right about this version, or whether the fustian in this play is to be pushed beyond the case of "warning parallel" to one of real portraiture of prototypes, each reader must decide for himself: that it was topical, however, I feel there can be no reasonable doubt.

The discussion of the next two plays carries us, however, into deeper and more dangerous waters of definite personal allegory. On 12 May, 1600, Essex wrote in a letter to the Queen (*State Papers, Elizabethan, Domestic,* 1598-1601, p. 435):

> The prating tavern haunter speaks of me what he lists; the frantic libeller writes of me what he lists; they print me and make me speak to the world, and shortly they will play me upon the stage.

Perhaps therefore it was Essex himself who gave the warning responsible for the censorial vigilance that detected treason in Daniel's play *The Tragedy of Philotas.* The plot is taken from Plutarch and centres about "a recalcitrant captain of Alexander," whom Daniel describes in the argument as "patient of trauell, exceeding bountifull, and one that loued his men and friends better than any Nobleman of the Campe: but otherwise; noted of vaine-glory and prodigalitie." (Dixon Wecter, *Timon of Athens, PMLA,* pp. 43, 708.) The play was, according to Daniel, conceived as early as 1596, but was actually written (at least three acts of it) in 1600: "neere halfe a year before" the riotous attempt of Essex in February, 1600. In other words, it is about contemporary with *Henry V*. Daniel's own account, from his *Apology*, is as follows (Chambers, *Elizabethan Stage*, III, p. 275):

Above eight yeares since [1596], meeting with my deare friend D. Lateware, (whose memory I reverence) in his Lords Chamber and mine, I told him the purpose I had for *Philotas*: who say'd that himselfe had written the same argument, and caused it to be presented in St. John's Colledge in Oxford; where as I after heard, it was worthily and with great applause performed. . . . And living in the country, about foure yeares since, and neere halfe a yeare before the late Tragedy of ours (whereunto this is now most ignorantly resembled) unfortunately fell out heere in England [Sept. 1600], I began the same, and wrote three Acts thereof,—as many to whom I then showed it can witnesse,—purposing to have had it presented in Bath by certaine Gentlemens sonnes, as a private recreation for the Christmas, before the Shrovetide of that unhappy disorder [Feb., 1601]. But by reason of some occasion then falling out, and being called upon by my Printer for a new impression of my workes, with some additions to the Civill Warres, I intermitted this other subject. Which now lying by mee, and driven by necessity to make use of my pen, and the Stage to bee the mouth of my lines, which before were never heard to speake but in silence, I thought the representing so true a History, in the ancient forme of a Tragedy, could not but have had an unreproveable passage with the time, and the better sort of men; seeing with what idle fictions, and gross follies the Stage at this day abused mens recreations. . . . And for any resemblance, that thorough the ignorance of the History may be applied to the late Earle of Essex, it can hold in no proportion but only in his weaknesses, which I would wish all that love his memory not to revive. And for mine owne part, having been particularly beholding to his bounty, I would to God his errors and disobedience to his Sovereigne might be so deepe buried underneath the earth, and in so low a tombe from his other parts, that hee might never be remembered among the examples of disloyalty in his Kingdome, or parallel'd with Forreine Conspirators.

That is Daniel's version, written after he had been "summoned before the Lords of the Councill" to answer for the treasonable application of his play to the Essex tragedy. Modern historians may justly, I think, suspect the sincerity of his stated reasons for putting aside the half-finished play in 1600. If he had intended an application to Essex, as his contemporaries believed he had, the tragedy of 1601 would have made either its stage presentation or its publication a danger not to be risked during the Queen's lifetime. A memorandum from the Privy Council, 10 May, 1601 (Stopes, *op. cit.*, p. 242), shows how very imminent such danger would have been:

> Certain players at the Curtaine in Moorfields do represent in their interlude the persons of some gentlemen of good desert and quality that are yet alive, under obscure manner but yet in such sorte that all the hearers may take notice both of the matter and the persons that are meant thereby. All are to be examined.

We have already quoted Bancroft's letter on this subject. Mrs. Stopes notes also the attempt of the authorities to suppress the ballads which reflected sympathy for Essex. She declares (*ibid.*, p. 221):

> The people responded by singing "Well-a-day" and other ballads in honour of the departed hero, who had carried the fame of England so far. [*Roxburgh Ballads*, I, nos. 402, 563, 571]. Richard Bancroft, Bishop of London, was on the hunt for this ballad, as if it had contained a pernicious heresy.

Even in 1604, as the event proved, the Lords of the Council, who had effected the destruction of Essex, were still suspicious of and hostile toward any possible demonstration in his favour. It is clear from a letter written by Daniel to the Earl of Devonshire (Chambers, *Elizabethan Stage*, III, p. 276) that Cecil was the particular person to object:

> First I tolde the Lordes I had written 3 Acts of this tragedie the Christmas before my L. of Essex troubles, as diuers in the cittie could witnes. I saide the maister of the Revells had pervsed it. I said I had read some part of it to your honour, and this I said having none els of powre to grace mee now in Corte & hoping that you out of your knowledg of bookes, or fauour of letters & mee, might answere that there is nothing in it disagreeing nor any thing, as I protest there is not, but out of the vniuersall notions of ambition and envie, the perpetuall argumentes of books or tragedies. I did not say you incouraged me vnto the presenting of it; yf I should I had

beene a villayne for that when I shewd it to your honour I was not resolued to haue had it acted, nor should it haue bene had not my necessities ouermaistred me.

Even as late as 1608, authority frowned upon Essex allusions on the stage. We know, for instance, that Chapman was driven into hiding under the protection of the Duke of Lennox, of whom he had begged a "shelter" against "the austerity of this offending time," because of the official objection to the Biron plays, at least, partly because he had ventured to treat of the forbidden subject of the Essex tragedy. Mrs. Stopes states *(op. cit.*, p. 221), though she does not mention her authority, that in these plays Chapman intended a "comparison between Essex and the Duc de Biron." Whether or not she is justified in interpreting Chapman's intentions in so large a way, it is nevertheless certain that the two cases were much alike. Of the Essex "conspiracy" Camden says *(Elizabeth* [1630], Bk. IV, p. 178):

This commotion which some call a fear and mistrust, others an oversight; others who censured it more hardly termed it an obstinate impatience and seeking of revenge; and such as spoke worst of it called it an unadvised and indiscreet rashness, and to this day there are few that ever thought it a capital crime.

With this statement it is interesting to compare one from the *Cecil Papers* (XCVII, 13) concerning the Biron parallel (Stopes, *op. cit.*, pp. 221-22):

After Biron had been condemned to death, it was found that he had not been guilty of any of these conspiracies for which he was arraigned; but only had offended the King by writing a discontented letter, and had given the charge of the army to one whom the King did not like. . . . Though Biron had offended in Law he might have been pardoned.

What Chapman wrote of Essex in the Biron play, we can now only guess. We do know that in the Fourth Act he had portrayed the Queen pointing out the head of the traitor Essex to the Duke of Biron, when the latter was on an embassy to England. When the play was finally published, after a most vexing obstinacy on the part of the censor to prevent it, lest he "drench his hand in danger" the text was ruthlessly cut. Act II, scene 2 was omitted entirely, because the French Ambassador had objected to the scene where the Queen of France boxed the ear of Mademoiselle de Verneuil; and Act V (Pt. 1) is obviously recast in order to give, in narrative form, a summary of the imprudent passages directly commenting upon Essex. We have already alluded to Chapman's indignation over "these poor dismembered poems."

It is the theory of Professor Dixon Wecter that the history of *Timon of Athens* offers a close parallel to that of *Philotas*. One of the chief difficulties in the discussion of this play is the complete lack of external evidence for the date. If the scholars who assume it to have been written between 1603-07 are correct, a plausible case for the parallel with *Philotas* may be worked out. In the following paragraphs, I am presenting Dr. Wecter's argument *(PMLA,* 43, pp. 401ff.).

Shakspereans need not be reminded of the exceedingly unsatisfactory text of *Timon.* It is obvious that the play has suffered a ruthless and crude revision—so ruthless and crude that critics are all but agreed it could not have been undertaken by Shakspere, but perhaps by Middleton sometime before 1607. The original design seemed to call for a soldier-hero, who had been in his heyday, not only a servant of the State, but privately had been absurdly generous to his friends. When, however, his hour of need came, he was banished by the Senate and deserted by all but his faithful steward and one Alcibiades, who had never been indebted to him. The logical *dénouement* would have required Timon to turn misanthrope, perhaps rebel, and for his friend Alcibiades to plead with the Senate for his reinstatement; and, failing that, to share his banishment. Instead of this simple design, we have a hodge-podge of irrelevances, *non sequiturs,* unfulfilled anticipations, and unintelligible additions. Timon is represented now as a private citizen, now as a soldier-hero, who assumes the right to send his steward to the senators to "bid 'em send o' the instant a thousand talents" to relieve his necessity. Learning of their refusal, he speaks of their "ingratitude," though the play makes no previous mention of services done. After he had returned to the forest, Alcibiades meets him apparently accidentally and reminds him how he has

. . . heard, and grieved,
How cursed Athens, mindless of thy worth,
Forgetting thy great deeds, when neighbour states,
But for thy sword and fortune, trod upon them.

This reference is especially interesting, as it is clearly an addition from the source material, which makes no suggestion of Timon's great services, military or financial, as a preserver of the State.

The "utter frustration of the Ventidius theme" is another unexplained wrench to the design. This matter, first noted by Mr. Fleay, is stated by Dr. Wecter as follows (*ibid.,* p. 705):

It is easy to see what Shakespeare meant to do with Ventidius. In the first scene he makes Timon, in affluence, ransom Ventidius from a debtor's prison with five talents. At the close of the second act, when the now insolvent Timon is appealing to his friends for help, he lets them send to Ventidius as a last and surest friend, now rich, for those five talents. We cannot think that Shakespeare meant to stop here. In a later scene, surely—after the other friends of Timon have deserted—he meant to show Ventidius denying the request. Such a refusal would have put the climax on the ingratitude of Timon's friends; and without it the part of Ventidius in the play is pointless. But before we reach the request to Ventidius we have seen it practically nullified. For the author of the banquet scene could think of no better way to open it than by making Ventidius offer to repay Timon's loan. With this error behind him, the author found it difficult to show Ventidius refusing Timon's appeal; so instead he merely mentions the refusal casually in the scene where he displays that of his own to Sempronius.

Perhaps the most unsatisfactory element in the whole play is the part played by Alcibiades. During the first two acts, he had very little to say—hardly a half-dozen lines, but he appears as the intimate and constant companion of Timon. Then suddenly in the middle of Act III, just before Timon invites "the rascals" to this insulting "feast," and therefore before his retirement, a scene is inserted showing Alcibiades before the Senate pleading most eloquently for a reversal of a hitherto unmentioned sentence of doom against a hitherto unmentioned and unnamed friend who has "in hot blood" but "with a noble fury and fair spirit" slain a man, also unnamed. Alcibiades claims that "setting his fault aside" his friend was "a man of comely virtues."

> Nor did he soil the fact [the murder] with cowardice,
> An honour in him which buys out his fault;
> But with a noble fury and fair spirit,
> Seeing his reputation toucht to death,
> He did oppose his foe.

When the Senate is obstinate, declaring that Alcibiades is "striving to make an ugly deed look fair" and that the unknown must die, Alcibiades plays his last card, exclaiming (Act III, sc. 5):

> Hard fate! he might have died in war.
> My Lords, if not for any parts of him,–
> Though his right arm might purchase his own time,
> And be in debt to none,–yet, more to move you,
> Take my deserts to his, and join 'em both:
> And, for I know your reverend ages love
> Security, I'll pawn my victories, all
> My honour to you, upon his good returns.

In view of such generosity–which in the play is not even tinged with suspicion of guilt–the answer of the Senate comes like a "tale told by an idiot":

> 'T is in few words, but spacious in effect
> We banish thee for ever.

This episode is irrelevant, unintegrated, and unintelligible.

Critics have pointed out many other such absurdities in this play, but, so far as I know, Dr. Wecter is the only one who has offered a plausible explanation. His theory is that in *Timon,*

> . . . Shakespeare wrote into the play the Southampton judgement on the crying injustice of the Essex affair, particularly the part played by Francis Bacon: and so transparent was his intention that the play was mutilated shortly after its composition when a contemporary event, the trouble over Samuel Daniel's *Philotas,* demonstrated that a public vindication of Essex would still be politically offensive,–not, probably to the King himself, but to certain powerful noblemen.

Dr. Wecter proceeds to draw the parallel between the noble but rash and prodigal Timon and the Earl of Essex, whom

Bacon described as "delighting in the press and affluence of Dependants and Suitors," against whom Bacon himself warned Essex by comparing him with the Duke of Guise "because he had turned all his estate into obligations; meaning that he had left himself nothing, but only had bound numbers of persons to him"; for, Bacon added significantly, "you will find many bad debtors." Bacon's description of Essex's chamber is certainly very like Timon's:

> His Chamber being commonly stived with Friends or Suitors of one kind or another, when he gave his legs, armes, and brest to his ordinary servants to button and dress him with little heed, his head and his face to his Barbour, his eyes to his letters, and ears to Petitioners, and many times all at once.

Again and again in his trial, these charges of reckless hospitality were urged:

> So likewise these points of his popularity which every man took notice and note of, as his affable gestures, open doors, making his table and his bed so popularly places of audience to suitors, denying nothing when he did nothing, feeding many men in their discontentments against the Queen and the State.

Essex's patronage to men of genius is of course notorious from the long list of dedications. His handsome treatment of Spenser is too well known for comment. To Sir Francis Allen, on whose behalf Essex had been soliciting the Queen, he wrote: "If I be so unfortunate that the Queen will break her word with me, for you, I will divide one house with you if you will live with me, or settle you in one, if I had but two in the world. For while I have my fortune, Sir Francis Allen shall have part of it."

But of all Essex's benefactions, the case of Bacon is most notorious. All the world now knows, since Dr. E. A. Abbott so carefully presented the facts in his *Bacon and Essex* (London, 1877), how "Essex befriended the slowly rising courtier for many years, wearied Elizabeth to exasperation with pleading for Bacon's advancement, and after Bacon's failure in 1594-5 to obtain the Solicitorship, assuaged his loss by giving him a piece of land worth upwards of £1,800." Again in 1597 we find him appealing to Essex for help, and receiving the earl's best efforts (Birch, *Memoirs,* II, 347-48); and yet, as we all know, Bacon found it impossible to hold with his former patron in his disgrace, and finally went the whole way in collecting evidence against him. If, therefore, Ventidius were intended as the type of arch-fiend of ingratitude to Timon, the parallel to Bacon and Essex would not be hard to credit, nor is it difficult to see why, under the hand of the censor, the part of Ventidius had to be dropped from the play.

Of course, the moment Essex's star began to sink, his creditors came upon him, clamouring for payment. Essex wrote to the Queen "of a number of hungry creditors who suffer me, in my retired life to have no rest." In pleading for the renewal of his patent for sweet wines, he cried out dramatically, "If my creditors would take for payment many ounces of my blood . . . you should never hear of this suit." So Timon bade his creditors to "tell out [his] blood" and declared that with five thousand drops he would pay Lucius' servant's debt of five thousand crowns. Timon's lack of restraint was really not more exaggerated than Essex's. Sir John Harington wrote of him: "The haughty spirit knoweth not how to yield, and the man's soule seemeth tossed to and fro, like the waves of a troubled sea."

In his passionate humiliation, Essex wrote, probably for the Queen's eye:

> Happy were he could finish forth his fate
> In some enchanted desert, most obscure
> From all society, from love, from hate
> Of worldly folk, then would he sleep secure;
> Then wake again and yield God ever Praise,
> Content with hips and haws and bramble-berries,
> In contemplation passing still his days,
> Where harmless robin dwells with gentle thrush;
> Quoth Robertus Comes Essexiae.

So Timon declares he is "so sick of this false world" that he will "love naught but even the mere necessities on it." He who had delighted in sumptuous banquets is now content with the "mast which the oaks bear," and the "scarlet hips which grow upon the briars." These and many more such passages do certainly constitute a plausible parallel to the sufferings and disillusionment of Essex, who declared that, "as for liffe, I hate it, and have lothed to live ainy tyme this twelvemonth and more." The unmitigated baseness of Timon's quondam friends, even of his servants, and the extravagance of his misanthropy have made this play seem to many readers an abstraction too far removed from the genus of "human kindness" to be really suitable for drama. Yet the desertions of Timon are not more sudden or more heartbreaking than those which daily surprised and disgusted the Earl of Essex and his sympathisers: the day before the trial, four of Essex's most intimate friends, Davies, Danvers, Blount, and Rutland, turned Queen's evidence. Dr. Wecter cites a letter from George Carleton to his brother Dudley testifying to the great surprise which these facile confessions evoked. Cecil, describing the trial scene, wrote to Winwood *(Memorials,* I, p. 300):

> Before he went out of the Hall, when he saw himself condemned, and found that Sir *John Davis,* Sir *Ferdinando Gorges,* Sir *Christopher Blunt* and Sir *Charles Davers,* [Danvers] had confessed all the Conferences that were held at Drury-house *by his direction, for surprizing the Queen and the Tower of London;* he then broke out to divers gentlemen that attended him in the Hall, *that his confederates who had now accused him, had been principall Inciters of him and not he of them, ever since* August last, *to work his Access to the Queen with force.*

So of Timon, Shakspere says (IV, ii, 10):

> So his familiars to his buried fortunes
> Slink all away; leave their false vows with him
> Like empty purses pick'd.

Perhaps none of the conspirators, except, of course, Southampton, came off with less odium than one of the Catholics in Essex's retinue, Henry Cuffe. Birch (II, p. 243) describes him as "a great philosopher" and Bacon, deriding his birth as "base," concedes him to have been "a great scholar." (*Declaration of Treason,* p. 15.) Wotton, who had a special hatred for Catholics, declares that his counsels were "slubbered over with a certain rude and clownish fashion that had the semblance of integrity."

Dr. Wecter finds in this man, who, whatever his churlishness, paid with his life for his friendship to Essex, the original of Apemantus. The following sample of his discourse, made from the scaffold from which he was hanged, is perhaps not too unlike the cynical style of Apemantus:

I am adjudged to Death for plotting a plott never acted; and for acting an Act, never by me plotted. The Law will have its course. Accusers shall be heard; Greatness must have the victory; Scholar & Martialist (whose Valor & Learning in Engld. shd have been priviledged) yet in Engld. must die like Dogs & be hanged. To dislike this is but folly; to gainsay it is but Time lost; to avoid it is impossible; But to endure it is manly: & to scorn it is magnanimity. The Prince is displeased; ye Law injurious ye Lawyers uncharitable; & Death terrible. But I ask pardon of ye prince, forgive ye Lawyer; beseech ye world to pardon me; & welcome Death.

Toward these men, however, Essex showed extraordinary patience, realizing, as he said at his trial, that they spoke as men that would save themselves. Against Cecil, and Ralegh, and Cobham, however, his indignation was without restraint. He had always rightly regarded Cobham as a "sycophant." Now he railed at the hated trio calling them "caterpillars" and "atheists." Speaking from the leads of his besieged house he declared (Stopes, *op. cit.*, p. 193):

I would thinke my death most honorable, if by my death I might lykewyse end their lives, and that I had done God, my prince, and my country good service by rooting out such Atheists and Caterpillars from the earth.

But, as Dr. Wecter observes, "the arch-recreant, like Ventidius the climax of ingratitude—one who in his penurious days had been aided generously by his patron, but now having risen to affluence himself deliberately repudiated his benefactor—this man is surely Francis Bacon."

It is not here a part of my duty to present Bacon's apologies; it is only necessary to point out, as Abbott (*op. cit.*, p. 249) has already done, "that Bacon was regarded by the men of his own day as a man who not content with deserting, attempted to injure and destroy his friend."

But, it will be objected, the Ventidius of the play does no

such thing. Dr. Wecter answers, in effect: true! and that is because the play, as we now have it, represents (1) the cuts made by the censor, and (2) the clumsy attempts of Middleton to patch it up again for presentation sometime after 1605. The frustration of the Ventidius theme, as hostile to Bacon, and the suppression of Alcibiades, as indiscreet for Southampton, were the result. Dr. Wecter sums up his argument respecting *Timon* as follows:

> I do not maintain the precarious thesis that Timon is in every particular a faithful portrait of the Earl, but rather that in building up the character of the Athenian lord Shakspere wrote into the play the Southampton judgement on the crying injustice of the Essex affair, particularly the part played by Francis Bacon; . . .

It is not possible here even to mention the scores of suggestions that have been made concerning further allusions to Essex and Southampton in Shakspere. The bibliographies of the *Shakespeare Association Bulletin* are crowded with them. It has been sought, with varying degrees of plausibility, in *Romeo and Juliet, As You Like It, The Merchant of Venice, A Midsummer Night's Dream,* all the *Henry* plays, *Julius Caesar, Troilus and Cressida, Hamlet;* indeed, it begins to look as though it might be suspected in any play. Miss Winifred Smith, in her study of Essex plays on the Continent *(PMLA,* 39 [1924], pp. 147ff.), refers to many such plays in French.

I turn now to a discussion of a similar episode in stage history under King James I.

CHAPTER TEN

Somerset Plays

THE WHOLE TRAGIC AFFAIR of the rise and fall of Essex was probably the most absorbing incident of English court life both socially and politically, between the Armada crisis and the debacle of Somerset's career in 1616. Passing over, for the moment, the other side of the story, that is, the literary campaigns carried on by Ralegh, Cobham, and Cecil against Essex, I turn now to notice several of the plays that almost certainly reflect the career of Robert Carr, one of the most notorious of James's minion-favourites. The list of such plays is hardly less impressive than the array of propaganda for Essex. Something of the history of Robert Carr must be known before we can judge of the suggested dramatic parallels.

Born of a gentleman's family in the neighbourhood of Edinburgh, he was probably from boyhood in some sort of service to the Court. His particular introduction to the attention of the King seems, however, to have taken place after the Court was moved to England—in fact at a tilting-match held in honour of the King's coronation anniversary. The office assigned to young Carr, was, according to Miss Lucy Aikin (*Memoirs of the Court of King James the First,* I, p. 325),

> . . . to present to the sovereign, according to established usage, the shield and device of his master; but as he was dismounting for this purpose, his horse started and threw him at the feet of the monarch, with his leg broken by the fall. James, who had been already captivated by his graces, was filled with grief at the accident; he instantly ordered his surgeons to give their assistance, and as soon as the tilting was over visited the sufferer in person. . . . The doting king visited him daily, occupied himself with his fortune, and even with his education, which he found miserably deficient, and soon exhibited him to the envying courtiers as the intercessor through whom all graces were henceforth to be sought.

The following extract from Sir Anthony Weldon (*The Court*

and Character of King James, ed. 1650, pp. 63ff.) will give the reader some idea of the tools which Cecil was willing to use to gain control over the King:

Lord! how the great men flocked then to see him, and to offer to his Shrine in such abundance, that the King was forced to lay a restraint, least it might retard his recovery by spending his spirits: & to facilitate the cure, care was taken for a choyce Dyet for himselfe, and Chirurgions, with his Attendants, and no sooner recovered but a proclaimed Favourite.

Then the *English* Lords, who formerly coveted an *English* Favourite (and to that end the Countesse of *Suffolk* did look out choyce young men, whom she daily curled and perfumed their breaths) left all hope, and she her curling and perfuming, all adoring this rising Sun, every man striving to invest himselfe into this man's favour (not sparing nor bounty nor flattery) which was not hard to be obtained, being naturally more addicted to the *English* then to the *Scotch,* in so much that he endeavoured to forget his native Country, and his Father's house, having none of note about him but *English,* and but one besides *English,* in any familiarity with him, which was Sir *Robert Carre* his Kinsman; but above all, was Sir *Thomas Overbury* his *Pythias,* then the strife between *Salisbury* and *Suffolk,* who should engrosse him, and make him their Monopoly; each presenting, proffering, and accumulating favours upon *Overburies* kindred, the Father made a Judge in *Wales,* and himself offered an office; but *Overbury,* naturally of insolent spirit, which was elevated by being so intimate with a favourite, and having wholly ingrossed that commodity, which could not be retayled, but by him and his favour; with a kinde of scorne neglected their friendships, yet made use of both.

Now was *Carre* Knighted, and made Gentleman of the Bedchamber, and *Overburies* pride rose with the others honours, still storming the Chapman, as they did by their cheap offices undervalue so precious a commodity.

Northampton finding himself neglected by so mean a fellow, cast about another way, and followed *Balaams* councell, by sending a *Moabitish* Woman unto him, in which he made use of *Copinger* a Gentleman, who had spent a faire fortune left by his Ancestors, and now for maintenance, was forced to lead the life of a Serving-man (that formerly kept many to serve him) and as an addition, the worst of that kind, a flat Bawd.

This Gentleman had lived a scandalous life, by keeping a Whore of his own, which for the honour of her Family I will not name, therefore was fittest to trade in that commodity for another, and in truth was fit to take any impression baseness could stamp on him, as the sequell of this Story will manifest; This *Moabitish* woman, was a daughter of the Earle of *Suffolk,* married to a young noble Gentleman the Earle of *Essex.*

This Train took, and the first private meetings were at Copingers house, and himself Bawd to their lust, which put him into a farre greater bravery for a time, then when he was Master of his owne, but it had bitternesse on all hands in the end. This privacy in their stoln pleasures, made *Copinger* a friend to *Northampton* and *Suffolk,* though but a servant to Viscount *Rochester,* for so now was he called, and now had they linked him so close, as no breaking from them.

Overbury was that *John Baptist* that reproved the Lord, for the sinne of using the Lady, and abusing the young Earle of Essex; would call her Strumpet, her mother and brother Bawds, and used them with so much scorne, as in truth was not to be endured by a fellow of his Rank, to persons of that quality, how faulty soever otherwise they were.

Then to satisfie *Overbury,* and blot out the name of Sin, his love led him into a more desperate way by a resolution to marry another mans wife, against this then did *Overbury* bellow louder, and in it, shewd himselfe more like an affectionate, then a discreet and moderate friend: had he compounded but one dram of discretion with an ounce of affection, he might with such a receipt, have preserved his own life, and their fortunes and honours.

This Countess of Suffolk was indeed an extraordinary woman. She seems to have been on friendly and co-operative terms with her husband *and* her lover, *and* her lover's other mistress, Lady Audrey Walsingham. Of the Constable of Castille and his machinations at the English Court, Weldon says *(op. cit.,* p. 27):

There was not one Courtier of note that tasted not of *Spains* bounty, either in gold, or jewels, and among them, not any in so large a proportion as the Countess of *Suffolke,* who shared in her Lords interest, being then a potent man, and in that interest which she had, in being mistress to that little great secretary (little in body and stature but great in wit and policy), the sole manager of State affaires; so it may be said, she was a double sharer.

The Countess of Essex, the daughter of the Earl and

Countess of Suffolk, seems to have been, vulgarly speaking, "a chip off the old block."

The following letter from Lord Thomas Howard to Sir John Harington *(Nugae,* i, 390), "marks," says Miss Aikin *(op. cit.,* I, pp. 326-330), "the maturity of the royal phrensy, as well as the vile adulation of his court."

My good and trusty knight;

If you have good will and good health to perform what I shall commend, you may set forward for court whenever it suiteth your own conveniency: the king hath often inquired after you, and would readily see and converse again with the "merry blade," as he hath oft called you since you was here. I will now premise certain things to be observed by you toward well gaining our prince's good affection: – He doth wondrously covet learned discourse, of which you can furnish out ample means; he doth admire good fashion in clothes, I pray you give good heed hereunto; strange devices oft come into man's conceit; some one regardeth the endowments of the inward worth, wit, valor, or virtue; another hath perchance special affection toward outward things, clothes, deportment and good countenance; I would wish you to be well trimmed; get a new jerkin, well bordered and not too short; the king saith, he liketh a flowing garment; be sure it be not all of one sort, but diversely colored, the collar falling somewhat down, and your ruff well stiffened and bushy. We have lately had many gallants who failed in their suits for want of due observance of these matters. The king is nicely heedful of such points, and dwelleth on good looks and handsome accoutrements. Eighteen servants were lately discharged, and many more will be discarded, who are not to his liking in these matters.

I wish you to follow my directions, as I wish you to gain all you desire. Robert Carr is now most likely to win the prince's affection, and doth it wonderously in a little time. The prince leaneth on his arm, pinches his cheek, smooths his ruffled garment, and, when he looketh at Carr, directeth discourse to divers others. This young man doth much study all art and device; he hath changed his tailors and tiremen many times, and all to please the prince, who laugheth at the long-grown fashion of our young courtiers, and wisheth for change every day. You must see Carr before you go to the King, as he was with him a boy in Scotland, and knoweth his taste and what pleaseth. In your discourse you must not dwell too long on any one subject, and touch but lightly on religion. Do not of yourself say, "This is good, or bad," but, "If it were your majesty's good opinion, I myself should think so and so." Ask no more questions than what may serve to discover the prince's thought. In private discourse, the king seldom speaketh of any man's temper, discretion, or good virtues; so meddle not at all, but find out a clue to guide you to the heart and most delightful subject on his mind. I will advise one thing;—the roan-jennet whereon the king rideth every day, must not be forgotten to be praised; and the good furniture above all, what lost a great man much notice the other day. A noble did come in suit of a place, and saw the king mounting the roan; he delivered his petition, which was heeded and read, but no answer was given. The noble departed, and came to court the next day, and got no answer again. The lord-treasurer was then pressed to move the king's pleasure touching the petition. When the king was asked for answer thereto he said in some wrath, "Shall a king give heed to a dirty paper, when a beggar noteth not his gilt stirrups?" Now it fell out that the king had new furniture when the noble saw him in the court-yard, but he was overcharged with confusion, and passed by admiring the dressing of the horse. Thus, good knight, our noble failed in his suit. I could relate and offer some other remarks on these matters. . . .

"You have lived to see the trim of old times, and what passed in the queen's days. These things are no more the same. Your queen did talk of her subjects' love and good affections, and in good truth she aimed well; our king talketh of his subjects' fear and subjection, and herein I think he doth well too, as long as it holdeth good. Carr hath all the favours, as I told you before; the king teacheth him Latin every morning, and I think some one should teach him English too; for he is a Scotish lad, he hath much need of better language. The king doth much covet his presence; the ladies too are not behind hand in their admiration; for I tell you, good knight, this fellow is straight-limbed, well-favored, strong-shouldered and smooth-faced, with some sort of cunning and show of modesty; though, G— wot, he well knoweth when to show his impudence. You are not young, you are not handsome, you are not finely; and yet will you come to court and think to be well-favored? Why, I say again, good knight, that your learning may somewhat prove worthy hereunto; your Latin and your Greek, your Italian and your Spanish tongues, your wit and discretion, may well be looked unto for a time, as strangers at such a place; but these are not the things men live by now-a-days. Will you say, the moon shineth all the summer? that the stars are bright jewels fit for Carr's ears? that the roan jennet surpasseth Bucephalus, and is worthy to be bestridden by Alexander? that his eyes are fire, his tail is Berenice's locks, and a few more such fancies worthy your noticing? Your lady is virtuous, and somewhat of a good housewife; has lived in a court in her time, and I believe you may venture her forth again; but I know those would not so quietly rest, were Carr to leer on their wives, as some do perceive, yea, and like it well too they should be noticed. If any mischance be to be wished, 'tis breaking a leg in the king's presence, for this fellow owes all his favor to that bout; I think he hath better reason to speak well of his own horse than the king's roan jennet. We are almost worn out in our endeavours to keep pace with this fellow in his duty and labor to gain favor, but all in vain; where it endeth I cannot guess, but honors are talked of speedily for him.

The rest of the story is too unsavoury to recount here in detail; it involves the murder of Overbury in the Tower by the agents of the Countess of Essex, the infamous nullity case, whereby she obtained a divorce from Essex, the King's action in creating Rochester Earl of Somerset that the Countess might marry him without loss of rank, the unparalleled magnificence of the wedding festivities for which almost every known poet then living made some contribution, and, finally the fall of the old favourite and the rise of the new.

Two things, however, it is important for us to keep in mind: first, the probable innocence of Somerset in the matter of the murder, and second, the disgraceful behaviour of the King in the whole conduct of the affair. It is more than probable that the case had never come up for trial, much less indictment, had it not been for the appearance on the scene of a new favourite with whom the King found it impossible to reconcile the old. Again it is Weldon who describes the rising sun *(op. cit.,* pp. 88-89):

For now began to appeare a glimmering of a new Favourite, one Mr. *George Villers* a younger Son (by a second Venter) of an ancient Knight in *Leicestershire,* as I take it, his Father of an ancient Family, his Mother but of a mean, and waiting Gentle-woman, whom the old man fel in love with and married, by whom he had three sons, all raised to the Nobility, by means of their brother-Favourite: this Gentleman was come also but newly from Travell [like Carr] and did beleeve it a great fortune to marry a Daughter of *Sir Rogers Astons* [the King's barber] &c., in truth it was the height of his ambition, and for that only end was he a hanger on upon the Court; the Gentlewoman loved him so well, as could all his friends have made her for her great fortune, but an hundred Marks Joynture, she had married him presently, in despight of all her friends; and no question would have had him without any Joynture at all.

But, before the closing up of this Match, the King cast a glancing eye towards him, which was easily observed by such as observed their Princes humour, and then the Match was laid aside, some assuring him a greater Fortune was coming to him, then one gave him his place of Cup-bearer, that he might be in the Kings eye; another sent to his Mercer and Tayler to put good cloathes on him; a third, to his Sempster for curious Linnen, and all as in-comes to obtaine Offices upon his future Rise; then others tooke upon them to be his Bravoes, to undertake his quarrels upon affronts put on him by Somerset's Faction, so all hands help to the piecing up of this new Favourite.

The story of the King's attempt to reconcile them is told in great detail by Miss Norma Solve in her *Stuart Politics in Chapman (University of Michigan Publications,* IV). Here it must suffice to state that when he found every effort at pacification between the rivals unavailing, he determined to rid himself of Somerset. His method of doing so is again recounted by Weldon. In describing the parting scene between the King and Somerset, after James had determined on the ruin of his quondam favourite, he says (*op. cit.,* pp. 102-03):

The Earle of *Somerset,* never parted from him with more seeming affection then at this time, when he knew *Somerset* should never see him more; and had you seen that seeming affection (as the Author himself did) you would rather have beleeved he was in the rising, then setting: The Earle when he kissed his hand, the King hung about his neck, slabbering his cheeks; saying, for Gods sake, when shall I see thee again? On my soule, I shall neither eate, nor sleep, untill you come againe; the Earl told him, on Monday (this being on the Friday), for Gods sake let me said the King, shall I? shall I? Then lolled about his neck; then, for Gods sake, give thy Lady this kisse for me; in the same manner at the stayres head, at the middle of the stayres, and at the stayres foot; The Earle was not in his Coach, when the King used these very words in the hearing of 4 servants, of whom, one was Sumersets great creature, and of the Bed-Chamber (who reported it instantly to the Author of this History) *I shall never see his face more.*

Contemporary opinion was much divided as to the Earl's guilt. Weldon himself, who does not often err on the side of charity, says *(ibid.,* p. 121-122):

Many beleeve him guilty of *Overburies* death, but the most thought him guilty onely of the breach of friendship (and that in a high point) by suffering his imprisonment, which was the high-way to his murther; and this conjecture I take to bee of the soundest opinion; . . . For the Gentleman himselfe, he had misfortune to marry such a woman, in such a Family, which first undermined his Honour, afterwards his life (at least to be dead in Law); nor did any thing reflect upon him in all his time of Favourite, but in, and by that Family; first in his adulterous marriage, then in so hated a Family, and the bringing in *Cranfield* and *Ingram,* as Projectors, all by his Wives and friends meanes; otherwise he had been the bravest Favourite of our time, full of Majesty imploying his time like a Statesman.

Weldon has a series of nicknames for the Countess—"old kettle" being the most frequent. He also called her "this Moabitish woman" and "the fatal Countess," which last sounds curiously like the title of a play. He further declares *(ibid.,* p. 86):

Somerset and that Faction bear all down before them, disposing of all offices (yet *Somerset* never turned any out as the succeeding favourite) but places being void, he disposed of them, and who would give most was the word, yet not by *Somerset* himself, but by his Lady and her Family, for he was naturally of a noble disposition, and it may be justly said of him, that never could be said of any before, or ever will be of any after him: he never got suit for himselfe or friends that was burdensom to the Commonwealth, no Monopolies, no Impositions.

In spite of the general scorn which historians have felt for the minions of James, it is important that for the most part

1615, Nov. **143.** Mistris Turner's Farewell to all women. A large wood-cut with two female figures; one representing *Mrs. Turner* in deep mourning; the other *Lady* Pride, lasciviously dressed out, and between both, these verses:

"Angell (turn'd Divell) Pride, by thee I fell,
"When heere on earth I dwelt, too the pit of Hell:
"Ye, spite of all thy Poysons, I am faire:
"Now in God's eyes, Women by me Beware."

Then follow some verses descriptive of Mrs. Turner and Lady Pride.

Printed for John Trundle.

The whole contained in a large oval border of very rude ornamentation.

1615, Nov. **144.** Mistres Turner's Repentance, Who, about the poysoning of that Ho: Knight Sir Thomas Overbury, VVas executed the fourteenth day of November last.

A long poem descriptive of her conduct at her execution, by T.B.

Printed at London, for Henry Gosson and John White, 1615.

they exonerate Somerset from the worst of crimes. Bishop Goodman says (Solve, *op. cit.*, p. 91):

> Now for the favorite Sir Robert Carr: truly he was a wise, discreet gentleman; as Sir Robert Cotton, the great antiquary, told me, he did very often send unto him for precedents, when as things were to be done in the State which he doubted whether they were lawful and expedient, and therefore did desire to have the example of former times for his warrant.

Lingard makes a similar testimony (*ibid.*, pp. 91-92):

> It is but justice to Somerset, to add what he says of his own services in a petition to Charles: that during the three years he was in power, he opposed all suits for honours and reversions of offices, lest the king and his successors should have nothing left to give in reward to their servants; that he found a resolution taken after the death of Salisbury, to disforest all the royal parks and forests, and to sell all the crown lands, reserving only an increase of rent; this also he prevented; that he never would receive of the king any gift of crown lands, or customs; and whatever he did receive, was such as either took nothing from the king or brought with it an increase to the revenue; and that he made himself many enemies by opposing both the suitors and the ministers for the advantage of the crown.

The anonymous author of *The Narrative History of King James,* who describes at length the briberies and insolencies of Somerset, concludes, nevertheless, that most of his enemies were stimulated by envy rather than other injury. The tract states that (Somers, *Tracts,* II, p. 268; Solve, *op. cit.*, p. 90):

> . . . his revenues were enlarged, and his glory so resplendent, that he drowned the dignity of the best of the nobility, and the eminency of such as were much more excellent, by which means envy (the common companion of greatness) procured him much discontent.

It is, however, not our business to vindicate the character of Robert Carr, but to acquaint the reader with the facts of his history and the contemporary attitude toward him. One of the most important of these facts is that Carr's destruction was planned and executed, not as an act of justice to the State, but as a political coup directed by a cabal of his hostile rivals. The most active members of this clique were Bacon (then Lord Chancellor), Treasurer Montague, Secretary Winwood, and—

certainly not least in the cabal—Queen Anne herself; and their *piece de resistance* was young Villiers. As formerly Cecil and the Countess of Suffolk had curled and perfumed the boys for the office of the King's minion, so now the new favourite, tricked out in all the effeminate fopperies intended to excite the sexually abnormal monarch, was presented to the King by the Queen, who had been induced by the enemies of Somerset, particularly Archbishop Abbott, to undertake the odious office. Birch *(The Lives and Characters of Illustrious Persons of Great Britain. . . . "Queen Anne,"* p. 56) asserts: "Whatever were the reasons, she put herself at the head of the faction against him (Somerset) which, upon the discovery of the murder of Sir Thomas Overbury, proved his ruin."

It is not necessary here to give in detail the procedure of Somerset's trial. The most impressive fact connected with it was the Earl's consistent, unalterable, and unshakeable protestation of innocence. Contemporary testimony bears ample witness to this fact. Amos, quoting the observations of an eyewitness at the trial, states (Solve, *op. cit.*, p. 37): "A thing worthy of note in him was his constancy and undaunted carriage in all the time of his arraignment, which, as it began, so it did continue to the end without change or alteration." Sir George More, Keeper of the Tower, stated that "He ever stood in his innocency and would never be brought to confess that he had any hand with his wife in the poisoning of Overbury, knew not of it, nor consented unto it." Bacon himself, who had been among the most fawning of Somerset's "slaves," now, spurred on by the new favourite and by the King to secure a conviction, admitted that in spite of his every endeavour, the case against the Earl "rested chiefly on presumptions." (*Ibid.*) But as the letters of Bacon prove beyond a doubt, both "James and Bacon agreed as to using fair means or foul in order to obtain a conviction."

Of course, the moment the King's face was turned from the Earl, all his old excesses and insolencies were recalled by the populace and he became, says Miss Solve, in the eye of all London, a monster, "not only of ingratitude to James and to his former friend, Sir Thomas Overbury, but also of the most horrible treachery and crime."

As in the case of Essex, it is not possible to note here all the plays which reflect one or more aspects of the story. Such reflections vary all the way from incidental allusion to elaborate and complete allegory, and the criticism involved is now friendly, now hostile. The most interesting case of friendly criticism, which really amounts to a case of special pleading for Somerset, is afforded in Chapman's *Tragedy of Chabot.* The full interpretation of this play has been admirably presented by Miss Norma Solve in her Monograph, *Stuart Politics in Chapman's Tragedy of Chabot.* In her essay, she has reminded us of two important facts which must be kept in mind when studying this problem: first, Chapman's theory of the moral end of literary art; and second, his labours for and devotion to Robert Carr. We have already referred briefly to the former fact, in mentioning Chapman's insistence upon art as the record of "memorable examples for the use of Policy and the state." In such purposes, he declares *(A Justification of Perseus and Andromeda,* p. 194):

. . . the poets in all ages, challenging as their birth-rights the use and application of these fictions, have ever been allowed to fashion both *pro* and *contra* to their own offenseless and judicious occasions. And borrowing so far the privileged license of their professions, have enlarged or altered the allegory with inventions and dispositions of their own, to extend it to their present doctrinal and illustrious purposes.

Chapman expresses the same theory in his dedication of *The Odyssey,* and in the *Letter to Bacon,* accompanying *The Georgics of Hesiod.* (Solve, *op. cit.,* pp. 10-11.)

In the face of such an avowed usage it is not to be wondered that Swinburne gives up in disgust the task of interpreting Chapman. He says of the allegory in *The Tears of Peace*: "The allegory is of course clouded and confounded by all manner of perversities and obscurities worth no man's while to elucidate or rectify." With this attitude, however, the modern student of the drama could not concur. It has certainly not been the point of view of Chapman specialists like Professor Mark Parrott or Miss Norma Solve. Without committing herself to an Essex parallel for Biron, Miss Solve says (*op. cit.,* p. 17):

The central moral interest of the Byron plays is the relations of subject to monarchy, of favorite to king, the duty of loyalty on the one side, and of justice on the other; that of *Chabot* is, in the words of Professor Parrott "the duty of the absolute monarch to respect the liberty of the loyal subject."

I do not know whether either Dr. Parrott or Miss Solve intended to imply a parallel to Heywood's *Royal King and the Loyal Subject,* but there is more than the title in this play to suggest such a comparison.

It is not necessary for us, at the moment, to review Chapman's relations with his former patron, Prince Henry, in whose household he had enjoyed a post from the year 1604 to the year of Henry's death, 1612. When, or under what circumstances, Chapman entered the service of Carr, we do not know. Our first intimation of the fact of Somerset's patronage of Chapman is in the dedication of *Andromeda Liberata* to the Earl and Countess, after their marriage in 1613. It is clear from certain passages that Chapman had written the poem as a definite commission. The poet declares:

> Nor will I fear to prostrate this poor rage
> Of forespoke Poesy, to your patronage,
> Thrice worthy Earl, and your unequall'd grace,
> Most noble Countess.

It is clear from other passages in this dedication that Chapman believed in the innocence and nobility of the Earl, and was no way moved by the flood of gossip and evil rumour concerning the murder of Overbury and the divorce of the Countess. He condemns the scandal mongers who hear only one side of the question and urges the Earl to go bravely forth "till scandal pine, and bane-fed envy burst." That Chapman was sincere in this point of view is evidenced by his dedicating his *Odesses* to Somerset even after his fall, and, as we shall see presently, by his urging his case in the *Tragedy of Chabot.* In this act of loyalty Chapman was almost unique among the former recipients of the Earl's favours. The language of subsequent dedications re-enforces our opinion of Chapman's sincerity. In the Epistle dedicating *Pro Vere, Autumni Lachrymae* of 1622 he addressed Somerset as "The Most Worthily Honoured and Judicially Noble Lover and Fautor of all Goodness and Virtue"; the *Hymns of Homer,* in 1624, were directed to "my ever Most-Worthy-to-be-Most Honoured Lord" Robert, Earl of Somerset, and signed "your Lordship's, ever most worthily bounden George Chapman."

While Chapman was thus proving his devotion to his ruined patron, affairs in the English court had undergone an almost complete change. Somerset's quondam secretary, but now his bitter enemy, Sir Ralph Winwood, had become Secretary of State. Villiers, "now first favourite, ruled the King without a rival," having—as Weldon remarks—"the Chancellor, Treasurer, and all great officers his very slaves." Bacon, who had been made Lord Chancellor, and Baron Verulam and finally Viscount St. Albans, was then within two months of the last advancement. Five months later he was accused by the House of Commons of "a collection of corruptions," found guilty and heavily sentenced. Two others in the "conspiracy" against Somerset were now enjoying at least a part of that high place that had once been occupied by Somerset alone. Of these the first was Sir Henry Montague, one of the Sergeants at the Trial, who had been rewarded for his work in that connection with the office of Lord High Treasurer. The second was Chancellor Ellesmere, then an old man and soon to resign his place to Bacon. He had acted as Lord High Steward in the trial, and it was against this latter appointment that Somerset had protested in a letter to the King to the effect that James had so far forsaken him as to turn over to his enemies the prosecution of his case. The personnel of the court presented, indeed, the complete triumph of Somerset's foes. The only person who seems not to have profited by the whole proceeding was Chief Justice Sir Edward Coke, who "it was thought for his over zealousness and his injudicious hinting of mystery and further crime, even involving the death of that sweet Prince Henry, was rebuked for his Indiscretion, and before the next year expired, removed from his Post." The result of the trial is, of course, known to all students of the period. The Countess confessed and Somerset "stood on his innocence," yet both were convicted and sentenced to death, but the sentence was not carried out. Lady Somerset was pardoned on 13 July, 1616; but as the Earl "had indignantly or coldly rejected all such promises of mercy held out to him before his trial in exchange for a confession, so now, still protesting his innocence, he refused a pardon. Consequently, though he had been freed from the Tower in January 1622, the judgment of death hung over his head for years, in fact until four months before the death of James, when he received and accepted a formal and full pardon."

Miss Solve believes that it was "after the conviction of Bacon and before Somerset had received a pardon—that is, after March, 1621 and before December, 1624, that . . . Chapman wrote *The Tragedy of Chabot,"* as his version of the fate of his admired patron. The source of Chapman's play was the ninth chapter of the sixteenth book of Pasquier's *Les Recherches* (1621): "Du Procéz estraordinaire fait, primierement à Messire Philippe Chabot Admiral de France, puis à Messire Guillaume Pauyet Chancelier."

The following summary of Pasquier's story is from Miss Solve's monograph (*op. cit.*, 64-66):

> The story of Chabot, as told by Pasquier, is very brief, and is all told in one short chapter, in less than four folio pages. It is introduced as a moral example, "in order," as Pasquier states, "to instruct all judges not to adapt their wills in judging to the singular wills of the Kings, their Masters." Such a moral, as well as political purpose would naturally enough attract the attention and interest of the moralist Chapman, and from its general application would invite him, with his allegorical habits, to apply it to a specific situation in England which was engaging his attention.
>
> From the statement of his moral, Pasquier jumps immediately into the heart of his story. Philip Chabot, favored by Francis I of France, had been showered with honors and titles, until the King, through mere whim, began to weary of him. This whim was strengthened into real displeasure, until one day an open break came and the King threatened to place him in the hands of the Judges. Chabot, not realizing his danger, and only conscious of his own right, defied the King to find any breach in his goods, his life, or his honor. This open challenge so displeased the King that he issued a commission against Chabot, and the case was put in charge of Chancellor Poyet. The remarkable thing about the trial was that there was no article by which the crime of felony or treason could be imputed to Chabot. There were only some

exactions unduly made by him on some fishers of Normandy under pretext of his admiralty. The judges were therefore inclined to be lenient, but the Chancellor, knowing the King's desire for a condemnation, treated the prisoner rudely and so threatened the Judges that, though the Admiral was not condemned to death, he was convicted and given a heavy sentence. However, in order to show that the judgment was forced, the judges wrote a *V* at the beginning of the verdict and an *I* at the end. The statement of arrest charged Chabot with infidelities, disloyalties, disobedience, oppression, contempt, and ingratitude. Pasquier here is moved to comment upon the latter accusation, as a vice which one naturally abhors but for which one hardly deserves to be brought to trial. The Chancellor had, however, used every means, sneering, rudeness, constraint to judges, and even the invention of a new crime, in order to please the King to whom he had promised "mountains and marvels." But the King who had desired a death sentence so that he might force Chabot to repentance, and so that he himself might afterward show mercy, ordered a pardon. The Admiral in answer only praised God that no real crime of felony and treason had been proved against him. Francis, astonished at such a statement, issued a new commission to investigate, and, upon seeing the procedure and documents which bore ample testimony to the truth of Chabot's answer, he restored Chabot to good fame and repute. But Chabot, shocked and embittered by the arrest, did not long survive, and two years later died.

The possibilities in this French story may be seen at once. The resemblances between the fortunes of Chabot and Carr are strikingly similar. A study of Chapman's changes in the source material, however, brings added weight to the argument in favour of Miss Solve's theories. These changes are detailed by Miss Solve (*op. cit.*, 73-79):

The first act in the play is almost entirely an addition, in which we have: a long defense of Chabot; the development of the rivalry between a rising and a falling favorite; an attempted reconciliation between these favorites on the part of the King; and its failure due to a plot against him by Chabot's enemies. The conspiracy to undermine Chabot as King's favorite and to replace him with one more pliant has no place in Pasquier. He attributes Chabot's fall to a mere whim, instead of to a plot. "Le Roy ne croyoit qu'en luy seul; entre ceux qui auoient son oreille. Toutes fois comme les opinions des Roys se changent sans sçauoir quelques-fois pourquoy, aussi commença-il avecques le temps de se lasser de luy, & en fin el luy despleut tout à fait." The only person mentioned in Pasquier as leagued against Chabot is Chancellor Poyet. In Chapman we have a faction of enemies made up not only of the Chancellor, but also of the Queen, Montmorency, the Treasurer, and the Secretary. So, although we have in Chapman's play the same haughty retort to the King which hastened Chabot's fall that we find in Pasquier, the other circumstances and causes have all been added.

In the trial scene we have several notable differences, although in main outline the similarity is quite evident. The Proctor-General is a new character, and although the sneers and rudeness of the Chancellor are largely transferred to him, Chapman owes no more than the barest suggestion for this character to his source. The long diatribe against Chabot is also an addition. Pasquier merely furnishes the basis of the charges, though even to these Chapman has added the lengthy accusation against Chabot of his "mighty fortune" and inordinate pride. Chabot's sentence, too, as Chapman gives it, is entirely unhistorical. The reading of the verdict is incomplete in Chapman as it is in Pasquier. But immediately after this incomplete reading, in Chapman's account of the trial, the Chancellor definitely alludes to a death sentence which has no authority either in Pasquier or in French history:

> *Chancellor:* Now, Captain of the guard, secure his person
> Till the King signify
> His pleasure for his death.

As a matter of fact, Chabot was fined 1,500,000 livres, banished for life without hope of recall, and his goods confiscated.

In Poyet's trial also we have a few distinct departures from Pasquier. The use of the same Proctor-General, furnishing as it does such nice irony in his complete reversal of attitude, is an addition, as well as his elaborate and wordy charge of corruption. The principal accusation against Poyet in Pasquier was, as we have already noted, his unjust treatment of Chabot, although there is mere mention of other charges. The sentences of Poyet in the two accounts are practically the same, with one slight change. Instead of a judgment of perpetual imprisonment which we find in Chapman, Pasquier tells of an imprisonment of only five years. In Chapman, Poyet confesses and humbly begs for the King's mercy, although in the French source there is no mention of such confession.

Other slight differences in Chapman's action are to be noticed in Chabot's haughty refusal of a pardon; in the belief that Chabot's hope of recovery after his vindication lay in the King's power; and in the pathetic last scene which portrays the death of the grief-stricken Admiral.

However, aside from the differences in the plot as developed in the first two acts of Chapman's play, the most striking differences are in the characters. And one of the most pronounced departures in character is in that of Montmorency, who is merely mentioned in Pasquier. Historically, Montmorency, as described by Professor Parrott, "appears to have been a violent, ambitious, and unscrupulous nobleman, and there is little or nothing in the accounts of his life to justify the favorable portrait presented to us in the play." According to Chapman's delineation, we have seen him young instead of approximately the same age as Chabot; gay and carefree instead of unscrupulously intriguing; impulsive rather than coldly calculating; amiable, agreeable, a little prone to too much flexibility, but honorable, honest, and personally charming. Instead of proceeding in the intrigue against Chabot, he deserts it after becoming convinced of the honor and uprightness of his opponent. When the King rebukes him for his former attitude, he impetuously admits his error, and continues in his supplications for mercy to the Admiral.

King: Why, you are the chief engine rais'd against him,
And in the world's creed labour most to sink him
That in his fall and absence every beam
May shine on you and only gild your fortune.
Your difference is the ground of his arraignment.

Montmorency: I would not have
It lie upon my fame that I should be
Mentioned in story his unjust supplanter
For your whole kingdom. I have been abused,
And made believe my suit was just and necessary,
My walks have not been safe, my closet prayers,
But some plot has persued me by some great ones
Against your noble Admiral; they have frighted
My fancy into my dreams with their close whispers,
How to uncement your affections,
And render him the fable and the scorn
Of France.

Queen: Brave Montmorency.

King: Are you serious?

Montmorency: Have I a soul or gratitude to acknowledge
Myself your creature, dignified and honour'd
By your high favours? With an equal truth
I must declare the justice of your Admiral
(In what my thoughts are conscious), and will rather
Give up my claims to birth, title, and offices,
Be thrown from your warm smile, the top and crown
Of subjects' happiness, than be brib'd with all
Their glories to the guilt of Chabot's ruin.

King: Come, come; you overact this passion,
And if it be not policy, it tastes
Too green, and wants some counsel to mature it;
His fall prepares your triumph.

Montmorency: It confirms
My shame alive, and, buried, will corrupt
My very dust, make our House-genius groan,
And fright the honest marble from my ashes.
His fall prepare my triumph: Turn me first
A naked exile to the world.

On this point, namely, the change in attitude towards Chabot, Professor Parrott remarks, "The friendly spirit displayed by Montmorency by these lines, and the regret he feels for the false position in which court intrigues have placed him, is, of course, quite unhistorical." Moreover, the historical Montmorency fell from power whereas in Chapman, instead of being dismissed and disgraced, he remains to the end of the play in high favor with the King.

Besides this difference between Chapman and his source in the character of Montmorency and his part in the action concerning Chabot, there is also a change in the character of the King. There is no intimation in the drama that Francis was weary of Chabot and broke with him as the result of a mere whim. Instead we find the break coming as a result of a conspiracy and the unbending pride and too strict justice of the Admiral. In place of a long discussion of court factions and intrigue against Chabot, we have in Pasquier one sentence which lays all the blame upon a fickle monarch. Apparently in Chapman then we have an attempt to remove the stigma of instability from the King and instead to place the blame upon the malicious and intriguing cabal of nobles leagued against the favorite. For in the drama even after the Admiral's insult to the signature of the King, the latter remains faithful to his Admiral. Not even the fiery malice of the Queen can move him to anger. It is only when he is hurt by the defiance of Chabot himself that he grows angry and in a moment of impulsive rage gives his favorite over to the law.

The whole last act, in which Chapman prolongs a situation in order to increase the pathos of Chabot's grief-stricken condition, offers another striking departure from the source. Again, all that the source contributes on this subject is condensed into one sentence: "Les coup toutesfois du premier arrest l'vlcera de telle façon qu'il ne suruesquit pas longuement." Actually Chabot was pardoned in March, 1541, and died in June, 1543, two years later, whereas Chapman has increased the pathos by moving the date forward so that he presents the death scene as though it followed immediately. Although in one way this is dramatically justified, by intensifying an emotion, in another it is an offence against dramatic structure. For the drama properly ends with the vindication of Chabot and the punishment of his enemy, and any explanation of such undue prolongation must be found in something aside from its dramatic fitness.

Besides expanding and changing the action and characters found in his source, Chapman adds several characters in his account: the faithful servant, Allegre, who is put to the rack for his master's sake; the Father, who serves as a foil for the character of Chabot, as the mouthpiece of his honor and integrity, and as one of the strongest elements of pathetic appeal; the Wife, who with the Father intensifies the pathos of the Admiral's position; the Secretary and the Treasurer, who strengthen the faction of Chabot's enemies; the Proctor-General, who helps to link the trials of Chabot and Poyet together; and the Queen, who by completely changing her attitude becomes one of the best witnesses for the uprightness of Chabot's character.

The question arises always in connection with these propaganda plays: how dared the dramatist to do it? In certain plays the question can be answered fairly easily. If, for instance, Richard II were recognized as a parallel for Elizabeth, there is, after all, at least as much flattery as criticism involved. Even the criticism is as much a plea for royal justice as a warning against royal tyranny. So with *Chabot,* the dramatist is careful to caress the King into a receptive mood by his sedulous praise of his good points and palliation of those that could be construed as mere weakness or foibles.

With many other plays, however, particularly those against the King, we are left in utter amazement at the intrepidity of the poets. As Sir Edmund Chambers notes (*Elizabethan Stage*, Vol. I, p. 325):

For some years after the coming of James the freedom of speech by the stage, in a London much inclined to be critical of the alien King, and his retinue of hungry Scots, was far beyond anything which could have been tolerated by Elizabeth. The uncouth speech of the Sovereign, his intemperance, his gusts of passion, his inordinate devotion to the chase, were caricatured with what appears incredible audacity, before audiences of his new subjects. "Consider for pity's sake," writes Beaumont, the French ambassador on 14 June, 1604, "what must be the state and condition of a prince, whom the preachers publicly from the pulpit assail, whom the comedians of the metropolis bring upon the stage, whose wife attends these representations in order to enjoy the laugh against her husband."

Samuel Calvert wrote to the same effect in a letter to Winwood, 28 March, 1605 (*Winwood Memorials*, ii, 54):

The Plays do not forbear to present upon their stage the whole course of this present time, not sparing either King, State or Religion, in so great Absurdity and with such great Liberty, that any would be afraid to hear them.

Apparently, however, the authors were not afraid to write them nor the players to perform them, for they continued to appear throughout the reign.

It will be convenient to examine some of these plays in a separate chapter.

CHAPTER ELEVEN

Miscellaneous Plays Against the King

Satires on the manners and morals of the King

CONSIDERING THE OFFENSIVENESS of the manners and morals of James I, the candour of the satirists is all but breathtaking, though, as a manner of fact, in his leniency towards acts of disrespect to his person, James's habit was the very opposite of the late Queen's. Whether his mildness in this respect was due to lack of wit or gall, or merely to regal superiority, I leave my readers to judge. At all events, the following anecdote from Howel *(Letters,* part i, let. xxx) illustrates his habit of forbearance:

> As I remember, some years since, there was a very abusive satire in verse brought to our king; and as the passages were a-reading before him, he often said, that if there were no more men in England, the rogue should hang for it. At last, being come to the conclusion, which was after all his railing,
>
> "Now God preserve the king, the queen, the peers
> "And grant the author long shall wear his ears!"
>
> this pleased him so well, that he broke into a laughter, and said, "By my soul, so thou shalt for me; thou art a bitter, but thou art a witty knave."

Perhaps the most offensive of all James's failings—certainly the most notorious—was his passion for boys. Speaking of the Earl of Carlisle, one of the King's Scottish favourites, Osborne says (*op. cit.,* pp. 274-275):

> He lay alwaies under the comfortable aspect of King James his favour, though I never found him in his bosome, a place reserved for younger men and of more indeering countenances: And these went under the appellation of his favourites or minions, who, like burning-glasses, were daily interposed between him and the subject, multiplying the heat of oppressions in the generall opinion, though in his own he thought they screened them from reflecting

upon the crowne: Through the fallacy of which maxime his son came to be ruined; it being unlikely any prince should abate in the account of his people, that hath no bodies expenses or faults to reckon for but his own. Now, as no other reason appeared in favour of their choyce but handsomnesse, so the love the king shewed was as amorously convayed, as if he had mistaken their sex, and thought them ladies; which I have seene Somerset and Buckingham labour to resemble, in the effeminatenesse of their dressings; though in w—— lookes and wanton gestures they exceeded any part of woman kind my conversation did ever cope withall. Nor was his love, or what else posterity will please to call it, (who must be the judges of all that history shall informe), carried on with a discretion sufficient to cover a lesse scandalous behaviour; for the kings kissing them after so lascivious a mode in publicke, and upon the theatre, as it were, of the world, prompted many to imagine some things done in the tyring-house, that exceed my expressions no lesse than they do my experience: And therefore left floting upon the waves of conjecture, which hath in my hearing tossed them from one side to another.

Every ill of the time was laid to the door of the Scottish minions who had followed James down from the north. They were called "beggarly rabble" and "caledonian boars" (Osborne, *op. cit.*, p. 217), and everywhere they were attacked by open insult and lampoon. On any wall or church door, one might see posted ballads like the following:

They beg our lands, our goods, our lives
They switch our nobles, and lye with our wives.
They pinch our gentry, and send for our benchers,
They stab our sargeants and pistoll our fencers.

Osborne says:

. . . [they] hung like horseleeches on him, till they could get no more, falling then off by retiring into their owne country, or living at ease, leaving all chargeable attendance to the English. The harvest of the love and honour he reaped being sutable to the ill husbandry he used in the unadvised distribution of his favours: For of a number of empty vessels he filled to compleat the measure of our infelicity, few proved of use to him, unlesse such as, by reason of their vast runnings out, had daily need of a new supply.

Even the King's ridiculous preoccupation with the hunt, in

which he behaved more like a buffoon in a holiday pantomime than like a monarch enjoying a regal sport, was laid to the door of the "straungers," as they were called. Osborne, who was, if anyone ever was, "typically English," declared (*ibid.*, pp. 195-97):

Now by this time the nation grew feeble, and overopprest with impositions, monopolies, aydes, privyseales, concealments, pretermitted customes, &c., besides all forfeitures upon penall statutes, with a multitude of tricks, more to cheat the English subject, (the most, if not all, unheard of in Queene Elizabeth's dayes,) which were spent upon the Scots: By whom nothing was unasked, and to whom nothing was denied; who for want of honester trafique, did extract gold out of the faults of the English, whose pardons they beg'd and sold at intolerable rates, murder it selfe not beinge exempted: Nay, I dare boldly say, one man might with more safety have killed another, than a raskalldeare; but if a stagge had been known to have miscarried, and the authour fled, a proclamation, with a description of the party, had been presently penned by the attourney-generall, and the penalty of his majesties high displeasure (by which was understood the Star-chamber) threatened against all that did abet, comfort, or relieve him. Thus satyricall, or, if you please, tragicall, was this sylvan prince against dear-killers, and indulgent to man-slayers. But least this expression should be thought too poeticall for an historian, I shall leave him dres'd to posterity in the colours I saw him in the next progresse after his inauguration, which was as greene as the grass he trod on, with a fether in his cap, and a horne instead of a sword by his side: how sutable to his age, calling, or person, I leave others to judge from his pictures, he owning a countenance not in the least regard semblable to any my eyes ever met with, besides an host dwelling in Anthill, formerly a sheppherd, and so metaphorically of the same profession: He that evening parted with his queene, and to shew himselfe more uxorious before the people at his first coming than in private he was, he did at her coach side take his leave, by kissing her sufficiently to the middle of the shoulders, for so low she went bare all the dayes I had the fortune to know her; having a skinne far more aimiable than the features it covered, though not the disposition, in which report rendered her very debonaire.

Though most of the court prostrated itself before this unregal person, there were some whose gorge rose at the spectacle and they boldly expressed their disgust in ballads and on the stage. Beaumont wrote to his master in 1608: *

> One or two days before, they had brought forward their own king, and all his favourites, in a very strange fashion. They made him curse and swear because he had been robbed of a bird, and beat a gentleman because he had called off the hounds from the scent. They represent him as drunk at least once a day, &c. He has upon this made order that no play shall be henceforth acted in London; for the repeal of which order they have already offered 100,000 livres. Perhaps the permission will be again granted, but upon condition that they represent no recent history, nor speak of the present time.

As Sir Edmund Chambers points out, this order, even if it had been carried out, "left the even more dangerous resource of allegory and of historical parallel still open to the seditious play-wright." Of this resource, such playwrights continued to take the fullest advantage. In fact, the portrayal of and descanting upon the vices of the King became so general that, it would seem, the censor gave up all attempt at real prevention and concentrated his efforts on the task of rendering the fustians technically sound. In so doing he gradually transformed the nature of his office from that of protector of the King and Court from criticism, to that of buffer between the acting companies and the objects of their attacks.

We have already reviewed the case of *Believe As You List,* which illustrates this attitude most convincingly; but there are many other less elaborate instances of the same practice—cases where the shafts of criticism are just as pointed, but where they are more ingeniously covered in outwardly irrelevant or inapplicable action. Such a case was *The Second Maiden's Tragedy.* The plot represents the love of a lady (unnamed) for a deposed king, Govianus, and the efforts of the usurping tyrant to force her to become his mistress. Whether or not the censor saw in this plot a parallel to the woes of Arabella Stuart, who was in love with a deposed king—or rather with a disallowed claimant—and who suffered the most unparalleled

* Gildersleeve, *op. cit.,* pp. 107-108. The French text is given in Chambers, *Elizabethan Stage,* III, pp. 257-58. Chambers says the letter was by M. de la Boderie, the French Ambassador. *(Ibid.,* I, p. 326.)

persecutions from the king, we do not know; but it is clear that the censor paid no attention to the possibility of such a parallel, but confined his attention to the deletions and reformations of passages expressing the general loathing of a court for a disgusting sovereign. A single example of such reformations by the censor must suffice. In Act V sc. ii, the expiring tyrant exclaims, "Your king's poisoned," and Memphonius rejoins, "The king of heaven be praised for it." Through this passage Sir George Buck drew his line, and substituted "I am poisoned," and made a cross in the margin to call attention to the necessary alteration. The text thus reformed was licensed for public performance 31 October, 1611. *The Second Maiden's Tragedy* coming, as it does, after the scandalous play referred to by the French Ambassador in 1608, reflects a nervousness on the part of the censor not noticeable in his dealings with earlier satires on the King. There are even indications that the censor sometimes rewrote an entire play himself. For instance, in Buck's Office Book there is the following entry (Massinger, *Works, ed. cit.,* xxi):

1620, Oc. 6.—For new reforming *The Virgin Martyr* for the Red Bull, 40s.

And in Herbert's Book:

1624, July 7.—Received for adding of a new scene to *The Virgin Martyr,* 10s.

Herbert's treatment of the play, *The History of the Duchess of Suffolk,* is similar. (See p. 192.)

Such a censorial attitude is in clear contrast to the indulgent policy of earlier years. Even the notorious case of *Eastward Ho!,* in which the King's Scottish accent and his Scottish retinue and his liberal knightings were openly jeered at, escaped the blue pencil entirely, and this was true not only of the first stage text, but the first printed quarto. Sir Edmund Chambers observed (*Elizabethan Stage,* III, p. 255):

I am inclined to think that it was the publication of the play in the autumn of 1605, rather than its presentation on the stage that brought the poets into trouble. This would account for the suppression of a passage reflecting upon the Scots (III, iii, 40-7) which appeared in the first issue of Q. 1 (cf. Parrott, ii, 862). Other quips at the intruding nation, at James's liberal knightings and even at his northern accent (I, ii, 50, 98; II, iii, 83; IV, i, 179) appear to have escaped censure. Nor was the play as a whole banned.

Whether or not Chapman and Jonson were really guilty of the offensive passages in this play, for which they were threatened with loss of ears and noses, or whether the blame belonged solely to Marston, it is certain that Chapman's previous plays abound in such scoffing allusions to the unwelcome strangers, who infest the land, and to the Jacobean knightings.* But indeed, allusions may be picked up in almost any play after 1604—in *Ram Alley,* of David, Lord Barry (Dodsley, p. 272), or in Middleton's *Mad World, My Masters* (I, i, 63; II, v, 41), or the anonymous *Somebody and Nobody* (1, 325); † or Day's *Isle of Gulls.*

It is obvious that this last named play contains more than an incidental gibe at the Scottish favourites. On 7 March, 1608, Sir Edmund Hoby wrote to Sir Thomas Edmondes (Chambers, *op. cit.,* III, p. 286):

> At this time (*c.* 15 Feb.) was much speech of a play in the Black Friars, where in the "Isle of Gulls," from the highest to the lowest, all men's parts were acted of two divers nations: As I understand sundry were committed to Bridewell.

The "two divers nations" in the play, i.e., the Arcadians and Lacedemonians, obviously stand for the English and Scotch; but the satire does not end here. The Induction makes it clear that some informer has charged the author with having "charactered a great man's life" in Damoetas; and Sir Edmund Chambers, following Fleay, observes that this royal favourite "a little hillock made great with other's ruins," inevitably suggests Sir Robert Carr. Fleay has pointed out that the play was published surreptitiously and that the characters who in the extant version are called the Duke and Duchess, had, in the original version been called King and Queen. (Gildersleeve, *op. cit.,* p. 101.)

* See, for instance, *The Widow's Tears* (IV, i, 28); *Monsieur D'Olive* (I, 263; IV, ii, 771); *Revenge of Bussy D'Ambois* (I, ii, 124).

† Sir Edmund Chambers says, "This play is probably Jacobean," but it is possible that the reference to the unwilling recipients of knighthood may refer to the liberal knightings of Essex.

Equally inevitable to Fleay and Gayley is the application of Beaumont's *Woman Hater* (1604) to the minion-loving king, and the *Hungry Courtier* (the sub-title to the *Woman Hater*) "a favourite on the sudden," to the newly advanced Carr. *

The prologue expresses the author's intention not to lose his ears, and the S. R. is careful to add that Sir George Buck's hand has been placed to it. These suggestions have not been argued in sufficient detail by competent scholars to justify our pressing the parallels; but the very titles of these plays could hardly fail to arouse suspicion as to their topical nature. The term "woman-hater" was regularly applied to the sodomites about the court. Weldon applies it to Sir Anthony Ashley, "who never loved any but boys," and to Sir Christopher Perkings, "a woman-hater that never meant to marry." Indeed, it is hardly any wonder that many wrong guesses were made regarding the fustian cloak that might, in such a "vipers' tangle" as the Court of James I, fit so many unworthy shoulders. An extremely interesting case of such a multiplicity of candidates for a given dramatic character is that of Marston's *Insatiate Countess*. In the quarto of this play in the National Library of Scotland, a contemporary hand has written on the tops of several pages the names of possible prototypes for this odious character. The Countesses named are: Shrewsbury, Roos, Bath, Castlemain, Sussex, Stamford, Lincolne (Dowager), Devonshire (Dowager). †

There is no contemporary statement explaining why the Sheriffs stopped Beaumont's *King and No King* (Gildersleeve, *op. cit.*, p. 224); but the title alone would have rendered the play suspicious.

The Spanish Peace

It is easy to understand how in such a Court contemporary criticism of the King and his minions would involve also the policies advocated by these minions. Prominent among such was the program of reconciliation with Spain, advocated by the King and supported by Buckingham, to the entire disgust of many "old courtiers."

* See also, Albert W. Upton, "Allusions to James I and his Court in Marston's *Fawn* and Beaumont's *Woman Hater*," *PMLA*, 44, (1929), pp. 1048ff.

† This fact was brought to my attention through the kindness of Mr. Harry Harvey Wood, the editor of Marston.

The plays which comment, directly or through foreign parallel, upon this policy of "Spanish Peace," which the heroes of Armada days regarded as a sign of the beastly decadence of the times, are indeed legion. There is hardly a play of Chapman's after 1604 that does not descant upon it, mourning "this declining kingdom," where "now all is peace, no danger," where the glorious deeds of 1588 are forgotten by "idle men" who "most practice what they may most do with ease, fashion and favour." (*Revenge of Bussy D'Ambois,* I, i.) Commenting on these protesting speeches from *The Revenge,* Professor Parrott says (*Tragedies of George Chapman,* p. 578):

It is not difficult to see in these speeches Chapman's lament over the degeneration of English character during the peace that followed the accession of King James. Chapman's sympathies, as became an old Elizabethan and a panegyrist of that 'thunderbolt of war,' Sir Horace Vere, were all with the war party.

In the first Act of *The Revenge,* Baligny declares:

Idleness rusts us, since no virtuous labour
Ends ought rewarded: ease, security,
Now all the palm wears: we made war before
So to prevent war; men with giving gifts,
More than receiving, made our country strong;
Our matchless race of soldiers then would spend
In public wars not private brawls, their spirits,
In daring enemies, arm'd with meanest arms,
Not courting strumpets, and consuming birthrights
In apishness and envy of attire.
No labour then was harsh, no way so deep
No rock so steep, but if a bird could scale it,
Up would our youth fly too. A foe in arms
Stirr'd up a much more lust of his encounter,
Than of a mistress never so bepainted:
Ambition then, was only scaling walls,
And over-topping turrets: fame was wealth;
Best parts, best deeds, were best nobility. . . .

As a matter of fact, the old courtiers attributed the odious Peace to the influence of the base new favourites. The earliest of these, Philip Herbert, brother of the Earl of Pembroke, must now be introduced into our narrative. The following account is from Miss Aikin's *Memoirs of the Court of King James the First* (I, pp. 203-206):

James's propensity to favoritism first displayed itself in England about this time, in the extraordinary bounties which he was pleased to lavish on Philip Herbert, brother of William, Earl of Pembroke. Osborne has described this personage, whom he served as Master of the Horse, as one of the most contemptible of mankind; and he supported his invective by some disgraceful anecdotes, founded indeed in fact, but highly coloured by exaggeration and malice. Lord Clarendon, in more measured terms, but not without that hostile bias which he uniformly exhibits with respect to the partisans of the parliament in the great contest of Charles's days, expatiates at some length on his character and fortunes. "The earl of Montgomery," says he, "being a young man scarce of age at the entrance of king James, had the good fortune, by the comeliness of his person, his skill and indefatigable industry in hunting, to be the first who drew the king's eyes towards him with affection; which was quickly so far improved, that he had the reputation of a favorite. Before the end of the first or second year, he was made gentleman of the king's bedchamber and earl of Montgomery; which did the king no harm; for, besides that he received the king's bounty with more moderation than others who succeeded him, he was generally known, and as generally esteemed, being the son of one earl of Pembroke and younger brother to another, who liberally supplied his expense, beyond what his annuity from his father would bear.

"He pretended to no other qualifications than to understand horses and dogs very well; which his master loved him the better for (being at his first coming into England very jealous of those who had the reputation of great parts), and to be believed honest and generous, which made him many friends and left him then no enemy." (Lord Clarendon's *History,* I, p. 59.) It appears that a brutal violence of temper, and a profligacy of manners which grew upon the feeble character of Herbert by long indulgence, procured him in after life the hatred of many, and the contempt of all men. But he was now in his zenith, and on occasion of his marriage, the favor of the king manifested itself in that unmeasured bounty which he delighted to shower upon the possessors of his affection. Lady Susan Vere, daughter of the earl of Oxford, and niece by her mother to the secretary, was the object of Herbert's choice. The parties, "after long love," were contracted without the knowledge of the friends on either side; but the king, "taking the whole matter on himself, made peace on all sides." Crown lands to the amount of more than 1000 £ a year were settled on the bridegroom, and masks and revels, in which no cost was spared, gave splendor to the celebration of the nuptials. The ceremony, as described in a letter from sir Dudley Carleton to Mr. Winwood, displays in lively colors the manners of the court and of the sovereign.

"On St. John's day we had the marriage of sir Philip Herbert and the lady Susan performed at Whitehall with all the honor could be done a great favorite. The court was great, and for that day put on the best bravery. The prince and duke of Holst led the bride to church; the queen followed her from thence. The king gave her; and she in her tresses and trinkets brided and bridled it so handsomely, and indeed became herself so well, that the king said, if he were unmarried he would not give her but keep her himself. The marriage dinner was kept in the great chamber, where the prince and the duke of Holst and the great lords and ladies accompanied the bride. The ambassador of Venice was the only bidden guest of strangers, and he had a place above the duke of Holst, which the duke took not well. But after dinner he was as little pleased himself; for, being brought into the closet, . . . he was then suffered to walk out, his supper unthought of. At night there was a mask in the hall, which for conceit and fashion was suitable to the occasion. . . . There was no small loss that night of chains and jewels, and many great ladies were made shorter by the skirts. . . . The presents of plate and other things given by the noblemen were valued at 2500 £; but that which made it a good marriage was a gift of the king's of 500 £ land for the bride's jointure. They were lodged in the council-chamber, where the king, in his shirt and nightgown, gave them a *reveille matin* before they were up. . . . No ceremony was omitted of bridecakes, points, garters and gloves, which have been ever since the livery of the court." (Winwood, II, p. 43.)

As all Elizabethans know, it was for this marriage that Jonson wrote his *Mask of Blackness.*

It will be seen from these contemporary comments that the king was intent upon enjoying himself in the revelry of English splendour after the austerity of his lean years in Scotland; and for such a revel, peace and freedom from the worries of war were essential. Concerning the king's Spanish Peace Policy, Osborne says (*op. cit.*, pp. 151-155):

He held his thoughts so intent upon play and pleasure, that, to avoyd all interruption likely to impede any part of the felicity he had possessed his imagination with from the union of these crowns, and to fit an example for his neighbours imitation, whom he desired to bring into the like resolution, he cast himselfe, as it were, blindfold into a peace with Spaine, farre more destructive to England than a warre: For it hath not only found that prince an opportunity to recover his strength, (much abated by the queens most happy successes at sea) but gave him a faire advantage to establish himselfe in the kingdoms of Portugall, and quiet the distempers of his owne people, that were, ever since the expulsion of the Moors, (to whom a major part of the subjects, together with their language, is undoubtedly allied,) much perplexed at the cruelty of the inquisition, and so upon all opportunities ready to call them back from the Barbary shore: Which could not have been so happily accomplished, but during so still a peace as the new reconciliation of the French king with the pope, and the pusillanimous temper of James did at that present afford him, and without which it had not been uneasy for a farre weaker neighbour to have tormented him in the bowels of his own estate, by the least fomentation they could have used.

And as this peace was of infinite consequence to the Spaniard, so he spared for no cost to procure it: And, to prevent the inserting any article that might obstruct his recourse to or from the Indies, (the magazine of strife,) either on this side or beyond the Line, (thought by the English commissioners not included, however the contrary was after pretended, and no farther disputed by King James, then with patience and a quiet submission of his subjects to their sense not rarely punishing such as transgrest, at their coming home,) he presented all, both Scotch and English, with gifts, and those no small ones; for by that, the Earle of Northampton, brother of Suffolke, had* he was alone able to raise and finish the goodly pile he built in the Strand, which yet remains a monument of his, &c. Nor are there a few other no lesse brave houses, fresh in my memory, that had their foundations, if not their walls and roofes plastered with the same mortar; though out of my will to name, who had rather be condemned by posterity, that are not likely to hurt me for this modesty, then expose myself to the mercy of the age I have the fortune to live in, by making my pen over familiar with my thoughts; since after times may better spare the knowledge of many things then we reveale them; only this I shall adde, as no improb-

* Osborne's grammar is so strange that the sense is often obscure. His meaning here is that by a single royal gift, Northampton had been able to build Suffolk House.

able conjecture made by many in those daies, that his catholick majesty was so frighted by the apprehension of a possibility that our king, according to the nature, no lesse then the obligation of his country might fall into a conjunction with France, that he would scarce at the time have denied him any thing, to the halfe of his Indies. And from hence all princes may calculate the vast difference that lies between a counsell suborned, and one free from corruption.

But the "old guard" detested these peaceful and, to them, supine tactics. They campaigned against the costly embassies which, the merchants declared, (Winwood, II, p. 46) profited them nothing, but cost them everything.

The reader will recall the extraordinary letter written by Lord Thomas Howard to Sir John Harington. (See p. 148.)

The ballad monger, the stage player, the pulpit preacher, and the court jester, all poured forth the same tale of the good old days of the late Queen when every hall was

Hung about with pikes, guns, bows
With old swords and bicklers, that had borne many shrewd blows.

The "old courtiers of the queen" were contrasted with the "flourishing young gallants" whose halls are

Hung round with new pictures that do the poor no good,
With a fine marble chimney, wherein burns neither coal nor wood.

The author of the ballad of *The Old and Young Courtier* (Percy's *Reliques* II, p. 318) adds, significantly, that the new courtier's "new study" was "stufft full of pamphlets and plays." We have already seen how Middleton's *Game at Chess* formed a part of this anti-Spanish propaganda. It is possible that the complaints of Gondomar in that connection may account for the series of restraints and punishments that followed. Massinger's *Spanish Viceroy* was unfortunately among those plays destroyed by Warburton's cook, but we are told that it was "supposed to have been full of allusions to Gondomar, the Spanish ambassador, and stood no chance of being licensed by the Master of the Revels." The players therefore resolved to act it on their own responsibility, and for this piece of insolence or of independence, were required to make a most humble apology to Sir Henry Herbert, and to sign a promise "not to act any play without your hand or substitutes hereafter, nor do anything which may prejudice the authority of your office." (Gildersleeve, *op. cit.*, p. 77.)

Whether for this act of boldness, or for another, Massinger, together with his collaborators in mischief, Nathaniel Field and Robert Daborne, was imprisoned. In their plight they wrote to Henslowe (Francis Cunningham, *The Plays of Philip Massinger*, pp. xi-xii):

To our most loving friend Mr. Philipp Hinchlow, Esquire, these: "Mr. Hinchlow, you understand our unfortunate extremity, and I do not think you so void of Christianity, but that you would throw so much money into the Thames as we request now of you; rather than endanger so many innocent lives; you know there is ten pound more at least to be received of you for the play, we desire you to lend us five pound of that, which shall be allowed to you, without which we cannot be bailed, nor I play any more till this be dispatched. It will lose you twenty pound ere the end of the next week, beside the hindrance of the next new play. Pray, sir, consider our cases with humanity, and now give us cause to acknowledge you our true friend in time of need. We have entreated Mr. Davison to deliver this note, as well to witness your love as our promises, and always acknowledgment to be ever

"Your most thankful and loving friends,

"Nat: Field."

"The money shall be abated out of the money remains for the play of Mr. Fletcher and ours.

"Rob: Daborne."

"I have ever found you a true loving friend to me, and in so small a suit, it being honest, I hope you will not fail us.

"Philip Massinger."

It was of course impossible to refuse a request at once so urgent, so reasonable, so modest, and so "honest," i.e., honourable; but still it is satisfactory to be able to transcribe the following endorsement, which I copy literatim in order to show the spelling of the names, which no doubt to a certain extent preserves the pronunciation:

"Rec. by me Robert Davison of Mr. Hinshloe for the use of Mr. Dauboern, Mr. Feeld, Mr. Messenger the some of *vl.*

"Robert Davison."

We do not know that Massinger had any part in the stinging satire of Henslowe in Day's *Parliament of Bees,* "being an allegorical description of the actions of good and bad men in our daies," but we feel sure he would have applauded the performance. Henslowe seems to have been as hard as the nails whose price he so carefully noted in his accounts. That the poor dramatists took their revenge in the portraiture of him as the Fenerator or Usuring Bee, scholars seem to entertain no doubt. Sir Edmund Chambers says (*Elizabethan Stage,* III, 288): "It is impossible to resist seeing with Fleay i, 115, in the Fenerator or Usuring Bee (p. 63) the portrait of Philip Henslowe." Like Henslowe, he is a "broker" and "takes up clothes"; and

> Most of the timber that his state repairs
> He hew's out o' the bones of foundered players.
> They feed on Poets braines, he eats their breath.

In a letter to Winwood 28 March, 1605 (*Memorials,* II, p. 54), Mr. Samuel Calvert described "a book lately published, but yet not to be had, *touching the late Peace,* wherein the Author, without Reservations or Respect, *discovers the whole Intention, nameth the Conplotters, and sheweth the Reasons why it was concluded."* He promises to send him a copy as soon as one can be procured. In the same letter Calvert describes the "great Execution done lately upon *Stone the Fool,* who was well whipt in *Bridewell* for a blasphemous Speech, *That there went sixty Fools* into Spaine, Besides my Lord Admiral and his two Sons."

In this case of discipline, it was, obviously, the satirized Admiral who acted, not the oft-insulted King. It was, however, another story when the King's own schemes were pilloried. One could, as Sir Edmund Chambers has said, "flout the Scots" upon the stage, or "beat the patriotic drum" against the Spaniards; but any criticism of what James was pleased to call his "kingcraft" was immediately resented and serious action taken. Thus, we learn that when Marston brought in the "Dutch Courtesan to corrupt English conditions," he suffered nothing worse than a temporary exile from London. We are told (A. Nixon, *The Black Year, 1606*) that he was "sent away westward for carping both at city and country." But when he jeered at the King's pet project for getting his silver from his own mines instead of from the Indian mines in America, he was in grave danger. In this statement, I am depending on Sir Edmund Chambers, who believes that Marston's arrest and imprisonment in Newgate on 8 June, 1608, was caused by his having had a share in a play at the Blackfriars which criticized the project to work the recently discovered mines at Hilderston near Linlithgow as a royal enterprise. On 11 March, 1608, Sir Thomas Lake wrote to Salisbury (*State Papers, Jacobean, Domestic,* I, XXXI, p. 73):

> His Ma*tie* was well pleased with that which your lo. advertiseth concerning the committing of the players y*t* have offended in y*e* matters of France, and commanded me to signifye to your lo. that for y*e* others who have offended in y*e* matter of y*e* Mynes and other lewd words, which is y*e* children of y*e* blackfriars, that though he had signified his mynde to your lo. by my lo. of Mountgommery yet I should repeate it again, That his G. had vowed they should never play more, but should first begg their bred and he wold have his vow performed, And therefore my lo. chamberlain by himselfe or your ll. at the table should take order to dissolve them, and to punish the maker besides.

James's attitude toward the Gowrie play is not dissimilar. Among other Scottish institutions which the English could not deride with impunity was the new holiday established by the King in celebration of his escape from the "Gowrie conspiracy." Students of history have long struggled over the details of this mystery, and many interpretations have been offered. It is, however, no part of my duty here to decide upon the guilt or innocence of the King, but rather to point out the contemporary opinion of the affair. "The only indubitable facts of the case," says Miss Aikin (*op. cit.,* I, p. 39), "are the following":

> That the king, who at this time was resident at Falkland, going out to hunt, was joined by Alexander Ruthven, brother of the Earl of Gowrie; and after the chase, followed by a small train, accompanied him to the mansion of his brother at Perth; and that an affray arose in the house, in which three of the King's attendants were wounded; and on the other side, the earl of Gowrie and Alexander Ruthven were slain.

The official report of the fracas issued by James was to the effect that he had been decoyed to a remote part of the house and there set upon by Ruthven, but had been rescued by his attendants. The details of the King's report do, indeed, seem improbable and absurd. Be that as it may, when James returned to Edinburgh, he issued an order through the privy council requiring the clergy of the city to collect their congregations, and "after relating all the particulars, to return solemn thanks to God for the providential escape of the King." But that incorrigible body of men replied through a chosen spokesman, that they were willing indeed to give thanks for the safety of their sovereign, but that they must be excused from entering into any details, and from promulgating in the house of truth things which appeared still dubious. (*Ibid.*, p. 41.) The King then caused a narrative of the affair to be published, but, we are told, "in spite of his utmost efforts, the clergy as a body, and not a few of the Party, persisted in their incredulity. Finally, however, partly by arguments, partly by threats, the preachers were all convinced, or silenced, except their leader Robert Bruce; against whom his majesty was pleased to maintain his own veracity by the unanswerable arguments of deprivation and banishment." Miss Aikin concludes (*ibid.*, pp. 43-44):

> On the whole, it is impossible, for various reasons, to believe that James went to the house of Gowrie for the purpose of attacking the brothers, or that he caused them to be slain without some immediate provocation; but it seems nearly certain, that for unknown reasons he distorted or disguised the real circumstances of the transaction, and concealed the most material ones.

It was, however, one of the most touchy subjects that could be broached in the King's presence, and there is something almost hysterical in his determination to have his version of the case not only the only accepted one, but, indeed, the basis of a national rejoicing. Osborne (*op. cit.*, pp. 276-77) gives a sprightly account of the English attitude toward the affair:

> Amongst a number of other novelties, he brought a new holy-day into the church of England, wherein God had publick thanks given him for his majesties deliverance out of the hands of Earle Goury: and this fell out upon the fift of August, on which many lies were told either at home or abroad, in the quire of Pauls church, of the

Long Walk: For no Scotch men you could meet beyond sea but did laugh at it, and the perepatetique politicians said the relation in print did murder all possibility of credit. But I will not wade further in this businesse, not knowing how dangerous the bottome may prove, being by all mens relations foule and bloudy: having nothing to palliate it but jealousy on the one side, and fear on the other; too weak supporters to keep upright so great a . . . . ., especially so far as to ruine a whole and noble family, for a fault knowne to be committed without the least question. Now, if anything farther deserved consideration, it is the misfortune of kings, who, once lapsed into a publick errour, cannot recall it, though the continuance of it reflect dishonour to God; not unpossibly the cause this held out all his raigne. Nor did any credit his son gave it justify it farther then ordinary report, which, in the generality, took it for a meer figment of state, and was buried with its author.

With a knowledge of the prevailing public opinion concerning the Gowrie mystery, we are not surprised to learn that the representation of the affair on the stage in December, 1604, met with instant disapproval. On the 18th, Chamberlain wrote to Winwood (*Letters of John Chamberlain,* I, p. 199, *Memoirs,* XII, Part I, American Philological Society, 1939):

The Tragedy of *Gowry,* with all the Action and Actors, hath been twice represented by the King's Players, with exceeding Concourse of all sorts of People. But whether the matter or manner be not well handled, or that it be thought unfit that Princes should be played on the Stage in their Life-time, I hear that some great Councellors are much displeased with it, and so 'tis thought shall be forbidden.

The play does not survive, and we have no further evidence of its offensive nature. However, that the offense lay in an inacceptable interpretation of the affair rather than in the fact of presentation is evidenced by the royal desire to have a similar delivery from danger presented on the stage. After the exposure of the Gunpowder Treason, we know that, among others, Jonson was engaged to write "upon the powder plot."

Though James was thus prompt to defend his own schemes, we shall see, in the following section dealing with stage criticism of Buckingham, how rarely he intervened in behalf of his minions.

Stage Criticism of Buckingham

A paragraph from Miss Gildersleeve's study will illustrate how comprehensive have been the suggestions concerning plays dealing with Carr's successor, George Villiers, Duke of Buckingham (*op. cit.,* pp. 123-24):

> Gardiner's paper on the *Political Elements in Massinger (New Shakspere Society Transactions,* 1876) points out in *Believe As You List* a striking analogy to Charles' attitude at this date towards his brother-in-law Frederick, Elector Palatine and titular King of Bohemia. In this play, as well as in several others, Gardiner thinks that Massinger was representing, under a thin disguise, current political events; and portraying them from the standpoint of the faction to which belonged his patrons, the Herberts, Earls of Pembroke and Montgomery. In the *Bondman,* for example, in the character of Gisco he satirized the Duke of Buckingham, then opposed by Pembroke; but in the *Great Duke of Florence,* some four years later, he exhibited toward the favorite the new and friendly attitude now felt by the brothers Herbert. *The Maid of Honor,* again, according to Gardiner, shows a striking similarity to the policy followed by Charles and James towards the Elector Frederick.

It is astonishing how many situations in French history seemed at this time to offer arresting parallels to the society and politics of Stuart England. Without suggesting any precise applications, Professor Parrott observes (*Tragedies of Chapman,* p. 575) that in the court of the last Valois there were, to Chapman's mind, "but too many analogies with that of the first Stuart king of England." He might equally well have extended the possibilities on the French side, to include the reigns of the early Bourbon kings. The story of the amazing career of the Maréchal d'Ancre could hardly fail to impress a favourite-ridden English court, even if the Maréchal had not been thought to represent an anti-Spanish faction. With the two elements combining, however, the news of his assassination was received in England as though it had been a report of a victory at the front. Bells were rung, a flood of pamphlets retailing the highlights of his story appeared over night, like leading articles in a morning paper, and, as soon as humanly possible, the whole course of his detestable life was acted on the stages of London. The following brief account of the Maréchal is given by Professor F. L. Lucas in his commentary on the *Duchess of Malfi* (*Complete Works of John Webster* [London, 1927], II, pp. 129-30):

Concino Concini, son of a Florentine notary, after spending a dissolute youth came to France in the train of Marie de Medici, the queen of Henri IV; and there married her *femme de chambre,* Leonora Galigai. This woman had an extraordinary influence over her mistress, and when the Queen became Regent after Henry's murder, the Regent herself was still ruled by Leonora; while Concini, though not liked by the Queen and perpetually at feud with his wife, in some strange way contrived to use the two women to make himself the chief power in France. The greater his influence became, the greater he made it, by pretending that it was even greater than it was, so that a sycophantic court flocked to the feet of this supreme dispenser of favours. In his hands the boy Louis XIII, already crushed by an indifferent mother, became a mere *roi fainéant* at the mercy of his Mayor of the Palace; whole armies were maintained in the usurper's pay; and some sudden stroke, whether arrest or assassination, was the only weapon left to the young king. On the morning of 24 April, 1617, Concini in the midst of his enormous suite was confronted by de Vitry, captain of the royal guard, and a few followers at the entrance to the Louvre; and, at the first sign of resistance to arrest, riddled with bullet and sword-thrust. The hated corpse was torn limb from limb in the streets of Paris; and throughout France, already partly in rebellion, the news roused wild enthusiasm. The old counsellors of Henry IV, Villeroi, Jeannin, du Vair, de Sillery were recalled, the Queen-Mother and Concini's tools disgraced or imprisoned. Marie de Medici had been the friend of Spain; and accordingly there were great rejoicings throughout Protestant Europe, so that in England not to share the general joy, was to brand oneself as "more than half Spanish." A dozen or more pamphlets in the British Museum still testify to the popular interest which occasioned this insertion in our play.

On 22 June, 1617, the Privy Council wrote to the Master of the Revels (Gildersleeve, *op. cit.,* p. 113):

We are informed that there are certain Players, or Comedians, we know not of what Company, that go about to play some enterlude concerning the late Marquesse d'Ancre, which for many respects we think not fit to be suffered. We do therefore require you. upon your peril, to take order that the same be not represented or played in any place about this City, or elsewhere where you have authority.

According to the Council, the play was thought unfit "for many respects." One of these may have been the possible displeasure of the French Ambassador, though, seeing that the French King assumed full responsibility for the Maréchal's death, it is difficult to see much reason for diplomatic reserve on the subject. There was, however, another reason for regarding with disapproval a play which portrayed an arch-sycophant who, by the most repulsive means, held sway over a decadent court, beridden by Spanish intrigue. George Villiers, now Duke of Buckingham, had risen to power—like Carr before him in the English Court and like the Marquesse d'Ancre in France—and, as we have seen in our earlier discussions of the *Game at Chess,* Buckingham was abetting the King's detested pro-Spanish policy.

There have been many attempts to identify this forbidden play. Fleay, taking the name de Vitry as a clue, argued with considerable plausibility for *Thierry and Thiodoret;* others, basing their decision on the obvious allusion to the recent purging of the French court by the King, in the first scene of the *Duchess of Malfi,* have decided for Webster's play. Whether or not this latter view is as "frivolous" as Professor Lucas declares it to be, (he maintains that the allusion was an addition tacked on to an earlier play to bring it up to date for a 1617 revival), still it remains an important witness to the English application of the Maréchal's character and policy to that of the reigning favourite in their own court. The passage is worth quoting (*Webster,* II, p. 37):

(Delio asks Antonio how he likes the French court, and Antonio replies):

I admire it—
In seeking to reduce both State and People
To a fix'd Order, the[ir] juditious King
Begins at home: Quits first his Royal Pallace
Of flattering Sicophants, of dissolute,
And infamous persons—which he sweetely termes
His Masters Master-peece (the worke of Heaven)

Considering duely, that a Princes Court
Is like a common Fountaine, whence should flow
Pure silver-droppes in generall: But if 't chance
Some curs'd example poyson 't neere the head,
Death, and diseases through the whole land spread.
And what is 't makes this blessed government,
But a most provident Councell, who dare freely
Informe him the corruption of the times?
Though some oth' Court hold it presumption
To instruct Princes what they ought to doe,
It is a noble duety to informe them
What they ought to fore-see.*

Before leaving the discussion of plays dealing with Buckingham, we ought to mention Professor Lucas' very interesting suggestion concerning the application intended by Webster in *Appius and Virginia,* concerning which he says (*op. cit.,* III, pp. 124-26):

The peculiar difficulty of dating *Appius* is due to its unusual lack of topical allusions. This lack I have tried to supply; and if the evidence I have to offer is not by itself very cogent, it has at least the advantage of agreeing with that of Sykes already given; for it indicates a date about 1625-7.

If we consider the plot of *Appius,* we find that it follows Roman history with unusual closeness, except in one respect—the famine in the camp. For this there is no historical basis at all. It may indeed be said that this famine was introduced simply because the impoverishment of Virginius is Appius' means of putting pressure on him. But then that means is never actually employed. Virginius is indeed impoverished; but the temptation to sell his daughter is never developed. And the sufferings of the troops are dwelt on in I.4, II.2, and IV.2, with an amount of detail particularly remarkable in a play which shows otherwise so little irrelevant episode, so few departures, for an Elizabethan drama, from its one main theme.

Now this starvation of troops in the field by the neglect of the home authorities is exactly what had been happening in the years 1624-5. In October-November, 1624, twelve thousand men were pressed in England to serve under Count Mansfeld in an effort to recover the Palatinate. Their rendezvous was Dover, but pay and

* Query: Had Voltaire been studying this passage when he decided to present the affair of Calas in a dramatic fustian before the King?

food were not forthcoming, and they were driven to pillage the countryside and "rob poor market-women." After much delay and suffering, in February, 1625, they were transported to Flushing, and thence to Gertruidenberg to starve. "All day long," writes Lord Cromwell, "we go about for victuals and bury our dead." Soon only three thousand were left; but even in June, 1625, their privations were still going on. They were left four days on the Dutch frontier with no bread at all. "Our Generall," Cromwell continues to Carleton on 7 June, 1625, (*State Papers, Holland,* 7 June, 1625), "studies his profit, and how to ruin us, I think. . . . Let us but command men that may not die as if we had killed them by giving them neither meat nor money, and we will go anywhere where our noble conductor dare send us; but to command a regiment starved, now not 220 men, I scorn it."

Commenting on the line "As Dutchmen feed their souldiers" (IV, 2, 38), Professor Lucas says: "Though the stinginess of the Dutch service was notorious in general: but it shows how easily remarks, even in this Roman play, become topical." He then continues (*op. cit.,* III, p. 125):

Nor were these the only forces of the English Crown that had to suffer from its incompetence and penury in these years. There are repeated accounts of soldiers and sailors clamouring in vain to Buckingham (like another Appius) for their pay. For instance, on Aug. 17th 1626, Mr. Pory writes to the Rev. Joseph Mead (Birch, *Court and Times of Charles I,* 1848, I, 141; cf. 174-8) describing how two hundred unpaid sailors from Portsmouth waylaid Buckingham, who promised them a hearing that afternoon and then gave them the slip. Similar episodes recurred for months. We may depend on it that had any of these victims strayed to the Bankside, they would have taken no slight interest in certain scenes of *Appius and Virginia.*

Professor Lucas adds, in a note: "Indeed, it does not seem to me impossible that Buckingham himself is aimed at in Appius." The plausibility of this suggestion is, in Professor Lucas' opinion, heightened by the fact that Webster left no room for doubt as to the application intended against Dr. Lamb, Buckingham's creature, in Act V, sc. 2, of *The Fair Maid of the Inne.* Fairobosco says to "the Clowne":

O my rare rascall! We must remove . . . Europe is to[o] little to be cozned by us, I am ambitious to goe to the East Indies, thou and I to ride on our brace of Elephants.

Clowne: And for my part I long to be in England agen; you will never get so much as in *England*—we have shifted many countryes, and many names: but [truant] the world over you shall never purse up so much gold as when you were in England, and call'd yourselfe Doctor Lambestones.

With this case of stage criticism of Buckingham in *Appius and Virginia,* it is interesting to compare a similar one, noted by the Master of Revels. The following anecdote is related by the Master in an entry under date of 4 June, 1638, concerning *The King and the Subject,* for which, it seems, he doubted the propriety of issuing a license (Cunningham, *The Plays of Massinger,* p. xvi):

At Greenwich, this 4th of June, 1638, Mr. W. Murray gave me power from the King to allow of *The King and the Subject,* and told me as he would warrant it.

Monies! we'll raise supplies what way we please
And force you to subscribe to blanks, in which
We'll mulct you as we shall think fit. The Caesars
In Rome were wise, acknowledging no laws
But what their swords did ratify; the wives
And daughters of the senators bowing to
Their will, as deities, &c.

Of this passage Sir Henry Herbert says:

This is a piece taken out of Philip Massinger's play, called *The King and the Subject,* and entered here for ever to be remembered by my son, and those that cast their eyes on it, in honour of King Charles, my master, who, reading over the play at Newmarket, set his mark upon the place with his own hand, and in these words—*This is too insolent and to be changed.* Note that the poet makes it the speech of a king, Don Pedro of Spain.

It is little wonder that Herbert could scarcely believe his ears when he received permission to license the play.

Plays About Arabella Stuart

Thus far in our study we have discussed only those plays for whose topicality there was some external evidence. Of the many plays whose plots suggest plausible applications to contemporary affairs, but for which exterior confirmations of the presence of fustian is lacking, we venture to include here two which *may* refer to the woes of Lady Arabella Stuart. The story of her persecution and death is told by Miss Aikin, in her *Life of King James I* (I, pp. 378ff.):

The nearness of lady Arabella Stuart to the English throne, subjected her to the obligation of forming no matrimonial connexion without the concurrence of the king; and a very weak and unworthy jealousy appears to have inspired James, as well as his predecessor, with the resolution of keeping her single. Against this species of tyranny she was much disposed to rebel; and, undeterred by a censure which had been passed on her a short time previously for listening to a clandestine proposal, she ventured to receive similar overtures from William Seymour, second son of lord Beauchamp and grandson of the earl of Hertford; on discovery of which, in February, 1610, both parties were summoned before the privy council and reprimanded. They proceeded notwithstanding to complete their marriage; which becoming a matter of notoriety, the lady was committed to private custody and her husband to the Tower. But the unfortunate pair continued to hold intercourse by means of confidential agents, and in June 1611, they concerted measures for their joint escape. Mr. Seymour, having disguised himself in mean apparel, walked unobserved out of the Tower behind a cart which had brought him billets, and made the best of his way to Lee, a small port in Kent, where he expected to find a French vessel in waiting.

The picturesque details of the lady's escape are given us in a letter from Mr. John More to Sir Ralph Winwood (*Memorials* III, p. 279):

On *Monday* last in the Afternoone my Lady *Arabella* lying at Mr. *Coniers's* House near *Highgate,* having induced her Keepers and Attendants into Securitie by the fayre Shew of Conformitye and Willingness to goe on her Journey towards *Durham,* (which the next Day she must have don,) and in the mean tyme *disguising herselfe by drawing a pair of great French-fashioned Hose over her Petticotes, putting on a Man's Doublet, a man-lyke Perruque with long Locks over her Hair, a blacke Hat, black Cloake, russet Bootes with red Tops, and a Rapier by her Syde,* walked forth between three and four of the Clock with Mr. *Markham.* After they had gon a foot a Myle and halfe to a sorry Inne, where *Crompton* attended with their Horses, she grew very sicke and fainte, so as the Ostler that held the Styrrop, said *that Gentleman would hardly hold out to London.* Yet being set on a good Gelding *astryde* in an unwonted Fashion, the stirring of the Horse brought Blood enough into her Face, and so she rid on towards *Blackwell;* where arryving about six a Clock, finding there in a Readiness two Men, a Gentle-woman and a Chambermaid, with one Boate full of Mr. *Seimour's* and her Trunks, and another Boate for their Persons, they hasted from thence towards *Woolich.* Being come so farre they bade the Watermen row on to *Gravesend,* There the Watermen were desirous to land, but for double Fraight were contented to go on to *Lee*: Yet being almost tyred by the way, they were faine to lye still at *Tilbury* whilst the Oares went a land to refreshe themselves. Then they proceeded to *Lee,* and by that tyme the Day appeared, and they discovered a Shippe at Anchor a Myle beyond them, which was the *French Barque* that wayted for them. Here the Lady would have lyen at Anchor expecting Mr. *Seimour,* but through the Importunitye of her Followers they forthwith hoisted Saile to Sea-warde. In the mean while Mr. *Siemour* with *a Perruque and Bearde of black Haire and in a tauny Cloth Suit,* walked alone *without Suspition* from his Lodging out at the great Weste Doore of the *Tower, following a Cart that had brought him Billets.* From thence he walked along by the *Tower Warfe* by the *Warders* of the fourth Gate, and so to the *Iron Gate* where *Rodney* was ready with Oares for to receive him. When they came to *Lee* and fownd that the *French* Ship was gon, the Billows rising high, they hyred a *Fisherman* for twenty Shillings to set them aboard a certain Ship that they saw under Saile. That Ship they found not to be it they looked for, so they made forwards to the next under Saile, which was a Shippe of *Newcastle.* This, with much ado they hyred for 40 *l* to carry them to *Calais*: But whether the *Collier* did perfourm his *Bargaine* or no, is not as yet here known. On Tewsday in the Afternoone my *Lord Treasurer* being advertised that the Lady *Arabella* had made an Escape, sent forthwith to the *Lievtenant* of the *Tower* to set straight *Guard* over Mr. Seimour; which he, after his *yare manner, would thoroughly do, that he would*: But coming to the Prisoner's Lodgings he fownd (to his great Amazement) that he was gonne from thence one whole Day before.

I may not omitt in this Relation to inserte the simple Parte of two silly Persons; the one called *Tom Barber* Servant to Mr. *Seimour,* who (believing his Master spake *bonâ fide,*) did according to his Instructions tell every one that come to enquire for his Master, *that he was newly betaken to* his rest being much troubled with the *Tooth-ach;* and when the Matter was discovered, did seriously persist to perswade Mr. *Leivtenant* that *he was gon but to lye a Night with his Wife, and would surely return thither of himself again.* The other, a Ministre's Wife attending *the Lady;* who seeing her Mistress disguise herselfe and slippe away, was trewly perswaded that she intended but to make a *private Visit* to her Husband, and did duly attend her Returne at the Tyme appointed.

Now the Kyng and the Lords being much disturbed with this *unexpected Accident,* my *Lord Treasurer* sent Orders to a *Pinnace* that lay at the *Downes* to put presently to Sea, first to *Calais* Roade, and then to scoure up the coast towards *Dunkerke.* This *Pinnace* spying the aforesaid *French Barke* which lay lingering for Mr. *Seimour,* made to her, which thereupon offered to fly towards *Calais,* and endured thirteen Shot of the Pinnance before she would stryke. In this Barke is the *Lady* taken with her Followers, and brought back towards the *Tower*: *Not so sorrye for her owne Restraynt, as she should be glad yf Mr. Seimour might escape, whose Welfare she protesteth to affect much more than her owne.*

Seymour did, as a matter of fact, escape, for when he found that her bark had sailed without him, he rode off to a collier "lying in the roads" by which he was safely landed in Calais. But the ill-fated lady never recovered her liberty. After four terrible years of imprisonment, we are told "she became distracted with the sense of her hopeless misery, and in that state died within the Tower in 1615."

There have been several rather venturous suggestions concerning the appearance of her sad story on the stage: Miss Winstanley believes that *Cymbeline* is Shakspere's plea for the lady during the first years of her last imprisonment. Professor Lucas suggests the *Duchess of Malfi* (*Webster,* II, p. 16):

While his [Webster's] audience watched The *Duchess of Malfi,* some of them must have remembered the real tragedy which was creeping to its close in the Tower, a few minute's walk away—whether Webster himself had thought of it or not . . . I do not wish to exaggerate the resemblances, though it will be seen that there are several: but it is perhaps a little surprising that the authorities did not feel the subject of the persecuted Duchess a dangerous one for popular sympathy.

We do not now know what allusions were contained in the *History of the Duchess of Suffolk* (1624), "which," says Herbert (Gildersleeve, *op. cit.*, p. 81), "being full of dangerous matter was much reformed by me . . . I had two pounds for my pains." Mary Tudor, who became the Duchess of Suffolk upon her long deferred marriage to Charles Brandon, had also suffered from the horrid tyranny of her brother in matrimonial affairs, so that a history of her persecutions might offer a possible parallel to those of Arabella. The date of the *History of the Duchess of Suffolk,* however, makes it unlikely that such a parallel was intended; and it seems hardly likely that as late as 1624 authority would be apprehensive about a tragedy that had come to a close in 1615. There were, of course, other Duchesses of Suffolk to whom the play might have referred.

Whether or not any of these suggestions should be credited, it is a fact that allusions to the affairs of the Lady Arabella were made on the stage during her own lifetime. In a despatch dated 8 February, 1610, the Venetian Ambassador reported that the Lady Arabella "complains that in a certain comedy the playwright introduced an allusion to her person and the part played by the Prince of Moldavia. The play was suppressed." Sir Edmund Chambers believes that the play which was objected to was *Epicoene,* for in Act V, i, 17 of that play there is an allusion to the Prince of Moldavia, who had visited London in 1607, and "is said to have been a suitor for Arabella." The plan was for Arabella to marry Stephan Bogdan, Pretender to Moldavia (in 1609). La Foole declares that Sir John Daw "has his box of instruments . . . to draw maps of every place, and person where he comes," and he swears that he has "drawn the pictures of the Prince of Moldavia and of his mistres, Mistres *Epicoene.*" "If," says Sir Edmund, (*Elizabethan Stage,* III, p. 371), "Jonson's text is really 'not changed from the simplicity of the first copy,' it is clear that Arabella misunderstood it, since Epicoene was Daw's mistress."

The Jacobean Puritan Plays

Concerning the plight of the Catholics at the accession of James, the author of the *Traditional Memoires on the Raigne of King James the First,* Francis Osborne, Master of the Horse in the household of the Herberts, the Earls of Pembroke and Montgomery, himself a Puritan, who later served in a position of trust under Oliver Cromwell, says (*op. cit.*, pp. 169-174):

He [James] left the poor catholickes in the wide field of Scottish cruelty, who did daily beg, sell, or exchange, such as preferred conscience before unreasonable compositions, remaining obstinate in their recusancy: which, in this excessive extremity, some either were so far indulged by others, or themselves, as to take their estates off from this Scotch book, did about this time go to church. Whilest King James stood so amazed at his present felicity, that the fleecing his subjects did seeme to concern him no more then it doth the lovesick bridegroome to loose all his gloves, ribbands, garters, and poynts, to the very single one that keeps all from, &c. For though the frequent petitions of these plundered people, no lesse then the recommendations of ministers of forraigne states, might for the present incline his heart (which, in its own nature, was not cruell), to commiseration, yet, upon a lively representation of that northerne puppet play, whose scenes they lay in the church of Rome, pretending the least candour used to those Canaanites would call his mothers sinnes to a new remembrance, and so conjure up the spirit of rebellion, against which there can be no apter sacrifice then the retainers to that community, which beautifies the vestries of Scotland &c. in the shape of a beast, &c. which once heard interpretated by a curtailed divine, he either durst not, or would not, abate this rigor, but rather increased their despaire by daily threats of worse, and invectives owned as written by himselfe, which, though some might consider as too theatricall to be reall, yet others, not so well versed in his majesties royall craft, and having possibly besides been swallowed by one of these harpies, that, like cormorants, will retaine the prey 'till their throats be cut, may be excused in part, if, finding their hopes deluded, they fell into despaire, especially hearing the uncessant cry made by the commons in the house of parliament, for a fresh supply of lawes against recusants, and all that lay but under the least notion of a popish affection: which was a latitude some extended as far as prelacy, others bounded it very little on this side anabaptisme: Though they saw them daily thrown into a denne of Scotchmen, which the court did already so naturally resemble, as nothing made penell by law, either in church or common-weale, but was by the king granted to his countrymen, and by them exacted to the uttermost farthing. Many in the meane time venting their spleen (capable of better imployment) in libels and songes, of one of which I remember two lines at this time, and may do more hereafter:

> In Scotland he was borne and bred,
> And though a beggar, must be fed.

This passage from contemporary history bears witness to many of the points I have tried to make in this study: (1) that the people were fearless in their use of political songs and libels, even against the King himself; and (2) that they made use of the stage in order to urge their point of view upon the King; and (3) that their use of stage propaganda was so far successful that it actually influenced the whole ecclesiastical policy of the King. We have already noted one example of stage propaganda for the opposite point of view, i.e., the private performance at the house of Sir John York, in which "scandalous play acted in favour of Popery," the Devil declared that all Protestants were eternally lost, and carried King James off on his back to the fiery lower regions. Though for this seditious play Sir John and his lady were fined and imprisoned, it is a fact that of the two extreme parties, Catholics and Puritans, it was the latter whom James detested most heartily. Osborne declares (*op. cit.*, 187-194):

> Now to take off the subjects eyes from observing the indulgency used by James in behalfe of the papists, whom, though he had no cause to love, he found reason enough to fear, a quarrell was rivived, (now almost asleep, because it had long escaped persecution, the bellowes of schism,) with a people stiled *puritans,* who meeting no neerer a definition then the name, all the conscientious men in the nation shared the contempt: Since under that generall terme were comprehended not only those brainsick fooles, as did oppose the discipline and ceremonies of the church, and made religion an umbrella to impiety, but such as out of meere honesty refrained the vices of the times were branded by this title; weaved of such a fashion, as it became a covering to the wicked, and no better than a foole-coat to men truly conscientious. . . . Court sermons were fraught with bitter invectives against these people, whom they seated in a classe farre neerer the confines of hell then papists; yet the wisest durst not define them. The king called them protestants scared out of their wits, others lovers of God, and haters of their neighbours; foolish and insignificant expressions: for had they held

them to the names of hypocrits, knowne and abominated by all, they would have been buried in contempt, and not risen, as since they have done, to the perpetuall detriment of church and state. . .

Thus hath the devell quenched (for what was but a rivulet then is now swelled to a land-floud), that zeale with hypocrisy, and its concomitants shame and reproach which in my fathers daies resisted the flames of the hottest persecution: For, to avoyd an imputation of puritanisme, (a greater rub in the way to preferment then vice,) our divines, for the generality, did sacrifice more time to Bacchus then Minerva; and being excellent company, drew the most ingenious laity into a like excesse: And for their ordinary studies they were schoole points and passionate expressions; as more conversant with the fryars then the fathers, scorning in their ordinary discourse at Luther and Calvin, but especially at the last, so as I heard a bishop thank God he never (though a good poet himselfe) had read a line in him or Chaucer. The same used this simile in a sermon at court, that our religion, like the kings armes, stood between two beasts, the puritan and papist, which perhaps admitted of a better construction then he meant. The last being, like the lion, easily knowne; but the first, sutable to a unicorne, never seen but in painting. Nor was this schisme any waies dangerous, till King James, (more it may be thought out of ostentation, to shew such parts as are nothing necessary, then reason of state, only requisite in a prince,) made it considerable, by putting it in competition with the doctrine generally profest, in a colloquie held before his royall person at Hampton Court; where he sinned so highly against the experience to be deduced from the French and Scots, who, by offering the unquestioned, or at least legall profession to arbitration, have brought their religious habit into such a motly, as 'tis scarce discernable which side is the right or with the most safety may be owned by the magistrate. Since till that dishonourable dispute, who should command, the diocesan or the priest, non did boggle at the surplice, crosse, ring; and so by consequence the Common Prayer Book, but out of pure conscience, and therefore unlikely to hurt any besides themselves; till the number increasing to such a proportion, made a visible profit appeare to so many as, wanting better imployment, could but conforme their mode, words, and looks to these precisians; though discrepant in heart from any thing the first owners of the title of *puritan* did commonly practice in their conversation towards God and man.

As Osborne shrewdly observed, the Puritan schism under James was a political, not a religious move; for those who "boggled" at the simple ritual of Episcopalianism "but out of pure conscience" were, indeed, few enough in number to hurt none but themselves. The issue of "preciseness" was, however, just the sort with which James felt himself competent to deal, and his vanity was fanned by the politically orthodox pulpit, from which, says Osborne, "came all our future miseries." He continues:

> The court-sermons informing his majesty, he might as Christs vice-regent command all, and that the people, if they denied him supplement, or inquired after the disposer of it, were presumptuous peepers into the sacred arke of the state; not to be done but under the severest curse, though it apeared likely to fall through the falsehood or folly of those at the helme: But, on the contrary, the other qualified preachers did fulminate against non-residency, profanation of the Lords day, connivance at popery, persecution of God's people, only inclusive in their congregations, and those that supplied the wants of such like saints as themselves, who maintained their families, and kept them in good plight out of the fasts they did weekly assigne, at first in private, and after before the face of the sunne, and all this without or against the leave of the magistrate. But if this should be prosecuted to its farthest extent it would moderate, if not expunge, all the vilany legible in story.

It will be seen from Osborne's account that James needed no special goad to urge him into action against the Puritans. The following "reasonable pretty jest," however, may have pricked him on to make to Jonson the suggestion "to write something against the Puritans." The story is told in a letter to the Earl of Shrewsbury (Aikin, *op. cit.*, I, 202-203):

> There was one of the king's special hounds, called Jowler, missing one day: the king was much displeased that he was wanted; notwithstanding, went a hunting. The next day, when they were on the field, Jowler came in amongst the rest of the hounds; the king was told of him, and was very glad; and looking on him spied a paper about his neck, and in the paper was written;—"God Mr. Jowler, we pray you speak to the king (for he hears you every day, and so he doth not us) that it will please his majesty to go back to London; for else the country will be undone; all our provision is spent already; and we are not able to entertain him longer." It

was taken for a jest, and so passed over; for his majesty intends to lie there yet a fortnight.

We have already alluded to Aubrey's statement concerning James's commission to Jonson, and to the Prologue and the Epilogue to *Bartholomew Fair,* which bear further witness to the same effect, i.e., that the play was intended as anti-Puritan propaganda. There is no evidence that the anonymous *Puritan* was a part of the same or a similar commission, but there is evidence that it was part of a literary campaign against the Puritans, which was immediately answered, both on the stage and in the pulpit. On 13 February, 1608, William Crashaw stated in a sermon at Paul's Cross (Chambers, *op. cit.,* IV, p. 249):

. . . now they bring religion and holy things vpon the stage; no maruel though the worthiest and mightiest men escape not, when God himselfe is so abused. Two hypocrites must be brought forth; and how shall they be described but by these names, *Nicholas S. Antlings, Simon S. Maryoueries.* [Names of characters in *The Puritan.*] Thus hypocrisie child of hell must beare the names of two Churches of God, and two wherein Gods name is called on publikely euery day in the yeere, and in one of them his blessed word preached euerie day (an example scarce matachable in the world): yet these two, wherein Gods name is glorified, and our Church and State honoured, shall be by these miscreants thus dishonoured, and that not on the stage only, but euen in print.

This last phrase, "even in print," might have referred to a whole series of anti-Puritan satires, such as those of John Taylor, the "water-poet," though, as far as I know, no definite dates have been assigned to the particular satires in his "gallimawfry of sonnets, satires, and epigrams" (the sub-title of Taylor's *Water-Work*), nor to the fourteen satires of the *Water-Cormorant, his Complaint.* In these early poems, abuses of the church were gravely chastized; but in *A Separatist* and in *The Praise of Hemp-Seed,* Taylor drives his shafts against the Puritans with a witty precision far superior to his much better known follower, Samuel Butler. The readers of *Hudibras* will recognize at once the original of the traditional jeer at exaggerated Sunday observances which later gave Charles II such pleasure (Hugh Walker, *English Satires and Satirists* [1925], p. 86):

Suppose his cat on Sunday kills a rat,
She on the Munday must be hanged for that.

I know of no seventeenth-century satire against the Puritans more devastating than Taylor's *Separatist.* Lines like the following should have endeared him to any Stuart:

Now enters next to play his oily part
A Saint in tongue, but a rough devil in heart:
One that so smoothly swallows his prey down,
Without wrath shewn or any seeming frown,
You'd think him shent he does't, in a psalm,
Or at his prayers, he's so mild and calm:
No noise, no trouble to his conscience cries,
For he devours his prey with heaved up eyes,
Stands most demurely swallowing down his bit,
And licks his lips with long grace after it.

The satirists took full advantage of the maxim: It is always easier and safer to prove one's opponent wrong than to prove oneself right. So the polemical plays continued one of the best weapons on both sides. While Dekker was harping on the old "no-popery" string in the *Whore of Babylon,* George Ruggle was writing "two other comedies, *Re Vere, or Verily* and *Club Law,* to expose the Puritans" (Chambers, *Elizabethan Stage,* III, p. 476); and Jonson wrote *Bartholomew Fair,* and some unknown author contributed the *Puritan;* and, like an earlier stage satire on the Puritan, the burden was: the preciseness of a few shall not deprive the rest of us from cakes and ale.

I turn now to the notice of a stage controversy that was begun in the last decade of Elizabeth's life, but which was carried on well into the next reign. This was, happily, not a political, but a literary fight, and the note is not propaganda, but personal satire. Alas! in those days even the poets submitted their quarrels to the arbitrament of such public opinion as could be influenced by the stage.

CHAPTER TWELVE

The War of the Poets

THE WAR OF THE POETS, or *poetomachia,* as it is usually called, was an almost inevitable phenomenon arising out of the regard of literature as a profession, in which the temptations to rivalry and competition were enhanced by the deeply entrenched habit of fustian. If you were edging for first place, or for a post which you felt you could fill better than its present incumbent, or if you were employed by an enemy of another poet's patron, an attack by your best weapon, your pen, was almost inevitable. We have seen how the Harvey-Lyly-Nashe quarrel grew from Harvey's resentment at Lyly's informing his patron, the Earl of Oxford, that he was the prototype for Tuscanismo. We hope we may be forgiven for a slight repetition in giving here in some detail the facts of this quarrel, as the whole episode illustrates both the cause and the procedure of such literary battles.

In 1580 Harvey had published some letters that had passed between himself and Spenser, under the title "Three Proper and wittie, familiar Letters, lately passed between two University men: touching the Earthquake in Aprill last and our English reformed versifying." In the second of these letters—the one purporting to deal with the earthquake, Harvey had vented his personal disappointment at failing to secure the public oratorship at Cambridge "in some reflections on the University and on Dr. Perne, their Vice-Chancellor in particular." In the third letter he "had introduced among his remarks on English versification, entitled *Speculum Tuscanismi,* some hexameters describing an Italianate Englishman." (Bond, *John Lyly,* I, p. 30.) Harvey was called before the Privy Council, where "the sharpest parts of those unlucky letters was over-read" and Harvey threatened with the Fleet, though apparently he escaped with a rebuke and an apology. Lyly, however, was apparently unsatisfied to let the matter drop; for when, in 1589, Bancroft hired Lyly and Nashe, and possibly others, to belabour Martin in his own style, the quarrel was resumed. *A Whip for an Ape* was probably the first anti-Martin pamphlet, and it was followed directly by Lyly's *Pappe With a Hatchet,* in which he not only alluded to the 1580 episode most offensively, but further taunted Harvey for his literary pretentions. "All his works bound close," says Lyly, "are at least sixe sheets in quarto, & he calls them the first tome of his familiar Epistles"; and he further declares that "for this tenne yeres have I lookt to lambacke him."

The plan of the anti-Martin campaign gave this long looked-for opportunity. It is not necessary here to discuss the problem of collaboration between Lyly and Nashe, either in the pamphlets or in the plays. Suffice it to note that they were collaborators, and that therefore Harvey's resentment was directed against the pair of them. Harvey's reply, (in the "Advertisement to Pap-Hatchett," *Works of John Lyly,* II, p. 213), makes it clear that the young controversialists had gratuitously included him in their "jerks" at the Puritan Penry. (See pp. 365ff.)

Harvey had indeed good reason to be afraid of a stage satire, for he had already been cruelly flouted in a play in his own University. On 6 February, 1581, shortly after he had been defeated by Anthony Wingfield for the Public Oratorship, the successful candidate was instrumental in staging the most outrageous lampoon on his rival. To be sure, Sir John Harington, who with Essex had witnessed the play of *Pedantius,* calls it "a pritie conceit" and declares it to be "full of harmless myrth"; but Nashe's description of the play in *Have With You* makes it clear that the mirth could not have been considered harmless by poor Harvey. Sir Edmund Chambers *(op cit.,* IV, p. 377) says:

There can be little doubt that Harvey was the butt of *Pedantius,* and hardly more that Wingfield was concerned with the satire. Nashe has two allusions to the matter. In *Strange News* (1593) he says that Harvey's verses were "miserably flouted at in M. Winkfields Comoedie of *Pedantius* in Trinitie Colledge." (*Works,* i, 303.) In *Have With You to Saffron-Walden* (1596) he says, "Ile fetch him aloft in Pedantius, that exquisite Comedie in Trinitie Colledge; where, under the chiefe part, from which it tooke his name, as namely the concise and firking finicaldo fine School master, hee was full drawen & delineated from the soale of the foote to the crowne of his head," and goes on to enumerate the principal traits of Harvey touched off by the actors, who "borrowed his gowne to playe the Part in, the more to flout him." (*Works,* iii, 80.) *

The reader will recall also the satire on Harvey in Huanabango of Peele's *Old Wives' Tale.* We can do no more than mention here the titles in the pamphlet war that flourished for more than fifteen years. Harvey replied, first with the *Advertisement to Pap-Hatchett.* Then his brother Richard Harvey took up the cudgels, in *Plaine Percevall, the Peacemaker of England,* absurdly avowing his "sweet-endeavour . . . to botch up a Reconciliation between Mar-ton and Mar-tother." Nashe replied with *Pierce Penniless.* Then Greene, whose ire was aroused by what he considered an attack on the London playwrights in Richard Harvey's *Lambe of God* (in this tract, Harvey had referred contemptuously to "the piperly Makeplaies and Make-bates" about London), retaliated by a general attack on all the brothers Harvey, in which he girded at the father for rope-making, at Gabriel for having been in the Fleet, at Richard for freedom with the wives of his parishioners at Saffron-Walden, and at John, who was a physician at Lynn. In less than a year appeared Harvey's *Foure Letters and Certain Sonnets,* "whose rancour against the dead men (Greene)," says Professor Bond, "and reproductions of details wormed out of his landlady while his body was lying scarce yet cold upstairs, have done more injury to his reputation than they could possibly inflict on the defenceless object of his attack." Nashe, in

* This case of purloining of a man's attire for the sake of a stage impersonation was, apparently, not an isolated instance of the impudent trick. A letter from Rowland Whyte to Sir Robert Sidney, 26 October, 1599, shows that the bold actors either stole the clothes of Sir Francis Vere, or had them copied exactly for their presentation of *The Victory of Turnhout.* Though their motive was obviously friendly, it is nevertheless clear that their act was done with neither the knowledge nor consent of Sir Francis Vere. The following letter from *The Sidney Papers,* II, p. 136, is quoted heré from Chambers, *Elizabethan Stage,* I, p. 323: "Two daies agoe, *The Overthrow of Turnholt,* was acted vpon a Stage, and all your Names vsed that were at yt; especially Sir. Fra. Veres, and he that plaid that Part gott a Beard resembling his, with a Watchet Sattin Doublet, with Hose trimd with Silver Lace. You was also introduced, Killing, Slaying, and Overthrowing the Spaniards, and honorable Mention made of your Service, in seconding Sir Francis Vere, being engaged."

Turnhout was taken from the Spanish by Count Maurice of Nassau, with the help of an English contingent, 24 January, 1598.

disgust, replied with *Strange News Out of Purgatorie,* which bore as its running-title *The Four Letters Confuted.* Harvey retaliated in *Pierce's Supererogation,* and *A New Letter of Notable Contents.* Nashe, after three years, thought he had done a finished job on Gabriel when he published *Have With You to Saffron-Walden,* but Harvey's rejoinder in *The Trimming of Thomas Nash* (1597) proved that the son of the rope-maker had not yet been fatally trussed up. It remained for "our fellow Shakespeare" to give them all a purge in *Love's Labour's Lost.* It is clear that he thought the whole business to be what Harvey had declared Lyly's *Pappe* to be, i.e., "ale-house and tinkerly stuffe, oddly muddled and bungled together in a mad-brain sort." At least, that is what he has represented it as being in his parody in *Love's Labour's Lost.*

Whether or not Dr. Rupert Taylor, in *The Date of Love's Labour's Lost* (New York, 1932), is right in regarding Armado as a satire on Gabriel Harvey, it is hardly disputable that in the lines of and about the absurd would-be courtier and his vulgar associates there are abundant echoes of the pamphlet war which we have been describing. Harvey's attempts to achieve his own fame and the extinction of his enemies by means of his Letters could hardly fail to occur to an initiated audience who had just been laughing over the pomposities of *Two Letters, Three Letters, Four Letters and New Letter,* when Dull brings in the first of a series of "letters" from the "magnificent Armado"—a man who "hath a mint of phrases in his brain," "a man of compliments," etc. The echoes would be the more amusing if they had just read *Have With You* (iii, 103), in which Nashe jeers at Harvey's "strange untraffiqu't phrases by him new vented unpacht"; and he declares that he "proceeds with complement and a little more complement, and a crust of quips, and a little more complement after that." The jest develops when the Courtiers declare they will use Armado for their sport. Nashe (iii, 79) had ridiculed Harvey's attempt to get employment at court, declaring that an unnamed courtier (Leicester) to whom he had applied, found him "more meet to make sport with than to be deeply employed." Similarly, the King protests (*LLL,* I, i, 174):

> I love to hear him lie
> And I will use him for my minstrelsy

Nashe had called Harvey an insulting Monarcho that out-acted the original Monarcho, and Boyet describes Armado as "a phantasm, a Monarcho, one that makes sport for the Prince and his bookmates"; and Longavelle concedes that Armado and Costard "shall be our sport." The King declares that "for interim to our studies (Armado) shall relate in high-born words the worth of many a knight from tawny Spain, lost in the world's debate." Harvey had, in *Four Letters* (i, 206) referred knowingly to Larizillo de Torimes, and in *Pierce's Supererogation* to Don Alonso d'Avalos, persons who, as far as an average reader is concerned, have been "lost in the world's debate." Again and again Harvey had hurled at his opponents the vague charge of "villany." "All is villany and vanity," he declared in *Pierce's Supererogation* (ii, 61); and in *Four Letters* (i, 224) he rages against "the abominable villanies of such base shifting companions"; and in *New Letter* (i, 289) he again harps on the "strange news of villany." Nashe had already poked fun at Harvey for this feeble charge in *Have With You* (iii, 15), so that when Dull announces, as it were, "out of the blue,"

> There's villany abroad: this letter will tell you more,

the audience must have tittered knowingly while they waited to hear the silly charges that were to follow. These parallels continue to point the wit right through the play, except in Act II. Some of the jokes are witty, some broad; all are in the recklessly insolent style of a Ménippean gallimaufry. Perhaps the most interesting are those jeering at Harvey's poor poetry. The Nashe pamphlets are full of gibes, burlesques, parodies; he hoots at Harvey's extemporal versifying on any and all subjects and occasions *(Have With You,* iii, 86), at his ridiculous alliterations, and his dusty moralizings. Harvey's sonnets are about as infelicitous as such poems could well be, and his clumsy treatment of the verse form known as "l'envoy," invited and received ample derision from his enemies.

In *Pierce's Supererogation,* Harvey had called Pern "a fox," Greene "the ape of Euphues" (Lyly), and Nashe "a bee" and "a pea-goose." Nashe had also been dubbed "a goose" by Anthony Chute in a poem appended to *Pierce's Supererogation.* Shakspere seems to have lighted a whole train of risible explosions when he made Armado burst into an extemporal envoy on being told that Costard had broken his shin. Costard pleads for a "plain plaintain" as a cure for his wound, and begs to be let off the envoy:

> O, sir, plaintain, a plain plaintain!
> no l'envoy, no l'envoy: no salve, sir,
> but a plaintain!

But Armado will not be done out of his envoy, which he explains as not a salve, but "an epilogue or discourse, to make plain some obscure precedence that have tofore been said." The example which he gives is a versifying, in the manner of Mother Goose, of the accusations used by Harvey against Nashe in *Pierce's Supererogation:*

> The fox, the ape and the humble-bee
> Were still at odds being but three,
> Until the goose came out of door
> And stayed the odds by adding four.

The list of such parallels could be extended to include almost every line of the comic scenes of *Love's Labour's Lost.* A full list of them has been presented by Dr. Taylor in the Appendices to his *The Date of Love's Labour's Lost.* Indeed, Shakspere seems to have done for Harvey in this play, what Nashe says he did for Penry in the *May Game of Martinism.* The description which follows has a general as well as a particular significance, as it illustrates the crazy methods of these satirists, in addition to offering a parallel to the *hors d'oeuvre* scenes of *Love's Labour's Lost* (Bond, *op. cit.,* I, p. 54, quoting Lyly, *The Return of Pasquill*):

> Howe whorishlie Scriptures are alleaged by them, I will discouer (by Gods helpe) in another new worke which I haue in hand, and intituled it, *The May Game of Martinisme.* Verie defflie set out, with Pompes, Pageants, Motions, Maskes, Scutchions, Emblems, Impreases, strange trickes, and deuises betweene the Ape and the Owle, the like was neuer yet seene in Paris-Garden. *Penry* the welchman is the fore-gallant of the Morrice, with the treble belles, shot through the wit with a Woodcock's bill, I woulde not for the fayrest horne-

beast in all his Countrey, that the Church of England were a cup of Metheglin, and came in his way when he is ouerheated, euery Bishopricke would prooue but a draught, when the Mazer is at his nose. *Martin* himselfe is the Mayd-Marian, trimlie drest vppe in a cast Gowne, and a Kercher of Dame *Lawsons,* his face handsomelie muffled with a Diaper-napkin to couer his beard, *and a great Nose-gay in his hande, of the principalest flowers I could gather out of all hys works.* [Italics inserted.] *Wiggenton* daunces round about him in a Cotten-coate, to court him with a Leatherne pudding, and a wooden Ladle. *Paget* marshalleth the way, with a couple of great clubbes, one in his foote, another in his head, & he cryes to the people with a loud voice, *Beware of the Man whom God hath markt.* I can not yet find any so fitte to come lagging behind, with a budget on his necke to gather the deuotion of the lookers on, as the stock-keeper of the Bridewel-house of Canterburie; he must carrie the purse, to defray their charges, and then hee may be sure to serue himselfe.

It is, of course, dangerous to accept as proved any of Fleay's identifications of dramatic characters. However, the equating of Ralph Roister of Ulpian Fulwell's *Like Will to Like* with Richard Edwards is not the worst of his guesses, and, if allowed, would add plausibility to the theory that the attack was answered by Edwards himself in *Damon and Pythias.* If this network of guesses should happen to be right, then the whole episode would offer another instance of such a venting of private grudges upon the stage as we have just seen in the play of *Pedantius.* This study, however, offers no scope for an examination of the reckless claims of Fleay.

A more purely literary quarrel is that between two Oxonians, John Rainolds, later President of Corpus Christi College, and Dr. William Gager of Christ Church. In a prolonged academic controversy over the suitability of student plays, Rainolds represented the more "precise" Puritan's disapproval, and Gager the more liberal humanistic tolerance or even enthusiasm. It was almost inevitable therefore that the time should come when the academic playwrights thought it well to challenge their opponent in public. Their champion was Dr. Gager. During one of the Christmas festivities of 1591-2, Rainolds was invited to be present at a performance of *Ulysses Redux* by Gager. He refused, and being pressed, gave his reasons. "It was not therefore," says Sir Edmund Chambers (*Elizabethan Stage,* I, p. 251), "unnatural that, when Gager appended to the *Hypolytus,* which was also given, a new apologetical epilogue in which arguments against the stage, very similar to those of Rainolds, were put into the mouth of one Momus, our theologian should infer that by Momus none other was intended than himself." In the long epistolary controversy which ensued, the debate was, as Sir Edmund observes, "a good deal complicated by topics of mere erudition, and by disputes as to whether Momus was really meant as a caricature of Rainolds. He adds *(ibid.,* p. 253):

It is with some skepticism that one reads the statement of the printer who gave Rainolds' share of the controversy to the world in 1599, that ultimately Gager 'let goe his hold, and in a Christian modestie and humilitie yeelded to the truth and quite altered his judgement.' My own conviction is that Gager would have subscribed to anything, in order to have done with receiving argumentative letters from Rainolds. But when Rainolds had disposed of Gager, he had to meet a fresh adversary in Alberico Genteli, an Italian who held the professorship of civil law at Oxford and had committed himself to a different view as to the force of the *praetorian infamia.* Between these two pundits the discussion continued for some time without contributing much elucidation of the main issue. Rainolds' book, the first line of the title of which was *Th'overthrow of Stage-Plays,* furnished many weapons later for the armoury of Prynne, and material for ridicule in the play *Fucus, sive Histriomastix,* produced at Queens' College, Cambridge, in 1623.

It is hardly to be wondered that, like Gabriel Harvey, Rainolds expressed his disapproval of "men . . . that haue not been afraied of late dayes to bring upon the stage the very sober countenances, grave attire, modest and matronelike gestures, and speaches of men & women to be laughed at as a scorne and reproch to the world." *(Ibid.,* IV, p. 245.)

Though they contribute important confirmation of the practice of personal satire on the stage, these academic plays are, on the whole, of less interest to students of Elizabethan drama than the plays of the London theatres. In this field, ignorance of the poets' quarrels cuts one off from much that is witty and pungent. I must crave the indulgence of Elizabethan scholars for repeating here a story which has been so often told elsewhere. The Marston-Jonson-Dekker quarrel is so essential a part of the thesis of this book that it is impossible to omit it altogether. The whole thing may possibly have arisen out of a mistake; i.e., what Marston had meant as a compliment to Jonson was taken by that bellicose poet as an intended insult, and hence the long quarrel, which ultimately involved many of the best known poets of the age. It all began with the writing or refurbishing by Marston of an old controversial play whose title was *Histriomastix, or, the Player Whipt.* The following description is from Sir Edmund Chambers' account (*Elizabethan Stage,* IV, pp. 17-18):

> As its whole substance is a satire on professional players, it must have been both produced and revived by amateurs or boys; and the same conclusion is pointed to by the enormous number of characters. The original matter is so full of the technical learning of the schools as to suggest an academic audience; I think it was a University or possibly an Inns of Court, not a choir boy, play. The theme is the cyclical progression of a state through the stages Peace, Plenty, Pride, Envy, War, Poverty, and Peace again. It is illustrated by the fortunes of a company of players, who wax insolent in prosperity, and when war comes, are pressed for soldiers. Their Poet Posthaste is clearly Munday and not, as Simpson and others have vainly imagined, Shakespeare. With him is contrasted the scholar-poet, Chrisoganus, a philosopher with whom the players will have nothing to do. . . . I agree with Small that Marston has given him Jonsonian traits, and that he intended to be complimentary rather than the reverse. I do not know that it is necessary to suppose that Jonson misunderstood this and took offence, for the real offence was given by *Jack Drum's Entertainment* in the next year.

Before, however, going on to this next step in the quarrel, we may pause a little over the portrait of Munday as Posthaste. Not even Gabriel Harvey has so suffered at the hands of his more clever contemporaries as Anthony Munday. As Sir Edmund says, "he was evidently a favourite mark for the satire of more literary writers, who depreciated his style and jested at his function as a messenger." He was probably resented the more intensely, as he "first was a stage player . . . [and] did play extempore," but with so little dexterity, we are told, that "those gentlemen and others which were present, . . . being wery of his folly, hissed him from the stage." (*A True Report of . . . M. Campion,* quoted by Chambers, *Elizabethan Stage,* III, p. 444.) Whereupon, "being discouraged, he set forth a balet against players." This was, to the dramatists who had a constant battle to maintain their position against the Puritan attacks, an unforgiveable disloyalty, so that even when he returned to the stage again, it was only to be treated with even deeper disdain. The anonymous author of *A True Report* ironically apostrophizes: "O constant youth! he now beginnes againe to ruffle upon the stage." His work in Rome, gathering material for a series of attacks on the Jesuits, and later his employment by Topcliffe against recusants, would lead naturally to his being regarded, at least by those sympathetic to Catholicism, as a base informer. He was finally made a Messenger of the Chamber and may have had a hand in the Archbishop's fight against the Marprelates. Be that as it may, his official duties seem not to have interfered with his literary productiveness, for he continued as translator of romances, maker of ballads, devisor of pageants, pamphleteer, and miscellaneous writer generally. He appears in Henslowe during various periods between 1594 and 1602, and though his opponents jeered at his dramatic efforts, Meres included him in 1598 as among "the best for comedy," with the additional compliment of "our best plotter." Nearly all the known facts about Munday are burlesqued in the character of Posthaste—his hack-writing, his balladeering, his extemporizing, his political employments, his lack of stage popularity. The players declare that "it is as dangerous to read his name at a play door, as a printed bill on a plague door" (Act IV, 165). The whole portrait, in the opinion of Sir Edmund Chambers, "agrees closely with the later portraits, by Jonson, and with the facts of Munday's career." * Discounting many attempts to establish further identifications, for instance, with Puntarvolo of *Everyman Out,* or Amorphus of *Cynthia's Revels,* or the In-and-In Medley of *The Tale of a Tub,* or Timothy Tweedle of *Jack Drum's Entertainment,* Sir Edmund concludes *(op. cit.,* III, p. 445): "But he may reasonably be taken for the Poet Nun-

* Dr. Kitchin, and others, favour equating Posthaste with Shakspere; see George Kitchin, *A Survey of Burlesque and Parody in English,* (Edinburgh, 1931), p. 65.

tius of *Everyman In* and the Antonia Balladino of *The Case Is Altered.*" As a matter of fact, Sir Edmund believes that the scene in which Balladino appears is an interpolation, added solely for the sake of presenting a satirical portrait of Munday. The chaff in Act I about Balladino's being "in print already for the best plotter" (referring to Meres' description of Munday), does, indeed, make the identification highly plausible.

But to return to the Jonson-Marston aspect of the quarrel: whether Chrysoganus was meant as an insult or compliment to Jonson, the fact is that Jonson was offended, and he retaliated in print by including in the published edition of *Every Man Out* (iii, I) what most scholars have taken to be a parody of Marston's "tumescent vocabulary." Marston replied by giving the world a satirical portrait of Jonson as Brabant Senior in *Jack Drum's Entertainment,* and in the following year another as Lampatho Doria in *What You Will.* In the former play Brabant Senior criticizes three "modern Wits" whom he calls "all apes and guls" and "vile imitating spirits." They are Mellidus, Musus and Decius. Sir Edmund Chambers says *(Elizabethan Stage,* IV, 21): "I take them to be Marston, Middleton, and Dekker, all writers for Pauls; others take Decius for Drayton, to whom Sir John Davies applied the name, and Musus, by a confusion with Museus, for Chapman or Daniel."

It is not necessary here to arbitrate these differences of opinion. It is more important to know that Brabant Senior and Lampatho Doria were fustian characters than it is to fix upon an identification for them. About the chief identification in Jonson's reply, however, there can be no doubt, for we have Jonson's own statement to Drummond that "he [Jonson] had many quarrels with Marston, beat him and took his pistol from him [and] wrote his *Poetaster* on him." With Marston as Crispinus, Jonson included Dekker as Demetrius Fannius, "a dresser of plaies about towne here," who had been "hir'd to abuse Horace and bring him in a play." As Sir Edmund observes, it "is Dekker who certainly associated himself with Marston as a victim of Jonson's arraignment, and wrote *Satiromastix* in reply." The final scene of the *Poetaster,* in which Crispinus, having been sentenced to a purge to cure him of his bad poetic manners, belches forth a whole page and a half of Marston's typical vocabulary, furnishes abundant internal evidence for the identification of Crispinus with Marston.

As yet there is too much disagreement among scholars to make safe a further identification of characters. There are in the play, however, many highly valuable testimonies concerning the practice of fustian drama. We have already alluded to the scene in which Jonson condemns Asinus Lupus to be fitted "with a pair of larger ears" for his "fierce credulity" in accepting a stupid and malicious gloss for a harmless emblem. This is, however, only one of many occasions which Jonson takes, in this play, to rail at informers and decipherers. When Caesar was informed of the treasonable meaning of the emblem, he asked:

> Who was it, Lupus, that informed you first
> This should be meant by us? Or was't your comment?

Lupus answers, strangely enough, considering that the treason in question was an emblem, not a drama:

> No, Caesar; a player gave me the first light of it indeed.

Tucca adds:

> Ay, an honest sycophant-like slave, and a politician besides.

When the player is summoned, Caesar sentences him to be whipped, and Virgil declares with satisfaction:

> Caesar hath done like Caesar. Fair and just
> Is his award, against these brainless creatures.
> 'Tis not the wholesome sharp morality,
> Or modest anger of a satiric spirit
> That hurts or wounds the body of the state,
> But the sinister application
> Of the malicious, ignorant, and base
> Interpreters, who will distort and strain
> The general scope and purpose of an author
> To his particular and private spleen.

Caesar replies:

> We know it, our dear Virgil, and esteem it
> A most dishonest practice in that man
> Will seem too witty in another's work.

We have already alluded to many protests of this kind, but this particular play is fairly bursting with Jonson's indignation against such spying and informing. He gives us, in Act IV, sc. I, a good notion of the tricks and sleights by which the practice was carried on. When Tucca has approached Demetrius and Crispinus to induce them to write a play "on Horace," he first shows how he (Tucca) has been irritated by Horace's satires, declaring that when once he (Horace) "drops upon paper against a man," that man lives to be the eternal scorn of every tankard-bearer, waterman, bawd, or baker's boy. "Fough! body of Jove!" he protests, "I'll have the slave whipt one of these days for his Satires and his Humours, by one cashier'd clerk or another." As we all know, Jonson did come to blows with Marston, though, according to Jonson, he did the beating. When Crispinus agrees to "undertake him"—that is, to put him in a play, Demetrius chuckles:

> Ay, and tickle him i' faith, for his arrogancy and his impudence, in commending his own things; and for his translating, I can trace him, i' faith. O, he is the most open fellow living; I had as lief as a new suit I were at it.

Tucca thereupon agrees to procure the necessary data for the satire. He says: "I'll give you instructions; I'll be your intelligencer; we'll all join and hang on him like so many horse-leeches, the players and all. We shall sup together; and then we'll conspire, i' faith." But Crispinus declares, ironically, "Do you hear, Captain? I'll write nothing in it but innocence, because I may swear I am innocent." While the play-writing is in progress, i.e., while Dekker is writing *Satiromastix, or the Untrussing of a Humourous Poet,* Lupus and a Player approach Maecenas and give him wind of a supposed treason by acting some scene before him; but Maecenas despises the information thus imparted, and Horace bursts forth:

> Was this the treason, this the dangerous plot
> Thy clamourous tongue so bellowed through the court?
> Hadst thou no other object to encrease
> Thy grace with Caesar, but this wolfish train
> To prey upon the life of innocent mirth
> And harmless pleasures, bred of noble wit?
> Away, I loath the presence of such as thou,
> They are the moths and scarabs of a state,
> The bans of empires, and the dregs of courts,

> Who, to endear themselves to an employment
> Care not whose fame they blast, whose life they endanger;
> And under a disguised and cob-web mask
> Of love unto his sovereign, vomit forth
> Their own prodigious malice, and pretending
> To be the props and columns of their safety,
> The guards unto his person and his peace,
> Disturb it most, with their false, lapwing cries.

Inasmuch as we are given no inkling of what the supposedly seditious scene was, it is possible that our present text has suffered a deletion at the hands of the censor. There is evidence that in the printing of the play, Jonson was somewhat "restrained" by "authority." He says at the close:

> Here, reader, in place of an epilogue, was meant to thee an apology from the author, with his reasons for the publishing of this book: but since he is no less restrained, than thou deprived of it by authority, he prays thee to think charitable of what thou hast read, till thou mayest hear him speak what he hath written.

A similar note appended to the last page of the first quarto of *Everyman Out of His Humour* leads one to wonder whether Jonson had not taken revenge against the decipherers of that play by introducing them and their machinations into a scene in the *Poetaster*. Jonson's note to *Everyman Out* says:

> It had another catastrophe or conclusion at the first playing which (διὰ τὸ τὴν Βασίλισσαν προσωποποιεῖσθαι) many seem'd not to relish it: yet that a right-ei'd and solide Reader may perceive it was not so great a part of Heaven awry, as they would make it, we request him but to look down upon these following reasons.

That Jonson had inserted a piece in the *Poetaster* to mock at those who had persuaded authority that there was offence in his former play, is, of course, mere conjecture, but it would offer a neat explanation of the otherwise unexplained sixth scene of Act IV.

An aspect of this play which has, I think, not been sufficiently emphasized by critics, is the ample testimony afforded by Jonson himself concerning his role as satirist. Throughout the play Horace makes it clear that he is satirist first, lyrist second, and only by grudging consent a player at all. When Trebatius urges the danger of writing satires like the *Poetaster,* Horace replies:

> . . . if to age I destined be,
> Or that quick death's black wings environ me;
> If rich or poor; at Rome; or fate command
> I shall be banished to some other land;
> What hue soever my sole state shall bear
> I will write satires still, in spite of fear.

The aristocratic young law-student, Ovid Junior, is careful to distinguish between poets who write dramatic poems for private performance and mere dramatists. When Ovid Senior hears that his son has written a tragedy for the common players, he is beside himself with rage and humiliation. "Ovid!" he exclaims, "whom I thought to see the pleader, becomes Ovid the play-maker!" In vain the son pleads that he is "not known unto the open stage," nor does he "traffic in their theatres"; but he acknowledges that "at request of some near friends, and honourable Romans" he has "begun a poem of that nature."

When Crispinus is trying to make friends with Horace, he boasts that he is, like Horace, a scholar, and he adds:

> Nay, we are new turned poet too, what is more; and a satirist too, which is more than that. I write just in thy vein. I am for your odes, or your sermons, or anything indeed.

The play reflects most amusingly the terror which the satirical playwrights inspired. Lupus assures Ovid Senior:

> Indeed, Marcus Ovid, these players are an idle generation and do much harm in a state, corrupt young gentry very much, I know it. I have not been a tribune thus long and observed nothing; besides, they will rob us, us, that are magistrates, of our respect, bring us upon the stages, and make us ridiculous to the plebeians; they will play you or me, the wisest men they can come by still, only to bring us in contempt with the vulgar and make us cheap.

Tucca complains that the fashion of plays for simple recreation is quite gone out and that nowadays, one can see on the stages "nothing but Humours, Revels, and Satires, that gird and f—t at the time." He has heard, he says, that

> You'll bring me o' the stage there; you'll play me, they say; I shall be presented by a sort of copper-laced scoundrels of you: Life of

Pluto! an you stage me, stinkard, your mansions shall sweat for't, your tabernacles, varlets, your Globes, and your Triumphs.

But Jonson persisted in the satire, and it seems clear from the Apologetical Dialogue appended at the close, that the victims furnished all the fireworks threatened in Tucca's speech. Nasutus says:

> I never saw the play bred all this tumult.
> What was there in it could so deeply offend,
> And stir so many hornets?

The Author replies, with, apparently, all the innocence of man's first wonder: "I never writ that piece more innocent or empty of offence." He admits it had "some salt," but declares it showed "neither tooth nor gall"; and he insists that it contained no circumstance "which in setting down" he could suspect "might be perverted by an enemie's tongue." When Polyposus expresses the general belief that the plays were directed against certain lawyers, captains, and players, Horace declares, "It is not so," and he labels as slanders all such imputations. True, he admits, his enemies had "for three years" provoked him "with their petulant stiles on every stage," until

> . . . [I] at last unwilling,
> But weary, I confess, of so much trouble,
> Thought I would try if shame could win upon 'em;
> And therefore chose Augustus Caesar's times,
> When wit and arts were at their height in Rome,
> To shew that Virgil, Horace, and the rest
> Of those great master-spirits did not want
> Detractors then, or practices against them.
> And by this line, although no parallel,
> I hoped at last they would sit down and blush.

Who, indeed, in such a context, could take seriously his protestation of "no parallel"? The fact is that Jonson overestimated his own ingenuity in the art of fustian, and had it not been for his very powerful patrons, he would have been driven off the public stage long before he was. As Asper, in *Everyman Out of His Humour,* he brags:

> Let me be censured by the austerest brow,
> Where I want art or judgement, tax me freely.

Let envious censors, with their broadest eyes,
Look through and through me.

But when the censor did begin to look through and through him, the result was that the plays were curtailed, and the poet imprisoned; and had it not been for his influential friends at Court, of whose favours he never tires to boast, he would have suffered the extremest penalties. As it is, he was driven from the public stage by one of his own victims. When Marston heard that Jonson was writing the *Poetaster* against him, he secured the help of Dekker, and possibly Shakspere, and between them, they managed to produce an almost, if not quite contemporaneous appearance of a rival satire in which Jonson as Horace is really laughed off the scene, at least temporarily. Act III, sc. i, of the *Poetaster* must, indeed, represent an actual incident of the war. Here Marston as Crispinus creeps up on Horace [Jonson] while he is composing the following lines:

Swell me a bowl with lusty wine,
Till I may see the plump Lyaeus swim
Above the brim:
I drink as I would write,
In flowing measure filled with flame and sprite.

Imagine what must have been Jonson's annoyance when his enemies at the Globe put on the following scene in *Satiromastix, or the Untrussing of a Humourous Poet*:

[*Horace sitting in a study behind a Curtain, a candle by him burning, books lying confusedly.*]

[Horace, to himself:]

To thee whose forehead swels with roses
Whose most haunted bower
Gives life and scent to every flower,
Whose most adored name incloses
Things abstruce, deep and divine,
Whose yellow tresses shine,
Bright as Evam fire . . .
O me thy Priest inspire!
For I to thee and thine immortal name,
In–in–in golden tunes,
For I to thee and thine immortal name,

In sacred raptures—flowing-flowing-swimming-swimming—
In sacred raptures swimming:
Immortal name-game-dame-tame-lame-lame-lame—
Pux! hath shame—proclaim—oh—
In sacred raptures flowing, will proclaim, not—
Oh me thy Priest inspire!
For I to thee and thine immortal name,
In flowing numbers filled with spight and flame—
Good! good! in flowing numbers filled with spight and flame.

This sad picture of the bombastic pedant belabouring his Muse for rhymes would be amusing enough even though it had no personal application; but the satire takes on salt and almost Attic flavour when we see how close is the parody, and when we imagine the glee with which the perpetrators must have watched the squirming of their victim. In *The Return From Parnassus* (II, iv, iii) Will Kempe is made to say, "O that Ben Jonson is a pestilent fellow; he brought up Horace giving the poets a pill, but our fellow Shakespeare hath given him a purge that hath made him bewray his credit." If Shakspere had no hand in *Satiromastix,* but was responsible for a now lost, but still severer drubbing to Jonson, we can only guess at the richness of the lost satire by the savour of that which it surpassed.

The academic plays known as the "Parnassus trilogy" are not primarily concerned with the Marston-Jonson quarrel, though in so highly topical a discussion of stage issues it would have been impossible to omit it altogether. As Dr. George Kitchin says (*op. cit.,* p. 63), "It meddles with the great poetomachia, but its scope is wider." Though the bibliography of this play is a long one, it is still quite unsafe to say anything very definite about it. Sir Edmund Chambers, can, as usual, be counted upon to state a conservative view of it (*Elizabethan Stage,* IV, p. 40):

The writer is much occupied with contemporary literature, but this does not justify the slapdash attempt of Fleay, ii, 347, to identify nearly all his characters with individual literary men. . . . The most that can be said is that there may be something of Marston in Furor Poeticus, and a good deal of Nashe, with probably also a little of

Greene, in Ingenioso, who ultimately takes flight, with Furor and Phantasma, to the Isle of Dogs (v. 3, 4).

> There where the blattant beast doth rule and raigne
> Renting the credit of whom ere he please.

Whomever Ingenioso may represent, it is clear that he is a writer of dangerous topical plays; for he observes to his friend (Act I, sc. 3):

> Faith, Academico, it's the fear of that fellow—I mean, the sign of the sergeant's head—that makes me to be so hasty to be gone. To be brief, Academico, writs are out for me to apprehend me for my plays; and now I am bound for the Isle of Dogs. Furor and Phantasma come after, removing the camp as fast as they can.

Precisely what the Isle of Dogs was meant to signify is never made quite clear. Furor says that when he arrives there he will take revenge on "Dan Phoebus," "sluttish Cynthia," and her "squirting boy Endymion," for allowing him to fall into a lousy state. Ingenioso realizes that this is, indeed, a "bold barking at the moon," but Philomusus reminds him that

> Exclaiming want, and needly care and cark,
> Would make the mildest sprite to bite and bark.

Phantasma is not quite sure it will be safe to bark in such terms, even in the Isle of Dogs. As he says,

> There are certain burrs in the Isle of Dogs called in our English tongue, men of worship; certain briars, as the Indians call them; as we say, certain lawyers: certain great lumps of earth, as the Arabians call them, certain grocers, as we term them.

Nevertheless, they all agree with Ingenioso:

> We three unto the snarling island haste,
> And there our vexed breath in snarling waste.

Furor says farewell to an unappreciative London, with all the pride of a Coriolanus:

> Farewell, my masters; Furor's a nasty dog,
> Nor can with a smooth glosing farewell cog.
> Nought can great Furor do but bark and howl,
> And snarl, and grin, and carl, and touse the world,
> Like a great swine, by his long, lean-ear'd lugs.
> Farewell, musty, dusty, rusty, fusty London;

Thou are not worthy of Great Furor's wit,
That cheatest virtu of her due desert
And sufferest great Apollo's son to want.

We have already noted the fact that the Recorder in this play is a satirical skit on Francis Brackyn. (*Elizabethan Stage,* III, p. 476.) It is, however, not possible, in a survey study of this kind, to enter into all the *pro* and *contra* evidence concerning the identities of most of the characters in this play. The same may be said for most, if not all the characters in the plays of the Poetomachia. That they are satirical portraits is conceded by almost all scholars; but few are agreed as to particular identifications. Occasionally we have a piece of outside testimony, such as Aubrey's statement concerning Volpone as Sutton; or The Alchemist as Dr. Dee; or Carlo Buffoono as Charles Chester; but for the most part, plausibility is our only guide; and till scholars present very detailed cases of plausibility, we must withhold our assent to definite identifications such as Hedon or Clove for Marston; or Anaides for Dekker; Crites for Jonson; Puntarvolo for Ralegh; Fastidious Brisk for Harvey; Bellamont for Chapman, etc., etc.

There is an almost devilish uncertainty connected with the great names of dramatic history. In the case of many an obscure figure in the sixteenth-century stage, there is no doubt concerning their identification. Thus, we know that Dekker's and Middleton's *Roaring Girl* was a dramatization of the bizarre life of Mary Frith (*ibid.,* p. 296); or again, that George Wilkins' *Miseries of Enforced Marriage* was "based on the life of Walter Calverley, as given in the pamphlets of 1605" (*ibid.,* p. 513); or Robert Yarington's *Two Lamentable Tragedies* was, as its title page indicates, the story of "the murder of Master Beech a Chaundler in Thames-streete, and his boye, done by Thomas Merry" on 23 August, 1594. But when a great and well-known dramatist like Ben Jonson is arrested "at the instigation of Northampton, his mortall enemie," and is "called before the Councell for his *Sejanus,* and accused of poperie and treason," as Jonson himself told Drummond (*ibid.,* p. 367), we are utterly unable to figure out the mystery.

The fact is, of course, that the study of the drama from the point of view of its social and political background has just begun. We hope that the present study will induce other students of the period to pursue the investigation much further in the cases of particular poets. We believe we have offered good and substantial reasons for believing that topicality in the drama was the rule rather than the exception, and we have also tried to show that these contemporary issues were normally presented under a mask or *prosopopoiea* of fancy or historical parallel. Fustian was, in other words, the normal device for avoiding prosecution for political propaganda or personal libel. The game was a dangerous one—dangerous enough to challenge the boldness and ingenuity of the cleverest men; and the result was a continued performance of unparalleled brilliance in literary history.

RALEGH AND MARLOWE

CHAPTER THIRTEEN

The Ralegh Legend

THE GREATEST OF MANY DISADVANTAGES in the kind of survey we have been making thus far is the absence of clear and detailed group pictures. In our attempt to show the wide-spread use of fustian for contemporary issues—its extent over a long period of time and over a wide area of space, and throughout the works of all sorts of artists, and upon every sort of stage—we have been obliged to sacrifice everywhere detail for panorama, and consecutive chronology for similarity of practice. Only so could we cover sufficient range to prove that the device was used by all poets, dramatic or otherwise, upon all stages, public or private, and for general as well as particular satire. We hope we have established this fact beyond all doubt, though we wish to state most emphatically that our study makes no pretence to be a complete history of the practice of fustian. Indeed, the materials for such a history are by no means yet available. Ground has been broken, considerable digging has unearthed much promising material, including, we hope, the foundation upon which such a history may one day be built. But the excavation has only begun, and it will be many years before the literary archeologists will be able to offer complete solutions of many fustian riddles in and out of the drama. If we have been able to convince our readers that the foundation is strong enough to bear the structures from which the miscellaneous and disordered fragments seem to have come—whether or not a given tentative reconstruction is acceptable—we shall have accomplished an important step.

There are many more steps to be taken, however, before we can properly apply the topical rather than the purely romantic formula to the rank and file of Tudor and Stuart drama, that is, before it can be asserted that topicality was the rule rather than the exception. We have seen that it is present in the works of practically all the dramatists—Gascoigne, Edwardes, Lyly,

Nashe, Peele, Chapman, Dekker, Day, Dayborn, Marston, Shakspere, Massinger, Middleton, Beaumont and Fletcher, Jonson, Munday, Webster, Tourneur, not to mention countless minor poets and anonymous authors. What we need now to enquire is whether or not the practice of topicality was the rule or the exception in the case of a given author, that is, were the plays of Lyly, Nashe, Jonson, Chapman, Dekker, Massinger, Marston, Middleton, Shakspere, etc., only occasionally topical, or were they usually so? Unfortunately we lack good modern editions of all too many of the great dramatists, and have hardly any at all of the less known ones. It is, however, patent to any student who has kept at all abreast in these matters that it is the experts, rather than the amateurs, who have been convinced concerning the preponderance of topicality in a given poet. Thus Professor Bond believes that it exists in almost every play of Lyly's; Gifford and Gardiner believe that it prevails in Massinger; Professor Parrott, without committing himself to detailed equations, has nevertheless stated clearly his belief in a generally intended parallel between the French politics exhibited in Chapman's plays, and the Court in which Chapman himself lived; Professor F. L. Lucas has suggested it, or entertained the suggestions of others, for most of the plays of Webster; and the editors of the Oxford Jonson have accepted it throughout his plays. It is too soon to prophesy what view the most recent editors of Shakspere will present when the Cambridge edition shall have been completed; but for as many plays as have been published, it is interesting to note that they have discussed seriously, and for the most part affirmatively, the presence of topical matter on a significant scale.

Aside from Greene, whose plays are only beginning to be worked on by modern scholars,* there is only one important dramatist in whose work, so far as I know, no such application has been sought. That poet is Marlowe. The isolation of his position in this respect is so striking, when once it has been brought to our attention, that our credulity is challenged, and we turn to our most recent studies of Marlowe to see what were his political and social backgrounds, and we find, to our

* See, for instance, Miss Ruth Hudson's study of Greene's *James IV and Contemporary Allusions to Scotland, PMLA,* 47, 652ff.

astonishment, that they have never been investigated, nor discussed in any fullness. Much has been made of Marlowe's murderers, but almost nothing at all of Marlowe's friends, associates, and patrons. Professor Tucker-Brooke, in his *Life of Marlowe* (p. 39) dismisses this whole group in a paragraph of five or six lines:

> Of men about London whom he might have met at Cambridge, Greene was an envier, and probably an enemy of Marlowe; Nashe was a friend.* Others with whom his name is particularly linked are Chapman and Chapman's intimate friend and fellow-poet, Mathew Roydon; Thomas Hariot, the mathematician and explorer; William, or Walter, Warner; and the young publisher-gentleman, Edward Blount.

Although Professor Tucker-Brooke admits that "this was excellent company," he passes on immediately to other matters without further discussion of them. Professor John Bakeless, in his book, *Christopher Marlowe* (New York, 1937), offers a chapter on the "Friends and Foes" of the poet. This is a more elaborate, if very informal, account of the Marlowe circle, but Dr. Bakeless does not attempt a serious appraisal of the influence of these men on Marlowe. In our opinion, however, before we can judge at all of the reflections of Marlowe's political and social background in his poetry, we must focus our attention somewhat closely upon these friends and colleagues, to see if we can learn something of their interests and Marlowe's possible share in them. This study, we feel, should be of interest to all students of Marlowe, whether or not they are persuaded concerning the reflection of this background in his poetry.

Before entering into the evidence which connects Marlowe with the group known as the Ralegh circle, we shall sketch in a character portrait of the protagonist who inspired, dominated, and very largely financed the activities of various members. Since this study does not aim to be, in any sense of the word, a biography of Ralegh, I have felt justified in emphasizing only those aspects of his personality and point of view which I feel, and which I hope to show, are reflected in Marlowe's poetry.

* References to Nashe in this study, *passim,* will show that this is untrue.

Perhaps not all the facts about Ralegh have yet been ferreted out from the archives of the period in which he lived, and it is possible that new light may influence our own appraisal of his character and career. There seems to be, however, abundant material easily available in the well known biographies, from which we can construct what may be called a poster-portrait or cartoon of him, easily recognizable to his contemporaries, in spite of, perhaps in some cases because of, the elements of caricature. In short, "the Ralegh legend" is easily come by, however shrewd a sifting may be required before we can arrive at the very truth about him.

No one would deny that during the years in which Marlowe must have known Ralegh, that is, from 1583-93, the two main issues on which Ralegh was concentrating his energies were: (1) the English campaign against Spain; and (2) possibilities of imperial expansion. These issues were, as a matter of fact, but two sides of the same political plan. It was Ralegh's passionate nationalism that made him the foe of the Queen's foes, who happened to be the French, Spanish, and Irish Catholics; and it was the same deep-seated emotion which made him determine to outrival those foes in the world of commerce as well as on the field of battle. Before the student of Marlowe can judge whether or not these particular enthusiasms were deliberately advertised and exploited in his plays, it will be necessary to set forth a somewhat precise description of Ralegh's position on both points.

Although, as Aubrey tells us, Ralegh was famed for his oratory and was "the ornament of the Juniors" while at Oxford, he first emerges into historical importance on the occasion of his accompanying his kinsman, Henry Champernoun, into France as one of a hundred mounted gentlemen volunteers sent by Elizabeth to the aid of the Prince of Condé, the Protestant leader. The Champernouns were connected by marriage with the Huguenot Comte de Montgomerie. It is obvious that in such an undertaking, under such Huguenot leadership, there would be afforded no check to an anti-Catholic prejudice. On the contrary, Ralegh's friendship for his cousin, and for one Jacques Le Moyne, whom he had met some time during his stay in France, doubtless strengthened a prejudice which was already strong enough to do violence to Ralegh's political acumen. Le Moyne was one of the survivors of the ill-fated Huguenot plantation in Florida. The tragedy of this early French experiment at colonization is succinctly described in Stebbing's *Sir Walter Ralegh* (p. 43):

In 1562 a French Protestant settlement had been attempted in Florida, Laudonnière reinforced it a couple of years later. But the jealousy of Spain was aroused. Pedro Melendez de Avila pounced down in 1565. He captured the forts. Eight or nine hundred Huguenots he hanged on the neighbouring trees as heretics, not as Frenchmen. Dominique de Gorgues, of Gascony, avenged their fate by hanging their Spanish supplanters in 1567, not as Spaniards, but as assassins. There the experiment at colonization ended. Neither Spain nor France had repeated the attempt. The whole land was vacant of white men.

Le Moyne was a distinguished artist and mathematician who performed for Laudonnière the same kind of service that, as we shall see, Hariot later did for Ralegh. We shall have occasion to say more of the friendship between this French Huguenot and Ralegh, when we are discussing the Virginia enterprise. Here I wish merely to point out that Ralegh's natural Protestant sympathies were not likely to receive any important check as a result of the contacts made on this French expedition.

There was, however, one aspect of war which Ralegh observed on this campaign, his reaction to which does full justice to his political perspicacity. I allude to his attitude toward civil wars, particularly those carried on under a mask of religion. As Stebbing observes (*op. cit.*, p. 10): "To Ralegh's keen sight the struggle would soon have displayed itself shorn of the glamour of religious enthusiasm. He regarded it simply as a civil war, by which 'the condition of no nation,' as he wrote later, 'was ever bettered.' " There could be, in his opinion, no such thing as a religious war, and he never tired of driving this lesson home to the English. In his "Discourse on War in General," (*The Works of Sir Walter Ralegh, Kt.* [Oxford, 1829], vol. vii, p. 284), he wrote:

History doth plainly tell us, that that furious war (which broke out in France) in the reign of Francis II, and which occasioned most barbarous murders, devastations, and such other calamities, (which are the common products of civil commotions, and by continuing near forty years had reduced France to the last misery), was begun and carried on by some few great men of ambitious and turbulent spirits, deluding the people with the cloak and mask only of religion, to gain their assistance to what they did more especially aim at. It is plain that the admiral Coligny advised the prince of Condé to side with the Huguenots, not only out of love to their persuasion, but to gain a party, and be made thereby the stronger.

Thus Ralegh wrote of the Huguenot hero, the Prince of Condé, but it need hardly be added, that with his background of strong Devonian Protestantism, the Catholic Church seemed to him the worst offender in this line. He adds:

Neither can any man think that the papists, out of the principle of the Christian religion, which enjoins us to be meek and charitable, did in few days' space cut the throats of nearly thirty thousand Protestants in France, many of whom were men of great fame and quality. . . . So that this Parisian massacre had no more religion in it than the Sicilian vespers, when in two hours' time all the French throughout the whole kingdom of Sicily were at once, with great barbarity, massacred, for no other reason but that the Sicilians might get their room.

Again and again Ralegh inveighs against the Crusades, especially against the Popes who prompted them. He declares (*ibid.*, p. 266) that:

It hath been their custom so shamefully to misuse the fervent zeal of men to religious arms, by converting the monies which they have levied for such wars to their own services, and by stirring up Christians one against another; yea, against their own natural princes, under the like pretence of serving God and the church.

Concerning the war between Pope Gregory II and the Emperor Leo III, he asks (*ibid.*, p. 270):

By what other art did the pope remove the siege, than by persuading the Lombards with a tale of Peter and Paul, that had consecrated the city of Rome with their precious blood? Thus was devotion made the cloak of treason, and thus did the popes first slip their necks out of the emperor's collar.

After Ralegh returned from France he soon took service in

Ireland, where again he was brought into contact with another aspect of Catholic action which he was sure to despise, namely, its fostering of "treasonable" rebellion. Nothing in his written works exceeds the rage with which he records the assistance given the Irish rebels by the Spanish forces of his most Catholic Majesty, and his biographers are faced with no more unpleasant task than the necessity of recording Ralegh's ferocity to the Spaniards who were compelled to surrender the Fort Del Ore while he was in partial command. The story is told by Oldys (*op. cit.*, p. 33):

While the lord deputy [Lord Grey of Wilton] lay before the fort, there arrived in the bay of Smerwick vice-admiral Bingham, and soon after Sir William Winter, admiral of the fleet, with fresh supplies. Hereupon the lord deputy resolved to besiege the fort by land, while the admiral should batter it by sea. But first the Spaniards were summoned to surrender at discretion. They answered, "They were sent, some from the holy father, who had given that realm to king Philip; and some from the king, who was to recover this land to the church of Rome, which by her majesty's means was become schismatical and excommunicate; therefore, in short, were obliged to retain what they had, and recover what they could." Nor did they omit the advantage they thought this parley would produce of finding the English unguarded, to make a sally upon them; but they were so disappointed through the vigilance and valour of Ralegh's company and that of Captain Denny, that such as were not left dead behind, were forced to retreat with more haste than good speed. The culverins and other pieces of ordnance being now landed, and a large mountainous bank laboriously cut through, for the carriages to pass to the place convenient for planting them, the deputy is said, by my author Hooker, to have given the enemy another summons by cannon-shot to surrender, and receive mercy. But they answered as before: thereupon the artillery was ordered to attack the fort both by land and water. Ralegh, as the same historian records, commanded the first three days after the opening of the trenches; and assaulted the fort so roughly from his battery, that he forced the Spaniards to several excursions; but they skirmished so warily, and hived again so nimbly, that there was no closing with them effectually. . . . But now the trenches for the full battery were drawn so near the Spaniards, and the English played their cannon so furiously and incessantly upon them from every side, that the enemy began to fear, somewhat prophetically, that what they had built for a garrison would prove their monument, and they should be buried alive in the ruins of it. Therefore, finding no succours arrive, they beat a parley, and hung out the white flag, crying out, *Misericordia, misericordia.* But the lord deputy would not listen to any treaty with the confederates of traitors and rebels; no, not so much as their departure with bag and baggage, or free passage to any one particular person; nothing but absolute surrender. . . . Then the said colonel did absolutely yield himself, the fort, with all therein; and craved only mercy, which it was not thought good (says my said author [Hooker]) to shew them.

At this point it would seem that Oldys could no longer approve of his hero and so he concludes with a much watered-down account of the massacre ensuing, and offers several tentative explanations. I give here, however, the summary of Hooker's account, by Stebbing (*op. cit.*, p. 17), who does not attempt to excuse or extenuate Ralegh's part in this atrocity, but he does point out that Ralegh's view as to "the shortest way" with the Irish rebels was by no means unique. It was identical with that of his superior, Lord Grey, who was entirely approved of and supported by his secretary, "the gentle Spenser." Stebbing says that after the unconditional capitulation of the garrison:

. . . Grey sent in Ralegh and Macworth, who had the ward of the day. They are stated by Hooker, in his continuation of Holinshed, to have made a great slaughter. Four hundred Spaniards and Italians were put to the sword. All the Irishmen and several of the Irish women were hanged. An Englishman and an Irish priest, who suffered the same doom first, had their legs and arms broken. Only the foreign officers were held to ransom. The act was that of the Deputy. Afterwards it was discovered that the massacre excited general horror throughout Europe. Attempts were made to repudiate sympathy with it on the Queen's part. Bacon wrote that she was much displeased at the slaughter. Her own letters to Grey comment on the whole proceeding as greatly to her liking. She expresses discontent only that she had not been left free to kill or spare the officers at her discretion. Ralegh cannot be accounted amenable for the atrocity. He is not named in Grey's despatch to the Council. But it would be folly to pretend that he disapproved it. Hooker, his eulogist, claims it for him as an eminent distinction. He cordially sympathized with Grey's ideal of a Mahometan conquest for Ireland.

This is, of course, from our point of view, terrific and unbearable; but if we would understand the temper of an audience that would thrill to the spectacle of *Tamburlaine* with all its gore and ruthlessness, and would experience satisfaction at the sight of the limbs of the enemy "capering in the air," we must face the fact that to otherwise decent people like Spenser and Ralegh, and many others, "ferocity to Irishmen was accounted policy and steadfastness." Ralegh protested again and again at the leniency of his immediate superior, the Earl of Ormond, who, though an Irishman, was loyal to the government, and was acting as Lieutenant of Munster; and he contrasts unfavourably the results of this mild policy with those of his half-brother, Sir Humphrey Gilbert, who had earlier (1569-70) been President of Munster during a similar uprising, but who had been recalled because of his savage treatment of the natives. Ralegh notes that during the two years of Ormond's rule the "traitors" of Munster had been multiplied by a thousand, whereas his brother Gilbert had been able with a third part of the garrison then in Ireland to suppress the trouble in two months. "Would God," he says, "Sir Humphrey Gilbert's behavior were such in peace as it did not make his good service forgotten and hold him from preferment he is worthy of!"

Although Ralegh did notable work in Ireland, he never looked upon the extermination of the natives there as a career, as he certainly did in the case of his Spanish activity. He thought meanly of the Irish as an unworthy enemy, and he got almost nothing in the way of plunder. Many years later he declared that when he was a captain in Ireland, a hundred foot and a hundred horse would have beaten all the force of the strongest provinces, for in those days the Irish fought only with darts, weapons that stood no chance whatever against the heavy ordnance of the English. He complained often of inadequate salary, and altogether made it clear that he regarded this Irish business as a mere stepping-stone to a better appointment. He wrote to Leicester in 1581, "I have spent some time here under the deputy, in such poor place and charge as, were it not for I knew him to be one of yours, I would disdain it as much as to keep sheep." He returned from Ireland in December, 1581, having been granted twenty pounds for his expenses, and, as all the world knows, though none knows *how,* he was speedily launched most auspiciously upon a court career that was soon to dazzle the eyes of his most sanguine admirers, as well as of his enemies. Preferments, grants, prizes followed in quick succession, in fact, so speedily as to put all his former patrons and promoters into a discomfiture of envy and alarm. Sir Robert Naunton describes how Ralegh very early broke away from his superior, Lord Grey, and set himself up as an unofficial, but highly regarded councillor in opposition to his chief. (*Fragmenta Regalia,* p. 49, in Arber's reprint of the 3d edition.) Naunton declares himself

. . . confident, that, among the second causes of his [Ralegh's] growth, (not denying, or rather acquiescing in his actions and accomplishments to have been first), that variance between him and the lord *Grey,* in his descent into *Ireland,* was a principall; for it drew them both over to the Councill Table, there to plead their cause; where he had much the better in the telling of his tale; and so much, that the queen and the lords took no slight mark of the man and his parts; for from thence he came to be known, and to have access to the Queen, and the lords; and then we are not to doubt how such a man would comply and learn the way of progression; and whether Leicester had then cast in a good word for him to the Queen, which would have done no harm, I doe not determine. But true it is, he had gotten the Queen's ear at a trice, and she began to be taken with his eloqution, and loved to hear his reasons to her demands; and the truth is, she took him for a kind of Oracle, which netled them all; yes, those he relied on, began to take this his suddain favour for an Alarum, to be sensible of their own supplantation, and to project his.

At all events, it is certain that Ralegh's humble apprenticeship was of short duration when once he had got a foot within the gates of the Court, and this fact is not inconsistent with his entire history. He was always too competent and too aggressive to be for any length of time subservient to any one. His own ideas pressed for utterance, and his own energy chafed restlessly under the restraint of organization, in which it often falls to the lot of a first-class person to be second or even lower in command to a person of third- or fourth-rate capacity. However that may be, by 1583 Ralegh had found a way to make himself "passing brave," that his appearance might be worthy of, and witness to his brilliant successes at court. An entry in the Middlesex Registers for 26 April, 1583, records the trial of one Hugh Pewe, gentleman, for the theft of "a jewel worth 80 pounds, a hat band of pearls worth 30 pounds, and five yards of damask silk worth 3 pounds, goods and chattles of Walter Rawley, Esq., at Westminster."

If one were to think of the value of these gewgaws in terms of their approximate modern equivalent (from five to ten times the rate of Elizabethan exchange), he could see that Mr. Ralegh, though not yet distinguished by the title of *Sir,* had no longer any need to compare himself with the much-disdained keeper of sheep. There are many such contemporary witnesses to Ralegh's sartorial elegance, descriptions of his exquisite armour, his impeccable taste in clothes, and his incomparable jewels. He was bitterly satirized by the Jesuit, Parsons, as "a courtier too high in the regard of the English Cleopatra, who wore in his shoes jewels worth 6600 gold pieces." This is, as Stebbing has observed, an obvious exaggeration; but it is all of a piece with the extravagant tradition which credits Ralegh with having worn a Court dress carrying 60,000 pounds worth of jewels. Of course, Ralegh was not unique in the display of sumptuousness; it was a fashionable requirement at Elizabeth's court; but it is significant that, amid such general lavishness, he should so manage to out-top all others in extremity of splendour as to render himself the subject of constant animadversion and a target for satire.

It must not be supposed, however, that his singularity of magnificence was alone responsible for his reputation. He was well made, and very handsome of countenance, and these were assets not easily to be forgiven among the rival minions of a virgin queen's court: but to his striking good looks he added a carriage of so much confidence, a manner so adroit, a wit so ready both for adapting himself to the moods of his royal mistress and for stimulating her self-esteem, that it was inevitable he should be feared and envied by his rivals as much as adored by those depending upon his success as a courtier. Naunton describes him in these early years, just after his return from Ireland, as having "a good presence in a handsome and well compacted person, a strong natural wit, and a better judgement; with a bold and plausible tongue whereby he could set out his parts to the best advantage."

Of all the kinds of stories about Ralegh, true and apocryphal, none are so plentiful as those which testify to his witty address, his turn for epigram, whether extempore or in verse, and his persuasive eloquence. There is no need here to retell Fuller's story of the Queen, the plashy place, and Sir Walter's "brain-wave" about the cloak, for there are others less hackneyed, which will serve our purpose as well. Incidentally, many of these anecdotes of Ralegh's instantaneous *retorte polite* reveal him in a role especially gratifying to the Queen, for it gave her an opportunity to show to all the Court that she was not only the inspirer, but the promoter of this fashion of felicitously mannered repartee. Indeed, according to Fuller, it was she who started the game, when she capped his line

Fain would I climb, yet fear I to fall

by scratching on the window beneath it

If thy heart fail thee, climb not at all.

Perhaps the most charming of all such little "duettos" is the one gleaned by "G. M.," in 1694 from an earlier unprinted MS, entitled *Apothegms of the English Nation.* It illustrates Ralegh's constant habit of using his position as favourite for the benefaction of others. Oldys says (*op. cit.,* p. 142):

> The truth is, Ralegh was so famous in these days for such like good offices, that the queen seems to have distinguished him by a title more honourable, in the proper sense it is to be here taken, than any other she conferred upon him: for one day, having told her he had a favour to beg of her, "When, sir Walter," said she, "will you cease to be a beggar?" To which he answered, "When your gracious majesty ceases to be a benefactor."

Almost the entire body of Ralegh's verse smacks of this epigrammatic flavour. Intellectual challenge was an instinct and became a habit with him. His mind naturally ran in a "counter, original" vein, and every utterance had a style peculiar to himself, though it has since been imitated by a whole school of wits, from John Donne through the Cavalier "Sons of Ben."

There are critics who lament the loss of passion under so much polish in Ralegh's verse. Be that as it may, there were plenty among his contemporaries to throw up their caps for this kind of polish, if not for a Pope of any kind. The Nymph's reply to Marlowe's *Passionate Shepherd* is an elaborate but especially engaging instance of this kind. I think not even Marlowe's most ardent admirer could fail to admit that Ralegh's is the wittier strain in the duet, which may, incidentally, constitute our earliest hint of a definite relationship between Ralegh and Marlowe. The poems are found copied out in a Commonplace Book belonging to John Thornborough, Chaplain to the Earl of Pembroke, for whose company Marlowe wrote *Edward II,* and possibly several other plays.* It may be interesting to note that Mrs. Thornborough was, according to Stephen Clapham, "very intimate" with Lady Audrey Walsingham, the wife of Marlowe's friend in Kent. (See p. 281.) Since none of these facts is dated, they may argue very little as to a personal relationship between Ralegh and Marlowe. At most, we cannot infer more than that the poems were handed about among mutual friends before their publication, though we might add that it would be a little odd for Sir Walter to bestow so flattering an attention upon a poem without making some friendly gesture to the poet who wrote it. But, as we shall see, there are other reasons for believing Marlowe to have been a member of the Ralegh circle.

Marlowe's enchanting, if conventional little *Pastoral,* is, of course, familiar to all, but it is printed here, lest the reader miss the tart contrast of Ralegh's *Reply,* which is anything but conventional.

Come, live with me and be my love,
And we will all the pleasures prove,
That grove or valley, hill or field,
Or wood and steepy mountain yield.

Where we will sit on rising rocks,
And see the shepherds feed their flocks
By shallow rivers, to whose falls
Melodious birds sing madrigals.

* See, Eleanor Grace Clark, *The Pembroke Plays,* (Philadelphia, 1928).

Pleas'd will I make thee beds of roses,
And twine a thousand fragrant posies;
A cap of flowers, a rural kirtle,
Embroider'd all with leaves of myrtle.

A jaunty gown of finest wool,
Which from our pretty lambs we pull;
And shoes lin'd choicely for the cold,
With buckles of the purest gold.

A belt of straw, and ivy-buds,
With coral clasps, and amber studs;
If these, these pleasures can thee move,
To live with me, and be my love!

Ralegh's Nymph replies:

If all the world and love were young,
And truth on every shepherd's tongue,
These pleasures might my passions move
To live with thee, and be thy love.

But fading flowers in every field
To winter floods their treasures yield;
A honey'd tongue, a heart of gall,
Is fancy's spring, but sorrow's fall.

Thy gown, thy shoes, thy beds of roses,
Thy cap, thy kirtle, and thy posies,
Are all soon withered, broke, forgotten,
In folly ripe, in reason rotten.

Thy belt of straw, and ivy-buds,
Thy coral clasps, and amber studs,
Can me with no enticements move,
To live with thee, and be thy love.

But could youth last, could love still breed;
Had joys no date, and age no need;
Then those delights my mind might move,
To live with thee, and be thy love.

This mood of witty disdain of "mere romance," this wilful subjugation of passion by *virtue* or "manliness," is revealed again and again in Ralegh's prose and verse. Writing to his son, he urges him not to allow his passion to enthral his judgment —"for that way lies misery." He admits that the great danger to be guarded against in women is their "beauty, by which all men in all ages, wise and foolish have been betrayed"; and he continues:

> Though I know it vain to use reasons or arguments to dissuade thee from being captivated therewith, there being few or none that ever resisted that witchery; yet I cannot omit to warn thee as of other things, which may be thy ruin and thy destruction. For the present time, it is true, that every man prefers his phantasy in that appetite before all other worldly desires, leaving the care of honour, credit, and safety in respect thereof: but remember, that though these affections do not last, yet the bond of marriage dureth to the end of thy life; and therefore better to be borne withal in a mistress than in a wife; for when thy humour shall change, thou art yet free to choose again (if thou give thyself that vain liberty) . . .

Though he admits that beauty is a *sine qua non* in a wise selection, he concludes by warning his son: "Have therefore ever more care that thou be beloved of thy wife, rather than thyself besotted on her." Ralegh's poetry is permeated with this antithesis—the power of Beauty to enthral, but the necessity for the man of affairs to keep his head. The following is one in point:

Now have I learned, with much ado at last,
By true disdain to kill desire;
This was the mark at which I shot so fast;
Unto this height I did aspire
Proud Love, now do thy worst, and spare not;
For thee and all thy shafts I care not!

What hast thou left wherewith to move my mind?
What life to quicken dead desire?
I count thy words and oaths as light as wind;
I feel no heat in all thy fire.
Go charge thy bows, and get a stronger;
Go break thy shafts, and buy thee longer.

In vain thou bait'd thy hook with Beauty's blaze;
In vain thy wanton eyes allure;
These are but toys, for them that love to gaze:
I know what harm thy looks procure:
Some strange conceit must be devised,
Or thou and all thy skill despised.

No one among the courtly poets wrote more rhapsodically of the Queen than Ralegh, and yet, when writing to his cousin Carew (about 1589) he scrupled not to show plainly how "business-like" such praises were. "The Queen," he writes, "thinks that George Carew longs to see her; and, therefore, see her." Apparently Carew took Ralegh's advice to heart, for we find him writing to the Queen when she was seventy years old, declaring his envy of "the blessing others enjoy in beholding your Royal person whose beauty adorns the world." Certainly Ralegh was behind the little comedy described by his friend Arthur Gorges in 1592, when Ralegh was in disgrace in the Tower for his secret marriage to Elizabeth Throckmorton. The following letter is transcribed from Miss Helen Sandison's article "Arthur Georges: Spenser's Alcyon" (*PMLA,* 43, pp. 657-58):

Honorable S:[r] I cannot chuse but aduertyse you of a straunge Tragedye y[t] this d[ay] had lyke to haue fallen owte betweene the Captayne of the Guarde, and the Lyietennaunt of the Ordenaunce; If I had not by greate chaunce cum*m*en a[tt] the very instant to haue turned it into a Com*m*edye. For vppon the re[port] of hyr Ma:[ts] beinge att S:[r] George Caryes; S:[r] W. Rawly hauing gazed an[d] syghed a longe tyme att hys study wyndow; fro*m* whence he mygh[t] discerne the Barges and boates aboute y[e] blackfryars stayers; soodayn[ly] he brake owte into a greate distemper, and sware y[t] hys Enymyes hadd of purpose brought hyr Ma:[tie] thethar, to breake hys gaule [in] sounder w[t] Tantalus Torment; that when shee wentt a way he myght see hys deathe before hys Eyes; w[t] many such lyke conc[eyts.] And as a mann transported w[t] passion; he sware to S:[r] George Care[w] that he wolde disguyse hymselfe; and gett into a payer of Oares to Ease hys mynde butt w[t] a syght of the Queene; or els he pr*o*test[ed] his harte wolde breake. But the trusty Iaylor wold non of y[t] for displeasing the hygher powers, as he sayde w[ch] he more respect[ed] then the feading of hys humor; and so flatly refused to p*er*mitt hyme[e]. But in conclusion vppon this disspute they fell flatt owt to collor[yq] outragius wordes; w[t] stryuing and struggling att y[e] doores, y[t] al[l] lamenes was forgotten; and in the fury of the conflyct, y[e] Iaylor [he] had hys newe perwygg torne of hys crowne. And ye[t heare] the battle ended not, for att laste they had gotten ow[te theyr daggers]; w[ch] when I sawe I played the styckler betwene theme, and [so] purchased such a rapp on the knockles, y[t] I wysht bothe theyr [pates] broken; and so w[t] much a doo, they stayed theyr brawle [to see] my bloodyed fyngers. Att the fyrste I was ready to breake wth laughinge; to see them too so scamble and brawle lyke mad[e] menn, vntyll I saw the Iron walkinge; and then I dyd my best to apease the fury. As yet I cannot reconcyle them by any p*er*swasions. for S:^{r} Walt: swears y^{t} he shall hate hyme for so restra[y]ning hyme fro*m* the syght of hys M^{rs} whylst he lyues; for y^{t} he knowe[s] not (as he sayd) whethar euer he shall see hyr agayne when shee is gonn the progress. And S:^{r} Georg, on hys syde swares y^{t} he had rather h[e] should lose hys longinge then y^{t} he wolde drawe on hyme hyr Ma. $^{[ties]}$ displeasur by such lyberty. Thys they contynew in mallyce and sn[ar]lynge, but I ame sure all the smarte lyghted on me [I] cannot tell wheare I should more alowe of y^{e} passionat lou[er] or the trusty Iaylor. But yf y^{r} selfe had seene it as I dy[d] yow wold haue byne as hartely merry and sorry; as Euar yow weare in all y^{r} lyfe for so shorte a tyme. I praye y^{u} pa*r*do[n] my hasty wrytten narration; wch I acquaynt y^{u} w^{t} hoping [yow] wyll be the peacemaker; butt good S:^{r} lett nobody kno[we] thearof. for I feare S:^{r} W. Rawly; wyll shortely growe [to be] Orlando furioso; If the bryght Angelyca perseuer agaynst [hyme] a l[y]tt[le] lon[ger.]

Y^{r} honors humbly to be com*ma*unded London in haste this wensdaye.

A Gorges

If yow lett the Q: Matie know hearof as y^{u} thinck good be it, butt otherwyse good S:^{r} keepe it secrerr for theyr credytts; for they know not of my discourse wch I could wyshe hyr Ma:^{tie} knewe.

In like manner and with a like intention of having Elizabeth see the effusion, Ralegh himself wrote in a note to Robert Cecil, appended to a requisition of cloth for new coats for his Yeoman:

My heart was never broken till this day, that I hear the Queen goes away so far off—whom I have followed so many years with so great love and desire, in so many journeys, and am now left behind her, in a dark prison all alone. While she was yet nigher at hand, that I might hear of her once in two or three days, my sorrows were the less; but even now my heart is cast into the depth of all misery. I that was wont to behold her riding like Alexander, hunting like Diana, walking like Venus, the gentle wind blowing her fair hair about her pure cheeks; sometimes sitting in the shade like a Goddess; sometimes singing like an angel; sometimes playing like Orpheus.

Only a Ralegh would have had the audacity to lug into so awkward a context such a patently official compliment. His arrogant assumption of both moods at once, i.e., of passion and of superiority to passion, is recognized by a contemporary critic, Arthur Puttenham. In his *Art of English Poesy,* (1589), he declared that "for ditty and amorous ode," Sir Walter Ralegh's vein was the "most lofty, insolent, and passionate." Lofty, insolent, and passionate his verse surely is!

It is, perhaps, not too much to say that before 1589, when Spenser, thanks to Ralegh's introduction, brought three complete books of his *Faerie Queene* to London, Ralegh was esteemed one of the best poets in England, especially at Court.

It must be admitted, however, that he apparently took no pains to atone for his dangerous gifts, or to placate those about him less highly endowed. Aubrey, who is not first-hand authority, but who knew several persons who knew Ralegh well, says: "He was a tall, handsome, and bold man; but his naeve was, that he was damnable proud. Old S^{r}. Robert Harley, of Brampton-Brian Castle (who knew him), would say, 't was a great question, who was the proudest, S^{r}. W. or S^{r}. Thomas Overbury, but the difference that was, was judged on S^{r}. Tho. side. . . . He had a most remarkable aspect, an exceeding high forehead, long-faced, and sour eie-lidded . . ." Aubrey also tells the story of how "old John Long, who then wayted on S^{r}. W. Long [a great friend of Ralegh's] being one time in the privy-garden with his master, saw the earle of Nottingham wipe the dust from Sir Walter R.s shoes with his cloake, in compliment." This story, like so many of Aubrey's, may be mere gossip, but the fact remains that a mere knight, who dared to be as proud as Ralegh, was not a comfortable person to have about, in a milieu where everyone was edging for first place. It is not to be wondered at that he was regarded, on the one hand, as "that glorious and gallant cavalier sir Walter Rawleigh," whom, as James Howell tells us, "his enemies confess" to be "one of the weightiest and wisest men that this island ever bred," and on the other hand, that he should have procured himself to be called "the best hated man of the world, in Court, city and country." Of course, these stories come from many sources—gossip, slander, and mere hearsay, and may be largely, if not wholly, untrue; but they bear witness to Ralegh's reputation as a "contemner and scorner," on the one hand, and on the other, as a beautiful *daemon* of absolutely irresistible winsomeness and fascination.

Again and again his contemporaries comment upon the power of his eloquence and personal magnetism to move even his enemies to his side. At his first trial in 1603 he furnished an overwhelming instance of this extraordinary power. Carleton says that he answered Coke and the rest of his accusers "with that temper, wit, learning, courage, and judgment, that, save it went with the hazard of his life, it was the happiest day that ever he spent." He was, as a result, almost acquitted. "In one word, never was a man so hated and so popular in so short a time." Roger Ashton, one whom James had commissioned to bring to him at Wilton House an account of the trial, said, "Never man spoke so well in the time past, nor would in the time to come," and he added, "Whereas, when he saw Sir Walter Ralegh first, he was so led with the common hatred that he would have gone a hundred miles to see him hanged, he would, ere they parted, have gone a thousand to save his life."

These suggestions alone would seem enough, both in variety and colourfulness, to indicate the outline of a significant personality; but they constitute the merest foreground for a portrait of Ralegh. All this might have been true of him before he did any of the things for which he is now famous—before he quarreled with Essex, or harried the Spaniards, or "ransacked the seas" while searching for the Northwest passage, or planted his colony in Virginia, (thus inaugurating the greater British Empire), or before he championed Udal, or nettled the theologians by his bold reasonings, or taught the English how to smoke tobacco in a silver bowl. But before describing these activities of Ralegh, we should like to introduce to our readers one or two other courtiers who, socially at least, were important luminaries in the Ralegh orbit.

CHAPTER FOURTEEN

The Triplicity That Denies the Trinity

To THE MALEVOLENT TONGUE of Lord Henry Howard, history owes the slanderous description of the trio of friends, Sir Walter Ralegh, Henry Brooke, eighth Baron Cobham, and Henry Percy, ninth Earl of Northumberland, as "the infamous triplicity that denies the Trinity." The libelous phrase was attached to the so-called "atheists" who, under the stimulus of Ralegh and the inspiration of his learned friend and tutor, Thomas Hariot, had devoted themselves to the study of astronomy and other branches of navigation science. This study will eventually have much to say of Sir Walter's "little academe"; for the moment, however, it seems best to isolate Lord Cobham from the group, since, except on the ground of a general persecution in which Lord Cobham shared alike with Ralegh and Northumberland, there is almost nothing in his personal history to account for his presence in the "school of night" picture. He was, however, the "Achilles' heel" of the enterprise as far as the Satirists went. Unlike Ralegh and Northumberland, Cobham had no political theory to foster, nor, so far as we know, had he any flair for science. He was neither "papist" like Percy, nor "free-thinker" like Ralegh. Indeed, it is difficult to see how so frivolous a person as Henry Brooke could ever have earned even a derisive title that implied serious thinking on his part, free or otherwise.

Historians have been so unanimous in their condemnation of this man that one is tempted, for the sake of fair play, to act the part of Devil's Advocate and challenge their authority. It is hard to accept, without indisputable evidence, Anthony Weldon's verdict of "silly Lord and a fool," and "a worthless Mortal known to have neither honour, virtue, principle, or veracity" (*op. cit.,* p. 28); or Stebbing's estimate of him as "garrulous, puffed up with a sense of his own importance, full of levity and passion, and morally, if not physically, a coward."

To temper these harsh judgments, one should keep in mind the fact that this man was honoured and trusted by the Queen, and that he was the intimate friend and companion of Ralegh and Northumberland and Cecil and Lord Grey and Sir John Stanhope and Sir George Carey and many others.

From the foregoing list of names, it will be clear to the student of the period that Cobham's friends and associates were almost exclusively members of the anti-Essex faction or Cecil party, under which informal label may be included all those who depended on Cecil rather than on Essex to procure them royal favours. The dark theme of bitter rivalry and enmity between these factions is woven into almost every episode of Marlowe's literary career, and forms, in a sense, a certain unifying thread which connects them all.

Unfortunately, however, there exists no direct link between Marlowe and Cobham. The relationship must be traced, if at all, through the fringe of the Ralegh circle. Henry Brooke was the son and heir of William Brooke, seventh Lord Cobham, a man of position and learning, a Knight of the Garter, a statesman and "a great patron of literature" (Vicary Gibbs, *Complete Peerage,* III, p. 349), who, at his death on 24 January, 1597, was the holder of many important posts, among which were those of Lord Chamberlain, Warden of the Cinque Ports, Constable of Dover Castle, and Lord Lieutenant of the County of Kent. The most persistent researches have not availed to discover the birth date of his eldest son, Henry, the subject of this study. The most recent *Complete Peerage* (Vicary Gibbs) does not even venture an approximate date. Does this little mystery seem to indicate that Lord Cobham kept his age a carefully guarded secret? Who can say? His long period of bachelorhood might have made such a course useful. The only authenticated portrait which I have been able to discover *

* Repeated searches in the files of the National Portrait Gallery in London and elsewhere have failed to locate any genuine portrait of Cobham other than the figure carrying the sword in the painting of Lady Ann Russell's wedding, now at Sherborne Castle. This blithe personality has generally been identified as Henry Brooke. Recently, however, through the kindness and efficiency of Mr. Louis Cohen, of the Argosy Bookshop, New York City, I have acquired a reprint of an engraving made of this "gallant courtier" when he was only "Henry Brooke, *Esquier.*" The portrait was made by Remigius Hogenbergh and bears the date 1582. The reprint was made from a unique original in the collection of

is one dated 1582, some fourteen years earlier than the date of the quarrel of which we are speaking. From this portrait one might guess him to have been in his middle forties.

As far as Essex and Cobham were concerned, in the complicated rivalry of the Court factions, the feud came to a head over the contest for the wardenship of the Cinque Ports, left vacant at the death of Lord William Cobham. In 1596 Rowland Whyte, in a letter to Sir Henry Sidney, dated 21 February, furnishes the first item in the story of this contest (*Letters and Memorials of State* . . . written and collected by Sir Henry Sidney, ed. by Arthur Collins, [1746], II, p. 18):

> My Lord Cobham is ill in Deed, and much fallen away, and now as I heare, his Sonne Mr Harry comes daily to the Queen, and the Father is willing to make Resignation of such places as he holds to the Queen, and to his Sonnes; especially the Cinque Ports.

The noble Lord had scarcely breathed his last before the scramble for his honourable posts began. Among these, the wardenship of the Cinque Ports was one of the most coveted. In spite of the great names entered in the list of contestants for the post—among them the Queen's closest relative, Baron Hunsdon, Shakspere's immediate patron, and Lord Buckhurst, and Lord Willoughby, and Sir Edward Wooton, and Sir Henry Sidney—the real battle was, from the beginning, between Essex and Cobham. Essex wanted the position for his protégé Sidney, and Cobham wanted it for himself. Early in the game, the Countess of Huntingdon, writing from the Court, told Rowland Whyte that she feared Cobham "would carry it away from all, for his favour was great and his friends in greatness and authority here." (*Ibid.*, p. 23.) Lady Essex, however, assured him that "she was of opinion that he should never have it, no worth being in him to deserve it." (*Ibid.*, p. 35.) Essex himself spared no pains in his opposition to the choice of Cobham, ever "laying before her Majesty his unworthiness and unableness to do her service" (*ibid.*, p. 24), and, at the same time, pressing the case for his own candidate, Sir Henry Sidney. In

---

Richard Hull, Esq., and published in 1791 by J. Thane. In its present form it is surrounded by a framing design bearing the inscription "S[r] Henri Brooke Cobham Knight," a title which, of course, could not have belonged to him at the date of the original portrait.

vain Sir Henry, through his secretary, offered Cecil "a fair suite of hangings to have it effected" (*ibid.*, p. 37), and to Cecil's wife "two coach mares," (*ibid.*, p. 37), and finally prevailed upon Lady Scudamore to present a pleading letter to the Queen. When the lady was asked if she knew the contents, she replied, untruthfully, in the negative; whereupon the Queen observed dryly, "Then it is much ado about the Cinque Ports." Lady Scudamore reported that her Majesty's comments while reading the plea for Cobham's rival was none other than "two or 3 Pughs"! (*Ibid.*, p. 97.) Again and again Essex used "all persuasions as a Councillor to make her Majesty see the dangers of those places [the Cinque Ports] and the necessity of a soldier to command them." (*Ibid.*, p. 97.) However, in 1597 Cecil was the better ally at Court. Whyte wrote on the last Saturday "nn [Lady Rich] says 200 [Cecil] does greatly labour 1500 [the Queen] for 30 [Cobham]," and "as for CC [Countess of Huntingdon]," he found "a beginning of feare in her to be seen to speak in it" [i.e., for Sidney] "for considering how Things stand now, all see in 200 [Cecil] Power to do Good and Harme, and all are fearful to displease." (*Ibid.*, p. 47.) Be it remembered that Cecil was Lord Cobham's brother-in-law, having in 1589 married his sister, Elizabeth Brooke. In spite of all that Essex could say or do to prevent it, in the end the plum went to Cobham "in respect of his friends," says Whyte, "and the particular good opinion she [the Queen] conceived of him, whom she used in some kind of service." (*Ibid.*, p. 97.) We are told that when the Queen informed Essex that Cobham should have it, the mortified favourite announced his intention of withdrawing from Court. Whyte described him as "mightely crossed in all things." *(Ibid.*, I, p. 357.) Certainly he made no attempt to hide his vexation, though it behooved him to make some sort of peace with Cecil when confronted with the *fait accompli*. Even this official peace was, however, beyond Essex's powers of dissimulation when he failed to win in a second contest, in which he had opposed to Cobham his friend Sidney for the place of Lord Lieutenant of the Shire of Kent. The particular scandal of this appointment lay in Cobham's comparative unfitness to levy soldiers, he being a courtier almost by profession, whereas his rival,

Sidney, was not only an experienced soldier, but, apparently, the choice of his fellow Kentish men. (*Ibid.*, pp. 24, 44, 62.) Rowland Whyte writes, on 5 November, 1597, to his master, "Surely, the peace concluded between the Earl of Essex and 200 [Sir Robert Cecil] I fear will burst out to terms of unkindness; My Lord Cobham, upon rumour of Ostend's besieging, to levy men in Kent, is made Lord Lieutenant of the shire; such power hath his friends in court that they are able to advance their allies." (*Ibid.*, p. 75.) When a second Armada became a real possibility, Cobham was given command of the army in Kent, a troop numbering 12,000 men. (*Ibid.*, p. 115.)

Politically speaking, therefore, at least from the point of view of the Essex faction, with which Shakspere undoubtedly allied himself, Cobham would not have been an impossible prototype for Falstaff, the unworthy recipient of the King's offices through the patronage of his "great" friends, the man who "waits at court for the obtaining of suits" (*I Henry IV*, I, ii, 80), the scandalous soldier whose military incompetence is evidenced in all his undertakings, but in nothing was so outrageous as in his levying of soldiers.

Socially speaking, the parallel is even more striking. If Falstaff is a satire on anyone, it must be on a philandering bachelor who is "some fifty odd" or "inclining to three score," "of a pleasing eye and a most noble carriage," and, to put the matter mildly, "little better than one of the wicked." (*I Henry IV*, I, ii, 106.) We have already noted that in 1582 Henry Brooke appears to have been in his middle or late forties. In 1596, therefore, he would be "some fifty odd" or "inclining to three score." A glimpse at his social career at court and elsewhere will convince the reader that his philandering qualifications for the role of Falstaff prototype are, if one may say so, first-class. On 7 March, 1596/7, Whyte reports that he has been "told very secretely today that the now Lord Cobham shall marry Mrs. Russell of the Privy Chambre." (*Ibid.*, p. 26.) Lady Anne Russell was one of the Queen's favored ladies-in-waiting, and it was, in fact, through her intercessions that the post of the Cinque Ports was finally manoeuvred into Cobham's possession. By the sixteenth of that same month, Whyte tells his master that he is "credibly informed that the Lord Cobham shall marry my Lord Oxford's daughter," and that he was to have with her £12,000"! (*Ibid.,* p. 30.) By 18 August, 1599, he wrote that "Mrs. Ratcliffe hath kept her chamber these four days, being somewhat troubled at my Lady Kildare's unkind using of her, which is thought to proceed from her love to my Lord Cobham." (*Ibid.,* p. 118.) The bewitching little Ratcliffe put on her "white satin gown, all embroidered, richly cut upon good cloth of silver, that cost £180" (*ibid.,* p. 48), and might have been successful in ensnaring the "old bird," had not her life been cut short in November by a fatal illness. In reporting her death and funeral on the thirteenth, Whyte adds, "Now that Mrs. Ratcliffe is dead, the Lady Kildare hopes that my Lord Cobham will proceed on his suit to her." (*Ibid.,* p. 141.) Meantime, 10 March, 1597/8 Whyte reports that there is a "speach that my Lord Cobham shall marry Spencers Daughter, and have with her £12,000." (*Ibid.,* p. 95.) But it was more than a year before poor Lady Kildare captured this astonishing "lady-killer," and then not until he had induced the Queen to give her a very sizable dowry. On 25 February, 1599, he was still, if not fancy-free, at least marriage-free, for on that date Whyte reported that "my Lord Cobham has wrenched his foot, and is not for the pains able to come abroad, which so much troubles the Lady Kildare that upon hearing Sir Walter Ralegh was newly come to court from him, just when the Queen's diet was sent for, she sent for him to come unto her in all haste, else the well-carving of the Queen's meat would be marred for the day." Whyte adds, *"res est solliciti plena timoris amor;* she wishes an end in it, but it seems he finds delay for it." (*Ibid.,* p. 172.) By 13 April, 1600, he was still stalling over the money settlement. Whyte writes that he understands Lord Cobham is "engaged in the matter of contract" with Lady Kildare. "But," he adds, "ere he will marry her, looks that her Majesty shall bestow something upon her, and he desires it may be land in exchange; if he will not, or cannot get Oteford Park, he means, as I hear, to get something of her Majesty round about it." (*Ibid.,* p. 187.) Finally, after rumours of secret marriage and seemingly endless negotiations about the dot, the marriage did take place on 27 May, 1601.

Students of the period need not be reminded of the fact that it was during these many months in which Lord Cobham was flourishing under the combined blandishments of the Ladies Fortuna, Kildare, and the Queen, that Essex lay prostrate under the frown of all three. There is abundant evidence that among the whole pack that brought Essex down, for no one did he feel so much hatred, such contempt and loathing, as for Cobham. In March, 1595/7, Whyte reported that Cobham "hearing how disdainfully my Lord of Essex speaks of hym in Public, doth likewyse protest to hate the Earl as much" (*ibid.*, p. 30); and in June he "made his Complaint to the Queen that My Lord Essex's Anger to him grew by doing of her Service and by doing her Commandments, and therefore he was assured that she wold protect hym and grace hym. Her Majesty byd hym not Doubt of it, and that no Man shuld wrong hym." (*Ibid.*, p. 54.) Birch tells us that Essex often referred to Cobham as "the sycophant," and that for him and a certain lady, whom he dubbed "the spider of the court," he entertained more contempt than for any person living. The equation of "the spider" with Lady Kildare would not be a bad guess; but, of course, it would be nothing but a guess. There is, however, no doubt about the hard names Essex hurled at his two chief enemies, Cobham and Ralegh. When he had made his last desperate gesture and had been, with his friends, driven back into his own house and surrounded by a posse of men led by Cobham and Ralegh, he came out on to the leads of the house, and there declaimed against that "caterpillar" and that "atheist," declaring: "I would think my death most honourable if by my death I might likewise end their lives, and that I had done God, my prince, and my country good service by rooting out such atheists and caterpillars from the earth." (C. C. Stopes, *op. cit.*, pp. 192-93.)

We have already alluded to Essex's bitter complaint that "The prating tavern haunter speakes of me what he lists; the frantic libeller writes of me what he lists; they print me and make me speak to the world, and shortly they will play me upon the stage." (*State Papers, Elizabethan, Domestic,* 1598-1601.) These words describe, of course, the methods of Essex's political rivals; but there is ample proof that Essex was playing the same game of literary and stage propaganda against his enemies. We have already noted in the first part of this study how Essex's cause was supported by songsters, balladiers, and dramatists, in particular by Daniels and by Shakspere. Camden tells us, that while in custody, preparatory to an investigation into his conduct, Essex's friends endeavored to excite and maintain popular feeling in his behalf. Bruce, the editor of Hayward's *Annals,* tells us in particular that "the conduct of the Queen's advisers, and through them, that of the Queen herself, was made the subject of unsparing condemnation; defamatory libels against them were spread abroad on every side." (*Hayward's Annals,* ed. by Bruce for the Camden Society, p. x.) When in November, 1599, the Lords of the Council made public declaration of the official charges against Essex, they made special mention of this literary campaign, outlining the steps to be taken "for the Reformation of divers Abuses offered to Her Majestie and her Councell." In a letter to Sir Robert Sidney, Mr. Francis Woodward described these abuses as follows (*Sidney Papers,* II, p. 146):

There are many dangerous Libells cast Abroade, in Courte, Cittie, and Countrey, as also by Table and Alehowse Talke Abroade, both in Cittie and Countrey, to the great Scandall of her Majestie and her Councell. And first my Lord Keeper (as his Place served) did declare that it was her Majesties Pleasure, and expresse Commandment, that all Gentlemen, and especially Justices of Peace, should repayre into the Countrey, not only to maynteyne Hospitalitie for the Relieff of the Poore, but that those which were Justices, and put in Aucthoritie for the Preservacion of the Peace, should chieflie, in this dangerous Tyme, see her Subjects kept in due Obedience, and to ponishe the Offenders. And that at this Tyme there were verry many sedicious People spread Abroade to breede Rebellion, who have not only bruted abroade many falce and slaunderous Speeches ageinste her Majestie and Councell, conserning the Marshallinge of the Affayres and State of Ireland; but also have throwen Abroade many scandelous Libells in the Courte, Cittie, and Countrey; Which Kinde of People, he did censure to be no better then Traytors: And thereupon did, in her Majesties Name, straightly charge all Judges, Justices, and other Officers, to make dilligent Enquiry, not only of such Persons as were Makers of such Libells, and Talkers of such sedicious Speeches, but also all those that did keepe Company with any such; to the Intente that they might not only receve due Ponishment therefore, but that thereby the Autors thereof might be the better boulted out, and known.

We have already drawn attention to one dramatic satire on this sort of spy work in the Egerton *Richard II.* The authorities were, however, wholly unable to stop this paper warfare. The plays were often made in private houses, and so were impossible to control. We should give much to know the names or subjects of the plays referred to by Whyte (*Sidney Papers* II, p. 91), in the letter of 15 February: "Sir Gilley Meiricke [Essex's steward] made at *Essex* House Yester night a very great Supper. There were at yt, my Ladys *Lester, Northumberland, Bedford, Essex, Rich;* and my Lords of *Essex, Rutland, Monjoy,* and others. They had 2 Plaies, which kept them up till 1 o Clock after Midnight." On 23 December, Roland Whyte states that "At Court, upon the very White Walles, much villany hath bene wrytten against 200." [Sir Robert Cecil.] Camden refers to the "most immoderate praise" of Essex, which was handed out from the pulpits by the clergy who sided with the once popular hero, now being, in their opinion, done to death by an ungodly, atheistic cabal. Could the character of Oldcastle-Falstaff have been part of that anti-Cobham propaganda which set out to inform the Queen how worthless a man it was to whom she intrusted the levying of soldiers, on whom she was willing to bestow offices, commands, lands and titles, honours of every sort, no matter how absurdly inappropriate? There is a certain amount of evidence leading to such a conclusion. In the first place, there is considerable justification for considering *I Henry IV* as Shakspere's second satire on the "school of night," *Love's Labour's Lost* being the first to mock "these earthly god-fathers of heaven's lights" who "give a name to every fixed star," but who "have no more profit of their shining nights that those that walk and wot not what they are." * The scene at Gadshill is studded with similar gibes. The "lads" in Falstaff's crew gaily dub themselves "squires of the night's body," and "gentlemen of the shade," and "minions of the moon"; and they admit that they "that

* The full discussion of the fustian element in *Love's Labour's Lost* is reserved for a later chapter (see pp. 335ff.). Here it is mentioned only to point the connection between the two attacks on the School of Night.

take purses go by the moon and the seven stars and not by Phoebus," and they boast that it is under the countenance of their "noble and chaste mistress the moon" that they steal. Hal and Poins are the brains of this "nightly enterprise," Falstaff is the booby.

As we shall subsequently see, the Essex faction carried on, through their poets, an elaborate literary campaign against the "school of night" and its poets Marlowe, Drayton, Roydon, and Chapman. By poems, plays, and pamphlets, such "fleshly poets" as Greene, Nashe, Harvey, and Lodge strove to discredit the excellence and to minimize the importance of the "high line" taken by the astronomical poets of the Ralegh circle. In this company certainly Cobham played the role of booby—Falstaff, and it was Shakspere who showed him up as the "dram of eale" that corrupted all the noble substance of their austere reputations "to its own scandal." But before we can accept with confidence the character of Falstaff as a satire on Cobham, it will be necessary to correlate the play somewhat more closely with certain known facts of Cobham's social and political history.

On 8 July, 1599, the Countess of Southampton wrote to the Earl, her husband, the friend and patron of Shakspere, appending to the letter the following postscript written upside down on the last page (*Cecil Papers,* CI, 16. See, Stopes, *op. cit.,* p. 160):

Al the nues I can send you that I think wil make you mery is that I reade in a letter from London that Sir John Falstof is by his Mrs. Dame Pintpot made father of a godly milers them, a boy thats all heade and veri little body; but this is a secrit.

On this news item, Sir Edmund Chambers says *(Shakespeare,* II, p. 198): "Lady Southampton's gossip is probably of some acquaintance whom she nicknames Falstaff. . . . One would guess at Henry Lord Cobham, but he appears to have had no children." There is something almost naïve in Sir Edmund's objection to the Cobham-Falstaff equation on the ground that he had no children. A man's illegitimate children are often enough lost to the records, especially those that are born rickety, as this one seems to have been. As we have seen, Cobham was not married at the date of this letter. In fact, his secret marriage did not take place until 21 May, 1600. A far stronger objection lies in the uncertainty regarding Cobham's extreme corpulence in 1599. In 1582, as we have noted, he was not fat. He was, in fact, rather handsome, elegantly attired, and dignified of bearing. One would guess him to be in his middle or late forties. If we knew more about *The Jealous Comedy,* the early play supposedly underlying Shakspere's *Merry Wives,* we might come closer to solving this mystery of "fat meat," which insists on intruding into any discussion of a prototype for Falstaff. *The Jealous Comedy* is the story of a befooled lover who was, as Sir Edmund Chambers says *(Shakespeare,* I, p. 426), "not a fat knight but a 'simpering lady-killer' with the characteristics of Joseph Surface." Such a description would, as we shall see presently, fit Lord Cobham to perfection and would, moreover, coincide with Falstaff's description of himself as "a goodly portly man, i'faith, and a corpulent, of a cheerful look, a pleasing eye and a most noble carriage." His age was "some fifty, or, by'r lady, inclining to three-score." He is much given to jokes at his own expense, and infinitely good-natured to those who abuse him. He is the intimate member of the Prince's own clique; he is put in charge of important military operations, including the levying of soldiers; and though he discharges these duties with complete irresponsibility, he seems never to get into serious trouble for his negligence or his knavery. From an unfavourable view, however, he is a sycophant, a swindler, a roisterer, a gourmand, a philanderer always pursuing women for the lowest reasons, that is, not for honourable love of them, but for their money or for the satisfaction of his insatiable lust. While hostess Quickly is obviously his mistress, out of whom he wheedles money continually by promising to marry her, still he carries on, or attempts to carry on, disgraceful flirtations with the Court ladies at Windsor on the one hand, and on the other, lolls in the embraces of a typical harlot like Doll Tearsheet. It seems safe to say that in spite of his wit, in spite of his good humour and his complacence, his faults are such as to make the role of prototype highly undesirable to one who would fain have been well thought on by his contemporaries. Since Lord Cobham does seem to have been the person who objected to the Oldcastle portraiture, it is necessary, in spite of the difficulty of Falstaff's avoirdupois, to examine all the evidence which might account for the protest.

Readers of Shakspere will not need to be reminded of the hilarious scene in Act II, in which Falstaff undertakes to play the King in the act of rebuking his naughty son. Falstaff and Hal are the principals, but Pintpot is the enthusiastic audience. It may, however, help to make the scene more convincing if we remind ourselves of the "quality" of Mistress Quickly. Contrary to the modern stage tradition, which presents her as a middle-aged wench presiding over a "pub," Shakspere makes it clear that his "hostess" is rather one of "Mrs. Warren's profession," a mistress of an elegant establishment, whose walls are hung with arras and whose dinner-service is of silver and gold of sufficient value, when pawned, to relieve the pecuniary embarrassment of a notoriously extravagant and self-indulgent companion of the Prince. While "low" enough to admit Doll Tearsheet into her house, she is at the same time socially "high" enough to be the trusted confidante of Anne Page; and she actually thinks it at least possible that she will be, one day, "my lady, thy wife" to Sir John Falstaff. These facts need to be kept in mind as we seek to study the parallel between the "Mistress Dame Pintpot" of the Countess's letter and the "good Pintpot" of Shakspere's merry scene.

As all students of Shakspere know, the character of the roistering knight appeared in Shakspere first, as he had in the anonymous *Famous Victories of Henry V,* as Sir John Oldcastle. The name was subsequently changed, first to Falstaff, and later merely to Buffone, as a result of a protest made by some member or members of the family of Lord Cobham, the direct descendant of Sir John Oldcastle, first Baron Cobham. About two years after the publication of the first folio, one Richard James, writing to Sir Harry Bourchier, tells us (Chambers, *Shakespeare,* II, p. 242):

> That in Shakespeares first shew of Harrie the fift, the person with which he undertook to playe a buffone was not Falstaffe, but Sir John Oldcastle, and that offence beinge worthily taken by Personages descended from his title (as peradventure by many others allso whoe ought to have him in honourable memorie), the poet was putt to make an ignorant shifte of abusing Sir Jhon Falstophe, a man

not inferior of Vertue, though not so famous in piety as the other, who gave witnesse unto the truth of our reformation with a constant and resolute Martyrdom unto which he was pursued by the Priests, Bishops, Monks, and Friars of those days.

At the close of *II Henry IV,* Shakspere adds an Epilogue, in which he promises the audience:

If you be not too much cloyed with fat meat, our humble author will continue the story with Sir John in it, and will make you merry with fair Katherine of France; where for anything I know, Falstaff shall die of a sweat, unless already a' be killed with your hard opinions; for Oldcastle died a martyr, and this is not the man.

The most interesting fact to be gathered from these remarks is that Shakspere was well aware of the true character of the Lollard martyr, Sir John Oldcastle, who was burned at the gallows at which he was hanged during the reign of Henry V, and, indeed, it would seem that the author was not even pretending to dramatize the life of that good man, nor even that of the good Sir John Falstolf, that "noble, valiant souldier" and "man of learning" for whose good works the students of "Maudlin Colledge in Oxford" were every day "bound to make memorie of his soul." Why, then did he select the name of Oldcastle for his frivolous old sinner, that mountain of infinite lust, that wily sycophant, that profiteering soldier, whose code in war was as unfair as his code in love? Our question may never be answered, but for those who believe that Shakspere would not have intended either Oldcastle or Falstaff as a satire on a contemporary nobleman, there is at least as difficult a problem to explain in Shakspere's slander of the decent dead.

Richard James was not the only one to object to this aspect of the situation. George Daniel of Beswick (*ibid.,* II, p. 243) made a similar protest against:

That Scandall (which has been throwne
Upon a Name of Honour) Charactered
From a wrong Person, Coward, and Buffone.
Call in your easie faiths, from what y'ave read
To laugh at Falstoffe, as an humor framed
To Grace the Stage, to please the Age, misnamed.

Fuller adds further testimony as to the unsuitability of both names for Shakspere's fat rogue. In his *Church History* (*ibid.,* p. 244) he says:

Stage-Poets have themselves been very *bold* with, and others very *merry* at the Memory of S[r] *John Oldcastle,* whom they have fancied a *boon Companion, a jovial Royster* and yet a *Coward* to boot, contrary to the credit of all Chronicles, owning him a *Martial man* of merit. The best is, S[r] *John Falstaffe,* hath relieved the memory of S[r] *John Oldcastle,* and of late is substituted *Buffoone* in his place; but it matters little what *petulant Poets* as what *malicious Papists* have written against him.

In his *Worthies,* Fuller protests against the outrage done to Sir John Falstophe Knight (*ibid.,* p. 224); he declares that

. . . the *Stage* hath been overbold with his memory, making him a *Thrasonical Puff,* & Emblem of *Mock-valour.*

True it is, *Sir John Oldcastle* did first bear the brunt of the one, being easily made the *make-sport* in all plays for a *coward.* It is easily known out of what *Purse* this black *peny* came. The *Papists* railing on him for a *Heretick,* and therefore he must also be a coward, though indeed he was a *man* of *arms, every inch of him,* and as valiant as any in his age.

Now as I am glad that *Sir John Oldcastle is put out,* so I am sorry that *Sir John Fastolfe* is *put in,* to relieve his memory in this base service, to be the *anvil* for every *dull wit* to strike upon. Nor is our Comedian excusable, by some alteration of his name, writing him *Sir John Falstafe* (and making him the *property* of *pleasure* for King *Henry* the fifth, to abuse) seeing the *vicinity* of sounds intrench on the memory of *that worthy Knight,* and few do heed the *inconsiderable difference* in spelling of their name.

We have already noted Shakspere's acknowledgement of Oldcastle's pious reputation, while disclaiming all intention to slander so good a man. It must be admitted, however, that such a statement may have been made with his tongue in his cheek, as was the case when Wentworth Smith tried to bring the Elector Frederick on the stage in his play called *The Hector of Germany, or the Palsgrave is a Harmless Thing.* When "authorities sterne browe" would not permit "to bring him, while he lives, upon the stage," the Prologue covered the situation by shamelessly claiming that the Palsgrave in this play was *not* Frederick. (Chambers, *Elizabethan Stage,* III, p. 493.) But his affirmation fooled no one.

There are, nevertheless, slight tags of evidence in support of the view that Shakspere did mean Falstaff, if not as a satirical portrait of Henry Brooke, eighth Lord Cobham, at least as an annoyance to his family. The whole question is intimately bound up with the problem of textual revision of the Henry plays, including the *Merry Wives;* but it is neither possible nor necessary here to enter into the morass of that Serbonian bog. Suffice it to mention one curious instance, described by Sir Edmund Chambers as follows (*Shakespeare,* I, p. 433):

> In one respect there has clearly been revision [of Merry Wives] at some stage. In Q, the disguised Ford takes the name of Brooke, and the connexion of meaning shows that this was the original name. In F, it is altered consistently to Broome. This is, I think, a bit of cautious censorship. Brooke was the family name of that Lord Cobham, to whose intervention the extrusion of Oldcastle from *Henry IV* was probably due.

What this proves, if anything, I am not quite sure, for the character of Ford, disguised or otherwise, is at no time confused with that of Falstaff. Perhaps this substitution of names means nothing more than that the Brookes were the persons offended by the Falstaff plays, and that, therefore, their names would best not be mentioned at all.

I have sometimes wondered if another of the revision problems in the *Merry Wives* could not be connected with the Ralegh-Cobham satire. The horse- and chain-stealing episode of Act IV, scene v, has generally been associated only with a satire on the Count of Mompergart, whose commandeering of horses under the Queen's warrant in 1592, caused some local irritation. (Chambers, *Elizabethan Stage,* III, pp. 452-53; *Shakespeare,* I, p. 427ff.) Certainly there is in *Merry Wives* some reference to this episode, but it is possible that in the main the allusion was aimed at another horse-stealing episode, which, though it happened in 1592, entered significantly into court gossip in 1595, by reason of the Interrogatories carried on at Cerne Abbas, in Dorset, on 21 March, 1594, against Sir Walter Ralegh. The depositions of these witnesses will be discussed in detail in connection with the account of Ralegh's "atheism." Here it suffices to mention only the deposition of Nicholas Jefferys, parson of Weeks Reges. This deponent declared (*Willoughbie His Avisa,* ed. G. B. Harrison [1926], p. 261):

That aboute some three yeres paste (1592) cominge to Blandforde out of Hampshire his horse was stayed and taken for a poste horse by Sr Walter Rawleigh and Mr Carewe Rawleigh: where this depon^t^ entreating to have his horse released for that he was to ride home unto his charge (from whence he had bene some tyme absent) to preach the nexte daye beinge sunday, whereunto Mr Carewe Rawleigh replyed, that he, this depon^t^ might goe home when he would; but his horse shoulde preach before him, or to that effecte.

In our play, Falstaff is closeted with a "wise woman of Brainford," who is being sought on a matter of chain-stealing by "one Nym"; and Falstaff screens his fellow rogue by a silly sophistry. This episode is followed immediately by a very cryptic allusion to a theft of horses from Bardolfe. Nashe's *Pierce Penniless* also refers to some "horses lately sworn to be stolen," and in *Summer's Last Will and Testament* he alludes to the chain borrowed from "my cousin Ned." That these fugitive chains and horses prove anything is, of course, doubtful; but it is possible that in the many revisions of *Merry Wives* some allusions to the pranks of Ralegh and his friend Cobham have been lost. Certain it is that Nashe and Shakspere belonged to the anti-Ralegh group, whose persecution began when Ralegh's friends got possession of the office of the Chamberlain.

By the death of their patron, Henry Carey, Lord Hunsdon, on 22 July, 1596, Shakspere's company lost their most powerful protector against the rigours of the law concerning stage-plays and players. On the very day of his death, an edict was issued prohibiting all plays throughout London and the pretended reason was fear of "increase in sickness," though the records show no evidence of plague. (Leslie Hotson, *Shakspere versus Shallow,* [Boston, 1931], p. 14.) Hunsdon was succeeded in office by William Brooke, seventh Lord Cobham, and Cobham was followed by Sir George Carey, the new Lord Hunsdon, the consistent friend and supporter of Ralegh and Cecil. The precise dates of their respective tenures may be useful. From 4 July, 1585, to 22 July, 1596, the office was held by Henry

Carey, Lord Hunsdon. From August, 1596 to 6 March, 1597, it was held by William Brooke, Lord Cobham. From 17 March, 1597, to 9 September, 1603, it was held by Sir George Carey, Lord Hunsdon. The old Lord Hunsdon had held the office of Chamberlain for more than ten years, and during his tenure the authors and players of interludes under his patronage seem to have flourished almost without restraint from the Queen. Whether this fact was due to the effectiveness of his defense or to his stupidity in not being aware of the presence of "dangerous matter," or to a general increase in the presence of such matter, we do not know. He was reputed to be almost illiterate, and indeed, it is surprising, when we consider the closeness of his relation to the Queen, to note how negligible a role he seems to have played in political affairs altogether. Nevertheless, during his lifetime few attacks upon his company of players are recorded at all, and there was no striking case of effective interference. Naunton says (*op. cit.,* p. 47), "He was fast man to his Prince, and firm to his friends and servants." With his death, however, all was changed. Almost immediately his stage company was ousted from their new playhouse in the Blackfriars. Among the signatories of the petition which led the Privy Council to forbid plays to be given within the "liberty," were the names of Lady Elizabeth Russell, and the new Lord Hunsdon. (Chambers, *Elizabethan Stage,* IV, p. 320; App. D, cvi.) In his account of the Chamberlain's company, Sir Edmund Chambers says (*ibid.,* II, p. 195), "At this time also (1596) the Corporations seem to have succeeded in finally and permanently expelling the players from the City inns which had long been their headquarters, and Nashe connects the persecution with the loss of 'their old Lord' by whom he doubtless means Lord Henry Hunsdon." Nashe specifically states that "now the players . . . are piteously persecuted by the Lord Mayor and the aldermen, and, however in their old Lord's time they thought their state settled, it is now so uncertain they cannot build upon it." Nashe also complains that he was disappointed of "an after harvest" he had expected "by writing for the stage and for the presse." (*Ibid.,* II, p. 195.) From that day also the plays of the Chamberlain's men began to "leak" into print, and Shakspere began his "fight with the pirates," after the surreptitiously printed quarto of *Romeo and Juliet,* in 1597, bearing on its title page the name of Lord Hunsdon's men. Several other quartos followed (for instance, *Richard II* and *Richard III*), described as having been played by the Lord Chamberlain's Men; but it is not certain that these quartos were pirated. Finally, on 28 July, the performance of the *Isle of Dogs* led to the inhibition of all plays (*ibid.,* II, p. 196), so that for the second time since their formation in 1594, the company had to travel.

Direct evidence concerning the relations between the new Lord Hunsdon and the company which had long been patronized by his father has not so far come forth out of the annals of the period, but an exceptionally interesting light may be thrown upon the whole matter somewhat circuitously by a study of Spenser's *Muipotmos,* which was dedicated "in a letter of exceptional ardour" to Elizabeth Carey, the wife of Sir George Carey. The title page of the poem bears the date 1590, so that its composition must have all but coincided with that of *Colin Clout,* Spenser's ardent plea for his friend and patron, Ralegh. The allegory of this delightful poem has never been indisputably established, but one of the most plausible interpretations would seem to indicate that Lady Carey was an earnest pro-Ralegh partisan in the Ralegh-Essex quarrel, described in the opening stanza as "a deadly dolorous debate between two mightie ones of great estate." Miss Harriet S. V. Jones (*A Spenser Handbook,* p. 114) outlines this interpretation, without self-commitment, as follows:

> Clarion represents Raleigh and may take his name from the house of Clare, with which some supposed that Raleigh was connected. The gay gardens in which the butterfly makes his home are then the Court, and Clarion's brilliant wings and elaborate armor represent the sumptuous tastes of the mighty Lord. Aragnoll, on the other hand, is Essex, symbolizing fittingly, in the eyes of Raleigh's friends, the envy of the Essex party that was focussed upon the Queen's favorite and that sought to destroy him.

It may not be amiss to remind the reader of a contemporary ballad against the Cecil faction, already described in the first part of this study. In it the new Lord Chamberlain, Cecil, and Ralegh are grouped together in a fierce satire on the enemies of Essex. From such an alliance it is, therefore, easy to infer the cause of the persecution directed at Shakspere's company from 1596 to the death of Lord Hunsdon.

From the date of their new organization in 1594, the Burbage group had shown itself to be consistently and unequivocally pro-Essex. Shakspere's devotion to Southampton is attested beyond any doubt by his dedication of *Venus and Adonis* and *Lucrece,* and, as we have seen, perhaps with less certainty, by his plea for Essex and Southampton in *Henry V,* in *Timon of Athens,* in *Richard II,* and others. It seems, at this late date, and in the face of the "gentle Shakespeare" tradition, almost a failure in *esprit de corps* even to inquire into the other and darker side of the picture. It would not offend any but the most bitter "anti-topicalists" to learn that Shakspere had warmly espoused the cause of the generous, ill-starred Essex; but who of us likes to believe that he was also a man of gall to his enemies, or to the enemies of his friends? Which of us would not hold out "till the last ditch" against the conclusion that the bitter iniquity of "Richard Crookback," or the snarling malice of hunchbacked Thersites, were meant as parallels for Cecil, the cripple? Let me hasten to say that the fight has not yet come to that point, as far as *Richard III* or *Troilus and Cressida* are concerned, though the war is still raging; but there is, undoubtedly, a certain amount of evidence leading to the conclusion that Shakspere did intend the characters of Launcelot Gobbo and Sir John Oldcastle as satirical parallels for the two worst enemies of Essex, Cecil and Cobham. The general connection between *The Merchant of Venice* and the famous trial of Dr. Ruy Lopez, in 1594, has long been recognized by Shakspereans, at least as far back as 1894, when there appeared in the *English Historical Review* (IX, p. 440) the article by A. Dimock, on *The Conspiracy of Dr. Lopez.* It is not my intention here to examine the plausibility for the identification of Lopez with the spirit of a wolf (Lupus) "hang'd for human slaughter" (Act II, sc. ii), or of Antonio of Venice with Antonio of Portugal, or the much-wooed Lady of Belmont with the universally courted Queen of England. For an implied satire on Launcelot Gobbo, however, there is a black-and-white reference that may be explained away, but cannot be thrown out on the grounds of "mere plausibility." Sir Edmund Chambers states the case as conservatively as possible (*Shakespeare,* I, p. 372):

> The Gobbo of the play seems likely to have inspired two malicious references by Francis Davison in letters of 1596 to an unnamed enemy of the Earl of Essex, who can only be the hunchbacked Robert Cecil. (T. Birch, *Elizabeth,* ii, 185, 204.) On October 27, he writes, "If he be vanquished . . . all the world shall never make me confess, but that bum-basted legs are a better fortification than bulwarks, and St. Gobbo a far greater and omnipotent saint than either St. Philip or St. Diego." And on November 10, he writes, evidently with reference to Cecil's appointment as Secretary of State, of the late instalment and canonization of the venerable saint. If I am right, the *Merchant of Venice* can hardly be later than the autumn of 1596, although, of course, it might have furnished Cecil's nickname sometime before.

This piece of direct evidence could perhaps be explained away by assuming that Cecil's nickname was bestowed upon him by his enemies *after* the play had appeared, but that such an application never existed in Shakspere's mind at all; just as, for instance, we might dub a furious motorist of our own day "Jehu," without implying that the Old Testament character referred to him. The difficulty with this explanation is that, without some outside hint from one of the initiated, it would be hard to see how the clown Gobbo could have seemed an inevitable parallel for the astute Cecil. We of the twentieth century, at least, are more accustomed to think of Gobbo as Jessica did, that is, "a merry devil," than as a graceless knave whose "conscience would serve him to run from his master," who habitually gulled his old father; one to whom "eleven widows and nine maids" was "a simple coming-in for one man," who, indeed, scrupled not to "the getting up of the negro's belly . . . with child." Yet when once the parallel has been suggested to us, these filthy characteristics, which do definitely mar the comedy, insist on being reckoned with as satire, particularly since they form so close a parallel to other contemporary satire on Cecil. Of the many scandalous broadsides circulated at his death, Osborne says (*op. cit.,* p. 235):

No wonder he met with no fairer encomiums, of which I shall relate these, not savouring so much of scurrility, though perhaps lesse of wit, than many did, then current:

> Here lyes throwne, for the wormes to eate,
> Little bossive Robbin, that was so great;
> Not Robin, good-fellow, nor Robin Hood,
> But Robin th' encloser of Hatfield wood.
> Who seem'd as sent from ugly fate,
> To spoyle the prince, and rob the state.
> Owning a mind of dismal endes,
> As trappes for foes, and tricks for friends.
> But now in Hatfield lies the fox,
> Who stank while he liv'd and died of the p–.

Before leaving the whole question of the connection between Oldcastle and the Cecil group, it is necessary to refer briefly to the play on the real Sir John Oldcastle, which gives, as the title page declares, the "true and honorable historie of the good Lord Cobham." As Sir Edmund Chambers observes (*Elizabethan Stage,* III, p. 307), "Clearly, the play was an answer to *Henry IV,* in which Sir John Falstaff was originally Sir John Oldcastle, and this is made clear in the prologue:

> It is no pampered glutton we present,
> Nor aged Councellour to youthfull sinne."

The play was written by Drayton, Hathaway, Munday, and Wilson in collaboration, and is, indeed, for modern readers a dull piece. To those, however, who had been annoyed by the slander of Sir John Oldcastle in the Henry IV plays, it apparently gave abundant satisfaction. Our first knowledge of the play comes from the letters from Rowland Whyte describing the visit of Vereiken, the Ambassador from the Archduke and the Infanta. He had come to England on a special mission to discuss a peace with Spain. (*Sidney Papers,* II, p. 165, 167, *et passim.*) From his arrival to his departure he seems to have been the special charge of the anti-Essex faction. A close follower of affairs at Court could not fail to notice how closely the rival factions held together in the weeks following Essex's arrest. Whyte notes, for instance, how "yesterday Mr. Secretary went to Dinner accompanied with the Earle of Shrewsbury, and Nottingham, the Lordes Tho. Howard, and Cobham, the Lord Grey, and Sir Walter Ralegh, and Sir George Carew." This list almost comprises the Cecil faction of 1599. Whyte notes, immediately following, that they who accompany the Earl of Essex are: "The Earl of Worcester, Rutland, Montgomery, Rich, Lord Harry [probably Lord Henry Howard]; but the last is held a Ranter." (*Ibid.*, p. 129.) Indeed, since Essex was under restraint at York House, all things seemed to be under the sway of Secretary Cecil and his train. During Vereiken's visit, it was Lord Cobham's coach that waited at Dover to bring the Ambassador to London (*ibid.*, p. 167); it was Sir Walter Ralegh who was "appointed to accompany hym to *Westmester* to see the Tombs and Singularities of that Place" (*ibid.*, p. 174); and again it was Cecil's friend Lord Hunsdon, who at Hunsdon House, Blackfriars, "upon Thursday, 6 May, feasted him, and made him very great, and a delicate dinner, and there in the After Noone his Plaiers acted, before Veriken, Sir John Old Castell, to his great Contentment." (*Ibid.*, p. 175.) There is a slight difficulty concerning the identity of this play because of the fact that the title page of 1600 describes it as "lately acted by the right honorable the Earle of Nottingham, Lord High Admirall of England his servants." In other words, though given at the house of Lord Hunsdon, the play was acted not by the Chamberlain's men, but by those of the Lord Admiral, the friend of Ralegh, Hunsdon, and Cobham, and the bitter enemy of Essex. (*Acta Regia . . . Rymer's Foedera,* Tom. XVI, p. 501.) This fact has led Sir Edmund Chambers to believe that the play which gave so much contentment to Lord Hunsdon was really *I Henry IV,* and not the new Oldcastle play. Such a view is, I believe, untenable, when one considers the close friendship between Lord Cobham and Lord Hunsdon at this date. It seems highly unlikely that Hunsdon would receive "great contentment" from a play which had clearly given great offense to his friend and ally Lord Cobham.

So far as I have been able to learn, there was never a shred of justification for Lord Howard's slander against the orthodoxy of Lord Cobham. The charge of heresy against so jaunty a person could have had no serious basis. The reader will recall that "Lord Harry" himself was held by Rowland Whyte to be "a ranter," and, as we shall see presently, it was he who became the disgusting tool used by Cecil for getting rid of all rivals in his scramble for political supremacy under James.

As the Queen's life drew to a close, Cecil managed to get all the aces into his own hand, and by 1600 he had already marked those he meant to finger from the pack. Chief among these were his former friends Ralegh, Cobham, and Northumberland, the "triplicity" under discussion in this chapter. It falls not within the scope of this study, however, to relate the life histories of these three friends, except in so far as their personalities, their interests, habits, tastes, and pursuits influenced the mind and art of Christopher Marlowe. Other aspects of their careers and persons may be studied in the excellent biographies of them that are readily available.

As already noted, it was the supposed atheism of these men that laid them open to the malicious slander of a jackal like Lord Henry Howard. The charge of atheism was, under the English Tudors, made indiscriminately against all critics of the new Protestant Episcopal prelacy, whether the criticism was spoken or only inferred, and whether it emanated from the Catholics or from the dictating clique which constituted Elizabeth's government in the last decades of the century. The label "atheist" was to that administration what the label "Trotskyite" is to the present Russian government of Joseph Stalin & Co., Ltd.

It is said that it was due to the "shrewd precepts and example" of Charles Paget that young Henry Percy was saved from the primrose path of social dalliance during his travel years in France. (Brenan, *op. cit.*, II, p. 35.) At an age when it is easy for young men of Percy's great wealth to squander not only their money but their strength and time, this susceptible boy was fortunate indeed to number among his respected friends so intelligent and high-minded a person as this devoted young Catholic zealot. When Walsingham's spy, the British ambassador, noted the "train of solemn personages" who frequented young Percy's apartment, he reported at once to London that the youth was surrounded with "Romish agents." Upon investigation these sober persons turned out to be merely "men of science," mathematicians, astronomers, chemists, and the like, who had been invited by Percy to help him in the various capacities of tutor and laboratory assistant. We are told that "he took up the study of history and the occult sciences with great avidity, devoting to reading and experiments as much of his time as he had formerly expended in less learned pursuits." Though he became in later life a serious and accomplished student of astronomy and mathematics, in these blithe student days he dabbled enthusiastically in all the traditional diversions of the alchemist and astrologer. Brenan says (*ibid.,* p. 35), "He purchased a crystal divining globe, cast his friends' horoscope with the ease of Nostradamus, and laboured hopefully to transmute the baser metals into gold." It was such activity that earned for Percy the name of the "Wizard Earl," the eighth Earl of Northumberland having died in the Tower during the summer of 1585, leaving his title and estates to Henry, his eldest son.

By 1586, Northumberland was back in London, where he installed himself in the family residence at Blackfriars. Here he set about rebuilding the library of his illustrious grandfather. The works of Machiavelli, Guicciardini, Holinshed, and many others were purchased, and the Earl's accounts showed every year heavier and heavier charges for the binding and cataloguing of books. He studied voraciously—architecture, archaeology, gardening, geography, military and political science, as well as astronomy and chemistry. To this laboratory he also added alembics, crucibles, furnaces, and "speculative glasses." Of these we shall have occasion to speak further in our discussion of Thomas Hariot.

No wonder the Puritans called him "wizard" and "conjurer." Aubrey tells how this stupid legend clung not only to the Earl, but to all his learned friends and protégés, and he records many instances which reveal the malice and stupidity of the persecution which dogged their heels.

In spite of slanders, however, the Earl was advanced in Her Majesty's favour, and on 23 April, 1593, he was installed in the chapel of Windsor Castle as Knight of the Garter "with due pomp and ceremony." Students of the period will recall that it was for this occasion that Peele wrote his *Honour of the Garter,* in the Prologue to which he apostrophized not only the "thrice-noble Earl of Northumberland," but also all the learned poets whose "heroical spirits" had been raised by patronage such as his. He praises his "admirable mathematical skill" and describes him as

> Familiar with the stars and zodiac
> To whom the heaven lies open as her book;
> To whose directions undeceivable,
> Leaving our schoolmen's vulgar trodden paths,
> And following the ancient reverend steps
> Of Trismegistus and Pythagoras,
> Through uncouth ways and inaccessible,
> Doth pass into the spacious pleasant fields
> Of divine science and philosophy.

Along with the fustian names of "Hobbin" and "great Hobbinal," which Dyce takes as referring here to Spenser, not to Harvey, Peele praises the other scientific poets who eschew the "trivial humours" that "pastime the world" by favouring "Pan and Phoebus both alike." He names Harrington, Daniels, Campion, Fraunce, and Watson, besides Marlowe, "the Muses' darling." It is pleasant to be able to record the prompt emolument of £3, which, according to the Sion House Rolls, was ordered to be given "to one George Peele, a poett, as my Lord's liberalities." As this study proceeds, the reader will realize that Peele has included, in this *Prologus Ad Maecenatem,* most of the poets who were the protégés of Northumberland, or Ralegh, or both. All joined in celebrating the scientific exploits of their patrons and thus earned for themselves the title of the *School of Night.*

The "old wives' tale" of the Earl's marriage to one who was "nor maid, nor wife, nor yet widow," * must be omitted here, however interesting to the student of Peele, lest the road to Samarcand become as circuitous as the long, long one to Xanadu.

It was, indeed a freak of irony that brought a sister of Essex into the circle of Ralegh's intimates; though, to be sure, it

* At the time of her marriage to Henry Percy, Lady Devereux's first husband (Sir Thomas Perrott) was still living, and no record exists to show that this union had ever been set aside. Brenan (*op. cit.,* II, p. 49), says that she was described by a contemporary as "nor maid, nor wife, nor yet widow."

would be easy to exaggerate the degree of intimacy between Northumberland and his wife. Brenan tells us that the Countess Dorothy chose to look upon her husband as an enemy almost from the beginning of their married life. Birch relates how she complained of his conduct wildly and incoherently to the suave and mock-sympathetic Francis Bacon. So shrewish and so curst she was, in fact, and so little able was the fiery Earl to endure her reproaches patiently, that during their first five years of wedded life, four formal separations were negotiated for the frenzied pair. Their biographer adds (Brenan, *op. cit.*, II, p. 63):

> As if any new cause of discord between them were wanting, it was supplied by the intrigues of the young Earl of Essex, Lady Northumberland's brother. Brother and sister loved each other with all the ardor of their wild headstrong natures, and the Countess entered eagerly into the network of plots and counterplots by which the sanguine Essex imagined he was playing the game of nations against trained hands like Robert Cecil. Not only did Northumberland look upon his brother-in-law as "of slender qualities, a mere royal minion," but he had at the same time a great regard for Sir Walter Ralegh, between whom and his rival favorite Essex there existed a cordial hatred.

Even at such times as the Earl and Countess were officially residing under one roof in town, the desperate husband kept a little "bachelor" villa out in the hamlet of Barking, where he and Ralegh and Drake and other sea-dogs like them, might retreat from the clamour of a scolding tongue. Lord Henry Howard relates in a letter to Bruce (*Secret Correspondence with James I,* 4 Dec., 1601), that on one occasion, when Northumberland and his friends were expressing their hostility to the Scottish succession, referring contemptuously to James as Essex's "great god," the Lady Dorothy replied that "rather than any other than King James should reign in this place, she would eat their hearts in salt, though she were brought to the gallows instantly." In her labours for James's succession the Lady Dorothy was the earnest collaborator of her more famous sister Penelope, whose intrigues for this cause we have already noted. It is only fair to point out that in 1601, the sisters of Essex had been under months of strain sufficient to cause taut nerves and uncontrolled tongues. We must remember too that Henry Percy, like so many of his ancestors, and in particular like Harry Hotspur, whom he much resembled, was naturally quick-tempered and impetuous, though whatever his ill success as a shrew-tamer, his pride kept him from discussing his domestic affairs in public; nor would he permit anyone else to do so. In fact, his notorious quarrel with Southampton arose out of this very circumstance. We are told (Brenan, *op. cit.*, II, p. 68) that Southampton,

> . . . "presuming upon his kinship" with the Devereuxes, sided somewhat too openly with the Countess of Northumberland against her husband, and even allowed himself—so said the gossip—"to speak disparagingly of the Earl." These things coming to Northumberland's ears, he sent one of his friends "in hot haste" to demand an explanation. But Southampton would vouchsafe neither explanation nor apology, and a hostile meeting was accordingly agreed upon. The Queen, however, heard rumours of what had taken place, and, on the very morning chosen for the duel, both principals were arrested by her orders, and haled before the Council. Here Southampton at length condescended to explain that his remarks had been grossly exaggerated, and some sort of reconciliation was patched up between the belligerent Earls.

There are many other stories illustrating the truculence and bellicose temper of the ninth Earl. On one occasion, after he and Cobham and Ralegh had succeeded in making themselves thoroughly annoying to Sir Francis Vere, commander of the British auxiliary forces in the Netherlands, Northumberland went so far as to strike his military superior, and later to challenge him to a duel. As on the former occasion, the Queen heard rumours of the affair and promptly commanded Northumberland "to forbeare any action against Sir Francis Vere, att that instant employed in her service." The Earl was so furious at this second inhibition, that he caused a declaration to be drawn up, and published in English, French, and Italian, to the effect that "Vere was a Knave and Cowarde, and that, in fleeringe and gearinge like a common Buffoon, would wrong men of all conditions, and had neyther the honestye or the courage to satisfye any!"

It must not be inferred, however, that the Earl of Northumberland fought only in petty causes and in no battles but his own. Nothing could exceed the courage and candour with which he defended the cause of religious toleration, in a period when to do so meant the risk of life and lands. Though not a Catholic himself, he wrenched from James VI, almost single-handed, a written pledge of leniency toward the persecuted Catholic tenantry of the North. He kept under his liberal patronage persons of all religious persuasions, and his doors were ever open to welcome those who brought and sought knowledge. Though he was proud—some say arrogant—to those of his own social order, despising their tortuous intrigues with their grotesque alternation of pomp and servility, yet with men of genius he doffed his rank and worked and talked with them as equals, the only difference being that he usually paid all the costs. The *Syon Household Accounts* bear witness to countless benefactions to writers, geographers, and physicians, as well as to schools and colleges. In his account of the conferring of the honorary degree of Master of Arts upon him in the year 1605, Anthony Wood (*Fasti Oxonienses,* Part I, p. 172), calls him "the most generous Count of Northumberland, a great encourager of learning and learned men, especially of Mathematicians; who, as others, have in high manner celebrated his worth." He was, in fact, as we shall see presently, a co-founder and co-patron of Ralegh's "Little Academe."

CHAPTER FIFTEEN

Sir Walter's Little Academe

AS AN UNDERGRADUATE, Ralegh had become keenly interested in the mathematical sciences, particularly algebra and astronomy. It is probable that, even at that early date, he was orienting his studies with a view to perfecting his knowledge of navigation. Be that as it may, very soon after his return from Ireland he invited one Thomas Hariot, a brilliant young mathematician and astronomer, fresh from the University, to act as resident tutor both to himself and to his growing band of sea captains, in the science of navigation. A letter to Ralegh written by Richard Hakluyt, himself an important promoter of British Imperialism and the science of navigation, in dedication of Peter Martyr's *Decades of the New World* (1588), is so generous a comment on the relationship between Ralegh and his protégés, that I subjoin a considerable extract from it:

> To you, therefore, I have freely desired to give and dedicate these my labours. For to whom could I present these *Decades of the New World* more appropriately than to yourself, who, at the expense of nearly one hundred thousand ducats, with new fleets, are showing us of modern times new regions, leading forth a third colony to Virginia, giving us news of the unknown, opening up for us pathways through the inaccessible; and whose every care, and thought, and effort tend toward this end, hinge upon and adhere to it? To whom have been present and still are present the same ideas, desire & incentives as with that most illustrious Charles Howard, the Second Neptune of the Ocean, and Edward Stafford our most prudent Ambassador at the Court of France, in order to accomplish great deeds by sea and land. But since by your skill in the art of navigation you clearly saw that the chief glory of an insular kingdom would obtain its greatest splendour among us by the firm support of the mathematical sciences, you have trained up and supported *now a long time,* [italics inserted] with a most liberal salary, Thomas Hariot, a young man well versed in those studies, in order that you might acquire in your spare hours by his instruction a knowledge of these

noble sciences; and your own numerous Sea Captains might unite profitably, theory with practice. What is to be the result shortly of this your wise and learned school, they who possess even moderate judgement can have no difficulty in guessing. This one thing I know, the one end and only consideration to place before you, that first the Portuguese and afterwards the Spaniards formerly made great endeavours with no small loss, but at length succeeded through determination of the mind. Hasten on then to adorn the Sparta [Virginia] you have discovered; hasten on that ship more than Argonautic, of nearly a thousand tons burthen which you have at last built and finished with truly regal expenditure, to join with the rest of the fleet you have fitted out.

Hariot's share in this particular venture of Ralegh's will receive fuller notice in the discussion of *Tamburlaine.* For the present it is sufficient to point out the fact of his early connection with the group. Henry Stevens, upon whose account of *Thomas Hariot and His Associates* (1900) I have leaned heavily in the ensuing paragraphs, concludes that Hariot was in Ralegh's service by 1582 "at latest." He declares (p. 81):

From this early time for nearly forty years, till the morning of the 29 October, 1618, when Raleigh was beheaded, these two friends are found inseparable. Whether in prosperity or in adversity, in the Tower or on the scaffold, Sir Walter always had his *fidus Achates* to look after him and watch his interests. With a sharp wit, close mouth, and ready pen, Hariot was of inestimable service to his liberal patron. With rare attainments in the Greek and Latin classics, and all branches of the abstract sciences, he combined that perfect fidelity and honesty of character which placed him always above suspicion even of the enemies of Sir Walter. He was neither politician nor statesman, and therefore could be even in those times a faithful guide, philosopher, and friend to Raleigh.

Stevens also states, without mentioning his authority (*ibid.,* pp. 82-83), that "Hariot is known to have spent some time in Ireland on Raleigh's estates there during the reign of Elizabeth, but it is uncertain when. It may have been between the autumn of 1586 and the autumn of 1588. . . . He was probably the manager of one of the estates there, as Governor White was of another in 1591-93."

With Hariot was associated, also one of Ralegh's pensioners, one Robert Hues (or Hughes?), an Oxonian, who had been with Hariot as an undergraduate at St. Mary's Hall. Under Hariot's inspiration, Hues became an eminent geographer and mathematician and a member of Ralegh's "school," to whose reputation he added considerable lustre by his *Tractatus de Globis,* which was financed by William Sanderson, but dedicated to Ralegh. Through the good offices of Sir Walter, Hues was introduced to the patronage of Sanderson, a rich and liberal London merchant, who had married Ralegh's niece. He was among the largest contributors to the 1584 Virginian expedition, and he continued throughout his life to be an ardent supporter of Ralegh's cause, both by investment and by his patronage of various geographical writers such as Hues, and, somewhat later, Molline and Hood. Since so little is known among students of letters about Robert Hues, I subjoin the brief sketch of him given by Stevens (*op. cit.,* p. 86):

> Robert Hues, who was an intimate friend and associate of Hariot, was born at Hertford in 1554. He became a poor scholar at Brazenose, and was afterwards at St Mary's Hall with Hariot. He took his degreē of Bachelor of Arts in 1579. He is said to have been a good Greek scholar, and, after leaving the University, travelled and became an eminent geographer and mathematician. He attracted the attention, probably through Raleigh, of that noble patron of learning Henry Percy, ninth Earl of Northumberland, who took him into his service, made him one of his scientific companions while in the Tower, supported him partly at Sion, intrusted him to instruct his children, and finally sent him to Oxford as tutor at Christ Church of his eldest surviving son, Algernon Percy, who on the death of his father on gunpowder treason day in 1632, became the tenth Earl of Northumberland. Hues died at Oxford, 24 May, 1632, and was buried in the cathedral of Christ Church, according to the inscription on his monument. He is mentioned by Chapman in his translation of Homer's Works (1616) as "another right learned, honest, and entirely loved friend of mine."

Two of the most intimate members of this very learned circle have yet to be introduced formally to the reader. These were Richard Hakluyt and John White. Henry Stevens declared (*op. cit.,* p. 50) that Ralegh "was blessed in his household, or at his table, or in his confidence, with four sterling adherents who stuck to him through thick and thin, through prosperity and adversity. These were Richard Hakluyt, Jacques Le Moyne,

John White, and Thomas Hariot . . . whom it is just to call Raleigh's Magi." This last is in reminiscence of the trio who were turned over to the patronage of Northumberland, after Ralegh's fall. Even during his long imprisonment in the Tower, Northumberland carried on his scientific researches, particularly in chemistry, with the help of Hues, Hariot and one Walter Warner, also a mathematician and philosopher, whose particular interest was what the Elizabethans called "alchemy," but which was, at least as far as these genuine scientists were concerned, "geological chemistry." It was Ralegh himself who dubbed this trio "the Earl's three Magi."

Hakluyt's introduction to this scientific group was somewhat circuitous. His interests and labours were from the beginning not in "pure science" but in science as an aid to discovery and imperial expansion. In this promotion of science, Ralegh had, as we have indicated, a special interest.

Ralegh may have known Hakluyt first at Oxford. Wood tells us that Ralegh went up to Oriel "in 1568, or thereabouts," and "after he had spent about three years in that house, left the University without a degree." That would be, then, about 1571 or 1572. Inasmuch as Hakluyt received his Bachelor of Arts in February 1574, and had already conceived a great zeal for "discovery," it is more than likely that the friendship between the two dates from their undergraduate days. In his Dedication of the first edition (1589) of the *Principal Navigations, Voyages and Discoveries of the English Nation,* to Sir Francis Walsingham, Hakluyt tells a pretty story of his first acquaintance with the noble science of Geography:

> I do remember that being a youth, and one of her Majesties scholars at Westminster, that fruitful nurserie, it was my happe to visit the chamber of Mr. Richard Hakluyt my cousin, a Gentleman of the Middle Temple, well knowen unto you, at a time when I found open vpon his board certaine bookes of Cosmographie, with an vniuersall Mappe: he seeing me somewhat curious in the view thereof, began to instruct my ignorance, by shewing me the diuision of the earth into three parts after the olde account, and then according to the latter & better distribution, into more: he pointed with his wand to all the knowen Seas, Gulfs, Bayes, Straights, Capes, Rivers, Empires, Kingdomes, Dukedomes, and Territories of ech part, with

declaration also of their speciall commodities, & particular wants, which by the benefit of trafficke & entercourse of merchants, are plentifully supplied. From the Mappe he brought me to the Bible, and turning to the 107 Psalme, directed mee to the 23 & 24 verses, where I read, that they which go down to the sea in ships, and occupy by the great waters, they see the works of the Lord, and his wonders in the deepe, &c. Which words of the Prophet together with my cousin's discourse (things of high and rare delight to my yong nature) tooke in me so deepe an impression; that I constantly resolued, if euer I were preferred to the Vniuersity, where better-time, and more convenient place might be ministred for these studies, I would by Gods assistance prosecute that knowledge and kinde of literature, the doores whereof (after a sort) were so happily opened before me.

When the opportunity came, he kept his resolution. He tells us, in the same letter, that when, not long after, he was removed to Christ Church in Oxford, his "exercises of duety first performed," he "fell to his intended course, and by degrees read over whatsoeuer printed or written discoueries and voyages [he] found extant, either in Greeke, Latine, Italian, Spanish, Portugall, French, or English languages." Moreover, in his office of public lecturer (at Oxford?), he tells us that he was "the first that produced and shewed the olde imperfectly composed, and the new lately reformed Mappes, Globes, Spheares, and other instruments of this Art for demonstration in the common schooles, to the singular pleasure, and general contentment of [his] auditory." He continues: "In the continuance of time and by reason principally of my insight in this study, I grew familiarly acquainted with the chiefest Captaines at sea, the greatest Merchants, and the best Mariners of our nation." In 1582, whether or not at Ralegh's instigation, he printed a book that would have endeared him to "the Shepherd of the Ocean," if he had not already been so, for it was a very able argument for the very policy Ralegh was pushing. It was entitled *Divers voyages touching the Discoueries of America, and the Island adjacent vnto the same, made first of all by our English men, and afterward by the Frenchmen and Britons: And certain notes of advertisements for observations, necessarie for such as shall heere after make the like attempt.*

The *Divers Voyages* was dedicated to Sir Philip Sidney, who by common interest in science and expansion, and by marriage alliance, had already become closely associated with the Ralegh group. Mr. James Augustus St. John, in his *Life of Sir Walter Ralegh* (1869, pp. 87-88) says: *

> With diplomatic skill, Ralegh bound to his interest the parties who each had separate schemes of his own to prosecute after the death of Gilbert. This was accomplished in part by his bringing about a marriage between Robert Sidney, the younger brother of Philip Sidney, and his lovely cousin, Barbara Gamage, the heiress of large estates by which Philip and his father-in-law Walsingham . . . were bound to his enterprise.

This marriage took place in 1584. Mr. St. John adds:

> It is not, perhaps, ascribing too much to beauty and wealth, and family ties resting on them, to suppose that Barbara had something to do in bringing about that accord which was witnessed in Parliament a few months later, when Walsingham and Sidney were on a committee to whom was referred the application for a confirmation of Ralegh's patent.

Perhaps it is not ascribing too much to beauty and family ties, but the fact remains that there were other good reasons for Sidney's interest in Ralegh's little academy. Chief of these was a common interest in science. Sidney had, as a matter of fact, a small clique of his own, in which there were several members who belonged also to the larger Ralegh group. It is no part of my purpose to enter into the controversy that has waged over the organization of the group known as the *Areopagus*. No one doubts that Sidney and his cousin, Fulke Greville, were the patrons of the group, and that it included at least one of Ralegh's warmest friends, Edmund Spenser. Sidney's biographer, Zouch, (*Life of Sidney*, p. 339) says that at the meetings of "this fellowship [i.e., the fellowship of the Areopagites] philosophical and metaphysical subjects were discussed, and the doors of the apartments in which they met, were kept shut." At least one such meeting behind closed doors is described by Bruno in his *Ash Wednesday Supper*. "We met," says Bruno, "in a chamber in the house of Sir Fulk Gre-

* See, Dr. Leonard Wood's Introduction to Hakluyt's *Discourse concerning Western Planting*, (Cambridge Press, 1877), XV, p. vii.

ville . . . to discuss moral, metaphysical, mathematical, and natural speculations."

Lord Brooke himself made more than one contribution to the Cult of the Intellect, which took its inspiration from Cynthia. Though he claimed, as did all the poets, that "my songs they be of Cynthia's praise," still his real inspiration was, as it was for Chapman, the glory of the life intellectual. Greville's *Treatise on Human Understanding* will show how naturally he would fit into the fellowship described by Zouch:

> The Mind of Man is this world's true dimension,
> And Knowledge is the measure of the mind;
> And as the mind, in her vaste comprehension,
> Contains more worlds than all the world can find,
>   So knowledge doth it selfe farre more extend,
>   Than all the minds of men can comprehend.
>
> A climbing height it is, without a head,
> Depth without bottom, way without an end;
> A circle with no line invironed;
> Not comprehended, all it comprehends;
>   Worth infinite, yet satisfies no minde
>   Till it that infinite of the Godhead find.
>
> This knowledge is the same forbidden tree
> Which man lusts after to be made his Maker;
> For knowledge is of Power's eternity,
> And perfect Glory, the true image-taker,
>   So as what doth the Infinite containe
>   Must be as infinite as it again.

It may be interesting to note in passing that Lord Brooke was himself in the habit of writing fustian plays about contemporary affairs. Concerning the Arguments of his Tragedies, he himself tells us, "they be not naked and casuall, like the Greeke, and Latine, nor (I confess) contrived with the variety and unexpected encounters of the Italians, but *near Level'd to those humours, councels, and practices, wherein I thought fitter to hold the attention of the Reader, than in the strangeness, or perplexedness of witty Fictions.*" [Italics inserted.] *

* For a full discussion of these fustian dramas, see Kuhl, "Political Matters in Elizabethan Drama," *Phil. Quart.*, 1928.

It was, therefore, not unnatural that Hakluyt should have chosen Sir Philip Sidney as the person most likely to help him and his patron in the fostering of a University foundation for a Chair in Navigation. In the Dedication of the *Divers Voyages* "To the right Worshipfull Gentleman Master Phillip Sidney Esquire," he descants at length upon the advantages ensuing to the Spaniards by reason of such a lectureship in Seville, and he concludes:

> I speake all to this ende, that the like order of erecting such a lecture here in London or about Ratcliffe in some convenient place, were a matter of great consequence and importance, for the saving of many men's lives and goods, which nowe through grosse ignorance are dayly in great hazard, to the no small detriment of the whole realme. For which cause I have dealt with the right worshipfull Sir Francis Drake, that seeing God hath blessed him so wonderfully, he would do this honour to himselfe and benefit to his countrey, to be at the cost to erect such a lecture: whereunto in most bountifull maner at the verie first he answered, that he liked so well of the notion, that he would give twentie pounds more before hand to a learned man to furnish him with instruments and maps that would take this thing upon him: yea, so readie he was that he earnestly requested mee to help him to the notice of a fitte man for that purpose, which I for the zeal I bere to this action, did presently, & brought him one, who came vnto him & conferred with him thereupon; but in fine he would not undertake the lecture, unlesse he might have fourtie pounds a yeere standing, and so the matter ceased for that time; howbeit the worthy and good Knight remaineth full constant, and will be, as he told me very lately, as goode as his worde. Nowe, if God shoulde put into the head of any noble man to contribute other twentie pounde, to make this lecture a competent living for a learned man, the whole realme no doubt might reape no small benefit thereby.

We shall have occasion, in our discussion of the Virginian enterprise in relation to *Tamburlaine,* to mention Drake's cordiality toward Ralegh's schemes; but in no real sense could Drake be said to belong to the intellectual aristocracy of "the Ralegh circle."

To the nucleus already described should be added three names: Laurence Keynes, Northumberland's steward, and explorer for Ralegh; Sir George Carey, who became Baron

Hunsdon and Lord Chamberlain, and Fernando Stanley, fifth Earl of Derby, whose courtesy-title of Lord Strange, is well known to students of Elizabethan drama. In Chapman's dedication to Roydon of *The Shadow of Night,* these three names are grouped for praise as special patrons of the scientific poets. Addressing Roydon as "my good Matthew," Chapman recalls:

> How joyfully ofttimes you reported unto me, that most ingenious Darby, deep-searching Northumberland, and skill-embracing heir of Hunsdon had most profitably entertained learning in themselves, to the vital warmth of freezing science, and to the admirable lustre of their true nobility, whose high-deserving virtues may cause me hereafter to strike that fire out of darkness [i.e., write a poem in their honour] which the brightest Day shall envy for beauty.

Sir George Carey was, as we have seen, the intimate friend of Cobham and Ralegh, and his relations with the Ralegh group were further cemented by his marriage with Spenser's cousin and admired friend, the Lady Elizabeth Spenser, daughter of Sir John Spenser of Althorpe. As early as 1582, he had been associated with Ralegh's anti-Spanish campaign, both in defense preparation of the Southern coast and in more aggressive acts of privateering against Spanish ships. Between the years 1585-86, two of his ships captured a vessel which he alleged belonged to Spain, but which was claimed by a Frenchman. In 1582 he was made Captain-general of the Isle of Wight and the stories of his rule there—for it was no less—are about as colourful as those of Ralegh in Ireland.*

In addition to the distinguished names already mentioned, there were many friends who were not actually dependents either of Ralegh or Northumberland, but who were constant visitors to the Martin Tower during the years of their joint imprisonment. Gerald Brenan says that these learned visitors:

> . . . assisted at his [Percy's] experiments, and remained for long or short periods as members of the *singular academy* [italics in-

* The reader should be cautioned against confusing Sir George Carey, or Carew, subsequently Baron Hunsdon, with Ralegh's friend and cousin Sir George Carew, subsequently Earl of Totnes. Up until the death of the "old Lord Hunsdon," in 1596, all references in *State Papers* are exceedingly confusing. I have tried, in my citations, to be very careful to distinguish between the two; but I herewith make a plea of indulgence if at any time I have mistaken the one for the other.

serted] which held its deliberations regardless of stone walls and iron bars. There was Nicholas Hill, the eminent philosopher and exponent of the Atomic Theory, who was afterwards forced to fly overseas because of his obstinate adherence to the "Romish persuasions," and to whom Ben Jonson alluded in one of his Epigrams (No. 34):

> . . . those *atomi* ridiculous
> Whereof old Democrite and Hill,
> One said, the other swore, the world consists.

There was also "the renouned mathematician," Nathaniel Torporley, rector of Salwarpe in Worcestershire, and Dr. John Dee, "now very old and feeble, who came from Richmond to visit his brother wizard." In his diary for 1583, Dee mentions Ralegh gratefully, and he records that he dined with him at Durham House in 1593; but it does not appear that Ralegh ever took the old astrologer very seriously. Especially associated with Northumberland was his friend and protégé, Thomas Allen, distinguished antiquary and philosopher, who had refused a bishopric under Elizabeth because of his stubborn loyalty to the Catholic faith, a combination of circumstances which brought him under the generous and fearless patronage of the ninth Earl. Both patron and protégé were hounded by slander and persecution. As Aubrey explains:

> In those dark times, astrologers, mathematicians and conjurers were accounted the same thing, and the vulgar did verily believe him [Allen] to be a conjurer. He had a great many mathematical instruments and glasses in his chamber, which did also confirm the ignorant in their opinion, and his servitor, to impose on Freshmen and simple people, sometimes affirmed that he should meet the spirits coming upstairs like bees.

The persecution of Allen, as we shall have occasion to note (see, p. 383), began in the early days of his service to Ralegh; for ignorance, bigotry, malice, and envy, all combined under the protection of a specious political orthodoxy to turn the fair fame of these renaissance scientists into the foul legend of criminal atheism.

It will be seen at once that these intimate friends of Ralegh and Northumberland formed a brilliant band of intellectuals, poets, painters, geographers, philosophers, astronomers, and mathematicians, all of whom have in one way or another contributed to the best cultural tradition of England. The story of the interrelation and artistic output of this little academy of supermen has never been told. In fact, few, if any, have realized that, deeply buried under the surface of their apparently unrelated exploits, and connecting them all, whether in the realm of poetry or science or exploration, there branched and flourished the golden vein of "deep Hariot's mine," in which, as Bishop Corbett said, there was "no drosse." So high a claim can hardly be made for all the persons who came under Hariot's influence; certainly it cannot be made for Marlowe and Chapman, the chief poets of the group. It is, however, to be hoped that the ensuing studies will at least open the way toward a better understanding of the relation between these most brilliant of poets and scientists.

There remains one name to be reckoned with among Marlowe's aristocratic patrons, though, so far as I have been able to discover, there is nothing to link him with the scholarly interests of the Ralegh circle other than a mutual patronage of the two most distinguished poet members, Marlowe and Chapman. I refer to Thomas Walsingham, with whom Marlowe was living at the time of his arrest in 1592. Certainly we do not know when or under what circumstances Marlowe's intimacy with the Walsinghams of Scadbury arose, but since he actually lived with "his friend T. Walsingham, in Kent," a sketch of that family will give us some notion of the poet's own social standing, and perhaps something of his literary life; for it seems clear that Walsingham was an admirer of Marlowe's poetry as well as a friend to his person. When Edward Blunt published the *Hero and Leander* fragment, he dedicated it to Walsingham with the following friendly assumption:

> I cannot but see so far into the will of him dead, that whatsoever issue of his brain should chance to come abroad, that the first breath it should take might be the gentle air of your liking; for since his self had been accustomed thereunto, it would prove more agreeable and thriving to his right children than any other foster countenance whatsoever.

Lady Walsingham apparently shared the good offices of patron with her husband, for Chapman wrote a special Dedicatory Epistle to her, which bears witness to her generosity to literary men. He says:

Such uncourtly and silly dispositions as mine, whose contentment hath other objects than profit or glory, are as glad, simply for the naked merit of virtue, to honour such as advance her, as others are hired to commend with deepliest politique bounty.

It hath therefore adjoined much contentment to my desire of your true honour to hear men of desert in court, add to mine own knowledge of your noble disposition, how gladly you do your best to prefer their desires; and have as absolute respect to their mere good parts, as if they came perfumed and charmed with golden incitements. And this most sweet inclination, that flows from the truth and eternity of Nobles, assure your Ladyship doth more suit your other ornaments, and makes more to the advancement of your name and happiness of your proceedings, than if, like others, you displayed ensigns of state and sourness in your forehead, made smooth with nothing but sensuality and presents.

This poor Dedication (in figure of the other unity betwixt Sir Thomas and yourself) hath rejoined you with him, my honoured best friend; whose continuance of ancient kindness to my still-obscured estate, though it cannot increase my love to him, which hath ever been entirely circular; yet shall it encourage my deserts to their utmost requital, and make my hearty gratitude speak; to which the unhappiness of my life hath hitherto been uncomfortable and painful dumbness.

By your Ladyship's vowed in
most wished service
George Chapman

It seems almost as if a wayward fate hung over Chapman's choice of patrons. Either they were done to death, like Ralegh; or disgraced and contemned, like Somerset; or died prematurely, like Henry, Prince of Wales; or, like Lady Walsingham, lived, to be sure, in comfort, but died, leaving to the world only her ill name. (See, p. 285.)

Though little is known of the public life of Thomas Walsingham before 1596, still, since "the child is father to the man," it is possible from the ampler records of his later years to reconstruct a fairly reliable portrait of him in the days when Marlowe was his guest at Scadbury. The substance of the following account is from Webb and Chalfont's *Annals of Chisle-*

hurst. Born in 1561, he was very nearly of an age with his poet friend. He was the third son of Sir Thomas Walsingham III, of Scadbury, who died in 1583, succeeded by his second son Edmund, the first son, Guilford, having predeceased him. The youth and young manhood of Thomas Walsingham IV were spent amid the stir of pre-Armada days, in the preparation for which the family at Scadbury was in almost daily collaboration with those of Chislehurst, Penshurst, and Cobham. Particularly concerned were these Kentish neighbours with the possibility of attack upon Rochester, lying just at the mouth of the Medway, and scarcely a mile from Cobham Hall. As part of the defense, a great chain was stretched across the river from Upnor Castle to the opposite bank just below Chatham, and the spirit of the defenders is well expressed in a letter of the Admiral's to Secretary Walsingham, in which he says, "God of His mercy keep us from sickness, for we fear that more than any hurt the Spanish will do." Ten years later, when England was threatened with a second Armada, similar precautions were taken, this time under the direction of the younger generation, Henry, Lord Cobham, Warden of the Cinque Ports, Lieutenant in Kent, and Constable of Dover Castle, and Sir Thomas Walsingham IV. The latter, with Sir Thomas Leveson, was sent with 1080 men to defend the chain, "five ships next the chain, whilst four others were to repair to Chatham Church." (*State Papers, Elizabethan, Domestic,* CCLX, 1596.) Nor was the anti-Spanish temper of these young men stimulated only by fear of invasion. We are told (Nichols, *Progresses of Elizabeth,* II) that in 1586, at the funeral of Sir Philip Sidney, friend and neighbour of the Walsinghams, Thomas' elder brother Edmund, together with William Sidney, carried a banner behind the supporters of the pall. At this time Thomas was twenty-two years old, and living with his unmarried brother Edmund, so that it is impossible for him not to have been interested in and thoroughly conversant with affairs in the Netherlands and in France, where Elizabeth was constantly, if often secretly, helping the Protestant and anti-Spanish cause by her assistance to the Prince of Condé and the young King of Navarre. Of her particular attitude toward the continental Protestants, more will be said in the chapter on the Holy League. Here it is sufficient merely to indicate something of the general political atmosphere that Marlowe must have breathed during his residence at Scadbury.

Strangely enough, the dates are not recorded either for the marriage or for the conferring of knighthood upon the new master of Scadbury (Edmund Walsingham having died in 1589), though it is certain that both had occurred before 1598. Much, however, may be gleaned from the careful gossip of Rowland Whyte concerning "the Lady Walsingham Junior"—so called in court documents to distinguish her from the Lady Walsingham, widow of Sir Francis. Her name was Audrey (or Etheldred) Shelton, daughter of Sir Ralph Shelton of Norfolk. She is often referred to in State Papers as Lady Audrey Walsingham. Her first documentary appearance is in 1597, on the occasion of the Queen's visit to Scadbury, there to spend at least one night, though it is obvious that Sir Thomas and his lady must have been at court for a considerable time before the honour of such an informal visit from the Queen would have been vouchsafed them. A letter from Cecil to Essex (*State Papers, Dom. Eliz.*, 1597) makes it clear that the visit occurred while the Court was at Greenwich, and not as part of a Progress. He writes, "I being at Greenwich and the Queen at Mr. Walsingham's." Her Majesty must have made it a gracious occasion, as she condescended to plant a commemoration oak, which is still standing in the avenue leading from St. Paul's Cray Common to the site of the old house, and some fig trees, reputed to have come from Marseilles. These are now dead, but were living as late as 1872, when they were pointed out to Queen Victoria on the occasion of her visit to Lord Sidney. *(Arch. Cant.*, XIII, 392.) It is said that in the old house at Scadbury two rooms retained to the last, in the eighteenth century, the names of "the Queen's apartment and that of the Maids of Honour." It is possible that Thomas was knighted as a result of this visit. Certainly in that year the Queen granted to him "the further demise of the manor of Dartford, with Cobham, Comb, and Chislehurst" for twenty-one years. Two years later, the Countess of Derby was entertaining Queen Elizabeth at her country place, Harefield (Nichols, *Progresses of Elizabeth*, III, IV, p. 591), and one morning, the weather proving showery and unfavourable for the many al fresco entertainments provided, "the Humble petition of a Guileless Lady" was presented to the Queen with a "Robe of Rainbows" by the Lady Walsingham. Mrs. Webb says that the verses which follow "were apparently of her own composition," but I know not upon what authority the claim is made. The verses commence with an extravagant compliment to the sixty-seven year old Queen:

> Beauties rose and Virtues booke
> Angells mind and Angells looke,
> To all Saints and Angells deare,
> Clearest Majestie on Earth,
> Heaven did smile at your faire birth.

The remaining lines relate how St. Swithin in heaven, being dissatisfied with the conduct of Iris in providing such rainy weather during her Majesty's visit, took her rainbow robes from her and had commissioned her Ladyship to present them to the Virgin Monarch.

In the roll for New Year's Day, 1599-1600, Sir Thomas and his Lady figure in a quaint collaboration, each giving the Queen "part of a petty-coat of clay-coloured satten, embroidered all over with branches of silver." The Lady received in return twenty-seven and one half ounces of gilt plate. (Nichols, *op. cit.,* IV, pp. 453, 591.)

During these last few years of Elizabeth's life, we have many glimpses of the social life of the Walsinghams, but all too few concerning the political career of Sir Thomas. In 1596 he was appointed Justice of the Peace for the Hundred of Rokesley (Lombarde, *Kent,* p. 31), and in October, 1597, Rowland Whyte wrote to his master, Sir Robert Sidney, concerning an affair which had come before Sir Thomas in his capacity of Justice.

It is not, however, until the accession of James that we see the Walsinghams as a political force to be reckoned with, and then it is Lady Walsingham, rather than her husband, who occupies the front of the stage. She was among the English ladies sent to Scotland to accompany the Queen to London, and in the same year Sir Thomas and his wife were appointed to the office of chief keeper of the Queen's wardrobe. Lady Walsingham was also made a lady of the drawing-chamber and granted a pension of £200 a year for life "for attendance on the Queen," and from many contemporary allusions, it seems that she was the ally and tool, if not actually the mistress of Cecil, to whose favours she probably owed these advancements. When Cecil died, the following lines came, says Osborne (*op. cit.*, p. 236), "from so smart a penne in the king's sense, that he sayd, he hoped the author would dye before hym; who it was God knowes":

Here lies Hobinall, our pastor while here,
That once in a quarter our fleeces did sheare.
To please us, his curre he kept under clog,
And was ever after both shepherd and dog.
For oblation to Pan his custome was thus,
He first gave a trifle, then offer'd up us:
And through his false worship such power he did gaine,
As kept him o' th' mountaine, and us on the plaine;
Where many a horn-pipe he tun'd to his Phyllis,
And sweetly sung Walsingham to Amaryllis.*

"It is possible," says Osborne, "posterity may find a key to these verses; if not, the loss is not much." The loss is, perhaps, more than Osborne realized. The editor of the *Memoirs* adds the following note:

Walsingham was the name of a popular tune. In an old play, to which we have mislaid the reference, mention is made of a "cobler teaching black-birds to whistle *Walsingham.*" But the Earl of Salisbury's favourite mistress was also named Walsingham; and hence the pun so much admired by James and by Osborne.

What a pity that we are not able to identify the play in which a cobbler taught the blackbirds to sing Walsingham! For Marlowe was not only the son of a cobbler, but he himself was constantly called "cobbler" by his contemporaries.

Lady Ann Clifford, in her diary, speaks of "My Lady Suffolk [wife of Lord Thomas Howard, Earl of Suffolk, and mother of the infamous Countess of Essex] and my yeonge Lady Derby, and my Lady Walsingham," as three ladies who were "the great favourites of Sir Robert Secill." In 1609 Lady Audrey was granted precedence of all ladies of her own rank at court, and nine years later she is referred to in a royal warrant

* This poem is ascribed to Ralegh by Mr. J. Hannah in his *Courtly Poets from Ralegh to Montrose.*

to pay her a certain sum of money, as His Majesty's "Valentine"! With more of this lady's history this narrative need not be concerned. Her importance lies only in the fact that she was part of the social clique in which Ralegh and Cobham and Cecil and the Howards moved, and that it was the circle in which Marlowe went, as a friend, if not almost as an equal. We cannot be certain that Marlowe knew her, but it is beyond doubt that Roydon and Chapman knew her well. Lady Walsingham may have been influential in getting Chapman's *Virginia Mask* put on at Court in honour of the Princess Elizabeth's nuptials. But of this mask, more later. (See, pp. 390ff.)

At the death of Sir Thomas IV, his son wrote of him in a Latin epitaph over his tomb, that he "was most wise in conducting the affairs of his country, most zealous for peace, most friendly towards his neighbour, most generous to the poor, and most famous for a liberal hospitality towards all." He might have been all these things except the last, and still have passed into absolute obscurity; but his patronage of Marlowe and Chapman, the two chief poets of the Ralegh group, places him in the list of the forever memorable. In 1605, Chapman's published version of *All Fools* was dedicated to his "long-lived and honourable friend Sir Thomas Walsingham, Knight." Three years later his Byron plays were dedicated to Sir Thomas and his little eight-year-old son. Chapman describes the latter as his "much-loved from his birth, the right toward and worthy gentleman . . . Thomas Walsingham, Esquire."

As I have indicated, I have been able to discover no direct connection between Sir Thomas and Sir Walter, but it will be obvious that they had many interests in common, including two of the most gifted poets in that age when gifted poets were by no means rare.

CHAPTER SIXTEEN

Virginia

IT WILL BE NECESSARY for us now to return to the special activities of Sir Walter's circle which were connected with his Virginia enterprise. All the training of Ralegh's young captains in the mysteries of navigation and all the scouting for funds for a chair or Foundation Lectureship in Navigation, undoubtedly formed a part of Ralegh's dream for a "new England on the shores of rich America."

Ralegh returned from Ireland in December, 1581, because the rebellion had been brought so thoroughly under control that it had become feasible to discharge a considerable portion of the English forces. He returned with despatches from Lord Grey and, as we have already noted, was promptly launched upon the most favourable of court tides. He was at once given several honourable employments. In 1581 he was a member of the escort provided by Elizabeth for Simier, Anjou's dexterous and all but successful agent in the affair of the French marriage. In fact, so acceptably, not to say seductively, had he done his proxy wooing, that it was rumoured he was in positive danger from certain Flushing pirates known to be in the pay of Leicester. At all events, the vessel containing the returning escort was chased for several hours, whether or not by Leicester's men. In *Leicester's Commonwealth,* we are assured that "Master Ralegh well knoweth it, being there present." More of this sort of thing fell to Ralegh's lot during the next year or so. He was sent again in February, 1582, as escort to Anjou himself, and returned from the Netherlands with special letters to the Queen from William of Orange, but it is clear that he set little store by these decorative jobs, keeping ever on the lookout for a more substantial preferment, something that would lead to a career not unworthy of his boundless energy, his keen attacking mind, and his restless imagination. The role of a Rosencrantz and Guildenstern, even if the errand were honourable, would not have satisfied this veteran of two wars, who had already tasted at the Queen's council table the wine of importance. There was no vision in this escorting, or Progress-attending business, hence no stimulus. Besides, his penchant for action and his pride demanded responsibility. He was a lover of power, not of place, which is, after all, a meaner thing. From his first coming to court, Ralegh had had constant occasion for observing this distinction; for while Elizabeth was shrewd enough in important affairs, like that of the exchequer and foreign relations, to depend upon sober, God-fearing men like Burleigh and Walsingham, who still took Scripture and Tully seriously, she amply consoled herself for this prudence by surrounding herself with a younger, flashier, altogether more joyous company. Occasionally one, such as her godson, Sir John Harrington, would emerge from this dressy group by a flash of wit; but too often they boasted only such fatuous advantages as a fine leg or the ability to execute a difficult figure in a dance. Hatton was especially famous for possessing both.

Against all this "superfluous sort of men" Ralegh set his wits and energy. He was too intelligent to spend his private hours concocting dreary runes like Hatton's "Book, bucket, and bodkin," yet his wit, his good looks, and his comparatively humble origin combined to keep him from rising quickly out of that group, to take his place among the serious statesmen of the Queen's Council. Even when more permanent occupation came in the form of a new captaincy in Ireland, the Queen kept him from busying himself much about it, instructing him to appoint a lieutenant while he was "for some considerations excused by Us to stay here." Not even when he was made Captain of the Queen's Guard and Warden of the Stannaries and Vice-Admiral of the West, was he satisfied, though this last office gave him at least one opportunity for action more to his liking. It became his duty to keep himself informed of the movements of all ships off the west coast of England. This meant mostly Spanish bottoms laden with treasure from all parts of the world, but especially from the Spanish cities of the Caribbean. Elizabeth had long made it clear to the initiated what practices she expected and approved for the English filibusters, as well as for those holding proper patents. Such famous sea-dogs as Hawkins, Drake, Frobisher, Cavendish, and Cumberland, not only ran no risk of her displeasure when they plundered the Spanish galleons and sacked the richest cities of the American colonies, but they found the treasure thus procured the best means to establish for them an immediate claim to her affectionate interest. After Drake's men had taken their "full pleasure both in the uttermost sacking and spoiling of all their household goods and merchandise" [i.e., of the Spanish colonists], they felt that they could "with much honour and reputation" [i.e., without considering themselves insulted by so paltry an offer!] then be satisfied to accept a ransom of "some xxvij or viij thousand pounds sterling"! (Hakluyt, *Principal Navigations . . . of the English Nation,* [Glasgow, 1903], X, p. 97.)

Yet, in 1585, England was still technically at peace with Spain; and if in 1585, much more so in 1580, when Drake returned from his voyage around the world laden to the hawse with gold ingots from the Peruvian mines, and the bejeweled and elaborately wrought plate and silken brocades with which the Spanish missionaries had made glorious their churches in the New World. There were quantities of native products such as pearls, spices, and drugs. Not only was his career of piracy, with all its savagery and sacrilege, condoned by his company, but the chaplain himself, after "offering up a prayer of thanksgiving," took it for granted that the sacred vessels stolen from the altars should be allotted to him as his appropriate share of the plunder! Drake himself was honoured by the Queen, who went to Deptford to meet him and knighted him there on his own ship. As Professor Sir Walter Raleigh says in his introduction to Hakluyt, "By this act, with full knowledge of what she was doing, she cast the die." From then on, all buccaneers sought to rival him whom his own people dubbed "The Master Thief of the Unknown World," but whom the terrorized enemy regarded as no less a scourge than Attila himself. Weldon tells us that the "Jesuits reported our nation to be ugly, and like devils, as a punishment to our nation for casting off the pope's supremacy; and they pictured Sir Francis Drake, generally half a man, half a dragon." This sounds like rubbish, but the fact is that Lope de Vega did actually write an epic poem entitled *El Dragoneta,* in which, we are told, "Sir Francis Drake's exploits are detailed, but with no friendly voice." But in England his treasure-laden ships were greeted in a very different style. The following ballad is typical of many:

I saw a ship a-sailing,
A-sailing on the sea,
And oh! it was all laden
With pretty things for thee!

There were comfits in the cabin,
And apples in the hold,
The sails were made of silk,
And the masts were made of gold.

The four-and-twenty sailors
That stood between the decks,
Were four-and-twenty white mice,
With chains about their necks.

The Captain was a Duck,
With a packet on his back;
And when the ship began to move,
The Captain said "Quack! Quack!"

In fact, Elizabeth fully shared the irritation felt by her boldest free-booters at the exclusive and, from their point of view, greedy and arrogant claims of the Spanish in the new-found World. M. Thomas Cates tells an amusing story which illustrates the English attitude toward the Spanish claims (Hakluyt, *op. cit.,* X, pp. 114-15):

Amongst other things which happened and were found at S. Domingo, I may not omit to let the world know one very notable marke & token of the insatiable ambition of the Spanish king and his nation, which was found in the king's house, wherein the chiefe governour of that Citie and Countrey is appoynted always to lodge, which was this: In the coming to the Hall or other roomes of this house, you must first ascend up by a faire large paire of staires; at the head of which staires is a handsome spacious place to walke in, somewhat like unto a gallery: wherein upon one of the wals, right over against you as you enter the said place, so as your eye cannot escape the sight of it, there is described & painted in a very large Scutchion the armes of the king of Spaine, and in the lower part of the said Scutchion, there is likewise described a Globe, containing in it the whole circuit of the sea and the earth whereupon is a horse standing on his hinder part within the globe, and the other forepart without the globe, lifted up as it were to leape, with a scroll painted in his mouth, wherein was written these words in Latin, *Non sufficit orbis*: which is as much as to say, as the world sufficeth not. Whereof the meaning was required to be knowen of some of those of the better sort, that came in commission to treate upon the ransome of the towne, who would shake their heads, and turn aside their countenance in some smyling sort, without answering any thing, as greatly ashamed thereof. For by some of our company it was tolde them, that if the Queene of England would resolutely prosecute the warres against the king of Spaine, hee should be forced to lay aside that proude and unreasonable reaching vaine of his: for hee should find more then inough to doe to keepe that which hee had alreadie as by the present example of their lost towns they might for a beginning perceive well inough.

The ogre in the story of *Jack and the Bean Stalk* is a popular chapbook version of this bug-a-boo, who gloats over his treasure on the top of his great "planting."

This Spanish policy of monopolizing the New World had been a festering thorn in the side of the English ever since Sir John Hawkins, in 1564, on board the Royal ship *Jesus of Lubeck,* had forced the ports of the Spanish Main to accept his cargo of Negro slaves in spite of the orders from King Philip that no English vessel be allowed to trade there. (*Ibid.,* VII, p. 48.) The development of this commercial rivalry through a long series of reprisals to an avowed and shameless policy of plunder is an exciting, if not too edifying story, and one that has been told often enough by the not-too-ashamed inheritors of the wealth and power thus gained. As Camden says (*ibid,* XII, p. 50), "When Drake and Hawkins reached home with their tale of Spanish treachery, military and seafaring men all over England fretted and desired war with Spain."

Indeed, this was precisely what Drake wanted, and he understood his countrymen well enough to feed their intense flame of Spanish hatred by adding the crackling fuel of rich plunder. Not only did he chase and rob every treasure-ship that sailed along the Spanish Main, but often enough turned land-thief as well, pillaging the cities, especially the churches, and robbing the great mule-trains that brought the yearly product of the Peruvian mines from Panama to Nombre de Dios. Tales of the loot spread like wildfire. "Incredible it is," says Camden (*ibid.,* XII, p. 51), "with how great alacrity they put to sea and how readily they exercised piracy against the Spaniards." When Drake returned to England in 1580, he was able to pay the investors in his enterprise a two-thousand-per-cent dividend (Conyers Read, *Mr. Secretary Walsingham,* [Oxford], III, p. 396), besides retaining a rich share for himself and his men. One aspect of his reception, however, troubled him and was not unnoted by others, viz., "some of the chief men at court refused to accept the gold which he offered them, as gotten by piracy." (Hakluyt, *op. cit.,* XII, p. 61.) It was not only that men like Humphrey Gilbert or Ralegh would have a naturally finer code than Drake, but the fact is that at the time of his first setting out to sea with Hawkins, Drake had his fortune to make and no reputation to lose, and certainly enjoyed the business of "singeing the King of Spaine's beard," as their exploits against Philip were later jocularly described. But long before he came back to England, Sir Humphrey Gilbert was a person of considerable standing, knighted, trusted and favoured by the Queen. Like many others at Court, both he and Sir Walter were much impressed by Drake's stories of El Dorado, the riches of the Indian and Peruvian mines; but it suited better with their notions of dignity and self-esteem to proceed by legal patent. Besides, why give oneself the troublesome, dangerous, and not too reputable task of stealing that which could be had freely and quietly, in domains not yet claimed by any rival Christian prince? At all events, so thought Richard Eden, as early as 1555. In the preface to his Translation of Peter Martyr's *Decades,* he informs the Queen (Mary) that from Florida northward to Newfoundland there are lands "not yet known but only by the sea-coasts, neither inhabited by Christian men"; but, as Professor Walter Raleigh points out (*op. cit.,* p. 35), "His suggestion that England should take possession of these was not likely to bear fruit while Mary reigned and Philip governed." It was, however, quite another matter when, in 1576, Humphrey Gilbert put before the covetous but practical Elizabeth a definite proposition for establishing a claim to these lands and placing thereon an English colony. In a notable *Discourse* presented to her in that year he confidently states (*ibid.*, pp. 35, 36), that there are

. . . divers very rich countries both civil and others . . . where there is to be found great abundance of gold, silver, precious stones, cloth of gold, silks, all manner of spices, grocery wares, and other kinds of merchandise of inestimable price, where both the Spaniard and Portugal, through the length of their journeys, cannot well attain unto. . . . We might inhabit some part of those countries, and settle such needy people of our country, which now trouble the commonwealth, and through want here at home are forced to commit outrageous offences, whereby they are daily consumed with the gallows.

He added the recommendation which made it possible for Elizabeth to grant him the patent he was seeking. This scheme, he declared, might be carried out "without injury done to any Christian prince, by crossing them in any of their trades, whereby they might take any just occasion of offense." Bacon had stated the average Englishman's point of view in his *Considerations touching a war with Spain* (*ibid.*, p. 72):

In money no doubt is the principal part of the greatness of Spain; for by that they maintain their veteran army; and Spain is the only State of Europe that is a money grower. But in this part, of all others, is most to be considered the ticklish and brittle state of the greatness of Spain. Their greatness consisteth in their treasure, their treasure in the Indies, and their Indies (if it will be weighed) are indeed but an accession to such as are masters by sea. So as this axle tree, on which their greatness turneth, is soon cut in two by any that shall be stronger than they at sea.

This was the argument which Drake and the early seamen had put into action, and Ralegh, of course, saw the importance of it. "By the abundance of treasure of that country," he wrote, "the Spanish King vexeth all the Princes of Europe, and is become in a few years from a poor King of Castile the greatest monarch of this part of the world." But he was not content merely to emulate Drake in his daredevil and spectacular role of romantic robber of this horde. Aside from the fact that his pride would have scorned a mere imitation, his intelligence could justly estimate the impermanence of such a policy of harrying and petty annoyance. "It is useless," he says, "to cripple the Spanish Navy; in a year the losses are repaired, and the King of Spain 'beginneth again like a storm to threaten ship wrack to us all. . . . It is his Indian gold that endangereth and disturbeth all the nations of Europe.' " (*Ibid.*, p. 73.)

The solution suggested, or rather promoted by his brother Gilbert, recommended itself to him as a more feasible, more dignified, more permanent, and in every way more worthy manifestation of Elizabeth's and of England's greatness. He declared later (*ibid.*, p. 72):

> It becometh not the former fortune in which I once lived to go journeys of picory; it had sorted ill with the offices of honour which by her Majesty's grace I hold this day in England, to run from cape to cape, and from place to place, for the pillage of ordinary prizes. . . . The King of Spain is not so impoverished by taking three or four port towns in America as we suppose.

But the constant burden of his song is: Let us get for Her Majesty a better, richer Indies of our own. In this program he was supported by a respectable minority, in and out of Court, who coveted the riches of the Americas, but who definitely felt squeamish about acquiring it through piracy. Among such, Hakluyt, though merely a burgher, was one of the most influential. Again and again we find him urging the comparison between the self-respecting methods of the Portuguese and Spaniards, who have colonies, and the free-booting practices of England and France, who have none. Portugal and Spain, he says, have found employment for all their subjects, so that these two nations breed no pirates, "whereas we and the French are most infamous for our outrageous, common and daily practices." (*Ibid.*, p. 36.) In the Dedication to Sidney already referred to, he observes:

> I Maruaile not a little (right worshipfull) that since the first discouerie of America (which is nowe full fourscore and Tenne yeeres) after so great conquests and plantings of the Spaniardes and Portingales there, that wee of England could neuer haue the grace to set fast footing in such fertill and temperate places, as are left as yet vnpossessed of them. But againe when I consider that there is a time for all men, and see the Portingales time to be out of date, & that the nakedness of the Spaniards, and their long hidden secretes are nowe at length espied, whereby they went about to delude the

worlde, I conceiue great hope that the time approacheth and nowe is, that we of England may share and part stakes . . . both with the Spaniards and the Portingale in part of America, and other regions as yet vndiscovered. And surely if there were in vs that desire to aduance the honour of our Countrie which ought to bee in euery good man, wee woulde not all this while haue foreslowne the possessing of those landes, which of equitie and right appertain vnto vs, as by the discourses that followe shall appeare most plainely.

In a later preface he reiterates, with renewed emphasis, his reasons for writing this book and those which followed in close succession. In the Dedication to Walsingham of the volume of 1598, he declared:

I both heard in speech and read in books other nations miraculously extolled for their discoveries and notable enterprises by sea, but the English of all others for their sluggish security, and continuall neglect of the like attempts, especially in so long and happy a time of peace, either ignominiously reported, or exceedingly condemned: which singular opportunity, if some other people our neighbors had been blessed with, their protestations are often and vehement, they would farre otherwise haue vsed.

Whether or not it was this volume or some friendly office on the part of Ralegh that procured for Hakluyt the patronage of the Admiral Lord Howard of Effingham, we know not; but the following year Hakluyt was appointed chaplain to Lord Howard's brother-in-law, Sir Edward Stafford, who went to France as English Ambassador in 1583. While in Paris, he found new opportunities for collecting information as to the Spanish and French voyages, "making," he says, "diligent enquiry of such things as might yield any light vnto our western discouery in America." These reflections he embodied in an essay entitled *A particular Discourse Concerning Western Discoueries,* and presented it to the Queen in manuscript, in 1584. This *Discourse* was first printed in 1877 by the Maine Historical Society, with a Preface and Introduction by Dr. Leonard Woods, and edited by Charles Deane.

With Hakluyt's *Divers Voyages,* of 1582, and his *Particular Discourse Concerning Western Discoveries,* of 1584, there should be noted another important contribution to the cause, namely, the account by Ralegh's friend, Sir George Peckham, of

Sir Humphrey Gilbert's expedition. It was published in 1583, entitled *A True Report of the Late Discoveries . . . of the Newfound Landes . . . By Sir Humphrey Gilbert.* Hakluyt had meant to join that expedition, but, as Dr. Woods suggests, "it was, however, probably thought that his services to the cause of Western discoveries and colonization would be greater in the post of observation and influence to which he was appointed," [that is, as Chaplain to Stafford]. While he was in Paris, the work of pushing the plantations was carried on at home. To Peckham's *True Report,* with the Introduction addressed to Sir Francis Walsingham, were attached nine complimentary poems, mostly by famous sea-captains who were generously helping Ralegh in his new project. Among these poems was one by Marlowe's intimate friend, Mathew Roydon. The Table of Contents makes it clear that the purpose of this discourse in eight chapters is to show that it is "lawfull & necessary to take possession of these colonies, to trade with the savages and to fortify these places," and it points out that "trading and planting" [i.e., establishing plantations] are not so difficult "as many would make it seeme to bee." To this intent Roydon wrote "to his fellow student":

> To prayse thy book because I am thy friende,
> Though it be common and thy due indeede;
> Perhaps it may some daintie eare offende,
> Reproofe repines that vertue hath her neede.
> Yet neverthelesse how ever thinges succeede,
> Sith to no other ende thy booke was made:
> All that I wish, is that thou mayest persuade.

Meanwhile, the enterprise was going forward. The six-year patent which Elizabeth granted to Sir Humphrey in 1578 had given him leave "to inhabit and possess at his choice all remote and heathen lands not in the actual possession of any Christian prince," but it was understood that he would strike out for the coast of the northern continent, with the intention of making a settlement somewhere between Florida and Newfoundland. The tragic fate of Sir Humphrey's first expedition is not a part of this history, but his second venture is pertinent in that it marks the beginning of Ralegh's lifelong pursuit of El Dorado.

Besides assisting at the council for Irish affairs, escorting Simier and Anjou to the Continent, and doing his bit to solace the Queen, Ralegh found time between January 1582 and the spring of 1583 to build a fine new ship which he christened the *Ark Ralegh* and in which he invested several thousand pounds. His obvious intention was to accept Gilbert's invitation to accompany him as vice-admiral; but the Queen, assuming the passion of a Dido for her Aeneas, peremptorily forbade him to go, and he had to let his ship sail without him. Sir Humphrey took possession of Newfoundland with the quaint ceremony of the water and hazel, but he was lost with his ship on the return voyage.

Ralegh at once sought and obtained a renewal of Gilbert's license in his own favour. In spite of the claims already made on Newfoundland by his brother, Ralegh decided to settle farther south, nearer the Indian mines which Drake and others reported, and where the climate was less difficult to contend with. There was, moreover, another element influencing his decision to settle further south. We have already noted Ralegh's friendship with Jacques Le Moyne, who survived the Huguenot massacre in Florida. How he escaped I do not know, but Henry Stevens (*op. cit.*, p. 37) tells us that he "landed destitute in Wales" and made his way to London where he "entered the service of Ralegh, who had lodged him safely in Blackfriars, where, under the name of James Morgan, he soon won considerable reputation as painter, engraver on wood, as teacher, and as art publisher or book seller." In 1586 Hakluyt and Ralegh co-operated in publishing the journal of Laudonnière, which, when translated by Hakluyt, appeared in 1587 under the title *A Notable History concerning four voyages made by Certain French Captains into Florida.** It is quite likely, therefore, that Ralegh was persuaded by Le Moyne that Florida was a fitter region for a plantation than the more northerly Newfoundland. At all events, he fitted out two new vessels and despatched them, under the charge of Captains Amadas and

* After Le Moyne's death in 1588, Theodore de Bry, the celebrated engraver of Frankfort, came to London and succeeded in purchasing from Le Moyne's widow a portion of her husband's drawings and paintings, together with his French version of the Florida expedition. See, p. 273, for connection between De Bry and John White, Le Moyne's successor.

Barlowe, on a reconnoitering trip to find a landing on the northern continent somewhere above the Gulf of Florida, and to report on the suitability of the region for the new colony he hoped to plant there. The report made by these two able and conscientious captains was such as to have intrigued a more phlegmatic imagination than Ralegh's. They landed on the Island of Wohokon, where, says the report, "we smelt so sweet and strong a smel, as if we had been in the midst of some delicate garden abounding with all kinds of odoriferous flowers." This fragrant breeze was discovered to have come from the sassafras, cedars, and cyprus trees that grew there in abundance. In fact, they found a land gloriously wooded, very fertile, and full of every kind of promise and "merchantible commodity," such as fish, skins, spices, grapes, and delectable new fruits; and above all, evidences of rare pearl fisheries. The report states that the chief's wife had about her forehead "a bande of white Corall, and so had her husband many times; in her eares she had bracelets of pearles hanging down to her middle (whereof wee delivered your worship a little bracelet), and those were of the bigness of good pease." (Hakluyt, *op. cit.,* VIII, p. 302.) Moreover when the King's brother, having taken a great fancy to a sword and other warlike gear, "offered to lay a great boxe of pearle in gage for them," the report says, "we refused it for this time, because we would not make them to know, that we esteemed thereof, until we had understood in what places of the countrey the pearle grew: which now your worshippe doeth very well understand." (*Ibid.,* p. 301.)

As a matter of course, they traded upon the simplicity of the natives in all their bartering, and made much of the advantages thus gained. They boasted of having exchanged a tin dish, which the chief coveted, for a gorget, "for twenty skins, worth twentie Crownes, or twentie nobles: and a copper kettle for fiftie skins worth fifty Crownes." As for gold and silver, it is clear that they stretched the truth as far as it would go. They declared that the chief "had upon his head a broad plate of golde, or copper, for being unpolished we knew not what mettal it shoulde be, neither would he by any means suffer us to take it off his head, but feeling it, it would bow very easily."

They would have liked to find a few nuggets along the shore, as Jacques Cartier said he had done along the river Saguenay, where, he declared (*ibid.*, pp. 237, 253), "are white Rubies, gold and other riches"; or they would fain have seen a few Indians "that sprinkled their bodies with the poulder of golde," as Sir Robert Dudley reported (*ibid.*, X, p. 208); but the evidence, and their responsibility to possible investors at home, did not seem to warrant their being too sure about these gold- and jewel-bespangled sands. As a matter of fact, the Exeter merchants whom Ralegh tried to interest in his next expedition were inclined to conservatism when it came to investing in so cautiously worded a security. There was, however, sufficient backing to enable Ralegh to equip a small fleet of seven sail, which he despatched in 1585 under the command of his cousin Sir Richard Grenville.

Professor Conyers Read says (*op. cit.*, III, pp. 406-407), "There is sufficient evidence to prove that Ralegh's Virginia voyages, like those of Sir Humphrey Gilbert before him, were not purely individual ventures, but were financed, in part at least, on the joint-stock plan." A passage in one of Lane's letters seems to suggest that Walsingham himself had invested in this venture of 1585, though Professor Read is cautious in his interpretation of this evidence. A calendar of the letter in question runs as follows (*ibid.*, III, p. 40):

> [Lane] has undertaken with good company to remain there [in Virginia] resolute rather to lose their lives than to defer possession of so noble a kingdom to the Queen, their Country and their noble patron, Sir Walter Ralegh, through whom and his Honour's [Walsingham's] most worthy endeavour and infinite charge an honourable entry is made to the conquest of.

The plan adopted seems to have been based on a earlier one, probably drawn up by Sir Humphrey Gilbert. Compare the following summary of a committee report on the colonizing venture of 1574, described in the *Calendar of Colonial Papers* (I, p. 1), as "Points set down by the Committees appointed in the behalf of the Company to confer with Mr. Carleil upon his intented discovery and attempt in the northern parts of America":

> The Committees are well persuaded that the country is very

fruitful; inhabited with savage people of a mild and tractable disposition, and of all other unfrequented places "the only fittest and most commodious for us to meddle withal." They propose that one hundred men be conveyed thither, to remain one year, who with friendly entreaty of the people, may enter into the better knowledge of the country and gather what commodities may be hereafter expected from it.

Similarly, Ralegh planned to leave there a colony of men who would have the hardihood to remain for a year and give the theory a fair trial. The settlement was to be under the governorship of Mr. Ralph Lane, with Captain Philip Amadas as his deputy. Ralegh took every possible care to insure the success of the expedition. He put the boldest, most courageous man he knew in supreme charge; and surely one of the uprightest, wisest, cleverest men in all England was his young friend and tutor, Mr. Thomas Hariot, whom he persuaded to go as the official geographer and reporter to the expedition. Did men suspect the reliability of the Virginia propagandists? They would now be confronted by a report so scientific and so transparently honest, that nothing but wilful incredulity could stand against it. Hariot's integrity was above suspicion.

The story of this first colony, the zest of its undertaking, the courage and loyalty of many of its members, and its sudden slump attendant upon the visit of Drake, has been told too often to need repeating here. All the world knows, too, how Ralegh refused to be discouraged, how he sent out a third (1586), then a fourth (1587) expedition, always intending to go himself but forcibly kept back by the Queen, till he had exhausted his resources. In 1589, he estimated that he had spent £40,000 on the Virginia plantation. Meanwhile he had the difficult task of sustaining a romantic interest in his far-away project, while he himself was compelled to stay prosaically at home. It would be truer to say that he remained at home, but not prosaically. For one thing, as we have seen, he instituted an elaborate campaign of advertising. He must get the thing talked about, he must convince investors, he must persuade the Queen that he had done, was doing, and would do her an incalculable service in Virginia. His first move was to publish a series of letters and reports concerning the expeditions and colonies, several of which we have already mentioned. Master Ralph Lane, on 2 September, wrote (Hakluyt, *op. cit.*, VIII, p. 319): "to M. Richard Hakluyt Esquire, and another gentleman of the middle Temple . . . from the new Fort in Virginia." This was to advertise the fact that this new country of her Majesty was "the goodliest and most pleasing territorie of the world," and were it once inhabited by Englishmen, "no realme in Christendome were comparable with it." He assures his readers that "what commodities soever Spaine, France, Italy, or the East parts doe yeild unto us, in wines of all sorts, of oyles, in flaxe, in rosens, pitch, frankinsence, corrals, sugars, and such like, these parts do abound with the growth of them all." Moreover, "sundry other rich commodities, that no parts of the world, be they West or East Indies have, here wee finde great abundance of." In particular there is a kind of flax "like silk, the same gathered of a grasse, as common there, as grass is here." In other words, silk in America will be as cheap and common as the coarsest linen at home. But these were all raw products, requiring time and labour for development, whereas many of the adventurers were looking for an immediate hundredfold, such as Drake had so dashingly achieved. For these, too, Master Lane had words of encouragement. He would lead men to believe that one might gather pearls like pebbles in Virginia. He tells of a native king who "had so great quantities of Pearle, and doeth so ordinarily take the same, as that not onely his own skins that he weareth and the better sort of his gentlemen and followers are full set with the sayd Pearle, but also his beds, and houses are garnished with them, and that he hath such quantity of them, that it is a wonder to see." He says he had a rope of black pearls "many of them . . . very great, and a few amongst the number very orient and round," but alas! he lost them with other things while "comming aboard Sir Francis Drake his Fleete." But the "King had great store of Pearle that were white, great, and round." (*Ibid.*, VIII, pp. 323, 357.)

Moreover, he has every reason to believe, though he does not actually say so, that the mineral the natives call Wassador, or copper, is really gold. At all events, the natives describe it as (*ibid.*, VIII, pp. 328-332):

. . . very soft and pale: they say that they take the saide mettall out of a river that falleth very swift from hie rockes and hils, and they take it in shallow water: the manner is this. They take a great bowle by their description as great as one of our targets, and wrap a skinne over the hollow part thereof, leaving one part open to receive the minerall: that done, they watch the coming down of the current, and the change of the colour of the water, and then suddenly chop downe the said bowle with the skinne, and receive into the same as much oare as will come in, which is ever as much as their bowl will holde, which presently they cast into a fire, and forthwith it melteth, and doeth yielde in five parts, at the first melting, two parts of metall for three parts of oare. Of this metall the Maugoaks have so great a store, by report of the Savages adjoining, that they beautifie their houses with great plates of the same.

Clearly Mr. Lane has read the showy accounts of the earlier navigators. In a Calendar of a "fragment of report of certain persons who travelled the aforesaid countries [of America] 1580" (*Colonial Papers,* I, pp. 1-2), the women are described as "wearing great plates of gold, covering their whole bodies like armour. . . . Of treasures, in every cottage pearl to be found and in some houses a peck. . . . Banquetting houses built of crystal, with pillars of massive silver, some of gold. Pieces of clean gold as big as a man's fist in the heads of some of the rivers . . . great abundance of silkworms." He is therefore making every possible inquiry as to the location of the "Mineral Countrey"; so far, he has found it only by report, and he dare not vouch for more than he has seen. Meanwhile he must not wet-blanket the cause at home by withholding these promising hopes of infinite riches to be picked up "without control" upon the American rocks. The truth is that he believes the mineral called Wassador to be copper, but he speaks of its paleness and softness in the hope of making investors at home think it gold. Note that toward the end of his report he inserts the following sentence to save his honour: "And touching the Minerall, thus doeth M. Youngham affirme, that though it be but copper, seeing the Savages are able to melt it, it is one of the richest Minerals in the World."

But in spite of these great possibilities, the little company was unable to resist the yearning for home when Drake offered them a chance to return. The story of these early years, particularly Ralegh's labours in England for his colonizing overseas, has never been adequately told, the tragedy of the Guiana voyage having quite overshadowed the romance of the earlier venture. It is not known what has become of the correspondence and other papers that must have accumulated during the last decades of the sixteenth century on the subject of Virginia. It appears, however, that neither the politicians nor the burghers were much moved by Mr. Lane's report. If Carew Ralegh had been unable to induce the Exeter merchants to join the company after the promising report of Amadas and Barlowe, how much less easily could Ralegh find investors and adventurers after the first little colony of 107 men had been unsuccessful, and after a year's trial had somewhat ingloriously returned with Sir Francis Drake? Ralegh had to contend not only with their failure to find gold, or even to vouch for it with any certainty, but also with certain malicious rumours spread abroad by a few disgruntled members of the colony itself. Difficulties of government had arisen almost immediately the little fleet embarked, owing, we are told by Master Lane (*Colonial Papers,* I, pp. 3-4), to the "intolerable pride and insatiable ambition" of their general "Sir Richar Greenefielde," of whom he has had "so much experience . . . as to desire to be freed from the place where he is to carry any authority in chief." Nor is this all. Even after Grenville left, there were unruly members who required keeping in order, and who were consequently dissatisfied with the adventure. Lane wrote to Sir Philip Sidney (*ibid.*), as "in the midst of an infinite business, having the charge of savages as well as wild men of his own nation, whose unruliness prevents his leaving them." These malcontents took their revenge by casting abroad disparagements of the new country, detrimental to Ralegh's plans for development. It was to counteract the bad effects of these rumours that Ralegh asked Hariot to make a further report of the country and its possibilities, to supplement the one already issued by Governor Lane. Hariot did so, and prefaced his remarks with what was intended for a scathing reproof to these unfair dealers. But poor Mr. Hariot had no gall at all! (Hakluyt, *op. cit.,* VIII, pp. 348ff.)

A brief and true report of the new found land of Virginia: of the commodities there found and to be raised, as well merchantable as others: written by Thomas Hariot, servant to Sir Walter Ralegh, a member of the Colony and there imployed a full twelve-month:

To the Adventurers, Favourers, and Welwillers of the enterprise for the inhabiting and planting in Virginia.

Since the first undertaking by Sir Walter Ralegh to deale in the action of discovering of that countrey which is now called and knowen by the name of Virginia, many voyages having beene thither made at sundry times to his great charge, as first in the yere 1584, and afterwards in the yeres 1585, 1586, and now of late this last yeere 1587: there have bene divers and variable reports with some slanderous and shamefull speeches bruted abroad by many that returned from thence: especially of that discovery which was made by the Colony transported by Sir Richard Grenville in the year 1585, being of all others the most principall, and as yet of the most effect, the time of their abode in the countrey being a whole yere, whereas in the other voyages before they stayed but six weeks, and the others after that were onely for supply and transportation, nothing more being discovered then had bene before. Which reports have not done a little wrong to many that otherwise would have also favoured and adventured in the action, to the honour and benefit of our nation, besides the particular profit and credit which would redound to themselves the dealers therein, as I hope by the sequel of events, to the shame of those that have avouched the contrary, shall be manifest, if you the adventurers, favourers, and welwillers doe but either increase in number, or in opinion continue, or having beene doubtfull renew your good liking and furtherance to deale therein according to the woorthinesse through cause of the diversity of relations and reports, many of your opinions could not be firme, nor the minds of some that are well disposed be setled in any certaintie.

I have therefore thought it good, being one that have beene in the discoverie, and in dealing with the natural inhabitants specially imployed: and having therefore seene and knowen more than the ordinary, to impart so much unto you of the fruits of our labours, as that you may know how injuriously the enterprise is slandered, and that in publique maner at this present, chiefly for two respects.

First, that some of you which are yet ignorant or doubtfull of the state thereof may see that there is sufficient cause why the chief enterpriser with the favour of her Majesty, notwithstanding such reports, hath not onely since continued the action by sending into the countrey again, and replanting this last yeere a New Colony, but is also, according as the times and meanes will afoord to follow and prosecute the same.

Secondly, that you, seeing and knowing the continuance of the action, by the view hereof you may generally know and learne what the countrey is, and thereupon consider how your dealing therein, if it proceed, may returne you profit and gaine, be it either by inhabiting and planting, or otherwise in furthering thereof.

And lest that the substance of my relation should be doubtfull unto you, as of others by reason of their diversitie, I will first open the cause in a few words, wherefore they are so different, referring my selfe to your favouravle constructions, and to be adjudged of, as by good consideration you shall finde cause.

Of our company that returned, some for their misdemeanour and ill dealing in the countrey have been there worthily punished, who by reason of their bad natures, having maliciously not onely spoken ill of their Governours, but for their sakes slandered the countrey it selfe. The like also have those done which were of their consort.

Some being ignorant of the State thereof, notwithstanding since their return amongst their friends and acquaintance, and also others, especially if they were in company where they might not be gainsayd, would seem to know so much as no men more, and make no men so great travellers as themselves. They stood so much, as it may seeme, upon their credit and reputation, that having bene a twelvemoneth in the countrey, it would have been a great disgrace unto them as they thought, if they could not have sayd much, whether it were true or false. Of which some have spoken of more than ever they saw or knew to be there. Other some have not bene ashamed to make absolute deniall of that, which although not by them, yet by others is most certainly and there plentifully knowen, and other some make difficulties of those things they have no skill of.

The cause of their ignorance was, in that they were of that many, that were never out of the island where we were seated, or not farre, or at least-wise in few places els, during the time of oure abode in the countrey: or of that many, that after gold or silver was not so soon found, as it was by them looked for, had little or no care of any other thing but to pamper their bellies; or of that many, which had little understanding, less discretion, and more tongue then was needfull or requisite.

Some also were of a nice bringing up, only in cities or townes, or such as never (as I may say) had seene the world before. Because there were not to be found any English cities, nor such faire houses, nor at their own wish any of their accustomed dainty food, nor any soft beds of downe or feathers, the countrey was to them miserable, and their reports thereof according.

Because my purpose was but in briefe to open the cause of the variety of such speeches, the particularities of them, and of many envious, malicious and slanderous reports and devices els, by our owne countreymen besides, as trifles that are not worthy of wise men to be thought upon, I mean not to trouble you withall, but will passe on to the commodities, the substance of that which I have to make relation of unto you.

Hereafter follows a report of the state and country of Virginia which is perhaps more amazing to posterity by reason of its accuracy and thoroughness, its far-reaching wisdom and insight, than it was dazzling to the shallow-pated multitude who could be lured thither only by an assurance of a get-rich-quick-and-easy proposition. It was a dignified and permanent way of dealing with one's detractors and enemies; but, like Hooker's stately reply to the Martinists, it was too ponderous a weapon for the kind of enemy Ralegh had to deal with. He must blaze the idea forth till it should be on the tongue of everyone. He must create an enthusiasm that would be contagious. He was practical enough to believe even then that it paid to advertise.

In the first place, he would display upon his own estates and person and those of his friends and relatives as many samples as possible of Virginia products. Hariot and Lane had discovered potatoes in Virginia; Ralegh grew them at Youghal, and great was the fame thereof. Hariot learned from the Indians the delectation to be found in smoking tobacco and he discoursed enthusiastically on its salubrious medicinal qualities; the passage is quaint enough to warrant quoting (*ibid.*, pp. 363-64):

There is an herbe which is sowed apart by itself: and is called by the inhabitants Uppawaoc: in the West Indies it hath divers names, according to the severall places and countreys where it groweth and is used: the Spaniards generally call it Tabacco. The leaves thereof being dried and brought into pouder, they use to take the fume or smoake thereof, by sucking it thorow pipes of clay, into their stomacke and head; from which it purgeth superfluous fleame and other gross humours, and openeth all the pores and passages of the body; by which meanes the use thereof not onely preserveth the body from obstructions, but also, if any be, so that they have not bene of too long continuance, in short time breaketh them, whereby their bodies are notably preserved in health, and know not many grievous diseases wherewithall we in England are often times afflicted. . . . We ourselves, during the time we were there, used to sucke it after their maner, as also since our returne, and have found many rare and wonderfull experiments of the vertues thereof: of which the relation would require a volume by itselfe: the use of it by so many of late men and women of great calling, as els, and some learned Physicians also, is sufficient witness.

So Ralegh smoked and got his friends to smoke. Northumberland's biographer, Gerald Brenan, says (*op. cit.,* II, p. 40) that Ralegh introduced into his [Henry Percy's] life "that which afterwards became one of its chief solaces–the use of tobacco. Northumberland was one of those men clearly intended by nature to be a smoker of the Indian herb. His hasty temper was soothed by its influence and his wits stimulated; and during the monotonous days of his captivity he found it a constant agreeable companion. After 1586 we find him (in the *Sion House MS Rolls*) buying quantities of tobacco from the Virginia merchants, and he possessed scores of pipes, some of them made from his own designing." Ralegh took infinite pains to give the practice vogue. We do not know that Ralegh hired Anthony Chute to advertise the new commodity on the stage, but it is obvious from Nashe's *Have With You to Saffron-Walden,* that he did so. Nashe declares that Chute "hath kneaded and daub'd vp a Commedie, called *The Transformation of the King of Trinidadoes two Daughters, Madame Panachaea and the Nymphe Tobacco;* and to approve his Heraldrie, scutchend out the honorable Armes of the Smoakie Societie." (*Works* [1596], III, p. 107.) Chute died about 1595, so that this *Comedie* must have been before that date, though we do not know the precise year. Before the end of the century the habit of smoking was so thoroughly intrenched that we can hardly pick up a play that does not allude to it, favourably or otherwise. Sir Edmund Chambers (*Elizabethan Stage,* II, p. 549) quotes passages from some half dozen plays illustrating this fact. Ralegh, too, designed exquisite pipes with silver bowls and took care to supply his friends and courtiers of influence with the leaf. In a letter to Sir George Carew, in Ireland, Sir John Stanhope excuses himself from sending any "tobacco, because Mr. Secretary and Sir Walter have stored you of late." It seems he did his best to induce the Queen to smoke, but if she had ever actually done so, the fact could hardly have passed without animadversion. She was, however, very curious to know the virtues and properties of the herb, and Oldys (*op. cit.*, I, pp. 74-75) tells an amusing story of a conversation Ralegh had with her on the subject:

> He [Sir Walter] assured her majesty he had so well experienced the nature of it, that he could tell her of what weight even the smoke would be in any quantity proposed to be consumed. Her majesty fixing her thoughts upon the most unpractical part of the experiment, that of bounding the smoke in a balance, suspected that he had put the traveller upon her, and would needs lay him a wager he could not solve the doubt: so he procured a quantity agreed upon to be thoroughly smoked; then went to weighing, but it was of the ashes; and in conclusion what was wanting in the prime weight of the tobacco, her majesty did not deny to have been evaporated in smoke; and further said, that "many labourers in the fire she had heard who had turned their gold into smoke, but Ralegh was the first who had turned smoke into gold."

At first people were shy of it. Even Ralegh's own servant was so astonished the first time he saw his master with "the smoke reeking out of his mouth" that he threw in his face a tankard of ale to put out the combustion that was inside him, and then ran downstairs to summon the family with repeated exclamations that "his master was on fire, and before they could get up would be burnt to ashes."

Elizabeth's sane attitude toward the new fashion contrasts favourably with the almost psychopathic intolerance of James I, who all but dripped foam at the mere thought of it, describing it in the concluding words of *A Counterblaste to Tobacco,* as "a custome loathsome to the eye, hatefull to the nose, harmfull to the braine, dangerous to the lungs, and in the blacke stinking fume thereof, neerest resembling the horrible Stigian smoake of the pit that is bottomlesse," and this in spite of the fact that the tobacco trade became a source of enormous revenue to the Crown. Aubrey tells us that when his "old yeoman neighbours" went to market, "they culled their biggest shillings to lay in the scales against the tobacco; now, the customes of it are the greatest his majestie hath." (*Ibid.*, III, p. 739.)

Samuel Rowland has an amusing description of a contemporary tobacco shop (c. 1610) in his *A Lying Knave*. Describing the "lying knave," who is, by the way, a great voyager, he says (Walker, *op. cit.*, p. 84):

> In a tobacco-shop, (resembling hell—
> Fire, stink, and smoke must be where devils dwell)
> He sits, you cannot see his face for vapour,
> Offering to Pluto with a tallow taper.
>
> . . . .
>
> Like an ill wind that grows fast, 't is come
> To stink in nostrils throughout Christendom,
> So that of most it may be truly spoke,
> Their tongues yield idle breath, their noses smoke.

It is not certain that these satires were directed at Ralegh, though the parallel throughout is highly plausible. *The Knave of Spades* (*ibid.*) is typical:

> God he neglecteth for the bar of gold,
> His soul for money every day is sold;
> To scrape and get his care is night and day,
> And in a moment death takes all away.

There are many other legends which illustrate Ralegh's devotion to tobacco—stories of how he smoked as Essex died, how he shocked the ladies by taking out his pipe at Sir Robert Pontz's, but we have noted enough for our purpose. We must not forget, however, that Marlowe is reported to have said "that all that love not tobacco are fooles."

Hariot also discoursed, in sedately elevated strain, of the rare and pleasant fruits to be had in the New World, and Ralegh planted on his own estates whatever of such rarities could be transported. In fact, there developed a great rivalry between Ralegh and Northumberland in the art of successful transplanting of such garden rarities at Sion and Sherbourne; but all this kind of personal advertising was for a court audience. Ralegh might intrigue investors and "favourers" among such, but he had need also for numbers of stout yeomen, men who could heave and haul, who were not too daintily bred to face the hardships incident to pioneering. The question was how to reach them. It was, I believe, at this point that the poets came to his assistance.

CHAPTER SEVENTEEN

The School of Night

THE LITERARY NAMES commonly associated with the brilliant young scientists of Ralegh's *Little Academe* are Spenser, Chapman, Roydon, Drayton, and Marlowe, with, perhaps, the addition of Arthur Gorges, a name not so familiar to students of literature as it might possibly be, had not most of his works been lost. We have already met him co-operating with Ralegh's other friend, Sir George Carew, in connection with the Orlando episode in the Tower. To students of Spenser he is known as "sad Alcyin" of the *Daphnaïda* and *Colin Clout,* who had married, very much against her father's will, little Douglas Howard, whom Spenser called "sweet Eglantine of Meriflure," the thirteen-year-old daughter of Viscount Binden Henry Howard. Gorges was connected with Ralegh not only by kinship but by lifelong friendship, dating perhaps from the time of their boyhood in Devonshire and later at Oxford and in public life. They served together in Parliament, and, according to Camden, were together on the Channel fleet the year of the Armada. We do not know definitely how early he became interested in navigation, but on the Azores voyage (1597) he was captain of Ralegh's own ship, the *Wastspight.* Of his poems so highly praised by Spenser, naught remains. Even his reputation has passed out of literary histories, though Spenser had declared him "fit to frame an everlasting Dittie." Of his prose works, many are lost and some have never been printed. From a list of the extant works, however, it is clear that his interests were Ralegh's interests and that his pamphlets constituted a series of brochures advertising Ralegh's imperial and naval policies, in the same sense that the various Reports of Hariot, Hakluyt, and Sir George Peckham had advocated them, save that their earliest date is slightly later than the early Virginian campaign. His importance for us lies more in his capacity as witness for the fact that poets did contribute to the advertisement of Ralegh's cause and point of view. We have noted Roydon's expression of good will toward Virginia in the sonnet prefixed to Peckham's *True Report.* A much more important poem, both intrinsically and historically, is Drayton's beautiful lyric *To the Virginian Voyage.* From his appearance on the literary horizon until long after Marlowe's death, Drayton proved himself the cordial and consistent friend of the entire group. No one, not even Chapman, has done more for Marlowe's posthumous reputation. The connection between this poem and the Virginia voyages has been noted by Professor J. Q. Adams (*Modern Language Notes,* 33, [1918], pp. 405ff.), but I believe he has hardly caught its full significance as a witness to Ralegh's patronage of poets who might help him to advertise Virginia. The whole poem is all but a verse paraphrase of Hariot's *True Report,* and might serve as an introduction to it, as Roydon's did to the *True Report* of Sir George Peckham. It is, in spite of its great beauty, so little known, that I am happy to have occasion to quote it here:

To The Virginian Voyage

You brave Heroique Minds,
Worthy your Countries Name,
  That Honour still pursue,
  Goe, and subdue,
Whilst loyt'ring Hinds
Lurke here at home, with shame.

Britans, you stay too long,
Quickly aboord bestow you,
  And with a merry Gale
  Swell your stretch'd Sayle,
With Vowes as strong,
As the Winds that blow you.

Your Course securely steere,
West and by South forth keepe,
  Rocks, Lee-shores, nor Sholes,
  When Eolus scowles,
You need not feare,
So absolute the Deepe.

And cheerefully at Sea,
Successe you still intice,
  To get the Pearle and Gold,
  And ours to hold,
Virginia,
Earth's onely Paradise.

Where Nature hath in store
Fowle, Venison, and Fish,
  And the fruitfull'st Soyle,
  Without your Toyle,
Three Harvests more,
All greater then your Wish.

And the ambitious Vine
Crownes with his purple Masse,
  The Cedar reaching hie
  To kisse the Sky,
The Cypresse, Pine
And use-full Sassafras.

To whose, the golden Age
Still Natures lawes doth give,
  No other Cares that tend,
  But Them to defend
From Winters age,
That long there doth not live.

When as the Lushious smell
Of that delicious Land,
  Above the Seas that flowes,
  The cleere Wind throwes,
Your Hearts to swell
Approching the deare Strand.

In kenning of the Shore
(Thanks to God first given,)
  O you the happy'st men,
  Be Frolike then,
Let Cannon's roare,
Frighting the wide Heaven.

And in Regions farre
Such *Heroes* bring ye foorth,
  As those from whom We came,
  And plant Our name,

Under that Starre
Not knowne unto our North.

And as there Plenty growes
Of Lawrell every where,
  Apollo's Sacred tree,
  You it may see,
A Poets Browes
To crowne, that may sing there.

Thy Voyages attend,
Industrious HACKLUIT,
  Whose Reading shall inflame
  Men to seeke Fame,
And much commend
To after-Times thy Wit.

Truly a poet attached to Ralegh's *Little Academe* could have looked out on no more thrilling company at any period of the world's history, and, as we hope to show, there seems a special felicity in the design which brought together the intellectual wealth of such a group, with so radiant an instrument for bodying it forth, as the poetry of Drayton, Chapman, and Marlowe. There seems to be almost a witchery to the luck these scientific poets enjoyed, for was not the moon, the chaste Diana, the incomparable Cynthia, to be equated with the Virgin Queen herself? And was there not implied in any esoteric worship of the planet a subtle but intriguingly original vein of compliment to the vainest of earthly goddesses? Lyly had long before given vogue to the identification, but now these young astronomers and star-gazers, these students of the School of Night, that grouped themselves about Ralegh and Northumberland, found, in their scientific jargon, a way of adding new and interesting point to the fashion.

Indeed, many believe that by his *Ocean's Love to Cynthia,* Ralegh was the originator of the strain "to Cynthia, the Lady of the Sea," as she is called in *Colin Clout*. Be that as it may, Ralegh swept the strings to this conceit until it took on a vogue of unparalleled popularity. His *Shepherd's praise of his Sacred Diana* is one of the most charming. Again, it is impossible not to see in the last lines of Ralegh's *Hymn to Diana,* an allusion to the same gossip which formed the subject of Chapman's *Hymn to Cynthia*:

Prais'd be Diana's fair and harmless light;
  Prais'd be the dews wherewith she moists the ground;
Prais'd be her beams, the glory of the night;
  Prais'd be her power, by which all powers abound!
Prais'd be her nymphs, with whom she decks the woods;
  Prais'd be her knights, in whom true honour lives;
Prais'd be that force by which she moves the floods!
  Let that Diana shine, which all these gives!

In heaven, queen she is among the spheres;
  She, mistress-like, makes all things to be pure;
Eternity in her oft-change she bears;
  She, Beauty is; by her the fair endure.
Time wears her not; she doth his chariot guide;
  Mortality below her orb is plac'd;
By her the virtue of the stars down slide;
  In her is Virtu's perfect image cast!
A knowledge pure it is her worth to know:
With Circes let them dwell that think not so!

Mention should be made also, in this immediate context, of his sonnets entitled *A Vision upon the Fairy Queen,* the second of which is herewith quoted:

The praise of meaner wits this work like profit brings,
As doth the Cuckoo's song delight, when Philomela sings;
If thou hast formed right true Virtue's face herein,
Virtue herself can best discern to whom they written been.
If thou hast beauty prais'd, let her sole looks divine
Judge if ought therein be amiss, and mend it by her eyne.
If Chastity want ought, or Temperance her due,
Behold her princely mind aright, and write thy Queen anew.
Meanwhile she shall perceive how far her virtues soar
Above the reach of all that live, or such as wrote of yore:
And thereby will excuse and favour thy good will,
Whose virtue cannot be express'd but by an angel's quill.
Of me no lines are lov'd, nor letters are of price
Of all which speak our English tongue, but those of thy device.

Similar contributions to the cult of Diana, Queen of the Sea, Queen of Mariners, Queen of Night, Queen of Chastity, and the like, poured in. Drayton, following the thought expressed in the last lines of Ralegh's sonnet, declared in the third eclogue in *The Idea*: *An Ode to Elizabeth*:

> The blessed angels have prepared
> A glorious crown for thy reward;
> Not such a golden crown as haughty Caesar wears
> But such a glittering starry crown as Ariadne bears.

Addressing the Queen with what Professor Oliver Elton calls "splendour and onset" (*Michael Drayton: A Critical Study,* p. 32), he cries:

> O, thou fair torch of heaven, the day's most dearest light,
> And thou, bright-shining Cynthia, the glory of the night;
> You stars, the eye of heaven,
> And thou, the gliding leven,
> And thou, O gorgeous Iris! with all strange colours dyed,
> When she streams forth her rays, then dashed is all your pride.

In the same vein and with the same intent Sidney wrote of Urania (*Arcadia,* 1588, Bk. I):

> Let us in such sort think, I say, that our poor eyes were so enriched as to behold and our low hearts so exalted as to love a maid who is such, that as the greatest thing the world can shew is her beauty, so the least thing that may be praised in her is her beauty. . . . But, indeed, as we can better consider the sun's beauty by marking how he gilds these waters and mountains than by looking upon his own face, too glorious for our weak eyes: so it may be our conceits (not able to bear her sun-sustaining excellency) will better weigh it by her works upon some meaner subject employed. And alas, who can better witness that than we, whose experience is grounded upon feeling? Hath not the only love of her made us (being silly ignorant shepherds) raise up our thoughts above the ordinary level of the world, so that great clerks do not disdain our conference? *Hath not the desire to seem worthy in her eyes made us, when others were sleeping, to sit viewing the course of the heavens;* [italics inserted] when others are running at Base, to run over learned writings; when others mark their sheep, we to mark ourselves? Hath she not thrown reason upon our desires, and, as it were, given eyes to Cupid? Hath in any but in her love-fellowship maintained friendship between rivals, and beauty taught the beholders chastity?

That is the new note; that is why Chapman declared that those who would sing "the majesty and riches of the mind" must cease "to prefer the painted cabinet [the face] before the wealthy jewels it doth store."

That Ralegh had approached Spenser with a request for poetry is hardly dubitable in view of Spenser's own account in *Colin Clout.* The letter of presentation to Ralegh makes it likely that *Colin Clout* was itself written in response to some such request. Spenser declared that his poem was a mere *intermezzo,* to sing "faire Cynthia's praises" albeit "rudely," till Ralegh should make known his own poem to Cynthia. Whether this is true or not, certainly the poem pays special tribute to "Cynthia the Ladie of the Sea" whose "Regiment" is "nought but sea and heaven" and whose sheep are faithfully protected by her devoted "Shepherd of the Ocean," Sir Walter Ralegh, "whose grace [with Cynthia] was great" and whose "bounty most rewardful." It is this last phrase particularly that sounds as if Ralegh had commissioned Spenser to write something.

All literary students know the story of Ralegh's introduction of Spenser to the Queen and of his sponsoring the greatest of all Cynthia poems, *The Faerie Queene.* A sentence or two from Spenser's introductory letter to Ralegh may perhaps induce the reader to bear with one more allusion to the Elizabethan habit of allegory and its place in the poetic theory of men like Spenser and Chapman. Having admitted that the *Faerie Queene* is a "continued allegory, or darke conceit," he opines:

> To some I know this Methode will seeme unpleasant, which had rather have good discipline delivered plainly in way of precepts, or sermoned at large, as they use, then thus clowdily inwrapped in allegorical devices.

Such, he says scornfully, are like those who prefer Xenophon to Plato! Sir John Harrington, in his Preface to the translation of *Orlando Furioso,* published in 1591, presses the same point of view even further:

> Men of greatest learning and highest wit in the ancient times did of purpose conceale these deepest mysteries of learning, and, as it were, cover theirs with the vaile of fables and verse . . . that they might not be rashly abused by prophane wits in whom science is

corrupted, like good wine in a bad vessel. [But] . . . a principall cause of all, is to be able with one kind of meate and one dish (as I may call it) to feed divers tastes, *for the weaker capacities will feed themselves with the pleasantnes of the historie and sweetnes of the verse, some that have stronger stomachs will as it were take a further taste of the Morall sence, a third sort, more highly conceited than they, will digest the Allegorie* [italics inserted]; so as indeed it hath been thought by men of verie good judgement, such manner of poetical writing was an excellent way to preserve all kinds of learning from the corruption which now it is come to since they left that mysticall writing of verse.

We have already seen how his practice conformed to his theory in the *Metamorphosis of Ajax*. Spenser could have written no more effective apologia for the practice of allegory which he used throughout his poetry. In the Letter to Sir Walter, expounding the author's "whole intention" in the *Faerie Queene* he says:

In that Faery Queene I mean glory in my generall intention, but in my particular I conceiue the most excellent and glorious person of our soueraine the Queene, and her kingdome in Faeryland. And yet in some places els, I doe otherwise shadow her. For considering she beareth two persons, the one of a most royall Queene or Empresse, the other of a most vertuous and beautifull Lady, this latter part in some places I doe expresse in Belphoebe, fashioning her name *according to your owne excellent conceipt of Cynthia* (Phoebe and Cynthia being both names of Diana). [Italics inserted.]

In a study so general as this, it would be impossible to enter the lists for the vindication of any particular interpretation of an episode in the *Faerie Queene*. No one will doubt, however, that the poet has well prepared the way for the "Ideal friendship" between Belphoebe, the daughter of Diana, and Timias, the man of honour, in Book IV, by his exalted praises of Britomart, the Lady of Chastity, in Book III. Elizabeth was to be made to glory in her chastity, and to exercise toward her weaker sisters, like Amoret, the daughter of Venus, her protective omniscience. *A Nymph's Disdain of Love* is one of the most graceful of Ralegh's own attempts to make the Queen enjoy the pose of "maiden-meditation" he had set for her:

Hey, down, a down, did Dian sing,
  Amongst her virgins sitting:
Than love there is no vainer thing,
  For maidens most unfitting:

When women knew no woe,
  But liv'd themselves to please,
Men's feigning guiles they did not know
  The ground of their disease.
Unborn was False Suspect,
  No thought of Jealousy:
From wanton toys and Fond Affect
  The virgin's life was free.

Hey, down, a down, did Dian sing, &c.

At length men used charms
  To which what maids gave ear,
Embracing gladly endless harms,
  Anon, enthralled were,
Thus women welcom'd woe,
  Disguised in name of love:
A jealous hell, a painted show,
  So shall they find that prove.

Hey, down, a down, did Dian sing,
  Amongst her virgins sitting:
Than love there is no vainer thing,
  For maidens most unfitting:
And so think I, with a down, down, derry.

In a more serious vein, Spenser, in his *Hymn in Honour of Love,* drives home the advantages of a purely intellectual passion:

Such is the power of that sweet passion,
And the refyned mynd doth new fashion
Unto a fairer forme vhich now doth dwell
In her high thought, that would itself excell.
Which he beholding still with constant sight,
Admires the mirror of so heavenly light.

The first stanza of the Third Canto (Book III) sings the same tune [italics inserted]:

Most sacred fyre, that burnest mightily
In living brests, ykindled first above,

Amongst th' eternal spheres and lamping sky,
And thence poured into men, which men call Love;
Not the same which doth base affections move
On brutish mindes, and filthy lusts inflame,
But that sweete fit that doth true beautie love,
And chooseth vertue of his dearest dame,
Whence Spring all noble deedes and never dying Fame.

It was platonic love, or, as Spenser tried to make the Queen believe, the love of Beauty, which Timias was offering Elizabeth, the "beauty of mind which is born of virtue," a variant of that "Religion of Beauty in Women," which has captured the imagination of many a patrician intellect before and after Ralegh. When stimulated by a truly noble intimacy, like that between Mrs. Herbert and John Donne, the "conceit" could arise to the transfiguring heights of mystic ecstasy. It does so in many of Donne's poems, and, as we shall see, by a dramatic miracle, in Tamburlaine's elegiac paean to Zenocrate; but it was a greater task than even Spenser could accomplish to depict his patron's real passion for Elizabeth Throgmorton on the same page with his official adoration of the Queen, and make the latter glow and vibrate with a convincing frenzy. However, what ingenuity and skill could do for such a case, Spenser did for Ralegh's *Idea,* in the Fourth Book of the *Faerie Queene,* concerning which Miss Jones says *(op. cit.,* p. 241):

Of the political allegory of the fourth book very little can be said with confidence. Indeed it is only in the Belphoebe-Timias episode that we find an historical situation at all clearly reflected. Its hero, whose name derives from the Greek adjective τίμιος, meaning "honorable," may be rather confidently identified with Raleigh; and Amoret would then be some lady for whose sake the great Sir Walter had incurred the displeasure of his Queen. The lady in question is probably Elizabeth Throckmorton, one of Elizabeth's maids of honor, whose secret marriage with the Queen's favorite in 1593 led to his banishment from Court. However, Queen Elizabeth's displeasure, like that of Belphoebe, was not protracted; and in 1596, the year in which Spenser published the second three books of the *Faerie Queene,* Raleigh, enjoying once more the royal favor, served as an admiral in the expedition against Cadiz.

It is not quite clear why Miss Jones has ignored Spenser's reason for the choice of the name Timias. Granting the *Idea* which he was trying to set forth, the name of Plato's noble Pythagorean was inevitable. Timaeus had laid bold claim to immortality through his "love of the beautiful." He declared (Jowett translation):

He, therefore, who is always occupied with the cravings of desire and ambition, and is eagerly striving after them, must have all his opinions mortal, and, as far as man can be, must be all of him mortal, because he has cherished his mortal part. *But he who has been earnest in the love of knowledge and true wisdom, and has been trained to think that these are the immortal and divine things of a man, if he attain truth, must of necessity, as far as human nature is capable of attaining immortality, be all immortal, as he is ever serving the divine power; . . . And the motions which are akin to the divine principle within us are the thoughts and revolutions of the universe.* [Italics inserted.]

This is a perfect expression of the Ralegh "doctrine" of the Cult of Diana, and is a more impressive "authority" for the "conceit" than the *Tre Dialoghi della Vita Civile,* of Cinthio, upon which Spenser leaned heavily for the Fourth Book.

The most forthright and argumentative of all the chroniclers of the new "doctrine of chaste love," (the title of "most winged" being reserved for Marlowe), was George Chapman. In a whole series of poems dedicated to various members of the Ralegh group, he set forth in his own dignified, scholarly way the ideals, the manners, the interests and exploits of this band of intellectual empire builders. If Chapman had been able, he would, I believe, have been a scientist, rather than a poet. The next best thing was a compromise, and Chapman became a scientific poet, whose muse sang *(A Cornet for His Mistress Philosophy)* not of "Love's sensual empery," but, like Lord Brooke, of "the majesty and riches of the mind."

I have already discussed Chapman's *Hymnus in Cynthiam,* in which he rebukes the detractors of Leicester and claims that the interest which Leicester had in the Queen was "all for astrology." Similarly the argument of the *Hymnus in Noctem* is devoted to a scathing reproof of those poets of "brass wits" and "golden foolery" who sell "her beauty's use / To rapes, adulteries and to all abuse." In contrast to these lascivious poets, there is, he says, a finer sort, "ennobled with a deathless love / Of things eternal, dignified above," who "proclaiming silence, study, ease, and sleep," have power to banish the tawdry triumphs of "haughty Day to the infernal deep"—

> Till thou (dear Night, O Goddess of most worth)
> Lett'st thy sweet seas of golden humour forth.

Then, under this noble influence, these poets of the Night "with meteors, comets, lightenings," will sing "the dreadful presence of our empress," who loves "music and mood" and the beauties of the mind; but "love she hates." This is the *leit motif* of the Night poets: Elizabeth can be worshipped properly only by those who approach her with the same intellectual attitude of awe and reverence with which the real astrologer (for so the astronomers of the sixteenth century called themselves), studies the wonders of the starry firmament. Therefore Chapman summons all the rarer sort of poets, those "endued with nimble and aspiring wits" to

> Come consecrate with me to sacred Night
> Your whole endeavors . . .
> Sweet Peace's richest crown is made of stars
> Most certain guides of honoured mariners.

Then, as if to establish the vogue of astronomical poetry in a place of permanent honour, he concludes:

> No pen can anything eternal write
> That is not steeped in humour of the Night.

Chapman not only illustrates the new mode, but he also supplies us with well documented reasons for attributing his astronomical imagery to the influence of the group in general, and of Hariot in particular. His Quarto of 1594 was entitled, with obvious reverberations, *The Shadow of Night,* and was dedicated to a member of the Ralegh circle in words which imply a relationship of great intimacy: "To my dear and most worthy friend, Master Matthew Roydon," whom he later calls "Sweet Matthew." Roydon had, as we have seen, already shown himself friendly to Ralegh's cause, by his sonnet prefixed to Peckham's *True Report;* but he remained, perhaps not unjustly, considering the indifferent poetry of the sonnet, only a minor literary member of the group. Apparently his poetic gifts were not such as to stir up his rivals to envy, as were Marlowe's and Chapman's. At all events Nashe, in his Preface to Greene's *Menaphon,* singles him out for special praise:

> There are extant about London many most able men to reuiue Poetry . . . as, for example, Mathew Roydon, Thomas Atchelow, and George Peele; the first of whom, as he hath shewed himselfe singular in the immortall Epitaph of his beloued Astrophell, besides many other most absolute inuentions (made more publike by euery mans praise, than they can be by my speech) . . .

In his enthusiasm for the persons and opinions of the Ralegh group, Roydon was, however, entitled to full-fledged membership. Chapman's dedication to him of the *Shadow of Night* not only makes this fact clear, but in addition, it defines the ideals and point of view of the Academy in a manner that is little short of a manifesto:

> It is an exceeding rapture of delight in the deep search of knowledge (none knoweth better than thyself, sweet Mathew) that maketh man manfully indure the extremes incident to that Herculean labour: from flints must the Gorgonean fount be smitten. Men must be shod by Mercury, girt with Saturn's admantine sword, take the shield from Pallas, the helm from Pluto, and have the eyes of Graea (as Hesiodus arms Perseus against Medusa), before they can cut off the viperous head of benumbing ignorance, or subdue their monstrous affections to most beautiful judgment.

He then expresses his scorn of "passion-driven men" who read "but to curtail a tedious hour":

> Now what a supererogation in wit this is, to think Skill so mightily pierced with their loves, that she should prostitutely shew them her secrets, when she will scarcely be looked upon by others but by invocation, fasting, watching; yea, not without having drops of their souls like an heavenly familiar.

But, he says, "I stay my spleen, when I remember" the glorious names of Stanley, Percy, and Carey, who represent the better cause. In a subsequent dedication to Roydon (*Ovid's Banquet of Sense,* 1595) he reiterates the point: "I only consecrate my strange poems to those searching spirits, whom learning hath made noble, and nobility sacred."

Particularly interesting as corroboration to other expressions of his own and Spenser's theory concerning the fustian nature of poetry, is the comment which he adds:

> But that Poesy should be as pervial as oratory, and plainness her special ornament were the plain way to barbarism, and to make the ass run proud of his ears, to take away the strength from lions, and give camels horns. . . . In my opinion, that which being with a little endeavor searched, adds a kind of majesty to Poesy, is better than that which every cobbler may sing to his patch. . . .
>
> Thus (not affecting glory for mine own slight labours, but desirous others should be more worthily glorious, nor professing sacred Poesy in any degree), I thought good to submit to your apt judgment, acquainted long since with the true habit of Poesy: and now, since your labouring with endeavour heaven-high thoughts of Nature, you have actual means to sound the philosophical conceits, that my new pen so seriously courteth. I know that empty and dark spirits will complain of palpable night; but those that before hand have a radiant and light bearing intellect, will say they can pass through Corinna's garden without the help of a lantern.

As in the *Hymnus in Cynthiam,* so in the *Shadow of Night,* he calls on true men to leave the perusal of what Lord Brooke calls "witty fictions," and instead:

> Come to this house of mourning, serve the Night,
> To whom pale Day (with whoredom soaked quite)
> Is but a drudge, selling her beauty's use
> To rapes, adulteries, and to all abuse.

Throughout his non-dramatic poems, Chapman has paid generous tribute to the whole group—to Roydon, to Hues, to Ralegh, to Marlowe, and very particularly to Hariot, for whom, as the chief inspirer of the Night Poets, he entertained a vaulting admiration. To his translation of *Achilles Shield* Chapman appended so lordly a eulogy of Hariot that one is tempted to quote it in full. It is addressed "To my admired and soul-loved friend, Master of all essential and true knowledge, M. Hariots." He describes him as one

> . . . whose depth of soul measured the height
> And all dimensions of all works of weight,
> Reason being ground, structure, and ornament
> To all inventions grave and permanent.

He praises his "clear eyes, the spheres where reason moves," and protests his one desire is to study under his inspiring tutelage:

> Rich mine of knowledge, O that my strange muse
> Without this body's nourishment could use
> Her zealous faculties, only t'aspire
> Instructive light from your whole sphere of fire!
>
> . . .
>
> Skill and the love of skill do ever kiss;
> No band of love so strong as knowledge is,
> Which who is he that may not learn of you
> Whom learning doth with his light's throne endow?

Chapman girds at the inferior unintellectual poets who "for profit" and "praise"

> . . . keep a squeaking stir
> With called-on muses to unchild their brains
> By wind and vapour;

and he looks forward to the time

> When thy true wisdom by thy learning won
> Shall honour learning while there shines a sun,
> And thine own name in merit far above
> Their tympanies of state that arms, or love,
> Fortune, or blood shall lift to dignity;
> Whom, though you reverence, and your empery
> Of spirit and soul be servitude—they think—
> And but a beam of light broke through a chink
> To all their waterish splendour; and much more
> To the great sun, and all things they adore
> In staring ignorance; yet yourself shall shine
> Above all this in knowledge most divine;
> And all shall homage to your true worth owe,
> You comprehending all, that all, not you.

What little evidence there is for the date of Chapman's entrance into the Ralegh circle would seem to indicate the early nineties rather than the late eighties. This fact, if it is a fact, may account for Chapman's enthusiastic espousal of the general interests of the group, and, at the same time, explain the absence of any direct propaganda in favour of Virginia before

1596, at which date he wrote what he called a "Carmen Epicum," entitled *De Guiana,* which was prefixed to Lawrence Keymis' *A Relation of the Second Voyage to Guiana.* This epic fragment has, even more than Drayton's poem, "splendour and onset"; in fact, it is characterized by an *élan* which we are more accustomed to associate with Marlowe than with the scholarly and sober Chapman:

Riches, and conquest, and renoun I sing,
Riches with honour, conquest without blood,
Enough to seat the Monarchy of earth,
Like to Jove's eagle, on Eliza's hand.
Guiana, whose rich feet are mines of gold,
Whose forehead knocks against the roof of stars,
Stands tiptoes at fair England looking,
Kissing her hand, bowing her mighty breast,
And every sign of all submission making,
To be her sister, and the daughter both
Of our most sacred Maid.

He calls upon the Queen:

Then most admired sovereign, let your breath
Go forth upon the waters, and create
A golden world in this our iron age.

Commenting upon her choice of Ralegh as leader of the New World enterprise, he admonishes:

Doubt not but your election was devine,
As well by fate as your high judgement order'd,
To raise him with choice bounties, that could add
Height to his height: and like a liberal vine,
Not only bear his virtuous fruit aloft,
Free from the press of squint-eyed Envy's feet,
But deck his gracious prop with golden bunches,
And shroud it with broad leaves of rule o'er grown,
From all black tempests of invasion.

Probably referring to the prosecution of Ralegh, in 1595, for atheism, he says:

You then that would be wise in wisdom's spite,
Directing with discredit of direction,
And hunt for honour, hunting him to death;

> With whom, before you will inherit gold,
> You will lose gold, for which you lose your souls.

Referring to the conservative opposition to the projected colony on the part of those who were fearful of the outcome, he says *(De Guiana)*:

> You that choose nought for right, but certainty,
> And fear that value will get only blows,
> Placing your faith in Incredulity:
> Sit till you see a wonder, Virtue rich:
> Till Honour having gold, rob gold of honour,
> Till as men have desert that getteth nought,
> They loathe all getting that deserves not aught;
> And use you gold-made men as dregs of men;
> And till your poison'd souls, like spiders lurking
> In sluttish chinks, in mists of cobwebs hide
> Your foggy bodies and your dunghill pride.

He contrasts the "incredulity, the wit of fools / That slovenly will spit on all things fair," with the attitude of the "patrician spirits," who smile on "brave endeavors." Such, he says, know they "cannot be kings of earth" as long as they "let the mines of earth be kings" of them. Such "will not be content like a horse to hold / A threadbare beaten way to home affairs." Such will "lift [their] eyes for guidance to the stars" in order "to possess / Your honour'd country of a general store." To such, he declares:

> You that are blest with sense of all things noble,
> In this attempt your complete worths redouble.

With direct address to Ralegh, he cries, "Oh, thou, heroic author of this act . . . that sustainst pain, charge, and peril for thy country's good," while "she, like a body numbed with surfeits / Feels not thy gentle applications / For the health, use, and honour of her powers. Yet," he promises, "shall my verse through all her ease-lock'd ears / Trumpet the noblesse of thy high intent." Of course, he mentions, in conclusion, "our Liege," who "at the most rare endeavor of her power," hath "blessed with her wonted graces / Th' industrious knight, the soul of this exploit / Dismissing him to convoy of his stars." Chapman makes it clear that he is not speaking merely of the Guiana voyage, but of the whole imperial plan for a "new Britannia" on the shores of "rich America," when he sings, in the conclusion of the poem, of the idyllic charms and glories of "Guianian Orenoque," where "healthful recreations strow the meads, / and make their mansions dance with neighbourhood," where

> . . . palaces and temples rise
> Out of the earth, and kiss the enamour'd skies
> Where new Britannia humbly kneels to heaven
> The world to her, and both at her blest feet
> In whom the circles of all Empires meet.

To some critics, I fear, so obviously practical an inspiration for poetry as a colonizing venture will seem to cheapen the high function of the Muse. They will resent even Chapman's own statement that his verse shall, through "ease-lock'd eares, trumpet the noblesse" of Ralegh's high intent. It is no part of my program to justify the poetic theory and practice of great Renaissance poets, like Spenser, Chapman, and others, whose work we have noticed. My duty is merely to point out the presence of current issues wherever I find them; and I do believe that in the poems we have just been reviewing, such topicality is beyond a shadow of doubt.

Chronologically, we should have discussed Marlowe's work for Ralegh before Chapman's. I have chosen the other order for the reason that the indubitability of Ralegh propaganda in Chapman seems to me to enhance the plausibility of such an element in Chapman's immediate predecessor, who was also the object of his generous admiration.

The names of Roydon, Hariot, and Chapman bring us a formal introduction of Marlowe into this charmed circle. We have noted Ralegh's reply to Marlowe's *Passionate Shepherd,* but, happily, there exists more positive evidence of Marlowe's connection with the group. When Kyd was arrested in 1593, he was charged also with atheism; but he repudiated the accusation, scorning that he should be thought to "love, or be familiar with one so irreligious" as Marlowe; and he declared that if the Lords of the Council wanted to know more of those with whom Marlowe *did* converse and consort, they should inquire of "Hariot, Warner, Roydon, and some stationers in Paul's

Churchyard," men whom we know now to have been intimate members of the Ralegh circle. We shall have occasion later to say something of these stationers at Paul's Churchyard; but here, as further evidence of Marlowe's connection with the group, we should mention the declaration made by Richard Cholmely to the effect that "Marloe told him that he hath read the atheist lecture to Sir Walter Ralegh and others."* These sworn statements regarding Marlowe's associates constitute a basis for the internal evidence we are about to present in proof of the influence of the group upon Marlowe's poetry.

All Hariot's contemporaries were well aware of the source of the inspiration vouchsafed to this special group of poets, and each made his own evaluation of the seed and the fruit. The cheap lucrative piety of many a poetaster-rival scrupled not to throw discredit on their successes by affecting to be shocked by their bold challenge of orthodoxy, and, as we shall see later, Nashe and Greene and Kyd joined the chorus of mockery for different motives. But the better poets understood the true source of the magic in the verse of the astronomical poets, and

* This Cholmeley was, apparently, a "professional libeller," and just such a "dangerous" popular satirist as we discussed at some length in the chapter on non-dramatic satire. Among other charges made against him when he was finally captured and imprisoned were (Tucker-Brooke, *op. cit.*, p. 65):

That he speaketh in general all evil of the (Privy) Council, saying that they are all atheists and Machiavellians, especially my Lord Admiral.

That he made certain libellous verses in commendation of Papists and Seminary priests, very greatly inveighing against the state, among which lines this was one: "Nor may the Prince deny that Papal crown."

That he had a certain book (as he saith) delivered him by Sir Robert Cecil, of whom he giveth very scandalous reports; that he should incite him to consider thereof, and to frame verses and libels in the commendation of constant priests and virtuous recusants. This book is in custody and is called an *Epistle of Comfort,* and is printed at Paris.

That he rails at Mr. Topcliffe [Richard Topcliffe, director of the Government's anti-Jesuit office. Not unjustly called "a monster of iniquity" by Tucker-Brooke] and hath written another libel jointly against Sir Francis Drake and Justice Young [Judge Richard Young, Whitgift's tool in religious persecutions, according to Tucker-Brooke] whom he saith he will couple together because he hateth them alike.

. . . .

That he saith and verily believeth that one Marloe is able to show more sound reasons for atheism than any divine in England is able to give to prove divinity, and that Marloe told him that he hath read the atheist lecture to Sir Walter Raleigh and others. . . .

bowed before it in reverent humility. For them Tamburlaine was famous not because he was an "Atheist . . . daring God out of his heaven," but because, as Drayton said in his poem *To Henry Reynolds, of Poets and Poesie,* its author "had in him those brave, translunary things that your first poets had." That, indeed, is the magic power that lifts the poetry of Marlowe, whatever his immediate intention may have been, into something so much more than "forespoke" poetry. Chapman's verse is splendid, learned, noble; Spenser's is mellifluous and full of high invention and other good things; but Marlowe's raptures were winged, or as Drayton put it, "all air and fire." These things were fetched, not from the mythical mines of "rich America," but from a finer source altogether—the rich vein of "deep Hariot's mine," in which, as Bishop Corbett said, "there was no dross." This is the mine of his great scientific knowledge and far-ranging intellect, before which Chapman bowed in profound and stirring admiration. Like Paracelsus, Marlowe could boast "Clay once cast into that rich mine should come up crusted o'er with gems." Though "free to all before," these notions, these *Faust Gedanken,* these intellectual experiments became "imbued" with Marlowe. What must have been a frequent, even casual query in a group of clever men bent upon serious astronomical research, becomes, in Marlowe, elevated into the rare atmosphere of metaphysical and spiritual speculation. Neither Marlowe nor his astronomical friends could fathom that Power

> . . . that never sleeps
> Nor is in one place circumscriptable,
> But everywhere fills every continent
> With strange infusion of His sacred vigour; . . .

but through the music of his verse and the dignity of his imagination, Marlowe has translated their query into the regions of mystic experience. Like him, we feel the "spirits of every element," shadowing "more beauty in their airy brows than have the white breasts of the Queen of love," wheeling round our "soul's centre" till we are awed by the majesty of the conception and purged by its "endless purity." This is what Chapman calls Marlowe's "most strangely intellectual fire" to find

. . . the eternal clime
Of his free soul, whose living subject stood
Up to the chin in the Pierean flood.

Whether Marlowe was actually present on the star-gazing nights at Durham House with the little Academy of Night, or whether his inspiration came directly from conversation with Hariot, he seems to have attained some glimpse of that mysterious horizon where Beauty and Truth and Mystery seem to dwell together in airy ease. At his death, Henry Petowe opined (Tucker-Brooke, *op. cit.*, p. 79):

But Marlo, still-admired Marlo's gone
To live with Beauty in Elysium, . . .

and he observed that Marlowe's constant wish "to be resolved into the elements" had been fulfilled:

Marlo, late mortal, now framed all divine,
What soul more happy than that Soul of thine!
Live still in heaven thy soul, thy fame on earth.

Marlowe's hero, Tamburlaine, was not above earthly rewards; he was, in fact, bent on a prodigious campaign for crowns and thrones; but the pinnacle of his desire, the aspiration which alone gives him permanent significance, is in that other world where "our bodies turn to elements" and "our souls aspire to celestial thrones." An earthly crown may have been the temporal occasion of Tamburlaine's more than famous question:

Is it not passing brave to be a king
And ride in triumph through Persepolis?

But what really stirs us in his rhapsody, is not the tawdry pomp of Persepolis, but the "state and majesty of heaven." Our own souls tingle with the realization of our "faculty" which can comprehend

The wondrous architecture of the world
And measure every wandering planets course,
Still climbing after knowledge infinite,
And always moving as the restless spheres. . . .

The "eternal clime of his free soul" is identified with "all things that move between the quiet poles." This "world of profit and delight, of power, of honour, of omnipotence," this "kingdom in the sky," Marlowe has realized for us with a compelling vitality that all but belies its airy abstractness. America, as we hope to show, may have been his subject, and Tamburlaine a poetic invention for his protagonist Ralegh; but one feels that, in the language of Broadway, Hariot "stole the show." Tamburlaine's passion to conquer the world becomes, under the influence of Marlowe's astronomical imagery, a symbol to signify the poet's search toward a vaster cosmos, his trapeze, on which he swings swiftly and with intense delight into a world of intellectual magnificence. Here he can play without restraint with the most impossible ideas. He can ride over "a bridge made through the moving air," or "teach the water to mount," or watch the meteors "run tilting round about the firmament," breaking their "burning lances in the air," or "batter the shining palace of the sun," or drive

> The horse that guide the golden car of heaven
> And blow the morning from their nostrils
> Making their fiery gait above the clouds. . . .

For him there is no "fairness" like to the "evening air, clad in the beauty of a thousand stars," especially "when that Ebena steps to heaven in silence."

It would be impossible, within the scope of a chapter, to show how saturated is Marlowe's language in astronomical allusion. It seems to be the only idiom adequate for his arrowy thought. In these "subtle regions of the air" he plays as nimbly and naturally as the disembodied spirit he is ever longing to be. For him, as for Chapman, death is a mere "resolution" into the substance of these elements. His is a world of "fiery circles," "brighter than the silver Rhodope," a realm of "restless spheres," "fiery exhalations wrapt in the bowels of a freezing cloud. / Fighting for passage," which "makes the welkin crack, and casts a flash of lightning to the earth," where "Auster and Aquilon with winged steeds / All sweating tilt about the watery heavens," where "airy comets" trail their "fiery spangled veils" across the sky, where "the moon begins to join in one her semicircled horns." In short, all that moves mysteriously, and burns and shines in the whole of "the glorious frame of heaven," Marlowe has rescued from the jargon of technical science and presented to us in this radiant imagery, through which, in some titanic fashion, he has identified the essences and processes of the vast cosmic principles of life with his own secret, vibrant, mysterious energy. Drayton said that he was "Fit to write passions for the souls below," but one cannot help feeling that so vital a language would only embarrass the "wretched souls" of the long dead. Far fitter he to write the passions of the Seraphim!

Many critics, including the editors of the *Cambridge Shakespeare,* have thought that Shakspere was taking a goodnatured poke at the School of Night in *Love's Labour's Lost.* We have already alluded to the satire on Harvey in Armado, but it is possible to argue plausibly for a more general satire in the plot as a whole. Chapman had discoursed most enthusiastically of "his Mistress Philosophy," whose "mind," he declared, "draws in the fires / Of her chaste eyes from all earth's tempting fuel." . . . "Her high deeds" are far above "the weak disjoint of female humours" and "the Protean rages of pied-face fashion" and the "courtship of antic gestures, brainless jests." With a magnificent renunciation he declares:

> Herself shall be my comfort and my riches
> And all my thoughts I will on her convert.

These ideas are even more strongly urged in the *Tears of Peace:*

> But this is Learning; to have skill to throw
> Reins on your body's powers that nothing know,
> And fill the soul's powers so with act and art
> That she can curb the body's angry part;
> All perturbations; all effects that stray
> From their one object, which is to obey
> Her sovereign empire; as herself should force
> Their functions only to serve her discourse;
> And that, to beat the straight path to one end;
> Which is to make her substance still contend
> To be God's image; in informing it
> With knowledge: holy thoughts, and all forms fit
> For that eternity ye seek in way
> Of his sole imitation; and to sway
> Your life's love so that he may still be centre
> To all your pleasures; and you here may enter

The next life's peace; in governing so well
Your sensual parts that you as free may dwell,
If vulgar raptures here as when calm death
Dissolves that learned empire with your breath.
To teach and live thus is the only use
And end of Learning.

Unless this poem existed in manuscript long before its publication, it could, of course, have no direct bearing on *Love's Labour's Lost.* My only purpose in quoting it here is to show how thoroughly characteristic of Chapman were the ideas ridiculed in Navarre's "Little Academe."

In *A Cornet for His Mistress Philosophy,* he declares that his "friendless verse" shall never envy the Muses who beautify "Fame's loose feathers." He declares:

Honour, and error, which the world bewitched,
Shall still crown fools and tread upon desert.

. . . .

And such as scorn to tread the theatre
As ignorant. . . .

Whether or not the following lines are a defense of Marlowe's intellectual stage poetry or that of some other "noble wit," they constitute a strong defense of the drama of intellectual ideas:

. . . the seed of memory
Have most inspired, and shown their glories there
[on the stage].
To noblest wits and men of highest doom,
That for the kingly laurel bent affair
The theatres of Athens and of Rome,
Have been the crowns, and not the base impair.
Far, then, be this foul cloudy-brow'd contempt
From like-plumed birds: and let your sacred rhymes
From honour's court their servile feet exempt,
That live in soothing moods and serving tunes:

We recall also the earnestness of his letter to Roydon, describing the "invocation, fasting, watching," that were required of Learning's votaries, and the studiousness with which they renounced fame and worldly honour. It is, therefore, not hard to believe that in the setup of Act I of *Love's Labour's Lost,*

Shakspere, the searcher of men's hearts and the chronicler of their passions, is puckishly mocking those who, with all the high seriousness of intellectual detachment, advocated a renunciation of "Love's sensual empery." The King must have had his tongue in his cheek when he harangued his followers:

> Therefore, brave conquerors—for so you are,
> That war against your own affection,
> And the huge army of the world's desires—
>
> . . . .
>
> Our court shall be a little Academe,
> Still and contemplative in living art.

Longaville replies:

> I am resolved; 't is but a three year's fast:
> The mind shall banquet, though the body pine.

Dumaine pledges:

> To love, to wealth, to pomp, I pine and die;
> With all these [his friends] living in philosophy.

Berowne, of course, objects, that it is very hard "to sleep but three hours in the night" when he was "wont to think no harm all night / And make a night, too, of half the day." And if to that austerity, they were to add "other strict observances"

> As not to see a woman in that term—
> Oh, these are barren tasks, too hard to keep
> Not to see ladies, study, fast, not sleep!

When the King insists, Berowne queries:

> What is the end of study? Let me know.

The King, with mock defense of what we should call "pure science," replies:

> Why, that to know, which else we should not know.

Berowne, defending common sense *versus* science:

> Things hid and barred, you mean from common sense?

The King:

> Ay, that is study's god-like recompense;

and he declares that for it, we must renounce all "the stops that hinder study quite." But Berowne, whom we might call a

Fleshly Poet in contrast to a Metaphysical Poet like Chapman, is unconvinced. He declares, with what has seemed to most critics a clear reference to the Astronomical School:*

These earthy godfathers of heaven's lights
That give a name to every fixed star,
Have no more profits of their shining nights
Than those that walk and wot not what they are.
Too much to know is to know nought but fame;
And every godfather can give a name.

Later in the play, when the King jeers at Berowne's "dark lady," Berowne calls for the "book" that he may swear

. . . beauty doth beauty lack
If that she learn not of her eye to look;
No face is fair that is not full so black.

To this the King replies:

O paradox! Black is the badge of hell,
The hue of dungeons and the school of night.

Nashe and Harvey also snarled enviously at the astronomical imagery of the Night Poets. In the preface to Greene's *Menaphon,* Nashe says,

I am not ignorant how eloquent our gowned aged is grown of late; so that euery mechanical mate abhorres the English he was borne too, and plucks, with a solemn periphrasis, his *vt vales* from the inkehorne; which I impute not so much to the perfection of Arts, *as to the seruil imitation of vainglorious Tragedians who contend not so seriously to excell in action, as to embowell the cloudes in a speech of comparison, thinking themselues more than initiated in Poets immortality, if they once get* BOREAS *by the beard and the heauenly* BULL *by the dew-lap.* [Italics inserted.] But heerin I cannot so fully bequeath them to folly, as their ideot Art-masters, that intrude themselues to our eares as the Alcumists of eloquence, who (mounted on the stage of arrogance) think to out-braue better pennes with the swelling bumbast of a bragging blanke verse. Indeede it may bee the ingrafted ouerflow of some kil-cow conceit, that ouercloyeth their imagination with a more than drunken resolution, being not extemporall in the inuention of any other meanes

* With this gibe it is interesting to compare the boast of Gulato in the pseudo-Chapman play *Two Wise Men and all the Rest Fools*: "I could turn Astronomer, and give names to any stars that want."

to vent their manhoode, commits the disgestion of their cholericke incumbrances to the spacious volubilitie of a drumming decasillabon. Mongst this kind of men that repose eternitie in the mouth of a Player, I can but ingrosse some deep read Grammarians, who, hauing no more learning in their skull than will serue to take vp a commoditie, nor Art in their braine than was nourished in a seruing mans idlenesse, will take vppon them to be the ironicall Censors of all, when God and Poetrie doth know they are the simplest of all.

It cannot be denied that this is an ill-natured attack upon the astronomical poets in general, but it must also be admitted that it is in part a fair criticism of Marlowe's dramaturgy. Certainly he strove not so seriously to excel in the "action" of his dramas as he did to hang his rhapsodies upon the clouds.

It is not strange that the rivals of the Night Poets should have been jealous of the high line taken by Chapman and Marlowe and others; but before we can understand how they came to use it as a device to link their names with the odious title of Atheist, we must glance at the history of one of the most notorious of the so-called atheists, and trace, if possible, his influence on Marlowe. I allude, of course, to Giordano Bruno.

CHAPTER EIGHTEEN

Atheism and the Bruno Scandal in "Doctor Faustus"

IT IS BARELY POSSIBLE that Marlowe had met Bruno before the latter was forced, because of atheistical charges made against him, to fly from England, though it is hardly likely. We have shown elsewhere (see, *Appendix,* pp. 463ff.) that Bruno's astronomical teachings, particularly his advocacy of the Copernican theory, could have had no influence on Hariot before 1600, and if not on Hariot, then hardly on Marlowe, Hariot's friend and admirer, who was, astronomically at least, his inferior. Bear in mind, therefore, that in 1583, when Bruno came to England, Hariot was barely twenty-three years old, and out of the University only three years. Though he was undoubtedly an unusually clever and knowing young man even at the age of twenty-three, we must not assume that he was therefore the experienced mathematician, astronomer, and geographer that he was in 1607-1609, when he was corresponding with the foremost mathematicians and astronomers of his day. The point at issue is the possible relation between Hariot's astronomical views in the late 1580's, and the astronomical knowledge exhibited by Marlowe in his plays, especially in *Tamburlaine, The Jew of Malta,* and *Doctor Faustus.* One meets, in almost any discussion of these plays, generalizations concerning Marlowe's adherence to the "old philosophy" or Ptolemaic system, and often these remarks are accompanied by an observation that such a fact argues strongly against the existence of any real intimacy between Marlowe and Hariot, since Hariot—so runs the argument—was England's foremost mathematician and astronomer, and would, therefore, surely have been conversant with and sympathetic toward the new and revolutionizing theories of Copernicus, especially since Giordano Bruno had been in Oxford lecturing on and defending Copernicus in 1583.

Even in the absence of any documentary evidence of the astronomical opinions of Thomas Hariot, such conclusions would seem to be based on a rather loose logic. Surely, to illustrate by a modern example, both Einstein and the theory of relativity were on the horizon several years before the curvature of space received any real prominence in undergraduate lectures, and it may be doubted if any serious student, even with the possible arrogance of youth to bolster him, would have felt competent to be the first to accept the theory after having heard one heated, certainly not dispassionate, lecture on it. That such a single opportunity to hear a discussion of Copernicus may have occurred to Hariot, is possible, but more than this is unlikely. Certainly during Hariot's undergraduate days no such exposition of the new philosophy would have been possible. When Bruno came to Oxford in 1583, two years after Hariot had left, he found things in a bad way. The University had become "a widow of true knowledge as far as philosophy and mathematics were concerned." The learning that had once flourished in England under the austere discipline of a monkish scholar like St. Bede, or even under the easier inspiration of an Erasmus, had fallen into the general degeneration that followed in the wake of Henry's destruction of Church foundations. Now Bruno found the place inhabited by "parrots," who, as Blake once said of Swedenborg, "told no new truth and repeated all the old lies." "Petty dissemblers," Bruno called them, "who spread foolishness," always trying to excuse the defects of "their divinity, Aristotle." As Bruno's biographer, William Boulting, observed *(Giordano Bruno,* [1914], p. 84), when once the English Universities were turned over to the sport-loving English gentry, "learning, which was almost confined to the priesthood," fled. Bruno declared that the dons "knew more about beer than about Greek," and that the graduates made themselves ridiculous by their dandyism. As for pedantry, he found it even worse at Oxford than at Geneva!

Bruno introduced himself to the Vice-Chancellor and the dons by presenting a manifesto, describing himself as: "Jordanus Bruno of Nolan, lover of God, doctor in a more perfect divinity, professor of a purer and more harmless wisdom, a philosopher known, esteemed, and honourably entreated by the foremost Academies of Europe, a stranger to none but churls and barbarians, the awakener of souls from slumber, the queller of presumptuous and recalcitrant ignorance, etc." The surprising thing is not that he failed to be invited to lecture on a stipend, but that he was allowed to talk at all.

He was, however, "allowed to hold a disputation with some learned doctors on the rival merits of the Copernican and so-called Aristotelian systems of the universe." According to his judgment, he achieved an easy victory over his conservative rivals; but he makes it clear that his teachings were not accepted by the "learned doctors." Indeed, according to his own version, he had literally cast his pearls before swine, and he was near coming to blows with his opponents in debate. He says they came armed, "not with prudence and power," but with "hearts that died of cold and learning that died of hunger," and he rages at the "incivility and discourtesy" with which his Oxford lectures were brought to an end. He all but fled to London, where, socially at least, he had better success. For several years he enjoyed the generous hospitality of Michel de Castelnau, the distinguished French Ambassador, with whom, he tells us, he went continually to Court. There he made himself acceptable to the Queen, first by giving her an opportunity to practice her Italian, for Bruno knew no English, and subsequently, by his enthusiastic contributions to the cult of Diana, the virgin queen. Indeed, at his trial, one of the most grievous accusations made was that he had "praised that hateful English heretic" (Elizabeth). Bruno's poetry is so little known that one is tempted to include here whatever is readily available in translation; but an economical selection must suffice. The following is the opening sonnet in the *Eroici Furori,* and is inscribed "to the most Virtuous and Delightful Ladies," meaning the Queen's ladies-in-waiting; but, of course, the highest praise is reserved for the "fair Dian" herself (translation from I. Frith, *Life of Giordano Bruno,* [London, 1887], p. 129):

O ye whose beauty decks the English Land!
Not mine the soul your sweet array to scorn;
And not to write you less be mine the hand,
Save when I write you women; for the morn,

The twinkling eve, and sable cove of night
Bore never children of the light
Fairer than ye, O stars of happy earth!
Spouses and daughters of angelic birth,
Not Envy's breath, and not her hand austere,
Withold your praise, and none your beauty mars,
Asps have no sting and venom no endeavour
Where, set on high, fair Dian doth appear
Above you like the sun above the stars;
And mine the task to do you homage ever.

So good a poet and so adroit a courtier was not without social contacts; nor indeed, was he too intellectual to enjoy them. The dedication of the *Eroici Furori* to Sir Philip Sidney (1585) reveals a relationship of genuine mutual esteem (*ibid.,* p. 128):

There is none more proper to receive the dedication of these discourses than you, excellent sir, lest I should hold a mirror to the blind and a lyre to him who is deaf, as I have done from want of heed, and as others do from habit. To you, therefore, they are presented, that the Italian may reason with him who has understanding; that verse may be under the countenance and judgment of a poet; that Philosophy may show herself in present nakedness to your fair understanding; that heroic things may be directed to an heroic and generous soul, such as that with which you are endowed; and that homage may be offered to one of such worth as is ever made manifest in you.

It may have been through Sidney that Bruno was invited by Fulke Greville to the dinner party already referred to, the famous Ash Wednesday Supper, which was meant to be a symposium on the Copernican philosophy. Bruno tells us in the *Cena de le Ceneri* (printed 1584) that his host had assembled a group of learned friends "to hear the reasons of his [Bruno's] belief that the earth moves," but as in the case of the Oxford disputation, Bruno's lack of tact and his irascibility of temper seem to have created so unfavorable an attitude in his audience that this meeting, too, broke up in disorder and incivility.

In his description of the group of disputants (*Opere Italiene,* 1907; *Cena de le Ceneri,* I, pp. 97ff.), Bruno has singled out one "knight," whom he calls *Torquato,* to be the speaker for the negative. He is pictured as bumptious and truculent; and, to the Nolan, he is a mere buffoon. This figure has never been identified by Bruno's commentators, but it is tempting, in the light of the Ralegh legend, to imagine it as a caricature of Ralegh, particularly since it is certain that Bruno viewed with hatred the English policy of imperial expansion advocated by Ralegh. In the *Spaccio,** Minerva suggests dispatching from heaven a certain constellation, by which she intends to signify the English slave-trading ships. She calls it "that true whale which swallows up living Bodies in one place, and then goes and spues them up on the most distant Shores, and opposite, contrary, and different Coasts of the Sea." A great many of the gods said (*ibid.,* p. 266):

> Let it go . . . with abominable Avarice, vile and precipitate Merchandizing, desperate Piracy, Plundering, Chicane, Usury, and its other wicked Hand-Maids, Servants, and Attendants. And let Liberality, Munificence, Nobleness of Mind, Communicativeness, Readiness to do Services, and their worthy Ministers and Servants, succeed.
>
> It is necessary, said *Minerva,* that it be granted and appropriated to some-body. Do with it what you please, said *Jupiter.* Then said she, let it serve some solicitous Portuguese, or curious and covetous Briton, that so with it they may go and discover other Countries and other Regions towards the West-Indies, where the sharp-sighted *Genoese* has made no Discoveries, and the tenacious and stiptick *Spaniard* has not set his foot: and thus successively, for the future, let it serve the most curious, solicitous and diligent Searcher of new Continents and Lands.

Bruno presents Torquato as asking questions that are not only silly and irrelevant, but which show that he has missed the whole drift of the Copernican argument. Torquato asks, "Where then is the sun?" and the Nolan replies that he may imagine it anywhere he likes. A very intelligent answer! But it is construed by Torquato to mean that Bruno does not know how to answer such a "poser." Then Bruno parodies: To the question "How many sacraments of the Church are there?" he replies with satirical irrelevance, "It is about the twentieth of Cancer and opposite the tenth or hundredth of Capricorn,

* This and other passages from the *Spaccio* are quoted from a translation printed in England in 1713, now very rare. I am indebted for the use of it to the generosity of Mr. John Purves, of the University of Edinburgh.

or on the campanile of St. Paul's!" When Torquato finally brings out a great diagram of the heavens in order to teach the Nolan both of Ptolemy and Copernicus, Bruno tells him his ignorance arises from having looked at the diagram without reading the text. If he had read the text, he would never have made the ludicrous error of mistaking the prick made by the compass for a dot representing the earth! The questions about the domain of the seven spheres of planets and Bruno's impatient dismissal of them as the "propositions of an infant," have a curiously familiar ring about them; one is almost tempted to translate, in the words of Dr. Faustus, "Tush, these are freshmen's suppositions!" At all events, Bruno's account leaves no room for doubt as to the uncompromising rejection of the New Philosophy by the learned guests of Lord Brooke. Bruno says, when they were departing, they expressed their felicitations not only to their host, but to each other, omitting only—and by deliberate intention to insult—any recognition of the guest of honour. With characteristic retort, Bruno sent his own servant after them bearing his own courteous compliments! What should we not give for a list of the guests of this dinner! At all events, Bruno's "Areopagite" friends, Greville, Sidney, Dyer, and Spenser may have formed a nucleus; and, if Ralegh happened to be in town, he would be almost sure to be among those invited. This feast of reason was precisely the sort for which he would have the keenest appetite. If Hariot was with Ralegh as early as 1583, it is even possible that he was brought along as the latter's chief oracle. But for all these hopeful guesses there is a disappointing lack of evidence. The only fact for us to bear in mind with certainty is that in his Oxford lectures and in his one recorded London discussion of Copernicanism, Bruno's attempts to create a favourable hearing for the New Philosophy in England were wholly unsuccessful.

In other respects, however, his notions and his fiery manner of discussion were not without influence. The precise date for the Ash Wednesday Supper is not known; Bruno's description of it was printed in 1584. In the same year he published another "strange dialogue," entitled the *Spaccio della Bestia Trionfante* (*Expulsion of the Triumphant Beast*). This is of special interest to the student of Marlowe because of the possible relation between it and the scandal concerning Ralegh's "School of Atheism." In this work, even a modern commentator assures us that under cover of an allegorical fustian "the mysteries of the faith are scoffed at. The Jewish records are put on a level with the Greek myths, and miracles are laughed at as magical tricks." This nineteenth-century misunderstanding of Bruno is exactly in tune with contemporary popular misapprehension of the great truths he was trying to promulgate. It is the same kind of crude conservatism that imagined Prometheus, the great servant of man, to be a rebel against Heaven. Bruno hardly scoffed at "the Mysteries of the faith"; but he did most unmercifully lash out against the theological pedants who insisted on justification by faith alone, independent of good works. Particularly angry was he at the conventional dons who where wont to equate faith with their own very limited understanding of God and His celestial cosmography. Bruno says through the mouth of Momus, in the First Dialogue of the *Spaccio* (p. 56):

> 'T will be a noble work to put an end to this dastardly Sect of Pedants, who without doing good according to the natural and divine Law, esteem themselves, and would be esteem'd by others to be religious Persons, and acceptable to God; and say that doing good is good, and doing evil is evil, but that doing good, or abstaining from evil, does not render them acceptable to God; but only hoping and believing according to their Catechism. I leave you to judge, O ye Gods, if there was ever such Ribaldry and Roguery as this in the world; . . .

In a magnificent passage in the Second Dialogue, Bruno shows his real philosophical tolerance of the many sects, which, though "staining the white radiance of eternity," do nevertheless represent attempts to diffuse that light for "the eyes of Understanding." The dialogue is between Saulinus and Sophia; in the following passage, Saulinus is speaking (*ibid.*, p. 85):

> I understand you *Sophia;* and know that 't is you who in various ways contemplate, comprehend, and explain this Truth, and the Effects of that heavenly Influence of your Being; which many aspire, endeavour, study, and earnestly contend to arrive at by divers steps

and degrees; which presents itself the very End and Scope of the different Studies of Mankind, and activates the diverse Subjects of intellectual Virtues according to different Measures; and to herself that one simple Truth which directs all men. And as there is none who has not some Notices of Truth, so there is none here below, who is perfectly able to comprehend it; because it is not comprehended and truly conceived by anything, but that in which it dwells essentially; and that is no other than *herself*: And therefore she is not seen externally, but in a Shadow, a Similitude, a Glass, and superficially; to which none in this World can approach by an Act of Providence, and Effect of Prudence, except your self, *Sophia*. However, she brings you many Sects, some of which admire her, others approve, others enquire, others suppose, others judge and determine: some by Sufficiency of natural Magick, others by superstitious Divination, others by way of Negation, others by way of Affirmation, others by way of Composition, others by way of Definition, others by way of Demonstration, others by acquir'd Principles, others by divine Principles, aspire for her. In the mean time, she who is present in no place, nor absent from any, cries aloud to them, and presents before the Eyes of their Understanding all things visible and invisible.

Marlowe, with a staggering carelessness of context, shows that he too is aware of this process of inferring from "outward forms the passion and the life" which only the true mystic experiences, as he contemplates "the endless power and purity" of God. With an irony that rivals Bruno, Marlowe makes the Turk declare that "His power everywhere fills every continent with strange infusion of His sacred vigour." Even so critical a tolerance as that shown by Bruno towards many sects, was dangerous in the days of early Reformation bigotry; but when he extended his liberalism to include "presumptuous" parallels between the legends of the Old Testament and those of Egyptian and Greek antiquity, he played directly into the hands of his enemies, the theologians. The Third Part of the Third Dialogue of the *Spaccio* is filled with these bold, challenging comparisons. A single sample will suffice to illustrate. Saulinus has asked Minerva to expound

. . . the Metaphor of the Raven, which was first found and figur'd in *Egypt,* and afterward taken up by the *Hebrews* in the form of History; with whom this Science transmigrated from *Babylon,* and travel'd from *Greece* in form of a Fable, dress'd up by the Poets. For the *Hebrews* speak of a Raven sent out of the Ark by a Man whose name was *Noah,* to see if the Waters were dry'd up, at the time when Men had drunk so much that they burst; and this Animal charm'd with so many dead Carcasses, remain'd and never return'd from its Message and Service: which appears quite contrary to the Accounts of the *Egyptians* and *Grecians,* which are to this purpose; That the Raven was sent from Heaven by one of the Gods call'd *Apollo,* to try if he could find any Water, at a time when the Gods were ready to die of Thirst; and that this Animal charm'd with Figs he found in his way, staid away many days, and at last came home late without Water and I believe he lost the Vessel too.

Soph. I will not at present put my self to the trouble of explaining to you the learned Metaphor: I'll only tell you, that the relation of the *Hebrews* and *Egyptians* answers all to the same Metaphor; for to say that the Raven went out of the Ark that was ten Cubits above the highest Mountain on earth, and to say that it went from heaven, is in my mind all one and the same. And that Men in such a Place and Region are call'd Gods, is not very strange; for being celestial, they may with little trouble be Gods. And that the *Jews* call the principal *Noah,* and the *Egyptians Apollo,* may be easily reconcil'd because the different Denominations concur in the very same Office of regenerating: for SOL ET HOMO GENERANT HOMINEM.

Though on the whole such comparisons are made in all philosophic sincerity, it cannot be denied that Bruno sometimes presented his material with a mischievous twinkle, knowing how irritating such information would be to the dour pedants whose gravity he particularly enjoyed mocking. Thus, while expounding this notion of the higher Pantheism, he says *(ibid.,* p. 234):

Divinity shows itself in all things: tho' 't is found and seen in the most abject things, for Ends proximate, convenient, and necessary to the divers Arts of human life; and for the most universal and excellent End in the greatest Things and general Principles; since every thing, as has been said, has the Divinity latent in it; for it unfolds and communicates itself even to the very meanest things according to their capacity. Without which Presence, nothing should have Being; for that is the Essence of Being from the first to the very last.

His illustrations, which are numerous, all tend to explain how certain very "abject things" come to be used as symbols of the Divine. Thus the wings with which Mercury adorns his hat are, though a part of a beast, symbolic of that "lightness" by which the gods "can raise themselves to the clouds." So, he says, do the successors of the ancients speak symbolically when they "call their young God a bleeding Pelican, a solitary Sparrow, a slain Lamb." This was, undoubtedly, playing with fire, but when he brought in Moses "horned" as the best possible illustration of this difficult "mystery," he went the "one step too far" that caused him to fly for his life. Inasmuch as I believe this naughty irony of Bruno's to be responsible for much of the myth surrounding the atheistical charges against Marlowe and Ralegh, I insert one or two typical passages from the Third Dialogue. Speaking of the pantheistic mystery he has just been expounding, Bruno makes Sophia say *(ibid.,* p. 239):

Nobody, either before or since, was ever able to express this more to the Life, than the Leader and Legislator of the *Jewish* People; that M[oses], I mean, who left the court of Pharaoh, after having receiv'd his Doctor's Degrees in all the Sciences of the Egyptians: Who in the number of his Signs surpass'd all the Professors of Magick. In what manner did he shew his Excellency, and Abilities for being a Divine Ambassador, and Representer of the Authority of the God of the *Hebrews?* Do you think it was by coming down from Mount *Sinai,* with the great Tables in his hands, in the form of a simple pure Man? No, no; it was by presenting himself venerable with two great Horns, which branch'd upon his Forehead; at which awful and majestick Presence, the Hearts of that vagabond People fail'd them, so that he was oblig'd to cover his face with a Veil: and this he did, that he might not make that divine and more than human Aspect become too familiar.

We are today so thoroughly accustomed to regard the horns of Moses as an august token of his having talked with God, that few indeed would find in the legend any irreverence or think it necessary to look up the source of it in a remote mistranslation, now irrecoverable, of the Hebrew *qāran.** However, the pedants who were too stupid to follow Bruno's argu-

* The *Encyclopedia Biblica* (ed. 2111, *Horn*) maintains that the Latin *"cornuta"* is the natural rendering of the Hebrew *qāran,* and the sense is "horned." Some have held that *qāran* may mean "to radiate light," but for this explanation there is no authority. For this note I am indebted to the Rev. Joseph Cattanack, of the University of Edinburgh.

ment, were acutely aware that he was insinuating a profane application of a holy mystery, and doing so in a spirit of intolerable mischievous levity. Bruno seemed to take a boyish delight in teasing the Professors of Divinity by alluding casually to the existence of men before Adam, whose "Memoirs and Records of about ten thousand years . . . are entire and round" *(ibid.,* pp. 245-56), and by equating the Hebrew fables with those of Egypt and Greece. Certainly when he mentions Noah and Silenus in the same breath, or compares the repeopling of the earth by Pyrrha and Deucalion after the flood, with the regeneration of life by Noah and his wife, assuming both to be fables representing the same mystery, or, as he says, "a Metaphor of some Truth worthy to be kept secret" (*ibid.,* p. 248), or when he assumes that the wonder done by Moses and Aaron before Pharaoh to have been mere legerdemain and Egyptian jugglery; when he suggests these things and many more, he knows, however serious and noble and philosophic his underlying purpose may be, that he is giving deadly offense to "those who presume to teach in the Chair or by Books [but who] have need to hear and be students," a set of men whom Bruno regarded as "fitter to feed Swine and Asses than reasonable creatures," that is, the undergraduates.

We shall see shortly how closely the pious reaction to Bruno's mockery is followed in the legends and accusations formulated both against Marlowe and Ralegh, with Hariot coming in for his share. The printer of these two works of Bruno's (as also of the four philosophical works) was a Frenchman, Thomas Vautrollier, a scholar who had come to England about the beginning of Elizabeth's reign, and first settled his printing office and book shop in Blackfriars. According to Ame (*Topographical Antiquities),* he married his daughter Jakin to his apprentice, Richard Field, of Stratford-on-Avon.* As Bruno's printer, he was certainly made to share the responsibility for the propagation of such "atheistical" views as were contained in the pages of these philosophical essays. Ame says (Frith, *op. cit.,* p. 126):

* McKerrow says it was his widow who married Field after the death of Vautrollier in 1587.

. . . he (Vautrollier) was the printer of Jordanus Brunus in the year 1584, for which he fled, and the next year being at Edinburgh, in Scotland, he first taught that nation the way of good printing, and there staid until such time as by the intercession of friends he had got his pardon, as appears by a book dedicated to the Right Worshipful Mr. Thomas Randolph, Esq., where he returns him thanks for his great favour and for assisting him in his distress, printed in octavo, 1587.

This definitely links Bruno with the Atheist scandal and both with the learned London stationer, Vautrollier. It may not be irrelevant to observe that in the sixteenth century, printing was often still in the hands of learned men, and it was not infrequent for printers to act as hosts to traveling scholars. Bruno himself actually lived, while in Frankfort, with the printer John Wechel. To be sure, tradition associates Marlowe with the stationers at Paul's rather than with any specific rendezvous in Blackfriars; but it is surely not stretching possibilities to think of Marlowe as a frequent visitor in a printing establishment in so theatrical a district as Blackfriars, as well as those in St. Paul's Churchyard. The shop of Vautrollier and Field, Ltd., would provide a picturesque channel through which the daring conversations of Bruno might reach the ear of Marlowe.

Bruno left London with Castlenau in 1585, and took up his residence in Paris, where he remained for seven months. His public lectures in the French capital met the same fate as in London; both ended in riots. Bruno therefore decided to try again to find a university sufficiently virtuous and enlightened to listen to his challenging argument with respect. This time he decided to try Wittenberg, in Saxony, probably hoping well from the foundation which had invited his old friend Gentile to lecture there. We are told that the professors received him cordially, and he was allowed to take private pupils on account of his poverty. In Wittenberg, Bruno ran squarely into a hive of seething controversy between the Calvinism of John Casimir, Regent of the Palatine Lines, and the Lutheranism of his brother-in-law, Christian I. Bruno's biographer, William Boulting tells us (*op. cit.,* p. 206) that Casimir "was busy coercing his own wife and his people into Calvinism, and this naturally aroused the indignation of the Saxon Lutherans." He adds that, strangely enough, Bruno's friends and supporters were of the "narrower Lutheran body." Never content with half measures, Bruno plunged into a defence of "Saxon Luther." He called him "the Mighty Hero," the "Bulwark against Papal tyranny," the "Hercules who dragged forth the monster with the triple crown, bursting open the steely gates of Hell, triumphing over the city guarded by triple walls and the nine-fold Styx." He declared that Luther "had seen the light" and had "confronted and overcome the adversary girt about with power," and had "despoiled him." As Professor Boulting observes, "Such words were not calculated to make any easier his desired reconciliation with Mother Church, nor would they add to the safety of that return to Italy which he soon had the temerity to effect." Professor Boulting also notes that the oratory of this speech "was probably the chief cause of the curious impression that by the 'beast' of the *Spaccio,* Bruno referred to the Pope." He also mentions a "tradition that seems to have arisen from this oration that he had written a paneygric upon the Devil." From such a defence of "Saxon Luther," it is easy to account for Bruno's receiving the title "Saxon Bruno."

From Wittenberg, Bruno went to Prague, seeking the patronage of Emperor Rudolf II, at whose court he had several friends, particularly Fabrizio Mordente and William of St. Clement, formerly Spanish Ambassador in France, but now accredited to the court of Rudolf. Bruno arrived about Eastertide, 1588, and on 10 June he dedicated to St. Clemente two little works bound together under the title *The Examination of Forms and the Combined Lamp of Raymond Lully, Doctor of All Knowledge and Almost Divine.* At the same time he promised that a "profounder Cabalistic Lamp" would soon follow; but it never appeared. It was in Prague that Bruno became engrossed in occultism. Boulting says (*op. cit.,* p. 215):

It may have been because he found so much attention paid to occult and astrological subjects at Prague that Bruno's interest was directed to the obscure operations of the mind in mathematics and those subtle sympathies in Nature concerning which the age was ready to believe almost anything. Magic meant to Bruno natural operations which are obscure and surprising, but of which, eventually, we may hope to learn the real character and laws. His mnemonic system was regarded as a species of occult science, for, quite apart from the Black Art, magical sciences were recognized as properly occupied with mathematics, physical sympathies, obscure causes and effects, such divine subjects as inspiration and prophecy, judicial astrology, metaphysical speculation, etc. Bruno had already exhibited interest in what the Church held to be a dangerous borderland between the lawful and the unlawful: in England he had written concerning the extraordinary effects wrought by the One Spirit in all things. He dedicated his *De Magia* to a pupil named Besler, a youth from Nurnberg, whose father had studied under Luther and whose brother gained distinction as a botanist. Besler continued to act as Bruno's copyist, and accompanied or followed him to Padua.

Bruno, the occultist, and his German servitor became famous throughout Europe. From Prague, he proceeded to Helmstedt, whence he was again ejected, and therefore, toward the middle of 1590, went on to Frankfort. By this time, Bruno's ill reputation had preceded him and he had difficulty even to find lodgings, not to mind permission to lecture in the University. Finally, through the intercession of John Wechel, the printer, an old friend of Sidney's, Bruno was granted asylum at a Carmelite monastery by a kindly prior who, though disturbed by Bruno's intellectual arrogance, gave him shelter, and, doubtless, his good prayers. He said charitably of Bruno, "He was a man of fine intellect and erudition—a universal man," but he added regretfully that "he professed to know more than the Apostles, and could, if he wished, make the whole world of one religion."

As we all know now, this year of residence in Frankfort was the last in which Bruno lived at liberty. In the fall of 1591, he accepted a long and hard-pressed invitation from the wealthy Venetian dilettante, Signor Giovanni Mocenigo, to come to Italy "to teach him the art of memory and discovery," and thereby flew, like the moth into the flame, straight into the fire of the Inquisition. Professor Boulting calls this Mocenigo "a treacherous and incapable dabbler." Bruno, who never learned to temper his windy dialectic to the lamb shorn of wit, obviously shocked his new patron by saying "far too much to a man of just sufficient intelligence to misunderstand and misrepresent; one whose affectation of a love of learning, friendliness and generosity disguised a stupid, superstitious mind, a treacherous heart and a mean and sordid disposition." At all events, Mocenigo denounced his learned guest to the Holy Office. Bruno was arrested and placed on his first trial in Venice on 26 May, 1592. By February of the following year, he was awaiting further trial in the Inquisitional prison in Rome. He was there at the moment of Marlowe's death on 18 May, 1593.

So far as I know, no one has ever suggested a political or fustian significance inherent in the early German Faust story, first published in Frankfort in 1587. Bruno's fame had certainly long had the character of a Faustus, or a Friar Bacon, or a Paracelsus legend, throughout Germany and Hungary. It is perfectly possible that the Faust story sprang into popular significance as a warning against Bruno. Be that as it may, the parallel between the two philosophers, the Bruno of history and the Faustus of Marlowe, is so striking that it is difficult to imagine how it could be missed by anyone familiar with the background of Bruno's career; and this would be true even if the so-called "additional scenes," in which "Saxon Bruno" appears as a character, were omitted from the play. It is not necessary here to enter the lists for or against the Marlovian authorship of these unpleasant scenes. The important fact to note, as far as this study is concerned, is that the kinship between the "atheist" Faustus and the "heretic" Bruno was established by the author of these scenes, whoever he was, and whenever he wrote. Faustus is represented as the defender and rescuer of "Saxon Bruno" and as the brazen "despoiler" of "the monster with the triple crown." It may be that the crudity of these scenes, with their crazy references to the personalities involved in Bruno's exploits, may be more readily traced to the garbled accounts of Bruno's continental legend brought back to London by Robert Browne and his Company, who were in Frankfort in 1592, acting in Marlowe's plays, than to Marlowe's own confusion. Incidentally, it is interesting to note that Marlowe's fame had already spread to the Continent. E. Mentzel, in his *Geschichte der Schauspielkunst in Frankfort am*

Main, (Boas, *Marlowe,* p. 44), quotes a Würtemberg merchant who spoke of the "dort im Inselland gar beruhmten Herrn Christopher Marlowe." This "Saxon Bruno" and the mysterious "Raymond of Hungary" have caused much perplexity to editors of Marlowe (Boas, *op. cit.,* p. 107), who have never heard of Bruno's residence in Saxony, nor of his connections with Raymond Lully, nor of his supposed antipapal exploits.

But, I believe, the influence of Bruno on Marlowe was not confined to his inference of a Bruno-Faustus parallel; it was the "heroic rapture" of Bruno, his soaring imagination, his daring dialectic, his passionate yearning for union with "the One that remains" when all the other temporal phases of our lives have passed, that was the something far more deeply interfused throughout the whole fabric of Marlowe's poetry that gives it its special incandescence, its "brave translucency," its "air and fire"—in short, its magic.

Both the prose and poetry of Bruno are shot through with the "conceit" so familiar to the readers of Marlowe, i.e., that which represents a mortal spirit longing to be "resolved" into the spirits of the elements. Tamburlaine yearns for that world where "our bodies turn to elements" and "our souls aspire to celestial thrones." He tells of the brilliance of the equipage with which, he says, "will I ride through Samarcanda street / Until my soul, dissevered from my flesh / Shall mount the milk-white way."

So too Faustus scorns the flashy triumphs of this world; the "dominion" for which he strives "stretcheth as far as doth the mind of man." These notions are everywhere in Marlowe, but Bruno had been saying these same things years before Marlowe had appeared on the literary horizon. "O worthy love of the beautiful!" sings Bruno, "O desire for the divine! Lend me thy wings; bring me to the day spring, to the clearness of the young morning; and the outrage of the rabble, the storms of Time, the slings and arrows of Fortune shall fall upon this tender body and shall weld it to steel." The following lines from one of the sonnets repeats the aspiration:

> While that the sun upon his round doth burn,
> And to their source the roving planets flee,
> Things of the earth do to the earth return,

And parted waters hasten to the sea,
So shall my spirit to the high gods turn,
And heaven-born thought to heaven shall carry me.

Sometimes it seems almost as if he longs to rise literally into the purity of the stratosphere, scorning the plight of Icarus precisely as Faustus did. To be sure, "treading on air" is a fairly common sixteenth-century conceit. The following sonnet is the work of Tansillo, the Neapolitan poet, but it is quoted by Bruno in the *Eroici Furori* as Sonnet XVI:

Winged by desire and thee, O dear delight!
As still the vast and succouring air I tread,
So, mounting still, on swifter pinions sped,
I scorn the world, and Heaven receives my flight.
And if the end of Ikaros be nigh,
I will submit, for I shall know no pain;
And falling dead to earth, shall rise again;
What lowly life with such high death can vie?
Then speaks my heart from out the upper air,
"Whither dost lead me? sorrow and despair
Attend the rash"; and thus I make reply,
"Fear thou no fall, nor lofty ruin sent;
Safely divide the clouds, and die content.
When such proud death is dealt thee from on high."

In just such physical terms does the Chorus describe the intellectual flight of Doctor Faustus, who

To find the secrets of astronomy
Graven in the book of Jove's high firmament,
Did mount him up to scale Olympus' top,
Where sitting in a chariot burning bright,
Drawn by the strength of yoked dragons' necks,
He views the clouds, the planets, and the stars,
The tropic zones, and quarters of the sky,
From the bright circle of the horned moon,
E'en to the height of *Primum Mobile*.*

* This doctrine of *Primum Mobile* was added in the Middle Ages to the Ptolemaic system. Sir William Gilbert, of Colchester, who was the only believer in Copernicanism in England in 1600 (see *Appendix*), has an amusing passage in his *De Magneto*, deriding the theory. (Bk. VI, p. 321 in P. F. Mottelay's translation, N. Y., 1893). This note was brought to my attention by my friend and former pupil, Miss Edith White.

In a later comment, Bruno again alludes to this "conceit" of flying:

As happens to one flying in the air, the higher he rises above the earth, the more he has of air beneath sustaining him; and, in consequence, he is the less exposed to the plagues of gravitation: thus he can fly the higher because he cannot return to the under world without painfully dividing the air, although he may consider it were easier to divide the depths of air about our earth than the heights of air about the other stars. Thus, with proficiency in this progress comes greater and greater facility in mounting aloft. For every part of bodies and of the said elements, when approaching their natural home, move with the greater impetus and potency; thus whether a man will or no, he must needs arrive there; and as we may divine bodies from parts of bodies, so we may judge of things intellectual by their objects, as their places, countries, and aims.

This *élan* so characteristic of Marlowe's poetry is everywhere throughout the works of Bruno, "repeated," as his biographer says, "with the innumerable decorations and enrichments of a luxuriant poetic fancy." Perhaps the finest of all the sonnets is the Twelfth, which is fairly "inspired" with that romantic pursuit of Beauty where it is most dazzling and dangerous. It is tragically prophetic of the prayer of Faustus:

The moth beholds not death as forth he flies
Into the splendour of the living flame;
The hart athirst to crystal water hies,
Nor heeds the shaft, nor fears the hunter's aim;
The timid bird, returning from above
To join his mate, deems not the net is nigh;
Unto the light, the fount, and to my love,
Seeing the flame, the shaft, the chains, I fly;
So high a torch, love lighted in the skies,
Consumes my soul, and with this bow divine
Of piercing sweetness what terrestrial vies?
This net of dear delight doth prison mine;
And I to life's last day have this desire—
Be mine thine arrows, Love, and mine thy fire.

Bruno's prayer was granted in the literal as well as the figurative sense; nor was the fire that burned his body more real than that "strangely intellectual fire" which glowed in his imagination, no less than in Marlowe's.

The parallel with Dr. Faustus is perfect. Like Bruno, he excelled "all whose sweet delight disputes / In heavenly matters of theology," but to the orthodox, he was "swoln with cunning, of a self-conceit" till "his waxen wings did mount beyond his reach / And melting, heaven conspired his overthrow." When, after the publication of his "atheistical" works, Bruno was forced to leave England, the official defenders of the faith sighed with relief, though we must believe that a finer spirit here and there wept with pity. Such might well have joined the Chorus at the conclusion of *Doctor Faustus:*

> Cut is the branch that might have grown full straight,
> And burned is Apollo's laurel-bough
> That sometime grew within this learned man.

We must not forget, as commentators upon Marlowe sometimes do, that this play is not a glorification of atheism, but a picture of the utter damnation which is the inescapable consequence of it. Mr. George Buckley, in his study of *Atheism in the English Renaissance* (1932, p. 135ff.) observes:

> It is perhaps worth noting of course that Doctor Faustus at the beginning of the play is made to say:
>
> Philosophy is odious and obscure;
> Both law and physic are for petty wits:
> Divinity is basest of the three,
> Unpleasant, harsh, contemptible and vile.
>
> and somewhat later, while working a charm:
>
> Within this circle is Jehovah's name
> Forward and backward anagramatis'd,
>
> thus reminding us of Parson's charge that Ralegh, in his school for atheists, taught the scholars to spell *God* backward. In the course of an interview with Mephistopheles, Faustus also says, "Come, I think hell's a fable."

Bruno had opined that "the fear of hell is more dreadful than the place itself would be." (Boulting, *op. cit.*, p. 245.) But *Doctor Faustus* was written to condemn such views, and therefore it is not quite fair to conclude, as Mr. Buckley does (*op. cit.*, p. 136), that "as the sixteenth century used the word, Marlowe was undoubtedly an atheist." Marlowe is not Bruno.

An explanation of Marlowe's motive for presenting such a didactic warning against atheism will, we hope, clear up the cause of this confusion, and account at the same time for his cruel debasing of the Bruno heritage; for although Marlowe undoubtedly romanticized Faustus' flair for intellectual conquest, he also brutalized it. After every allowance has been made for possible additions by other hands, it is still certain that the curse of vulgar necromancy is written large over the whole design. The point of the tragedy is to show how "learning's golden gifts" have been betrayed by intellectual arrogance into a pursuit of the cheapest kind of black magic, conjuring, "anagramatizing" the name of God, and the tricks of legerdemain. This is not worthy of Faustus, whose early aims were to comprehend "the end of every art," to "be resolved of all ambiguities," to lure the "flowering pride of Wittenberg to swarm to his problems"; but it is the logical denouement of the plot. Faustus' career is pictured for us as an "example of evil." If Marlowe rises above his plot and makes us care so much for his great protagonist that we resent the conclusion, the fault is one which we ought to find easy to forgive. Is not Faustus at his best worth a dozen well made plays or edifying examples? Our affirmative can be emphasized by recalling a parallel. As we like Shakspere the better for his inability to keep Shylock down to his role of pure villain, or Milton for a like weakness towards Satan, so we are happy to see in Faustus, evidence that Marlowe understood the beauty as well as the more obvious fiasco of a career like Bruno's. Marlowe had his reasons for drawing Faustus "devilish."

It may be worth noting in passing the record of a play on the continent (Leopold Prowe, *Nicolaus Copernicus,* Berlin, 1583-4) poking fun at the Copernican system and its originator, written by an Elbing schoolmaster, a Dutch refugee from the Inquisition, and given by the villagers of Elbing. Dr. Dorothy Stimson, in her study, *The Gradual Acceptance of the Copernican Theory of the Universe* (Hanover, N. H., 1917, p. 32), mentions this play, which seems to be an interesting parallel to *Doctor Faustus,* though the comparison has not been noted by Dr. Stimson.

Certain scholars (notably Mr. Sebastian Evans, in *Macmil-*

lan's Magazine, XLII, pp. 145ff.) have argued that Spenser's Mutability Cantos were written for the same purpose, i.e., to put on record the poet's disapprovel of Bruno.

In their desire to throw discredit on the new fashion of astronomical poetry, Nashe, Greene, Harvey, Lodge, and subsequently Kyd, all poetaster rivals, saw in the Bruno tragedy the possibility of a charge which, if nothing worse, would smear the authors of the fashion. Greene launched the attack by the publication of the *Planetomachia,* in 1585. This pamphlet strives, by means of a story which is more interesting in its psychology than clear in its allegory, to describe the dangers of Astronomy, or, as he usually calls it, "astrology." The pamphlet is dedicated to Leicester, and is described in *The Epistle* (*Life and Works of Robert Greene,* ed. by Grosart for the Huth Library, V, p. 7), as follows:

> Although my ignoraunce might iustly abash me from troubling your honour with such friuolous trash: yet duetifull and humble affection wherewith I finde my selfe bound to such a worthie patrone of good letters, hath emboldned me to present your Honour with this Pamphlet, being a Planetomachia or generall opposition of the seuen Planets. wherein is Astronomically decyphered their nature & essence, and plainly sheweth (that sith euery man is naturally borne vnder the influence and irradiate constellation of one of these wandering starres, and that one is alwaies predominate in the configuration of euery natiuitie) what proper qualities each particuler Planet doth appropriate. . . . But as Horace alwaies sung his satyres vpon the Lute, and Phidias painted blacke Vulcan sitting in an Iuorie Charriot: as Protagines carued the counterfaite of Irus in a wedge of gold: and Demosthenes sawsed his weightie inuectiues with some pretie & plesaunt inuentions. So (right Honorable) I haue mixed melancholie with Musicke, and tempered the brawles of the Planets with plesaunt though tragical histories.

In fairness to Greene, we must point out that in this early "simple censure of Astrologie" he does not condemn Astronomy theoretically, but only the improper use of it. Citing Tully's *Somnium Scipionis,* he says (*ibid.,* p. 17):

> Thrice vnhappy then wee, he thought, who are not delighted with this sweet and pleasant contemplation, whose minds are not moued with the wonderfull works of God and Nature. He is a foolish beast,

not a man, sayth Plato, whiche is not delighted with the studie of Astronomie: whereof God himselfe is the author. . . . But [he warns], no marvel though the ignorant do inveigh against this sacred science, when as the learned men themselues do neither make account of Astrologie, nor yet exercise it: But when by chaunce they happen vpon any that do for want of skil prognosticate anything amisse, they straight condemne the starres and hate Astrologie it selfe: iudging it rather false and friuolous, than either true or necessarie: much like them which hearing an unskilfull Musition sing, rashly without reason doe despise Musicke it self.

Giving examples of good and bad astrologers, he says (*ibid,* p. 21):

As for *Dedalus* the *Athenian,* I esteeme him to be a perfect Astrologer, in which Science he greatly excelled in his time, and instructed his sonne therein. But *Icarus* tickled forward with the heate of youth, and trusting too much in his vnperfect skill, began at first to search the deapth of Astrologie, and to wade so farre in the intricate misteries thereof, that climing too hie he erred from the trueth, and fell headlong into the deepe Sea of supernatural conceipts: whereof the Gretians said he was drowned in the Sea called *Mare Icarium.*

After 1584, it would have been extraordinary if Greene's readers had not been reminded at this point of Bruno, who, as we have seen, not only compared himself to Icarus, but who had already fallen into the sea of disgrace. There was, at this date, no definite allusion to Marlowe.

The attack on the School of Night and its sister, the imperial enterprise of Ralegh, is, however, far more definite in Nashe's *Terrors of the Night* (1594), published within a few months of Chapman's *Shadow of Night.* He alludes in the "Epistle Dedicatorie" to "a number of men . . . who pursuing the high way to the Indies, have perisht in lingring expectation before they could get thither." The body of the pamphlet is a full-front attack on the worship of the "spirits of every element" which, Marlowe had declared, "shadow more beauty in their airy brows than do the white breasts of the Queen of Love." Nashe declares (*Complete Works of Thomas Nashe,* ed. by Grosart for the Huth Library, III, p. 230):

The spirits of the earth are they which crie, all bread and no drinke, that love gold and a buttoned cap above heaven. . . . If with their earth-plowing snowtes they can turn vp a pearle out of a dunghill, it is all they desire. . . . There is no citie merchant, or country purchaser, but is haunted with a whole hoste of these spirits of the earth. The Indies is their Metrapolitaine realme of abode.

As for the spirits of the aire, which have no other visible bodies or form, but such as by the vnconstant glimmering of our eies is begotten; they are in truth all show and no substance, deluders of our imagination, & nought els. Carpet knights, politique statesmen, women & children they most converse with. Carpet knights they inspire with a humor of setting big lookes on it, being the basest cowards vnder heaven, couering an apes hart with a lion's case, and making false alarums when they mean nothing but a may-game. Politique statesmen they priuily incite, to bleare the worlds eyes with clowds of common wealth pretences, to broach any enmitie or ambitious humor of their owne vnder a title of their cuntries preservation to make it faire, or fowle when they list to procure popularity, or induce a preamble to some mighty peece of prowling, to stir vp tempests round about and replenish heaven with prodigies and wonders, the more to ratify their avaricious religion.

Alluding to certain "great famous conjurers and cunning men," he says (*ibid.*, p. 249), that they live "by telling of newes, & false dice, and it may be he hath a pretie insight into the cardes also, together with a little skill in his Jacob's staffe, and his Compasse: being able at all times to discover a new passage to Virginia." In all this fulmination, the general attack seems quite clearly against Ralegh, the "carpet knight," the enthusiastic stargazer and colonizer. The following excerpt seems to glance not only at Ralegh's rustication in 1592 and subsequent temporary postponement of the Virginia plan, but to his being what Aubrey called "sour-eie-lidded":

Questionless this is an unrefutable consequence, that the man who is mocked of his fortune, he that hath consumed his braines to compasse prosperitie, and meetes with no countervaylement in her likenesse, but hedge wine and lean mutton, and peradventure some halfe eid good looks that can hardly be discerned from winking; this poor piteous perplexed miscreãt either finallie despaires; or like a lanke, frost-bitten plant, looseth hys vigor or spirit by little and little; anie terror, the least illusion in the earth, is a *cacodaemon* vnto him. His soule has left his bodie, for, why, it is flying after these ayrie allurements: which when they vanish to nothing, it lyke wise vanisheth with them.

Professor Tucker-Brooke refers to Nashe as Marlowe's friend. I do not myself know of any evidence leading to such a conclusion, but if it does exist, it would need to be very strong to counteract the evidence supplied in this virulent attack upon the Ralegh group. There are other instances of Nashe's hostility to Marlowe. (See pp. 336ff.)

Both Marlowe and Chapman were subjected to repeated attacks because of their connection with the free-thinking, scientifically-minded men of Ralegh's Little Academe. Not only was their flair for precise astronomical nomenclature held up for ridicule, but they were repeatedly accused of atheism, a charge not to be laughed off lightly, since in those troublous times a conviction meant a horrible death. The story of the rivalry between the Ralegh and the Essex factions has many an ugly chapter, but perhaps none so intolerable to the literary student as that which reveals the low part played by certain men of letters toward whom we have an old habit of respect. Were it not essential to our "case," we should be more than content to draw the veil over the whole sordid episode of the so-called atheism of the Ralegh group.

The story begins with an anecdote concerning one of Ralegh's most decent acts—an errand of justice, in the execution of which he was, for the moment, allied with Essex. I allude to the trial and condemnation of John Udal. We shall best understand the complications in which Ralegh was involved as a result of his generous gesture to save Udal, if we glance for a moment at the events immediately preceding Udal's trial.

It would be pretentious to attempt to give here a full account of the religious problems under Elizabeth, for they were endless. The Catholic problem will be noticed briefly in connection with *The Jew of Malta,* but here I need only remind the reader of certain facets of the Puritan side of the question, some of which have already been noticed in a previous chapter. This party was, like most parties, divided against itself. One faction, the more conservative element, was content with reforming certain obvious abuses in an elaborate ecclesiasticism.

The other branch of the party was definitely radical. It wished to do away with episcopacy, root and branch. These men called themselves Separatists. The attitude of the Queen toward this *mêlée* is fairly clear: she was the head of the Church, but it was of the old Church as far as organization and ceremony were concerned. She had defined her position officially, early in her reign, by the promulgation of two Acts, the Act of Supremacy, and the Act of Uniformity. Both were passed in 1559. The first Act was properly called the *Act for Restoring the Ancient Jurisdiction* [of the Crown] *over the State Ecclesiastical and Spiritual.* This Act established the Queen, not the Pope, as the head of the Church in England, though she diplomatically declined to resume the title which her father had enjoyed, thereby avoiding offence to the Catholics, who thought the title belonged only to the Pope, and to the Separatists, who thought it belonged only to Christ. The second Act, properly called the *Act of Uniformity of Common Prayer,* prescribed an invariable ritual to be used in Anglican services. Elizabeth realized, as James did later, that "Presbyterianism and monarchy agree about as well as God and the Devil." The Act of Supremacy was not imposed on the laity in general; only the clergy and holders of civil office were compelled to take the oath. Mass and Presbyterian conventicles were alike prohibited, but no private person had to swear against his conscience. Indeed, it was Elizabeth's boast that, though for political reasons she demanded outward conformity, she "made no windows in men's souls." Though the law compelled everyone to go to an Anglican service on Sunday, the punishment in case of disobedience was only twelve pence for the poor. It is clear therefore that the Queen's ideal was, as usual, a middle course. It was necessary for her very claim to the throne to keep the Catholic Church powerless in England, but she was distinctly opposed to radical measures. She had to be above the Pope to save her legitimacy, and the only way to establish it as a "fact" was through a national church; but persecution was no part of her plan until she was forced to it by a train of circumstances over which she had no control. The first massacre of Protestants in France occurred in 1562, arousing so great a tide of sympathy in England that Elizabeth was pushed into sending aid to the Huguenots—not, however, without exacting Havre in payment! Incidentally, it may be well to remember that it was on this little French expedition that Ralegh got his first military experience. He had enlisted, at the age of seventeen; but long before he returned, a "seasoned warrior" of twenty-three, he had learned once and for all that there is no such thing as a religious war, and that of all kinds of civil war, the most odious is that which masks its unworthy political motives under a pretence of religion. Whether or not the *Massacre of Paris* was written at Ralegh's suggestion, or inspired by the accounts of his friend Le Moyne, it is obvious that the play is a dramatization of his passionate conviction that civil wars, especially those masking under a hypocritical guise of religion, are, of all things in the world, the most odious and idiotic. Commentators on this play have made much of Marlowe's success with the hero-villain type; but to regard the Guise as the hero, or even the protagonist of this piece, is, it seems to me, to miss the point of the whole thing. This is not a tragedy of character, but of a State embroiled in civil war. Here there are no heroes; even the slain Admiral is in no sense the hero of the play. All participators in the action are villainous examples of the iniquity we have been discussing, i.e., the use of religion as a disguise of political and personal ambition. Indeed, the Guise says as much in his famous soliloquy:

> Religion! O Diabole!
> Fie, I am ashamed, however that I seem,
> To think a word of such a simple sound
> Of so great matter should be made the ground!

Anjou himself plays double all the way through; he stabs with the Guise all during the massacre and is quite as active as anybody; but when Navarre and the Prince of Condé come on the scene, he pretends that he had nothing to do with it—that he is, in fact, horribly shocked:

Navarre: My lord, they say
That all the Protestants are massacred.

Anjou: Ay, so they are; but yet, what remedy?
I have done what I could to stay this broil.

Navarre: But yet, my lord, the report doth run
That you were one that made this massacre.

Anjou: Who, I? You are deceived; I rose but now.

Then at the end of the play, Anjou, who had in the beginning suggested sending the head and hands of the Admiral as "a present to the Pope," dies with the roundest antipapal curses on his lips:

Agent for England, send thy mistress word
What this detested Jacobin hath done.
Tell her, for all this, that I hope to live;
Which if I do, the papal monarch goes
To wreck and th' antichristian kingdom falls;
These bloody hands shall tear his triple crown,
And fire accursed Rome about his ears;
I'll fire his crazed buildings, and enforce
The papal towers to kiss the lowly earth.
Navarre, give me thy hand: I here do swear
To ruinate that wicked Church of Rome,
That hatcheth up such bloody practices;
And here protest eternal love to thee,
And to the Queen of England specially,
Whom God hath bless'd for hating papistry.

The story of the civil wars in England is similar in many ways. As in France, these wars had their origin in the formation of two parties, as mentioned above. In high places the extreme Protestant side of the feud was championed by Walsingham, toward whom, as a consequence, Elizabeth showed a marked coolness, even denouncing him as a "damned little Puritan" for his zeal. This party forced the extension of the Act of Supremacy to include members of the House of Commons, schoolmasters, and lawyers.

Far more to the Queen's liking was the policy advocated by Archbishop Whitgift, who was strongly antipapal, but who was unimpeachably "sound" in the matter of the Anglican hierarchy. Whitgift was all but a "high Churchman," and his most effective weapons were literary rather than military. His first tool in his fight with the Extremists was his protégé, Richard Hooker. Hooker had early made himself *persona grata* with the Archbishop by his weekly debates (for his sermons were almost literally that) with the Presbyterian, Walter Travers, co-lecturer with Hooker at the Temple. The burning questions of ecclesiastical policy were discussed by Hooker from the Anglican point of view in the morning sermon, and refuted by Travers at Evensong, so that the congregation were wont to say, "The forenoon sermon spake Canterbury, the afternoon Geneva." It goes without saying that "Canterbury" had the last word, for Whitgift forbade Travers' sermons altogether. Meantime, however, the gauntlet for Geneva was taken up by two zealous Separatists, Henry Barrow and John Greenwood. In 1593 they had been in gaol for over six years. Suddenly the Archbishop's patience with the whole controversy reached a breaking point; on 21 March he caused these two men to be indicted for felony, and on 6 April they were duly hanged. But this was only the beginning of the fierce anti-Puritan policy urged by Whitgift, henceforth consistently till his death. The feud between the Churchmen and the Puritans finally reached a crisis, at least dramatically speaking, in the episode known as the Martin Marprelate controversy. It is probable that the Marprelate tracts (so called because of their declared intention to *mar the prelates)* were written by more than one person; but it is certain that the big gun in the battle was fired by one John Penry, a young Welshman who was contemporary with Marlowe at Cambridge when he took his Bachelor's degree in 1584. Penry's avowed purpose was to prove the illegality of the episcopate. He quoted Scripture, with chapter and verse, to prove "that according to the New Testament, the officers of the Church were to be pastors, doctors [teachers], elders, and deacons and these alone"; that it was especially forbidden for these to be "lords" [Lord Bishops] in the Church; that the above-mentioned officers and none else were to have to do with preaching the Word, administering the sacraments, ordaining ministers, excommunicating, and administering all other Church censures and punishments. These were the tenets of Martin; but a mere statement of them gives the reader no notion of the peppery pen wielded by this clever pamphleteer. Martin walked on anything but a *via media.* He did not hesitate to declare that "all our Lord Bishops are petty popes, and petty usurping Anti-Christs," and he says he thinks "if they will still continue to do so, that they will breed young Popes and Anti-Christs: *per consequens,* neither they nor their brood are to be tolerated in any Christian commonwealth." *Sic quod* Martin Marprelate! Nor was this the worst of his charges. As usual, the noise of the fray was roused on petty points—the question of the indispensability of vestments and other "popish ceremonial," the "wanton lives" of the clergy, their general want of learning, their indolence and neglect of those under their care. These colourful accusations, combined with a witty, often scurrilous language, assured Martin of a popular audience, one whose clamours sounded much louder than any reverberations caused by the ponderous impact of Hooker's *Ecclesiastical Polity,* or *An Admonition to the People of England,* of Thomas Cooper, Bishop of Winchester. It was clear that Martin should be not only answered adequately, but outrivalled. Hence, therefore, with the heavy-gaited, wordy moralizations and denunciations of the parsons! At least this was the idea conceived by Richard Bancroft, Archbishop Whitgift's secretary, who forthwith secretly invited John Lyly, Thomas Nashe, and perhaps several others, to "give it back" to Martin in his own style. They responded first by a series of pamphlets, the tenor of which is well illustrated by their titles: *Pappe with a Hatchet; A Counter Cuf to Martin Junior; An Almond for a Parrot; Martin's Month's Mind; Mar-Martin; A Whip for an Ape; A Mirror for Martinists;* etc. The pamphlets are, however, only a background for the excitement produced when the war began to be enacted on the stage. The dissenters jeered at these specially engaged actors, calling them "rogues and vagabonds dressed in the Queen's liveries," and they derided Bancroft for his somewhat unorthodox commission, not hesitating to dub his highchurch policy as popery, and circulating scandalous lampoons and limericks against him. On one occasion, when he was shown such a libel, we are told by Fuller that he, "nothing moved thereat," bade it be "cast . . . to an hundred more that lie in a heap in my chamber." One of these broadsides, written at his death, is preserved, but not approved of by

Osborne (*op. cit.*, p. 65); it glances at his commission to the dramatists:

Bancroft was for plaies,
Leane, Lent, and Holy-daies,
But now undergoes their doome:
Had English ladies store,
Yet kept open a back dore
To let in the strumpet of Rome.

The laugh, however, was on the other side when Martin, dressed like a monstrous ape "with a wolf's bellie, cats clawes, &c." (Nashe's *Almond,* p. 22), was brought on the stage and "wormed and lanced to let the blood and evil humours out of him." We have already noted one account of the *May-Game of Martinism* (Part I, p. 204), but there are many others in the Marprelate pamphlets. *The Return of Pasquill* gives the following (Sig. C iij, quoted by Bond, *Lyly,* I, p. 53):

Methought *Vetus Comoedia* began to pricke him at London in the right vaine, when shee brought forth *Diuinitie* wyth a scratcht face, holding of her hart as if she were sicke, because Martin would have forced her; but myssing of his purpose, he left the print of his nayles uppon her cheekes, and poysoned her with a vomit, which he ministerd vnto her to make her cast vppe her dignities and promotions; . . .

As Sir Edmund Chambers remarks, "the savage Aristophanic invective was surely in full swing." Nashe brags of the part played by the dramatists, in the final rout of Penry. In *Martin's Month's Mind (ibid.,* I, p. 52), he tells how Martin [Penry] had been "drie beaten" by Cooper's *Admonition;* then "whipt that made him wince" by *A Whip for an Ape;* then "made a May-game vpon the Stage"; and at length "cleane Marde by *Marre-Martin.*" This last was, apparently, a second play that had been penned but never performed. Lyly in his *Pappe* describes the play, of which there is now no other record. The fustian device for the action was apparently taken from the *Book of Esther.* Lyly says (*ibid.,* I, p. 53):

Would it not bee a fine Tragedie, when Mardocheus shall play a Bishoppe in a Play, and Martin Hamman, and that he seekes to pull downe those that are set in authoritie aboue him, should be hoysted vpon a tree aboue all other?

A note in the margin reminds the reader that "If it be shewed at Paules, it will cost you foure pence: at the Theater two pence: at Sainct Thomas a Watrings nothing." But all this "have-at-you," "free-for-all," "rough-and-tumble," was turned into scandal when it became whispered about that the bishops were behind this dreadful horseplay. Protest rose on every hand. Harvey, of course, objected because of Lyly's authorship, wondering, he said, how the ecclesiastics could be driven "to entertain such an old light-headed fellow as [Lyly] for their defence." Bacon, in an Essay written about 1590, expresses the "hope that my Lords of the clergy have non-intelligence with this interlibelling, but do altogether disallow that their credit should be thus defended" (*ibid.,* I, p. 51). "To leave," he says, "all reverent and religious compassion towards evils or indignation towards faults; and to turn Religion into a Comedy or Satire; to search and rip up wounds with a laughing countenance; to intermix Scripture and Scurrelity, sometimes in one sentence; is a thing far from the devout reverence of a Christian, and scant beseeming the honest regard of a sober man." It was reported that "Mr. Tilney utterly misliked" of the whole proceeding. The result was that *Mar-Martin* was withdrawn, to the delight of Penry, but to the disgust of Lyly and Nashe. Nashe protested in the *Return of Pasquill (ibid.,* p. 53), against the "slye practice that was used in restraining" the play, and Lyly in *Pappe (ibid.,* p. 52) opined: "Would those comedies might be allowed to be plaied that are pend and then I am sure he [Penry] would be decyphered, and so perhaps discouraged." Martin, of course, capitalized this rebuff to the players. In *The Protestation of Martin Marprelate* (*ibid.,* I, p. 50), he taunts "all the rymers and stage-plaiers, which my Ll. of the clergy had suborned against me, [for that] I remember *Mar-Martin,* John a Cant, his hobbie-horse was to his reproche, newly put out of the Morris, take it how he will, with a flat discharge for ever shaking his shins about a May-pole againe while he lived."

The *May-Game* must, however, have accomplished all that the Bishop had hoped. Strype, in his *Life of Whitgift,* says that the course which was taken "did principally stop Martin's and his fellows' mouths."(*Ibid.,* p. 50). At all events, shortly after

1589, Penry was forced to flee to Scotland where he remained for nearly three years.

In the meantime his antiprelatic mission was taken up by another zealous reformer, this time the learned Hebraist, John Udal. Udal's style was not so spicy as Penry's, but his lack of discretion was, perhaps, equal. At all events, he dared to say in print, in 1590, that the bishops "cared for nothing but the maintenance of their dignities, be it the damnation of their own souls, and infinite millions more." Stebbing gives the following account of his treatment (*op. cit.*, p. 55):

> He was tried for treason, since the Bishops, it was averred, governed the Church for the Queen. A jury convicted him of authorship of the book. The Judges iniquitously held that to amount to a conviction of felony. They therefore sentenced him to death. He prayed Ralegh to intercede with the Queen to commute his punishment to banishment "that the land might not be charged with his blood." Ralegh accepted the office, and Essex combined with him. . . . They saved the enthusiast's neck; but he died in the Marshalsea, pending a dispute whether he could safely be permitted to carry his anti-prelatic zeal and immense learning into a chaplaincy in Guiana.

In this offer of a chaplaincy in Guiana, we see Ralegh taking a brave step which led to a popular linking of him in action, if not in sympathy, with one of the most hated of the heretical groups, the Martinists. We shall see presently how quick his enemies were to recognize in this generosity an instrument for his undoing.

When Kyd was arrested, 12 May, 1593, under suspicion of a connection with the anti-alien posters on the Dutch Church wall, his rooms were searched and his papers seized. Kyd declared that they were "waste and idle papers" which he cared not for, and which, unasked, he delivered to the authorities. Among them, however, was one document which not only brought Kyd into further difficulties, but also implicated Marlowe, and, indeed, the whole Ralegh group, in a series of official charges of atheism. The document was a three-page fragment copied out from a book by one John Proctor, concerning *The Fal of the late Arrian* (1549) and is now in the British Museum (Harleian MSS 6848), under the following endorsement:

12 May, 1593
vile heretical Conceiptes
denyinge the deity of Jhesus
Christ our Saviour found
amongst the papers of thos
kydd prisoner
which he affirmeth that he
had from Marlowe.

This, apparently, fixed the legend of the "Arian blasphemies of the stage-poet Christopher Marlowe," which was still current in 1716, as appears from an allusion from Myles Davis in that year. In the light of the background we have just sketched in, it will be seen how serious, nay, how deadly, was the attack levelled against Marlowe, Hariot, and Ralegh by Nashe in *Pierce Penniless,* as early as 1592. Nashe, we have seen, had had his hand in on the Martinist controversy since 1589, but now he adds a new victim to his list of criminal heretics—Martin (Penry), Barrow, Greenwood, yea, and the new Arians [i.e., Marlowe, Hariot and Ralegh], to all of whom allusion is made in the following cataract of rhetorical abuse so characteristic of Nashe:

> Another misery of Pride it is, when men who have good parts, and bear the name of deep scholars, cannot be content to participate one faith with all Christendome, but because they will get a name to their vain glory, they will set their self-love to study to invent new sects of singularity, thinking to live when they are dead, by having sects called after their name, as Donatists of Donatus, Arrians of Arrius, and a number more new faith founders that have made England the exchange of Innovations and almost as much confusion of Religions in every quarter as there was of tongues in the building of the Tower of Babel. Whence, a number that fetch the Articles of their belief out of Aristotle and think of heaven and hell as the Heathen Philosophers, take occasion to deride our Ecclesiastical State and all ceremonies of Divine worship, as bugbears, scare-crows, because (like Herod's soldiers) we divide Christ's garment amongst us in so many pieces, and of the vesture of salvation make some of Babie's and Apes coats, and others straight trusses and devil's breeches, some gally-gascoines or shipman's hose like the Anabaptists and adulterous Familists, others with the Martinists, a hood with two faces to hide their hypocrisy; and to conclude, some

like the Barrowists and Greenwoodians, a garment full of the plague which is not to be worn before it be new washed.*

Hence Atheists triumph and rejoice and talk as profanely of the Bible as of Bevis of Hampton. I hear say there be Mathematicians abroad that will prove men before Adam, and they are harboured in high places who will maintaine it to the death that there are no devils.

The accusation implied in the last paragraph was quite clearly levelled at the Hariot-Ralegh group. But Greene makes the object of his attack more obvious still in the Preface to *Perimedes the Blacksmith* (1588), (Chambers, *Elizabethan Stage,* III, p. 324):

I keep my old course to palter up something in prose, using mine old poesie still, *Omne tulit punctum,* although lately two Gentlemen Poets made two mad men of Rome beat it out of their paper bucklers: and had it in derision for that I could not make my verses jet upon the stage in tragical buskins, every word filling the mouth like the faburden of Bo-Bell, daring God out of heaven with that Atheist Tamburlan, or blaspheming with the mad priest of the Sun. . . . Such mad and scoffing poets that have poetical spirits, as bred of Merlin's race, if there be any in England that set the end of scholarism in an English blank-verse, I think either it is the humour of a novice that tickles them with self-love, or too much frequenting the hot-house (to use the German proverb) hath sweat out all the greatest part of their wits. . . . I but answer in print what they have offered on the stage.

Of this passage, Sir Edmund Chambers says: "The references here to Marlowe are unmistakable." The "Atheist Tamburlan" is, of course, obvious; but in the following chapter I venture to suggest also that the "mad priests of the sun" may be a reference to a Marlowe invention. Elsewhere (*The Pembroke Plays; A Study in the Marlowe Canon,* 1938), I have stated my reasons for identifying the "two gentlemen poets" with Marlowe and Lodge. Sir Edmund notes further that "in 1589 Greene published his *Menaphon* (S. R. 23 Aug.), in which he further alluded to Marlowe as the teller of 'a Canterbury Tale; some propheticall full-mouth that as he were a Cobler's eldest

* The items of apparel which he derides refer to the distinguishing features of costume affected by various heretical sects.

son, would by the last tell where another shoe wrings.' " *(Ibid.,* p. 324.)

The part which Lodge played in the quarrel has never been clearly understood; nor is it now. If my guess concerning the authorship of the *Wounds of Civil War* is correct, Lodge and Marlowe did come together on at least one literary job; but the existing evidence seems to connect Lodge with Marlowe's enemies rather more closely than with his friends. His association with Greene is, of course, well attested, both by their collaboration on *A Looking Glass for London and England,* and by Lodge's entrusting to Greene the manuscript of *Euphues His Shadow.** Greene was not, as we have seen, friendly to Marlowe.

With Marlowe's intimate friend Roydon and with his admirer Drayton, however, Lodge seems to have been on friendly terms, though even here the evidence points to acquaintance rather than to intimate friendship. In the third eclogue of *A Fig for Momus,* Golde (anagram for Lodge) is conversing with Wagrin (anagram for Guarini). Golde complains of lack of patrons to encourage poetry and reward poets; Wagrin tells him that he would get on much better if he would "surcease the wandering Cynthia to pursue" and appeal instead to the enlightened few "that honour poesie and wit adore." Such a one, he declares, is the patron of Donroy (anagram for Roydon). This patron can hardly be other than Ralegh. His final injunction is to "follow the harvest where thy Donroy gleans." There is, alas, no indication that Lodge ever acted upon this advice. Instead, there seems to be some indication that he held himself aloof from both Ralegh and Marlowe. It is possible that the attack on the too ambitious Laurus in *Catharos: . . . A Nettle for Nice Noses* was meant for Ralegh. Laurus was like those who "thirst after promotion vehemently without moderation." He "liveth on the water as well as on the land." He was "a shipman the greatest that could be." Such phrases might well point to Ralegh, though the identification is not certain. More convincing is the possible attack on Marlowe in *Wits Miserie and the Worlds Madness.* The character of Derision seems to follow the Marlowe legend so closely as to be all but labeled

* See, Edward A. Tenney, *Thomas Lodge,* Cornell Studies, 1935, p. 126.

"Marlowe." After describing his affectation of fine clothes, his haughtiness and his quarrelsomeness, Lodge reveals his Catholic abhorrence of such irreverent flippancies as were ascribed to Marlowe by Kyd and Baines. Lodge's character of Derision is one "whose meerest profession is Atheisme"; for whom "It is meat and drink when he is mocking another man"; "Christ his Saviour is a Carpenter's son. Christian Galileans in contempt. Nay such blasphemy uttereth he betwixt the Holy Ghost and the blessed and Immaculate Virgin Mary as my heart trembleth to think them and my tongue abhorreth to speak them."

The date of the composition of *Wits Miserie* is uncertain; but the date of its publication (1596) places it near enough to the atheist scandals of 1593 in London, and 1594 at Cerne Abbas, to justify our suspicion of an intended jibe at the Ralegh group and at Marlowe in particular.

This girding at atheism was a wonderful new engine with which to batter down the unrivalled vogue of the Astronomical poets, providing a much more deadly thrust than the vague jibe at the "vain-glorious Tragedians, who contend not so seriously to excell in action as to embowell the clouds in a speech of comparison, thinking themselves more than initiated in Poet's immortality if they but once get *Boreas* by the beard and the heavenly Bull by the dewlap." Good cause had these rival poets for jealousy. Not even Shakspere had written anything before *Love's Labour's Lost* to be compared with this stirring new "music of the spheres" that came so crisply and authentically from the choir of poets who fetched their inspiration directly from England's finest mathematician and astronomer. Small men, like Greene, Nashe, and Harvey, would not scruple to tilt at such genius with the poisoned lance of slander for a weapon; but real men of all ages have been captivated and held enthralled by the great strain that flowed from the pen of the first "first-class" poet of the English Renaissance. As Professor Tucker-Brooke observes:

> Numberless readers must have paralleled the experience which J. R. Lowell describes: "With him I grew acquainted during the most impressionable and receptive period of my youth. He was the first man of genius I had ever really known, and he naturally bewitched me. What cared I that they said he was a deboshed fellow?

nay, an atheist? To me he was the voice of one singing in the desert, of one who had found the water of life for which I was panting, and was at rest under the palms. How can he ever become to me as other poets are?"

Drayton had earlier voiced the same sentiment in a tribute already quoted in part:

> Neat Marlowe, bathed in the Thespian springs,
> Had in him those brave translunary things
> That your first poets had; his raptures were
> All air and fire, which made his verses clear:
> For that fine madness still he did retain
> Which rightly should possess a poet's brain.

To the rival group, however, the charge of atheism seemed to hover over all the scenes of scientific discourse between Ralegh and Hariot and their group, like the skeleton in a *danse macabre,* ensnaring their unwary steps into a design of tragic death.

It is not possible to establish any certain chronology of the events which follow, nor, perhaps, to decide who is the teacher and who the pupil in what must have been a series of symposiums on the subject of the inspiration of the Scriptures; but what is clear is that the whole Ralegh group was implicated. Kyd was the one who precipitated the avalanche. As soon as he had declared that the "atheist" fragment found in his room belonged to Marlowe, a warrant was issued (18 May) "to Henry Maunder, one of the messengers of her Majesty's Chamber, to repair to the house of Mr. Tho. Walsingham in Kent, or to any other place where he shall understand Christofer Marlow to be remaining, and by virtue thereof to apprehend and bring him to the Court in his company. And in case of need, to require aid." But the aid was not necessary. The minutes of the Privy Council for 20 May state that on "This day Christofer Marley of London, gentleman, being sent for a warrant from their Lordships, hath entered his appearance accordingly for his indemnity therein; and is commanded to give his daily attendance on their Lordships, until he shall be licensed to the contrary." This was on Sunday, 20 May. On the Monday following, was scheduled the trial of John Penry, for felonious heresy, which was, as we have already indicated, quickly shuffled through and Penry was hanged on 29 May. This was, I believe, the danger signal that warned Marlowe to make his escape. Accordingly, he left London on 30 May, as I believe, to make his way to Dover and hence out of the country. Roydon apparently did the same thing. Kyd says: "He [Marlowe] wold perswade with men of qualitie to goe vnto the King of Scotts whether J heare Roydon is gon and where if he had liud he told me when J saw him last he meant to be." As we now know, Marlowe was shadowed as far as Deptford. There, unable to shake off his unwelcome escort, he provoked the fray in which he was killed.

Marlowe safely out of the way, Kyd felt himself free to ingratiate himself with the Powers by "informing" concerning Marlowe. Accordingly, he took his pen in hand and delivered himself as follows: *

At my last being with your Lordship to entreat some speeches from you in my favour to my Lord, who (though I think he rest not doubtful of mine innocence), hath yet in his discreeter judgment feared to offend in his retaining me, without your Honour's former privity; so is it now right honourable that the denial of that favour (to my thought reasonable) hath moved me to conjecture some suspicion, that your Lordship holds me in, concerning Atheism, a deadly thing which I was undeserved charged withal, and therefore have I thought it requisite, as well in duty to your Lordship, and the Laws, as also in the fear of God, and freedom of my conscience, therein to satisfy the world and you:

The first and most (though insufficient surmise) that ever as therein might be raised of me, grew thus. When I was first suspected for that Libel that concerned the state, amongst those waste and idle papers (which I cared not for) and which unasked I did deliver up, were found some fragments of a disputation touching that opinion affirmed by Marlowe to be his, and shuffled with some of mine (unknown to me) by some occasion of our writing in one chamber two years since.

My first acquaintance with this Marlowe, rose upon his bearing name to serve my Lord, although his Lordship never knew his serv-

* British Museum Harleian MS 6849, fol. 218; quoted here from Tucker-Brooke, *op. cit.*, pp. 103ff., but without regard to the line formation of the original MS. The spelling, also, has been modernized.

ice, but in writing for his players, for never could my Lord endure his name, or sight, when he had heard of his conditions, nor would indeed the form of divine prayer used duly in his Lordship's house, have quadred with such reprobates.

That I should love or be familiar friend with one so irreligious, were very rare, when Tully saith, *Digni sunt amicitia quibus in ipsis inest causa cur diligantur,* which neither was in him, for person, qualities, or honesty; besides he was intemperate and of cruel heart, the very contraries to which, my greatest enemies will say by me.

It is not to be numbered amongst the best conditions of men, to taxe or to upbraid the dead, *Quia mortui non mordent,* but this much have I with your Lordship's favour, dared in the greatest cause, which is to clear myself of being thought an Atheist, which some will swear he was.

For more assurance that I was not of that vile opinion, let it but please your Lordship tc enquire of such as he conversed withal, that is (as I am given to understand) with Hariot, Warner, Royden, and some stationers in Paul's churchyard, whom I in no sort can accuse nor will excuse by reason of his company, of whose consent if I had been, no question but I also should have been of their consort, for *ex minimo vestigio artifex agnoscit artificem.*

Of my religion and life I have already given some instance to the late commissioners and of my reverend meaning to the state, although perhaps my pains and undeserved tortures felt by some, would have engendered more impatience when less by far hath driven so many *imo extra caulas,* which it shall never do with me.

But whatsoever I have felt right honourable this is my request not for reward but in regard of my true innocence that it would please your Lordships so to [use] the same and me, as I may still retain the favours of my Lord, whom I have served almost this VI years now, in credit until now, and now am utterly undone, without herein be somewhat done for my recovery. For I do know his Lordship holds your honours and the state in that due reverence, as he would no way move the least suspicion of his loves and cares both towards her sacred Majesty, your Lordships, and the Laws, whereof when time shall serve I shall give greater instance which I have observed.

As for the libel laid unto my charge I am resolved with receiving of the sacrament to satisfy your Lordships and the World that I was neither agent nor consenting thereunto. Howbeit if some outcast Ishmael for want or of his own dispose to lewdness have with pretext of duty or religion, or to reduce himself to that he was not born unto by any way incensed your Lordships to suspect me, I shall beseech in all humility and in the fear of God that it will please your Lordships but to censure me as I shall prove myself, and to repute them as they are indeed *Cum totius injustitiae nulla capitalior sit quam eorum, qui tum cum maxime fallunt id agunt ut viri boni esse videantur,* for doubtless even then your Lordships shall be sure to break [up] their lewd designs and see into the truth, when but their lives that herein accused me shall be examined and ripped up effectually, so may I chance with Paul to live and shake the viper off my hand into the fire for which the ignorant suspect me guilty of the former shipwreck. And thus (for now I fear me I grow tedious) assuring your good Lordship that if I knew any whom I could justly accuse of that damnable offence to the awful Majesty of God or of that other mutinous sedition toward the state, I would as willingly reveal them as I would request your Lordship's better thoughts of me that never have offended you.

Your Lordship's most humble in all duties

Th. Kydde

Poor Thomas Kyd! One feels through this wordy, incoherent epistle a certain manly desire to "inform" no further than was absolutely necessary to save his life. It is likely that he had already been subjected to the rack. But the Council obviously was not satisfied; so, probably to save himself further racking, Kyd decided that the repetition of some of the current gossip about Marlowe could do no harm to the dead poet, and might, perhaps, be the means of his own safety. Accordingly he wrote further to Puckering (Brit. Mus. Harleian MS 6848, fol. 154; Tucker-Brooke, *op. cit.,* p. 107):

Pleaseth it your honourable Lordship touching Marlowe's monstrous opinions as I cannot but with an aggrieved conscience think on him or them, so can I but particularize few in the respect of them that kept him greater company. Howbeit in discharge of duty both towards God, your Lordships, and the world, thus much have I thought good briefly to discover in all humbleness. First, it was his custom when I knew him first, and as I hear say he continued it in table talk or otherwise to jest at the divine scriptures, gibe at prayers, and strive in argument to frustrate and confute what hath been spoke or writ by prophets and such holy men.

1. He would report St. John to be our Saviour Christ's Alexis. I cover it with reverence and trembling, that is, that Christ did love him with an extraordinary love.

2. That for me to write a poem of St. Paul's conversion, as I was determined, he said would be as if I should go write a book of fast and loose, esteeming Paul a juggler.

3. That the prodigal Child's portion was but four nobles, he held his purse so near the bottom in all pictures, and that it either was a jest or else four nobles then was thought a great patrimony, not thinking it a parable.

4. That things esteemed to be done by divine power might have as well been done by observation of men, all which he would so suddenly take slight occasion to slip out, as I and many others in regard of his other rashness in attempting sudden injuries to men, did overslip, though often reprehend him for it, and for which God is my witness as well by my Lord's commandment as in hatred of his life and thoughts I left and did refrain his company. He would persuade with men of quality to go into the k of Scots, whither I hear Royden is gone and where if he had lived, he told me, when I saw him last, he meant to be.

From these two documents alone, forced as they were, we get a fairly vivid sketch of Marlowe's personality—bold, challenging, learned, intelligent, full of witty irreverence, with a mischievous, undergraduate delight in shocking the stodgy. The indulgence in insolence and leg-pulling, with never a care for discretion, was with him apparently a favourite form of recreation. From Bruno he may have got many heretical ideas, as well as a habit of buffooning dialectic. The charges made against Marlowe and the group by Richard Baines, whether they are true or hearsay, help to fill out the picture. The following is labeled "A note Containing the opinion of one Christopher Marly Concerning his damnable Judgment of Religion, and scorn of Gods word." * It is usually referred to as the *Baines Libel:*

That the Indians and many Authors of antiquity haue assuredly writen of aboue 16 thousand yeares agone wheras Adam is proued to haue lived within 6 thousand yeares.

He affirmeth that Moyses was but a Jugler & that one Heriots being Sir W Raleighs man Can do more then he.

That Moyses made the Jewes to travell xl yeares in the wildernes (which Jorney might haue bin done in lesse then one yeare), ere

* Brit. Mus. Harleian MS 6848, fols. 185-86; Tucker-Brooke, *op. cit.*, pp. 98-100. I have omitted the words scored through in the original.

they came to the promised land to th' intent that those who were privy to most of his subtilties might perish and so an everlasting superstition Remain in the hartes of the people.

That the first beginning of Religioun was only to keep men in awe.

That it was an easy matter for Moyses being brought vp in all the artes of the Egiptians to abuse the Jewes being a rude & grosse people.

That Christ was a bastard and his mother dishonest.

That he was the sonne of a Carpenter, and that if the Jewes among whome he was borne did Crucify him theie best knew him and whence he came.

That Christ deserved better to dy then Barrabas and that the Jewes made a good Choise, though Barrabas were both a thief and a murtherer.

That if there be any god or any good Religion, then it is in the papists because the service of god is performed with more Ceri-monies, as Elevation of the mass, organs, singing men, Shaven Crownes, & cta. That all protestants are Hypocriticall asses.

That if he were put to write a new Religion, he would vndertake both a more Excellent and Admirable methode and that all the new testament is filthily written.

That the woman of Samaria & her sister were whores & that Christ knew them dishonestly.

That St. John the Evangelist was bedfellow to Christ and leaned alwaies in his bosome, that he vsed him as the sinners of Sodoma.

That all they that loue not Tobacco & Boies were fooles.

That all the apostles were fishermen and base fellows neyther of wit nor worth, that Paull only had wit but he was a timerous fellow in bidding man to be subject to magistrates against his Conscience.

That he had as good Right to Coine as the Queen of England, and that he was acquainted with one Poole a Prisoner in Newgate who hath greate Skill in mixture of mettals and hauing learned some things of him he ment through help of a Cunninge stamp maker to Coin ffrench Crownes pistoletes and English shillings.

That if Christ would haue instituted the sacrament with more Ceremoniall Reverence it would haue bin had in more admiration, that it would haue bin much better being administred in a To-bacco pipe.

That the Angell Gabriell was baud to the holy ghost, because he brought the salutation to Mary.

That one Ric Cholmley hath Confessed that he was perswaded by Marloe's Reasons to become an Atheist.

These thinges, with many other shall by good & honest witnes be approved to be his opinions and Comon Speeches and that this Marlow doth not only hould them himself, but almost into every Company he cometh he perswades men to Atheism willing them not to be afeard of bugbears and hobgoblins, and vtterly scorning both god and his ministers as J Richard Baines will Justify & approue both by mine oth and the testimony of many honest men, and almost al men with whome he hath Conversed any time will testify the same, and as J think all men in Cristianity ought to indevor that the mouth [of] so dangerous a member may be stopped, he saith likewise that he hath quoted a number of Contrarieties oute of the Scripture which he hath giuen to some great men who in Convenient time shalbe named. When these thinges shalbe Called in question the witnes shalbe produced.

Richard Baines

It is extraordinary how closely this caricature of Marlowe resembles the legendary Ralegh. When the hounds of intolerance were cheated of their quarry by the debacle of Deptford, they set out in full halloo to bag the great boar himself. After all, the time was most opportune, for not only had they a crowd of actual witnesses against Ralegh, but they could take him at a special disadvantage by reason of his being in disgrace at Court, on account of his marriage to Elizabeth Throckmorton. He was, in fact, rusticated on his beautiful new estate at Sherborne, in Dorset. There, one evening shortly after Marlowe's death in the summer of 1593, Sir Walter and his brother, Carew Ralegh, dined with Sir Ralph Horsey and the Reverend Ralph Ironside, Vicar of Winterbottom, and his friend Mr. Whettle, Vicar of Forthington. With so clerical a company it is not surprising to learn that the talk drifted to religious subjects, particularly the question of the immortality of the soul. Apparently unterrified by all the bruit of heretical persecutions, the Raleghs showed their usual scepticism and impatience with the theological quibbles of the Schoolmen, much to the confusion of the parsons and the scandalized amazement of the other guests, Sir Ralph Horsey in particular. The following is the account of the dinner given by the Reverend Ralph Ironside himself and signed by Sir Ralph Horsey: *

Wednesdaye sevenight before the Assises sumer Laste I came to Sr George Trenchard*es* in the afternone accompayned wth a fellowe minister, & frinde of myne mr Whittle Viccar of fforthington. There were then wth the Knight, Sr Walter Rawleigh, Sr Raulfe Horsey, Mr Carewe Rawleigh, Mr John ffitziames, &c. Toward*es* the end of supp*er* some loose speeches of Mr Carewe Rawleighes beinge gentlye reproved by Sr Raulfe Horsey in these word*es* *Colloquia prava corrumpunt* bonos mores. Mr Rawleigh demaund*es* of me, what daunger he might incurr by such speeches? wherevnto I aunswered, the wages of sinn is death, and he makinge leight of death as beinge com*m*on to all sinner & reightuous; I inferred further, that as that liffe wch is the gifte of god through Jesus Christ, is liffe eternall: soe that death wch is pr*o*perlye the wages of sinne, is death eternall, both of the bodye, and of the soule alsoe. Soule qu*o*th Mr Carewe Rawleigh, what is that? better it were (sayd I) that we would be carefull howe the Soules might be saved, then to be curiouse in findinge out ther essence. And soe keepinge silence Sr Walter request*es* me, that for there instrucc*io*n I woulde aunswer to the question that before by his brother was pr*o*posed vnto me. I have been (sayeth he) a scholler some tyme in Oxeforde, I have aunswered vnder a Bachelor of Arte, & had taulke wth diuines, yet heithervnto in this pointe (to witt what the reasonable soule of man is) have I not by anye beene resolved. They tell us it is *primus motor* the first mover in a man &c. Vnto this, after I had replied that howesoeu*er* the soule were *fons et principium,* the fountaine, beginninge and caws of motion in vs, yet the first mover was the braine, or harte. I was againe vrged to showe my opinion and hearinge Sr Walter Rawleigh tell of his dispute & schollershipp some time in Oxeforde I cited the generall definic*io*n of *Anima* out of Aristotle 2° *de Anima* cap: 1°, & thence a *sub*iect*o proprio* deduced the speciall definic*io*n of the soule reasonable, that it was *Actus primus corporis organici* an*i*m*antis humani vitam ha*b*entis in pot*entia: It was misliked of Sr Walter as obscure, & intricate: And I wth all yealded that though it coulde not vnto him, as beinge lerned, yet it must seme obscure to the most prsent, and therfore had rather saye wth devines plainly that the reasonable soule is a speritual & im*m*ortall substance breathed into man by god, wherby he lyves & moves & vnderstand-

* Quoted from G. B. Harrison's edition of *Willobie His Avisa,* Bodley Head Quartos, XV, London, 1926. App. III, pp. 265ff.

eth, & soe is distinguished from other Creatures; yea but what is that speritualL & im*m*ortall substance breathed into man &c. saieth S[r] Walter; the soule q*uot*h I, naye then saieth he you aunswer not like a scholler. Herevppon I endevoured to prove that it was schollerlike, naye in such disputes as these, vsuall, & necessarye to runne *in circulum* par*t*lye because *definicio rei* was *primum et imediatum principuum,* and seinge *primo non est prius,* a man must of necessetie come backwarde & p*ar*telye becawse *definicio & definitum* be nature recipr*o*ce the one conv*er*tiblie aunsweringe vnto the question made vppon the other. As for example, if one aske what is a man? you will saye he is a creature reasonable & mortall; but if you aske againe: what is a creature reasonable & mortall? you must of force come backewarde, and aunswer, it is a man; *et sic de ceteris.* But we have principles in our mathematickes sayeth S[r] Walter, as *totum est minus quamlibet sua* p*arte.* And aske me of it, and I can showe it in the table, in the window, in a man, the whole beinge bigger then the *p*ar*tes* of it. I replied that he showed *quod est,* not, *quid est,* that it was but not what it was; secondlye, that such demonstrac*i*on as y[t] was against the nature of a mans soule beinge a sperite. For as his thing*es* beinge sensible were subiecte to the sence; soe mans soule beinge insensible was to be discerned by the sperite. Nothinge more c*er*taine in the worlde then that there is a god, yet beinge a sperite to subiecte him to the sence otherwise then perf*ec*ted it is impossible. Marrye q*uot*h S[r] Walter these 2 be like for neither coulde I lerne heitherto what god is; M[r] ffitziames aunsweringe that Aristotle shoulde say he was *Ens, Encium.* I aunswered that whether Aristotle dyinge in a feavor shoulde crie *ens encium miserere mei,* or drowninge him selfe in Euripum shoulde saye *quia ego te non capio tu me capies,* it was vnc*er*taine, but that god was *ens entium* a thinge of thinge havinge beinge of him selfe, & geivinge beinge to all creatures, it was most c*er*taine, and confirmed by god him selfe vnto moyses. Yea but what is this *ens entium* sayeth S[r] Walter? I aunswered it is God. And beinge disliked as before S[r] Walter wished that grace might be sayed; for that q*uoth* he is better then this disputac*i*on. Thus supp*er* ended & grace sayed, I dep*ar*ted to Dorchester w[t] my fellowe minister, and this to my rememberance is the substance of that speach w[ch] S[r] Walter Rawleigh & I had at Wolveton.

Ralphe Ironside

No wonder Bruno snorted at the Oxford method! No one now knows how the story of this dinner party got to London, but it is certain that, when it did, it was immediately slipped into a folder with considerable other evidence of atheism that was being collected there by Ralegh's enemies. In March, 1594, a commission, "emanating from Her Majesty's Commissioners for Causes Ecclesiastical," was appointed to inquire into the alleged heresies in the county of Dorsetshire, and on this commission sat, beside Sir Ralph Horsey, Lord Thomas Howard, Ralegh's most malicious enemy. The interrogatories which were put to the witnesses in the course of this investigation show how general was the gossip about Ralegh's atheism and how similar was his legend to that of Marlowe. The reader will recall, for instance, that Baines declared, in obvious recollection of the *Spaccio,* that Marlowe affirmed "that Moses was but a juggler and that one Hariot can do more than he"; and "that Moses made the Jews to travel 40 years in the wilderness, which journey might have been done in less than one year"; and "that it was an easy matter for Moses being brought up in all the arts of the Egyptians to abuse the Jews, being a rude and gross people." So here, when the investigation in the "alleged Atheism and Apostacy of Dorset" was made at Cerne, charges were made against Sir Walter and "his man," Thomas Allen, for the like flippant remarks about Moses. For instance, Robert Ashebourne of Sherbourne, Churchwarden, deposed (*ibid.,* p. 265):

> That he hath harde reportes, that a man of Thomas Allens, whose name he knoweth not cominge from Lyllington with certaine women of Sherborne, spake certaine wordes in derogacion of moyses, that he had manye whores, and other speches to the like derogacion of moyses and the scriptures.

The full story of this scandalous conversation was given by Grace Brewer and Elizabeth Whetcome. (*Ibid.,* p. 271.)

There are several other general lines of accusation that appear in both sets of testimony. One of these is concerned with their enthusiasms for tobacco. Baines says that Marlowe declares that "all that love not tobacco are fools." Thomas Norman, of Weymouth Melcomb Reges, minister, said that "his friend Mr. Jones saw Mr. Allen tear two leaves out of a Bible to dry tobacco on."

Another set is about the learned "free-thinking" that characterized the group. Baines says that Marlowe insists that there exist "writings of about 16,000 years ago, whereas Adam is proved to have lived only 6,000 years ago"; and "that all the Apostles were fishermen and base fellows, neither of wit nor worth; that Paul only had wit, etc."; and that "almost in every company he cometh, he persuadeth men to Atheism, willing them not to be afraid of bugbears and hobgoblins and utterly scorning both god and his ministers."

On these latter points, the charges against the Raleghs are pretty well documented. Nicholas Jeffreys, parson of Weeke Reges, had not only heard "by reporte . . . that Sr Walter Rawlegh and his retenewe ar generallye suspected of Atheism, and especially one Allen of Portland Castle Leiftenant, And that he is a great blasphemer & leight esteemer of Religion" (*ibid.*, pp. 260-261), but he had had a first-hand experience of the Ralegh scorn, if not of God, certainly of His ministers. (See above, p. 381.)

In general, the stories about the brothers show Carew to have been far less guarded in his speech than Sir Walter, and, possibly, Allen may have been more reckless than either. Nashe had declared that there were those "harboured in high places" that would maintain it to the death that there were no devils, etc. This is precisely what Allen did, according to the deposition of John Dench, Churchwarden of Weeke Reges, who said (*ibid.*, p. 263):

. . . that he hath harde one Allen Leiftennant of Portland Castle when he was like to dye, beinge perswaded to make himselfe reddye to God for his soule, to aunswer that he would carrye his soule vp to the topp of an hill, and runne god, ruñe devill, fetch it that will have it, or to that effecte.

Baines had pointed out the iniquity of prefacing one's remarks concerning God with an *if clause;* but to this comparatively mild sin Allen is reported to have added the most shocking, unedifying blasphemies. Francis Scarlett, minister of Sherborne, said that he had heard someone say (*ibid.*, p. 264):

. . . that Allen sayde when he was a hawkinge, and that it rayned; That if god were in the bushe there he woulde pull him out wth his teeth, or to the like effecte.

In all these reports the names of Hariot and Marlowe are continually being brought in to share the odium of Sir Walter's supposed heresy. As early as 1592, Robert Parsons, the Jesuit, had said (*ibid.*, p. 209):

Of Sir Walter Ralegh's School of Atheism, by the way, and of the Conjurer M thereof the diligence used to get young gentlemen to this school wherein both Moses and our Saviour, the old and new Testament are jested at and the scholars among other things taught to spell God backwards.

The Conjurer M is sometimes taken to refer to Marlowe, though it well may be an abbreviation for Master. However, it does seem that Marlowe was one of the most enthusiastic of these young radicals, and was, in fact, more indiscreet than any of them. We recall the words of Richard Cholmely (p. 329) to the effect that "Marlowe was able to show more sound reasons for atheism than any devine in England is able to give to prove divinity."

Was this "atheist lecture" the Arian pamphlet that was found in Kyd's room? It is possible that some light may be thrown on the question by Sir John Harington, who concludes the Prologue to the *Metamorphosis of Ajax* by a mock litany to "the black saintes," i.e., to a group of heretics, under fustian terms, "whose names begin with A." Some of these, he tells us, "denied the Godhead of Christ with Arrius, some the authoritie of the Bishops at Aerius," etc. (including 11,000 Anabaptists!). If the names stood for anyone, obviously Marlowe would be a good candidate for one of those "who deny the Godhead with Arrius."

In view of a recent correspondence in the *Times Literary Supplement* * concerning the identification of the Aetion of *Colin Clout* with Marlowe, one is tempted to see in "Sauntus Aetius" also a reference to Marlowe, who was said to be the owner of the Arian pamphlet found in Kyd's room. After all, Aetius is not a wider variant of Aetion than Morley of Marlowe, or Hinchly of Henslowe, and so forth.

The slander about spelling *God* backwards stuck to the group for many years in spite of the fact that Marlowe had scotched

* See letter of Mr. Arthur Grey in 24 January, 1935, and a reply by Mr. W. L. Renwick a week later.

the snake by damning the trick in *Doctor Faustus*. Aubrey says that Hariot was a deist and taught his doctrines to Sir Walter, to Henry, Earl of Northumberland, and to some others, but that Ralegh himself was scandalized with atheism. In all the stories which find place in the myth of Ralegh's atheism, Ralegh's own attitude is pictured as one of genuine, dignified challenge and philosophical inquiry, quite free from the reckless buffoonery of many of his admirers, such as Allen or Olliver, his servants, or Marlowe, or his brother Carew. Aubrey says: "He was a bold man and would venture at discourse which was unpleasant to the Churchmen"; and we have seen him in the act at the dinner of Sir George Trenchard, when he put old Ironside into such a logical corner about the soul. But Aubrey adds:

> I remember the first Lord Scudamore sayd 't was basely said of Sir Walter Ralegh to talk of the anagram of Dog [and that] in his speech on the scaffold I heard my cousin Whitney say (and I think 't was printed) that he spake not one word of Christ, but of the great and incomprehensible God with much zeal and adoration, so that he concluded that he was a-Christ not a-theist.

In spite, however, of Ralegh's edifying death, his enemies continued to spread the slander of his atheism. The following libel is one of several quoted by Dr. J. Hannah in his Introduction to *The Courtly Poets from Ralegh to Montrose* (London, 1870, xxiv):

> Water thy plants with grace divine,
> And hope to live for aye;
> Then to thy Saviour Christ incline;
> In him make steadfast stay;
>
> *Raw* is the reason that doth *lie*
> Within an atheist's head,
> Which saith the soul of man doth die,
> When that the body's dead.
>
> Now may you see the sudden fall
> Of him that thought to climb full high;
> A man well known unto you all,
> Whose state, you see, doth stand *Rawly*.

Again and again these threads cross: Ralegh, Spenser, Hariot, Bruno, Marlowe, Roydon, Chapman, Northumberland, Warner, Hues, and many others. Even if Kyd had not told us in so many words that Marlowe's confrères were "Hariot, Warner, Roydon, and some stationers in Paules churchyard," we should be able to get a fairly good notion of the personnel of the group from these continued references. The threads may seem, to some scholars, frail, but there are many of them. We should give much to know more of Marlowe's relations with the "stationers in Paules churchyard." Judging from the tenor of their pamphlets, and from the records of conflicts with the censoring authorities, (see below, pp. 428ff.), their stalls must have been the scenes of daring conversations, in which, it would seem, Marlowe delivered himself with something of the strut and eloquence of his most famous protagonist. While living, no man could tame his wild flights, or rival them, but when once he was safely dead, Gabriel Harvey was not above taunting him with mortality. In a very muddy sonnet, he asks:

> Is it a Dreame? or is the highest minde,
> That euer haunted Powles, or hunted winde,
> Bereaft of that same sky-surmounting breath,
> That breath, that taught the Timpany to swell?
> The graund Dissease disdain'd his toade Conceit,
> And smiling at his tamberlaine contempt,
> Sternely struck home the peremptory stroke,
> He that nor feared God, nor dreaded Diu'll,
> Nor aought admired, but his wondrous selfe:
> Like Iunos gawdy Bird, that prowdly stares
> On glittering fan of his triumphant taile:
> Or like the vgly Bugg, that scorn'd to dy,
> And mountes of Glory rear'd in towring witt:
> Alas: but Babell Pride must kisse the pitt.
>
> *L'enuoy*
>
> Powles steeple, and a hugyer thing is downe:
> Beware the next Bull-beggar of the towne.

In another sonnet, entitled *Gorgon, or the wonderfulle yeare,* he mocks: "Weepe Powles, thy Tamberlaine voutsafes to dye."

Marlowe's intolerance and pride, like Ralegh's, won him more enemies than his free-thinking did, but the latter was the more vulnerable point of attack. In the body of the *New Letter of Notable Contents,* 1593, Harvey identifies Greene with Julian, and Marlowe with Lucian; then he observes (Tucker-Brooke, *op. cit.,* p. 112):

Plinyes, and Lucians religion may ruffle, and scoffe awhile: but extreme Vanitie is the best beginning of that brauery, and extreme Miserie the best end of that felicity. Greene and Marlow might admonish other to aduise themselues.

This sounds almost like a text for *Doctor Faustus!* Incidentally, the passage identifying Greene with Julian, and Marlowe with Lucian, contains what may be an oblique gibe at Bruno. Harvey says that he would hate to call Nashe "an Aretine that paraphrased the inestimable bookes of Moses and discoursed the Capricious Dialogues of rankest Bawdry . . . that recorded the history of S. Thomas of Aquine, and forged the most detestable Blackebooke *de tribus impostoribus mundi.*" This last reference is to a hypothetical book proving Moses, Christ, and Mohammed to have been impostors. Scholars are not sure that there ever existed such a book, but the sixteenth century not only took its existence for granted, it was actually ascribed, among others, to Bruno. (Buckley, *op. cit.,* p. 85.)

Far be it from me to attempt to settle the date of *Doctor Faustus.* Suffice it to observe that any date between 1585 and 1592 would bring it within the time limits of the Bruno-Marlowe-Ralegh atheist scandal. The Faust story had begun to be popular in England as early as 1589, as is attested by the entry in the S. R. (28 February, 1589) of "a ballad of the life and deathe of Doctor Faustus, the great Congerer." There is, of course, no proof that the popularity of the theme depended on its fustian nature; but I know of no reason to think it might not be so. The play was certainly going well in 1594, since Henslowe records eleven performances of it between 30 September, 1594, and 8 February, 1594-5.

At all events, we have seen the group was being persecuted on two strangely antithetical charges: dangerous free-thinking on the one hand, and "popery" on the other. Ralegh himself had, so far as I know, never been accused of this latter, but Marlowe had, as we have seen by the charges in the *Baines Libel,* and in the fact that in 1587 he all but lost his Cambridge degree on this ground. Northumberland was not only reputed to be an atheist, a member of the "triplicity that denies the Trinity," but was in fact a practising Catholic, or, as it was called in the sixteenth century, a confirmed Papist. He was repeatedly persecuted as such. Thomas Norman (Harrison, *op. cit.*, p. 263) concluded his testimony against the Ralegh group by saying that he "harde of one Herryott of S[r] Walter Rawleigh his howse to be susspected of Atheisme"; and when Hariot died of a cancer, his enemies saw in his suffering a judgment of God upon his lack of faith.

The play *Doctor Faustus* is an answer to both charges: It proves that the Ralegh group knows an "atheist" when they see one, and that they abhor him duly, and are properly sensible of the warning conveyed in his damnation. Whether or not Marlowe was responsible for the horseplay circus in the papal court, these scenes certainly make it clear that the author, or authors, can be guilty of no penchant for popery. They would, moreover, help to localize the fustian and to win for the author much popular enthusiasm. Marlowe and Ralegh may both have enjoyed Bruno's spicy dialectic in 1585; they may even have imitated him in his bold challenge of the sanctity of the Scriptures, and in his merciless satire of the clergy; but if by 1592 their relish of this sort of thing had got them into bad odour, so that it behoved them to disclaim all adherence to that "vile persuasion," they could not have chosen a better means of advertising their orthodoxy than a presentation of an atheist's damnation on the stage. Nor could they have picked a more effective "example of tragedy" than the very person who had taught them this dangerous form of amusement. I do not mean to suggest that the tragedy of *Doctor Faustus* is a dramatization of Bruno's career; rather I should put it this way: that in bodying forth the horror felt by them for the crime of atheism, Marlowe has made vivid his fictitious example by reminding his audience of a real personality whose monstrous atheism had so recently brought his complete disgrace and downfall. *The English History of Doctor Faustus* gave Marlowe the story with its Goliardic flavour; the brilliant intellect and "heroic rapture," even the "conceits" of Giordano Bruno endowed his protagonist with that touch of romance and modernity that won for him an immediate and lasting popularity.

It would be indiscreet to press the suggestion further. I turn now to consideration of the case for *Tamburlaine*.

CHAPTER NINETEEN

"Tamburlaine"

IT IS CERTAINLY not possible to say, in the absence of documentary evidence, whether Ralegh invited the promising young poet of "passionate shepherd" life, still fresh from Cambridge, to help him by exploiting upon the stage "the good newes" from the American Indies, or whether the promising young poet was enterprising enough to do it on his own initiative as a bid for Ralegh's favour and patronage. We have seen that Ralegh had actually hired Thomas Churchyard to write a play in the cause of Leicester, and he may have had something to do with *Sir Thomas Moore* and the tobacco play of Anthony Chute, though of this there is no positive evidence; but whether or not he deliberately commissioned Marlowe to dramatize his project for endowing Her Majesty with a new kingdom in America must remain an open question.

It is, however, worth noting that plays on the subject of Virginia did exist, under both Elizabeth and James. *The Conquest of the West Indies,* by William Houghton and John Day (*c.* 1600), is a case in point, though it must not be assumed that this play was friendly to the enterprise. There is, however, a very important instance of such a play, written by a member of the Ralegh circle and presented at court under circumstances which make its special application to Ralegh highly probable. I refer to Chapman's *Virginia Mask,* called in the records, *"The Masque of the Middle Temple and Lincoln's Inn"* (1612/13). The idea underlying this magnificent ballet was the enthronement of Honour by the help of Riches, who places her Virginian mines at the disposal of "A learned King," who, like the sun in the skies, is "the flaming . . . to poore dimme stars." The stage sets, designed by Inigo Jones, are thus described by Chapman (*Progresses of King James,* II. p. 570):

First, there appeard at the lower end of the Hall, an artificiall rock, [representing the Virginian gold mines] whose top was neere as high as the Hall itself. . . . All this rocke grew by degrees up into a gold-colour: and was run quite through with veines of gold. On the one side whereof, eminently raised on a faire hill, was erected a silver temple of an octangle figure; whose pillars were of a Composed order, and bore upon architrave, freese, and cornish, over which stood a continued plinthe, wheron were advanc't statues of silver. Above all was a coupolo or type, which seem'd to be seal'd [ceiled] with silver plates. . . . About this temple hung festones wreath'd with silver from one pillars head to another. Besides, the freese was enricht with karvings, all shewing greatnes and magnificence. On the other side of the rocke grew a grove, in whose utmost part appear'd a vast, wither'd, and hollow tree, being the bare receptacle of the baboonerie.

The dialogue is interspersed with choral singing by the Phoebades, or Priests of the Sun. These are the Virginian Indians, whose custom it is "to adore the sun setting." These "priests of the sun" may throw an interesting light upon "that mad priest of the sun" which Greene coupled with "that atheist Tamburlaine." Had Marlowe written a play idealizing the beauty of the Indian sun-worshippers? At all events, I see no reason for connecting the "mad priest of the sun" with the *Interlude of the life and death of Heliogabalus,* entered upon the *Stationers' Register* on 19 June, 1594. (Chambers, *Elizabethan Stage,* III, p. 324.) As far as my own knowledge goes, Heliogabalus, in spite of his name, had nothing to do with American Indian sun-worshippers. He was referred to, fairly often, by the Elizabethans as a type of monstrously wicked ruler. Thus Robert Greene, in the *Spanish Masquerado,* speaking of the worldly cardinals of Rome (*Works of Greene,* V, p. 261) says:

Then gluttony is seene in their sumptuous banquets, which exceede in such riotous abundance: to pamper themselves, not to feed the poore, that the Monsters of Rome, their predecessors in belly cheare, Heliogabalus, Commodus, Iulianus, & Lucillus, Emperors and Senators, neuer surpassed in this vice these peevish shavelings.

The description of the action of the Mask continues:

After the speech of Plutus . . . the middle part of the rocke began to move, and being come some five paces toward the King, it split in pieces with a great crack, and out brake Capriccio . . . [a Man of Wit] . . . The peeces of the rocke vanisht, and he spake as in his place.

At the singing of the first song, full, which was sung by the Virginian Priests called the Phoebades, to six lutes (being used as an Orphian virtue, for the state of the mines opening); the upper part of the rocke was sodainly turn'd to a cloude, discovering a rich and refulgent mine of golde, in which the Twelve Maskers were triumphantly seated, their Torch-bearers attending before them; all the lights being so ordred that, though none were seen, yet had their lustre such vertue, that by it the least spangle or spark of the Maskers' rich habites might with ease and cleareness be discovered as far off as the seate. Over this golden mine, in an evening sky, the ruddy sunne was seen ready to set; and behind the tops of certain white cliffes by degrees descended, casting up a banke of clouds, in which a while he was hidden; but then, gloriously shining, gave that usually observed good omen of succeeding faire weather. Before he was fully set, the Phoebades (shewing the custome of the Indians to adore the sun setting) began their observance with the song, to whose place wee must referre you for the manner and words. All the time they were singing, the Torch-bearers holding up their torches to the sun, to whom the Priests themselves and the rest did, as they sung, obeisance; which was answered by other musique and voices, at the commandment of Honor, with all observances us'd to the King, &c.

In the printed version of the Mask, all the dialogue of the baboons was omitted, to Chapman's intense disgust. Possibly the baboons were intended as a satire on the unworthy adventurers who had been to Virginia, but who had been too "nice" to do the hard work required in pioneer life, and so had returned disgruntled, and had avenged themselves for the harsh treatment they had received by slandering the enterprise. Chapman's description of the costumes for the baboons throws some light on his intention. The rich procession of Gentlemen Maskers was followed at "a fit distance" by

. . . a mocke maske of baboons, attired like fantastical travailers in Neopolitane sutes and great ruffes, all horst with asses and dwarf palfries, with yellow foot-clothes, and casting cocle-demois about, in courtesie, by way of lardges; torches boarn of either hand of them lighting their state as ridiculously as the rest nobly.

In contrast to these, the chief maskers were attired "in Indian habits all of a resemblance," the costumes obviously modelled on White's drawings of the Indian chiefs—though of course heightened for the purpose of the ballet:

. . . the ground cloath of silver richly embroidered with golden sunnes, and about every sunne ran a traile of gold, imitating Indian worke; their bases of the same stuffe and work, but betwixt every pany of embroidery, went a rowe of white estridge [ostrich] feathers, mingled with sprigs of golde plate; under their breasts they woare bawdricks of golde, embroidered high with pearle; and about their neckes ruffes of feathers, spangled with pearles and silver. On their heads high spriged feathers, compast in coronets, like the Virginian Princes they [re]presented. Betwixt every set of feathers, and about their browes, in the underpart of their coronets, shined sunnes of golde plate, sprinkled with pearle, from whence sprung rayes of the like plate, that, mixing with the motion of the feathers, shewed exceedingly delightfull and gratious. Their legges were adorn'd with close long white silke stockings, curiously embroidered with golde to the middle-legge; and over these (being on horsebacke) they drew greaves or buskins embroidered with gould, and interlace't with rowes of fethers, altogether estrangefull and Indian-like. In their hands, set in several postures as they rode, they brandisht cane darts of the finest gould. Their vizerds of olive-collour, but pleasingly visag'd, their hayre blacke and large, waving downe to their shoulders. Their horses for rich shew equall'd the Maskers themselves, all their caparisons being enchac't with sunnes of gould and ornamentall Jewells; to every one of which was tackt a scarffing of silver, than ran sinnuousely in workes over the whole caparison, even to the daseling of the admiring spectators. Their heads no less gracefully and properly deckt with the like light skarffing that hung about their eares wantonly dangling. Every one of these horses had two Moores, attired like Indian slaves, that for state sided them, with swelling wreaths of gould and watched [watchet] on their heads, which arose in all to the number of a hundred.

The musicians, "the choicest of our Kingdom," were drawn in "two carrs triumphall . . . every part inricht with silver and golde." They were

. . . attirèd like Virginean priests. . . . Their robes were trickt up before, strange hoods of heathers and scallops about their neckes, and on their heads turbants, stucke with severall-coloured feathers, spotted with wings of flies of extraordinary bigness like those of their countrie.

The Torch-bearers' habits were likewise of the Indian garb, but more extravagant than those of the maskers, all showfully garnisht with several-hewed [hued] fethers; the humble variety wherof strucke off the more amplie the Maskers' high beauties, shining in the habits of themselves; and reflected in their kinde a new and delightfully-varied radiance of the beholders. All these sustain'd torches of the Virgine-wax, whose staves were great canes all over gilded; and these (as the rest) had every man his Moore attending his horse. The Maskers, riding single, had every Masker his Torch-bearer mounted before him.

The "application" of all this to Ralegh's Virginia enterprise was, I believe, obvious, if not to everybody, at least to those to whom it was specially directed. It was, like the plea for Somerset in *Chabot,* the strongest argument that Chapman could conceive in order to induce the King to spare the life of one of the best "men of wit" in his kingdom. It was, as the lines of the dialogue imply, an attempt to buy Capriccio's life with "a wedge of gold," in other words, an attempt to persuade the King that he owed to Ralegh, the chiefest source of all his wealth, namely, the mines of his new found world.

Objections against the play were voiced immediately, but Chapman stood to his guns. He protested against the suppressing of the baboon episode by the printer; and he concluded [italics inserted]:

To answer certaine insolent objections made against the length of my speeches and narrations, being (for the probability of all accidents, arising from the invention of this Maske, *and their application to the persons and places, for whome and by whome it was presented*) not [only] convenient, but necessary, I am enforct to affirme this, that, as there is no Poem nor Oration so generall, but hath his one particular proposition, nor no river so extravagantly ample, but hath his never-so-narrow fountaine, worthy to be nam'd; so all these courtly and honoring inventions (having Poesie and Oration in them, and a fountaine, to be exprest, from whence the rivers flow) *should expressively arise out of the places and persons, for and by whome they are presented;* without which limits they are luxurious and vaine. But what rules soever are set downe to any art or act (though without their observation no art nor act is true and worthy), yet are they nothing the more followed, or the few who follow them credited. Every vulgarly-esteemed upstart dares breake the dreadfull dignity of antient and autenticall Poesie, and presume Ludicrously to proclame, in place thereof, repugnant precepts of their own spaune. Truth and Worth have no faces to enamour the lycentious, but Vaine-glory and Humor. The same body, the same beauty, a thousand men seeing; only the man whose blood is fitted hath that whiche he calls his soule enamoured. And this out of infallible cause; for men understand not these of Menander,

. . . est morbus opportunitas
Animae, quod ictus, vulnus accipit grave.

But the cause of [some] men's being enamoured with Truth, and of her slight respect in others, is the divine Freedom; one touching with his apprehensive finger, the other passing The Hill of the Muses (which all men must clime in the regular way to Truth), is said of ould to be forcked. And the two points of it, parting, are *Insania* and *Divinus Furor*. *Insania* is that which every ranckbrainde writer and judge of poeticall writing is rapt withal, when hee presumes either to write or censure the height of Poesie, and that transports him with humor, vaine-glory, and pride, most prophane and sacrilegious; when *Divinus Furor* makes gentle and noble the never-so-truly inspired writer,

Emollit mores, nec sinit esse feros.

And the mild beames of the most holy inflamer easily and sweetly enter, with all understanding sharpenesse, the soft and sincerely humane; but with no time, no study no meanes under Heaven, any arrogant, all-occupation devourer (that will, chandler-like, set up with all wares, selling Poesie's nectar and ambrosia as well as mustard and vinegar). The chaste and restrain'd beame of humble Truth will never enter, but only grase and glaunce at them, and the further fly them.

Thus, in a typical utterance, spake Chapman, the loyal friend to the Virginia enterprise, and the stout defender of the theory of practical purposes in poetry. The topicalists, who are regarded by some scholars as positively insubordinate in their persistent search for the "narrow fountain" of local and contemporary "application," whence flowed the general rivers of Tudor and Stuart poetry, have at least this consolation: They are in the excellent company of literary critics, such as Chapman, Lyly, and Spenser, who do not hesitate to label the detractors of their theory "vulgarly esteemed upstarts, ludicrously proclaiming repugnant precepts of their own spawn."

In view of these defenses, therefore, it does not seem to require a great mountain of faith to enable us to believe that the predecessor and friend of Chapman, and a member of his social and intellectual coterie, may have contributed an earlier stage production to the cause of their common patron. At all events, if Marlowe did not make some contribution to the Virginian project, he was the only literary member of the group not to do so. We have already noted Drayton's *Virginia Voyage;* Chapman's *De Guiana,* and the poems to Hariot; Roydon's poem attached to Sir George Peckham's *True Report;* Spenser's paean to the Shepherd of the Ocean in *Colin Clout,* and his further plea for Ralegh in the Timias episode of the *Faerie Queene,* to say nothing of the ceaseless prose works of Hariot, Hakluyt, and Le Moyne. In view of these definitely motived poems written by Marlowe's friends, it would be strange if the cause of empire, the *élan* of conquest and the rich materialism to be gained therefrom were to find no reflection in the poetry of the most brilliant literary member of the group. Such a detachment on the part of any poet would be unlikely, but on the part of a person of Marlowe's gifts and temperament truly little short of an impossibility. Even if we believe that for Marlowe the inspiration of Timur's conquest of the East was more vital and stirring than the project of Western Empire which was being so strongly urged by his friend and patron, still it could hardly be that the rich detail of "western plantation" literature could fail to give added point and reality to the story of the remote conquest of Tartary. As the old story of Dr. Faustus gained in Marlowe's play a richness of texture and surface-brilliance from the contact of Marlowe's mind with that of a real, vivid, contemporary "atheist" like Bruno, so we believe that the story of Tamburlaine has gained a similar verve and reality from the association of its author with the aspiring mind of Ralegh and his friends. I myself am inclined to believe that the relation between Marlowe's plays and his patron was even more definite; but I realize that in attempting to show how Tamburlaine's career of Eastern conquest was a fustian for the contemporary spirit of empire-building that animated the group in which Marlowe moved, I am venturing upon unbroken ground, and that I shall not be able to carry all of my readers the whole way with me. I think, however, that they will have no difficulty in admitting that *if* Marlowe had wished to write a play exploiting Ralegh's Virginian Enterprise, or at least one whose motive was to inspire admiration and emulation of it, his idea would surely have been to represent the new world in a twofold light: first, as a vast source of dazzling, easily obtained wealth for Englishmen; and secondly, as an instrument of titanic proportions for quashing the pretensions of Spain in the world of commercial rivalry. Marlowe would, accordingly, cast about him for a myth or legend which would body forth, or, if you will, dramatize these ideas. He would not have far to seek; for, as we have seen, he was by no means the first Englishman who had needed a bad name and a desperate metaphor with which to vilify the Spaniards. A glance at contemporary pamphlet literature may help us to understand how easy it would have been for Marlowe's audience to equate the pagan obstructors of Tamburlaine's conquest of the East with the Spanish forces who opposed the English expansion in the new western world.

For all Europe in a vague way, but for Spain in particular, there had been, since the first of the century, three major objects of fear and hatred: the Turks, the Moors, and the Jews. A word or two will remind the reader of the reasons for each of these sixteenth century phobias.

Until after the battle of Lepanto, when the Ottoman empire received its first important check in the course of its invasion of Europe, the burden of European defense against the Turk rested upon the small but sturdy shoulders of Venice. The capture of Constantinople, in 1453, was for the Othmani a mere beginning of their conquest of Europe. All the city states of the Italian peninsula had to keep a constant vigilance against the encroachments upon their frontiers, but Venice, both because of her outlying possessions, such as Cyprus, and because the Turk had most to fear from her commercial and maritime rivalry, had to bear the brunt of the defense. The fact is, she alternately fought and traded with her adversary. Some one has said of her, "She traded when she could and fought when she coudn't"; but when Venice actually entered into a treaty with the victors of Constantinople, all Europe rose in scandalized protest. The world said that Venice, the beautiful, fair-haired Bride of the Adriatic, had wedded the loathsome Turk to her own destruction, that sooner or later he would betray and ruin her. We shall shortly have occasion to show how this "fable" was used by Cinthio in his *Hecatomythi,* but first we must account for the confusion of Turk with Moor in the popular rhetoric of the period.

With the rise and fall of the Moorish empire in Spain, the general reader is probably less familiar than with the Ottoman invasion of Europe. It needs, therefore, no apology to subjoin the following brief account of the background of the wars of Granada, the substance of which is taken from S. P. Scott's *History of the Moorish Empire in Europe* (III, pp. 255-288). Obviously it is impossible within the scope of this chapter to give even the briefest history of the Moors in Spain. It must suffice to state broadly that the race came into the fearful odium under which it suffered during the sixteenth century, as a result of a persecution instigated by Charles V. The original causes were, of course, complex, but the crux of the matter was that all Mohammedans, whether Moorish or Turkish or Arab, within the jurisdiction of the Spanish Crown, should become Christian. With papal sanction, Charles V issued a proclamation requiring the Moors, under mysterious, unspecified penalties, to become Christians within ten days. The Turks had already submitted to a compulsory baptism—1600 of them at one time, according to one chronicle, though this is probably gross exaggeration. The Moors, however, offered more resistance. They decided to endure exile, and accordingly went about selling their goods and chattels. But this did not suit Charles, who promptly forbade both sales and departure, leaving to the Moors the choice of apostasy or armed resistance. Most of them submitted to compulsory baptism, which naturally gave rise to certain reactions which Catholics were certain to construe as malignant blasphemy. "Allah be praised!" shouted one who felt no drop of the baptismal waters, "not a drop defiled me."

The result of all this enforced orthodoxy was that by the middle of the sixteenth century there no longer remained within the limits of the Spanish peninsula a single individual who dared openly to acknowledge his belief in the creed of Mohammed. The Moors, however, were wealthy and their lords corrupt, so that there arose a scandal on a gigantic scale: as the Catholics under Elizabeth bought their exemptions from Protestant services, so the Moors bought their exemptions from the hated Mass. This was a fatal mistake; they no sooner began to bribe the officials in this way than they were arrested by other more greedy officials for bribery. Gradually it became impossible for the Moors to live in peace. The enemies of the Church have insinuated that the Inquisition found no difficulty in discovering heresy in a person whose villa or palace was wanted for a monastery. Be that as it may, the Moors, especially in Granada, offered a stubborn resistance. Every time a group of Moors was condemned to expiate their heresies in an *auto-da-fé,* information was promptly sent to Barbary and an equal number of Christian captives perished by fire: hence the legend of the cruelty of the Moors to their Christian prisoners. As time went on, the recriminations became aggressive. Many of the bolder Moors, whose property had been confiscated, betook themselves to the mountains where they organized themselves into bands of outlaws under the name of Monfis. These men not only habitually robbed the wealthy on the mountain highways, but, in the event of some new outrage in the capital, they would swoop down into the city by night and take what revenge they could, bearing away the wives and children of their enemies, and leaving in the squares and highways the mutilated corpses of every Christian they encountered. These bands of Monfis soon grew into a large and powerful organization, so that at last they were able to contemplate an insurrection against Spanish rule that would be more than a retaliatory raid. It was an obvious step for these rebels to enlist the sympathy of other Mohammedans, and the rulers of Fez, Algiers, and Constantinople were persuaded to make common cause with these persecuted Moors, and accordingly promised help. The plans were carried forward with an amazing efficiency. Under pretence of soliciting funds for a hospital, trusty emissaries were despatched to every Moorish community in the kingdom, and it is known that approximately 110,000 families were thus visited. It is a considerable testimony to their ability and integrity that among the multitudes who shared the secret, for which a traitor would have received a fortune, not a single individual abused the trust. Arms were purchased in Algiers and avenues of communication were organized and perfected. They lacked only a leader who should serve as a symbol of the political entity of their race. The idea was good, but their selection of a king was bad. It fell upon one Don Fernando de Valor, a young man of Granada, of amiable disposition, and clever enough, but of prodigal and licentious habits. The choice was determined by his happening to belong to an ancient line of Moorish princes. He was crowned and invested with the royal insignia with all the ceremonial of the ancient rites. His new subjects rendered him obeisance; he named the dignitaries of his court, and the assemblage invoked the blessing of heaven upon the servant of Allah and the representative of the Prophet. His full title was *Muley-Mohammed-Ibn-Ommeyah,* King of Granada and Andalusia. The ceremony was, however, a farce, through which the Moorish citizens of Granada saw only too well. Intolerable as their condition was, they were unwilling to trust to this profligate youth so dangerous an honour as the leadership of the rebellion.

In the country and the mountain districts, however, the new King was hailed with wild enthusiasm, with the result that these men could not be restrained until the proper signals came from the capital, which, as I have said, was slow to act because of lack of confidence in the King. An appalling tempest of rebellion seemed to break out simultaneously in every settlement of the Sierras, and the excesses and atrocities committed by these insurgents are too terrible to relate. The reader may think that the horrors of *Tamburlaine* and *Titus Andronicus* are beyond human credulity, but they are as nothing compared with the outrages of mutilation, torture, and sacrilege that were devised and perpetrated by these enraged Moors. As nuns and monks got the worst of it, it is small wonder that the legend grew up in the sixteenth century whereby the Moor was regarded as the very incarnation of blasphemy, hypocrisy, sacrilege, and insatiable bloody fury. Alarms very soon reached the capital, and the Christians rose in a panic of retaliation. In the campaign that ensued every consideration of military virtue, of pity, of humanity, was cast aside. We are told that the Christians fought with an energy dictated by fanaticism and rapacity for plunder, the Moors with all the reckless courage of despair. Scott declares that even the plain-spoken old chroniclers of the time recorded their shame as they wrote of the outrages inflicted by the savage Spanish volunteers. The result was that the army of Muley-Mohammed-Ibn-Omeyah was finally beaten and dispersed, and forced to retire to the mountains where they quickly gathered force for a second attempt. Before this reorganization could be effected, however, Ibn-Omeyah was killed by one of his own councillors in a private quarrel respecting a beautiful slave. There is no doubt that he was unscrupulous, licentious, and cruel, and my only interest in him is that I believe him to have contributed largely to the English legend of the inconceivably wicked Moor whose death is made more hideous than his life by his diabolical bragging of his crimes. Such monstrosities are to be found in the characters of Aaron in *Titus Andronicus,* and Ithamore in the *Jew of Malta,* or Eleazar in *Lust's Dominion.* When Ibn-Omeyah's enemies had finally bound him and thrown him into a corner from which he could watch them plundering his apartment, the Spanish chronicler says (Luis Coloma, S.J., *The Story of Don John of Austria,* [London, 1912], p. 194):

> He followed them with bitter speeches which revealed the depth of his fury and the blackness of his heart: That he never intended to be a Moor except to avenge himself on one or the other; that he had hanged his enemies, friends and relations; cut off their heads, taken their women, stolen their property; and as he had fulfilled his desires and vengeance, now they were taking theirs; but not for all this could they take away his heartfelt satisfaction. And when he heard that Ibn Ibu was designated to succeed him, he said that he died content, because Ibn Ibu would soon find himself in the same situation as he was in at that moment. . . . At daybreak his two enemies took him to another room and there strangled him with a cord, each pulling an end, and in the morning they took him out and buried him in a dung hill as something despicable.

No one who had read this chronicle, it seems, could fail to see in this bold, bad, crafty, blasphemous man, with his horrid lust and his diabolical pride in his infamy, the ancestor of Aaron and Ithamore and Eleazar. I must not be understood to imply that Ibn-Omeyah or Al-Habaqui furnished the precise models for the wicked Moor of the drama. To the sixteenth century, Turk, Moor, and Jew were interchangeable names for the Infidel, and, needless to say, Turkish corsairs of the Mediterranean furnished many a a colourful addition to the legend. The mere name of Barbarossa [Khair-ed-in Pasha] was, like Tamburlaine's, enough to scare the foe. But Ibn-Omeyah was closer at hand than Barbarossa or Piale.

As I have already noted, Ibn-Omeyah's successor was Ibn Ibu, a man of real ability and integrity, who, if he had not been betrayed by his own chief minister, might have led the wars to a satisfactory Moorish victory. On the Spanish side, there was also a new and better leader, the distinguished, capable, adored half-brother of the King, Don John of Austria, whose victories both at Galera and at Lepanto won for him the title of First Soldier in Europe. It is possible that the episode of Olympia in *II Tamburlaine* is an echo of the terrors of Galera, where many parents killed their children, and husbands their wives, to save them from the fury of Don John's soldiers.

The rest of this war is highly interesting to the student of the drama in general, but there is no need to speak further of it here, except to mention one other famously iniquitous man who certainly contributed to the sixteenth century legend of the atrocious Moor. This was Al-Habaqui, the chief minister of Ibn Ibu, who played a loathsome part of braggart and traitor and villain, until he was seized by the Turkish allies of Ibn Ibu and strangled.

For the Jews, a like persecution produced a like result. From the date of their technical expulsion from Spain to the Moorish wars of the sixteenth century, they were identified by the Spaniards with the other pagans within their gates. At first the persecution created that strange and significant phenomenon "Maranism," or crypto-Judaism, that is, a public acceptance of Islam, or Christianity, as the persecutors varied, combined with a private fidelity to the rites of Judaism. As a matter of fact, the treatment of the Jews under the dominion of the Moors in Andalusia was far more lenient than during the period succeeding the fall of the kingdom of Boabdil. Professor Israel

Abrams says *(Encyclopedia Britannica,* 11th ed., vol. 17, p. 668; vol. 15, p. 405):

> The reconquest of Andalusia by the Christians, associated towards the end of the fifteenth century with the establishment of the Inquisition, introduced a spirit of intolerance which led to the expulsion of the Jews and Moors. The consequences of this blow were momentous; it may be said to inaugurate the ghetto period. In Spain Jewish life had participated in the general life, but the expulsion, while it dispersed the Spanish Jews in Poland, Turkey, Italy, and France, and thus in the end contributed to the Jewish emancipation of the French Revolution, for the time drove the Jews within their own confines and barred them from the outside world.

No reader of Chaucer will need to be reminded of the fearful religious animosity that gave rise to the story of St. Hugh of Lincoln. No charge was too odious to bring against the Jews—ritual murder, torture of children—all these hateful myths were accepted for truth by a bigoted and terrified world of Gentiles.

These, then, were the enemies of Christendom: the Turks, the Moors, and the Jews. The train of thought and circumstance through which the anti-Turkish, anti-Jewish, anti-Moorish rhetoric was finally fused into an elaborate anti-Spanish and anti-Catholic metaphor, offers one of the most curious of the phenomena of sixteenth-century history; and the study of it furnishes an instructive initiation into the devious arcana of myth-making.

We have already noted the fact and the nature of the commercial rivalry existing between Spain and England; but this was only a chapter in the story of this gigantic sixteenth-century quarrel. Into the vortex of it were finally drawn most of the major issues of European politics—the strangling wars between Catholics and Protestants, the rise of the Dutch Republic, the execution of Mary Stuart and the revenge of the Holy League, the struggle between England and Spain for naval supremacy, the conflicting policies of expansion, and the absorbing riddle of the English succession. In all these matters, it was natural that Protestant England should ally herself with the rising tides of Protestantism on the continent, particularly, as we have seen, with the policies of the Prince of Orange, of Henry of Navarre, and of the Catholic, but antipapal city-state of Venice. To all these, Spain was the archenemy; and since the common people of Castile were very largely of Jewish or Moorish mixture, it was an easy step for their adversaries to link the atrocities of Moorish and Jewish tradition to those more recent ones along the Spanish Main or in the torture chambers of the Holy Office. Rightly or wrongly, the Protestants of the sixteenth century believed that it was the Moorish and Jewish blood in the Spaniard that accounted for his penchant for atrocious, bloody deeds. The tracts of the time are full of this notion. The following extracts from some of these will show how prevalent and commonplace it really was.*

(1) The *Apology* of William the Silent, published in 1580, and sent by him as his official defense to almost all the courts of Europe. This led to the Abjuration of 1582, in which the States General, meeting at The Hague, repudiated the power and authority of Spain. In the following quotation he is describing the nature of the Spanish. [Italics inserted throughout.]

> The Duke of Alva hath willingly bathed himself in our blood and in the blood of all Christians, *carrying a Turkish heart within him. I will no more wonder at that which all the world believeth, to wit, that the greatest part of the Spaniards and especially those that count themselves noblemen, are the blood of Moors and Jews, who also keep this virtue of their Ancestor, who sold for ready money down told the life of our Savior,* which also maketh me to take patiently the injury laid upon me.

(2) *The Anti-Spaniard,* a tract published in 1590 by an anonymous French gentleman, who declares himself a Catholic, but who wishes to prove that the Spanish King is the origin of all the troubles in France.

> Shall the Country of France become servile to the commandment of the Spaniard? Shall France be added to the title of this King . . . *of this demi-Moore, demi-Jew, yes demi-Saracen?*

(3) *The Flower de Luce,* a manifesto by a Frenchman against Spain, supposedly P. Forget. It was translated into English in

* Passages from these sixteenth-century pamphlets are quoted from Miss Lilian Winstanley, *Othello, the Tragedy of Italy,* pp. 66ff.

1593. This exhorts France to gather strength and defend her king:

In how short space shall we see these Spanish forces cut in pieces? *all these garrisons of Moores dyed in their own blood?*

(4) *A Treatise Paraeneticall by a Pilgrim Spaniard beaten by time and persecuted by Fortune.* This exhortation was specially addressed to Henry IV (Navarre) and was translated into English in 1598. The Pilgrim Spaniard dwells on the universal hatred felt for the Castilian, even in the other provinces of Spain.

As to the Castilians, *they are descended of the Vandals, the Jews and the Moors; and their language is in a manner all one with that of the Moores and their pronunciation all one or much alike.*

Later, after a long list of Philip's crimes, including the murder of Don John and of Elizabeth de Valois, Philip's French Queen, the Pilgrim Spaniard asserts:

The Castilians are descended of the Moores and Jews (for these two peoples live mingled pell-mell together) and their pronunciation of their language is after the Moorish fashion, seeing that the Moors have inhabited their country so many years and yet at this present possess and occupy a great part of Castile.

(5) *A Brief Discourse of the Spanish State,* by Edward Daunce, a Dutchman, published in English in 1590. Like the other authors quoted, the writer describes the Spaniards as being of Moorish descent, and therefore cruel, suspicious, and treacherous. He then compares them with the Othmani, or Turks:

All other creatures and even beasts spare those of their own family; *but the family of the Othmani and the Spaniards alone are distinguished by this: that they will kill their own children and their chaste wives.*

(6) *The Hecatomythi* (Seventh Myth of the Third Decade) of Giraldis Cinthio (1565, in Italian), offers another curious instance of the fusion of Turk and Moor. Cinthio calls his tale the *Story of the Wicked Moor,* but Shakspere shifts the name to *Othello,* which suggests "little Turk," though the etymology is, obviously, vague. This story is too well known to Shak-

sperean scholars to need quotation here. It will be clear from these brief excerpts that the confusion was not limited to Turks and Moors. All dark races were jumbled together "pell-mell," and ultimately made to stand for "popery" in general and "Jesuitry" in particular. Falstaff's joke about "Turk Gregory" *(I Henry IV,* V, iii, 46) is a well known instance of such application. Moors are called Egyptians, Egyptians Moors, Moors are called Indians, are even made sun-worshippers. In short, the dark races stood for the heathen, and the heathen were heretics, and heretics were, in the polemical language of the period, those whose beliefs diverged from the norm established by Whitgift's authority. Thus, Barnabe Googe concludes his tirade on the Church in the fourth book of *The Popish Kingdom* (1570) with these words:

> So mayst thou both the Turks and Moores,
> Call Catholics as well.

It is interesting to note the fact that this long and outrageously libellous attack on the Catholic Church was part of Burleigh's propaganda for the Protestant cause. Googe was a cousin of Burleigh's, whose retainer he was. There are many more such instances to be found in the literature of the time. Miss Winstanley has noted many of them, including those here mentioned, and I have referred to others in the chapter on the Holy League; but these will suffice to show the existence and prevalence of the popular identification of the Catholic Spaniards with Turks, Jews, and Moors.

I return now to the workshop of Christopher Marlowe in Middlesex and try to reconstruct the process of making the play of *Tamburlaine.* Granting that Marlowe's ideas of conquest were associated with what he heard and read daily concerning English imperial expansion, it would not be too much to expect that he would see in the enemies of his ideal conquering hero a symbol or parallel to the forces likely to obstruct the English program in the New World, i.e., the Spaniards. If he wished, therefore, to discuss this subject in the grand manner of epic idealization, he would naturally choose from history some splendid heroic conqueror who would embody his own, or perhaps his patron's energetic spirit of conquest, and his attention is directed toward Turkish sources because of the association, already established by the pamphleteers, between the Spanish enemies of England and the pagans of the Moslem world.

It is impossible to say how conscious such a creative process would be; the roads to Xanadu are devious and obscure even to the traveler himself, as any student of sources will realize; and the paths herewith suggested, after an interval of several centuries, are, needless to say, necessarily tentative and subject to correction in the light of new discoveries. I believe, however, that it is safe to say that the creative mind rarely works with wholly abstract material, and that therefore the enemies of Marlowe's epic hero may have had in them something of the contemporary enemies of Marlowe's own experience; but whether it was the Spaniards that suggested Turkish foes to him, or the Turkish-Moorish foes that suggested the Spanish, who can say? For the sake of convenience, I have imagined the former case, but a reversed process would be quite as intelligible. I reconstruct, therefore, the first step.

The poet will let the Turk represent Spain. But he must have a particular story or fiction to give verisimilitude and character to his drama. The story of Lepanto would be inevitable were it not that the hero in this case was a Spaniard. No, he must find a scourge of the Turks who would not be confused with the Spanish, whom it was his particular wish to abuse under the thin disguise of Turk. Accordingly his attention was drawn to another famous rout of the Turks, the battle of Ancora, in Bithynia, in the early fifteenth century, when Bajezet, the head of the Turkish Empire, was utterly defeated, routed, and captured by the resplendent, irresistible Timur, the Lame. Rarely in the history of literary composition has an author hit upon so happy a fiction for his idea. Here was every opportunity for striking parallel between the protagonist of his fiction and the protagonist of his idea. Ralegh, the Shepherd of the Ocean, who with Drake had long been known as the Scourge of Spain and terror of the Irish, was a kind of Timur, splendid, arrogant, full of successful conquest, of a vaulting ambition, ruthless to his enemies, extravagantly generous to his friends, shrewd, brilliant, showy, irresistible. The fustian coat was an all but perfect fit. Accordingly, Marlowe wrote down his *Dramatis Personae: Bajazeth, Emperor of the Turks,* with his allies the *Kings of Fez, Morocco, and Argier,* against whom fought *Tamburlaine, a Scythian Shepherd,* with his friends *Techelles* and *Usumcasane.* This is the theme-major of his dithyramb; but before he had finished the strain, his resonant ear had caught and woven into it, as it were by ample orchestration, a score of arresting minor motifs. It could hardly fail that many such would be associated with a personality as vibrant and complex as Ralegh's. His ruthless way with rebels, his inordinate love of splendour, his devotion to poetry, his moving oratory, his code of "virtu" *vs.* "passion," his pride and ambition, his romantic gesture of knightly service for his Queen—all these fill the pattern out till the political theme of anti-Spanish sentiment is all but lost in the boom of personal panegyric for Ralegh, the magnificent. Not that there lacks plenty of Turk-killing! Their carcasses lie about the pages of *Tamburlaine* in "hugey heaps," in "pyramids," their "shattered limbs . . . hang in the air as thick as sunny motes"; he makes whole cities to "caper in the air"; but when we close the book, happily these horrors are forgotten while there rings in our ears Tamburlaine's unforgettable paean in praise of beauty, the *élan* of his "aspiring mind," the majesty of his countenance "who sleeps each night with conquest on his brows," his celestial imagination holding continual intercourse with "the spirits of every element" that shadow such mysterious "beauty in their airy brows." This is, of course, as it should be. Ralegh himself signifies for us now, because of these magic qualities, rather than for his program against the Spaniards. Just so the fiery ichor that stirs in the veins of Tamburlaine animates us too with a vigour, a sense of expansion and release from things mundane, that far transcends the temporal occasion of his particular ecstasy. Miss Ellis-Fermor, in her recent edition of *Tamburlaine* (pp. 19ff.), gives the following summary of the character of Timur as he was revealed in the early fifteenth century travel reports, such as those of Clavijo or Schiltberger:

He inherited, as a member of a military caste, the tradition of the great line of Tartar Khans, with their genius for tactics and military discipline. . . . He had courage and tenacity unsurpassed even among Mongols, and the power of binding to him, by his generosity, his severe yet even justice and his charm, men of the highest ability whom his watchful and sympathetic judgment unfailingly discerned. National temperament and the hard battle of the first half of his life combined to make him ruthless. He slaughtered, where necessary, in cold blood and upon a scale horrifying to western nations. Yet his empire, when it was established, was orderly and peaceful. . . .

The picture of his capital, Samarquand, in Clavijo's narrative, equals in its colour and beauty Marco Polo's earlier pictures of the Court of Kublai; a city with fair and open streets, rich with trade and crafts, lying in a fertile land from which waggons of wheat and barley and fruit, horses and herds of fat-tailed sheep poured daily in; with far-stretching suburbs of houses and palaces surrounded by orchards and gardens, and, far out into the plain, the villages and settlements of the captives of war that he had gathered from every nation he had subdued. The gates of the palaces were glorious with blue and golden enamel, the hangings of woven silk, gold-embroidered and decorated with jewelled plaques and silk tassels; the tents, in which the Tartars still for the greater part lived, were of richly coloured silks fur-lined; huge erections three lances high that looked from a distance like the castles of Europe. Merchants from all lands poured into this city with leather and fur from Russia, with the matchless silks of China, with rubies from the north; the perfumes of India scented its streets. Such splendour was there, says Clavijo, as could not have been seen in Cairo itself. From every land that he had conquered Timur had brought the masters of its most famous crafts, all to the enriching of this city of Samarquand, the treasury of the eastern world. . . . Such was the man who had dared everything possible to his imagination and had never faltered; who had endured desert and mountain warfare, victory and defeat, from boyhood to the age of seventy years; who had raised up this golden city in Tartary and had stripped the ancient cities of Persia and Anatolia; who had slaughtered a million people in Baghdad and built their heads into a pyramid for his own memorial, yet had spared the libraries, mosques, and hospitals there and sent its scholars in custody to Samarquand. Such was "the sweet fruition of an earthly crown" upon the brows of the great Khan Timur.

This was precisely what Marlowe needed. In the scientific reports from Virginia, written by Amadas and Barlow, Lane and Hariot, Ralegh and his servants had been hampered by their sense of honour and responsibility to the investors in their enterprise. There they had had to keep a fairly well drawn distinction between what their credulity, stimulated by their great hopes, led them to *accept* as true, and what with their own eyes they had seen, and therefore *knew* to be true. But here in the Tartar story no one could say where allegory left off and pure dramatic fiction took up the strain. Here, under cover of his fustian coat, the poet could prank his hero out in a splendour more fantastic than any exaggeration dreamed of by the least scrupulous of the early chroniclers of El Dorado. Hariot dared not claim he had seen the natives in Virginia rolling in gold-dust and scattering pearls like pebbles, or plating their houses in gold; but Marlowe might insinuate as much of this as he liked, and there is no denying that he took an unrestrained advantage of the opportunity. Gold! Did the English want gold from the Western World? Well, let them have it, and so he pours it forth: "liquid gold," "massy gold," "wedge of gold," "whole chests of gold," "rivalled gold," "beaten gold," "burnished gold," "yellow gold," "gold ingots," "gold rings," "gold chains," "gold curiously wrought," "nets of gold," "robes of gold," "helmets of gold," "coats and cloaks of gold," "roofs of gold," "sheets of gold," "wagons of gold," and gold *ad infinitum, ad absurdum.* Nor does he leave the reader in any doubt of the source of all this gold. Tamburlaine may pretend to strut about the Asian plains, but lest there should be any doubt in the minds of his audience as to his real conquests and the actual sources of his wealth, he tells them plainly, in his promise to Zenocrate [italics inserted]:

A thousand galleys manned with Christian slaves
I freely give thee, which will cut the straits,
And bring Armadoes from the coast of Spain
Fraughted with the gold of rich America.

In *II Tamburlaine,* just before "the scourge of God must die," he calls for a map, saying:

Give me a map; thus let me see how much
Is left for me to conquer all the world.

After reviewing his already accomplished conquests, in Asia, Scythia, and elsewhere, he cries:

Look here, my boys; see what a world of ground
Lies westward from the midst of Cancer's line
Unto the rising of this earthly globe,
Whereas the sun, declining from our sight,
Begins the day with our Antipodes!
And shall I die, and this unconquered?
Lo, here, my sons, are all the golden mines,
Inestimable drugs and precious stones,
More worth than Asia and the world beside;
And from th' Antarctic Pole eastward behold
As much more land, which never was descried,
Wherein are rocks of pearl that shine as bright
As all the lamps that beautify the sky!
And shall I die, and this unconquered?

The thought of all that gold in America is still hovering in his restless mind when he writes *Doctor Faustus,* where he declares [italics inserted]:

From Venice shall they drag huge argosies,
And from America the golden fleece
That yearly stuffs old Philip's treasury.

Hariot had found crystal quartz in abundance, and of this Marlowe is even more fantastically prodigal than of the gold. He advertises its possibilities and impossibilities to a point of delirium. He will have "crystal armour," "crystal livery," "crystal gates," "crystal robes," "pavings of bright crystal," "molten crystal," yea, a "whole crystal world."

Both Hariot and Lane had learned to judge of pearls by their weight, and by their whiteness and roundness. Black pearls, in the "new found world," were in great abundance and were considered "naught," but the number of those which were "very large" and "very orient [white] and round" was, according to Hakluyt's *Chronicles,* small enough to make their value all but priceless. So Marlowe rings the changes on this theme, not only in *Tamburlaine,* but in all the early plays. Tamburlaine's men "sweat with carrying pearl and treasure on their backs"; they drink "liquid gold . . . Mingled with coral and with orient pearl"; Faustus has his emissaries "ransack the ocean for orient pearl"; Barabas says his warehouses are filled with "whole chests of gold in bullion and in coin," and he "knows not how much weight in pearl, Orient and round"; and he has "a pearl so big, So precious and withall so orient, As be it valued but indifferently, The price thereof will serve to entertain Selim and all his soldiers for a month." So it is with all of Hariot's reported treasures. Marlowe goes quite off his head about the silk-possibilities described by Hariot. Not only is Zenocrate to be clad habitually in silk, even when sledging "amid the frozen pools," but in Tamburlaine's newly conquered world "the townsmen mask in silk and cloth of gold," Faustus "will have them fill the public schools with silk, Wherewith the students shall be bravely clad." Unlike Chapman, the "plain-living" side of "high-thinking" seems to have had small appeal for this scholarship-boy of Canterbury's famous public school.

Hariot had discovered many new fruits in America and Ralegh had planted orange trees in the garden of his wife's uncle, Sir Francis Carew, at Beddington, but in Marlowe's fustian world, his humblest Tartar soldiers may "glut" themselves with "the dainties of the world," and Faustus realizes that the best place to get his "pleasant fruits and princely delicates" is in the "corners of the new-found world." Marlowe's readers need not be reminded further of his enthusiasm for easily gained wealth, "picked up . . . without control." Nothing that Ralegh's reconnoiterers found worthy of note but finds a use in the transports of the splendour-intoxicated Tamburlaine. Silks, spices, drugs, fragrant woods, rare fruits and plants, new wines, ivory—oh, much ivory!—rubies, sapphires, plumes—it is all here, enlarged, enflamed, transfused in the alchemy of Marlowe's extravagant imagination. The point needs no further labouring.

There are, however, other points of resemblance between Ralegh and Tamburlaine which may not be so easily recognized and which may, indeed, have been less consciously inserted. I mention them because they fill out the character of Tamburlaine and enhance our interest in his fustian role. All the characteristics that we found in an earlier chapter to be a part of the Ralegh legend, appear in the design for Tamburlaine—his "working words," his shameless flattery of the fair sex, his love of poetry, his code of "virtu" versus "beauty," his "frowning brow," his arrogance, his severity with his enemies, his generosity toward his friends, his love of splendour, and his flair for "the state and majesty of heaven." All these distinctions, acutely felt but shrewdly idealized by Marlowe, gain for Tamburlaine, as I believe they did for Ralegh, a hearing that would never otherwise have been vouchsafed to one whose methods and manners were open to criticism along so wide a front. Here we may, perhaps, insert a *caveat*. It is a mistake to push the parallels too far. Zenocrate, for instance, serves Tamburlaine as a romantic excuse for his wild conquests, and as the queenly recipient of his plunder, a role that must have been meant to suggest Elizabeth, and to flatter her; but this must not be taken to indicate that Ralegh meant to kidnap and wed the Queen, as did Zenocrate. The fustian rarely fits as closely as that.

CHAPTER TWENTY

The Holy League and "The Jew of Malta"

THOUGH THE CHRONOLOGY of Marlowe's plays has never been fixed with any certainty, scholars have been inclined to settle upon the year 1589 for *The Jew of Malta.* It was certainly written after 1588, for the Prologue contains a reference to the death of the Duke of Guise, who was murdered on 23 December of that year. There exists, however, no external evidence for placing it before 26 February, 1592, when it appears in Henslowe's *Diary,* other than the general belief that since Henslowe failed to mark it "ne," probably it had already been some time on the boards. My own opinion, based on what I believe to be the topical element in the play, would place it subsequent to the famous Siege of Paris, in 1590. The likelihood of this dating will depend upon the degree of likelihood in the interpretation of the play herewith presented.

While Marlowe was advertising America on the stage, and Hariot and Hakluyt were writing it up in learned prose, and Ralegh and Northumberland were smoking it into the nostrils of the court, the rivalry between Spain and England was growing daily more intense. Ralegh knew how to play up his cause in such a way as to make Englishmen believe that, at all costs, "rich America" must be saved from the "overweening" and "greedy" Spaniard.

The stage, the press, and the creation of a personal legend at court were Ralegh's legitimate means of advertisement; but his hands were not always so white. If he was to see the colonizing venture through, he must have money—ever so much more money than he could produce from his own revenues, even more than he could get by securing investors. Where so obvious a source as these same Spanish galleons that were already freighted with the rich cargoes from these same Americas? Drake had already shown the way, for as a result of sheer, shameless piracy he had not only enriched himself, but, as we have seen, had been able to pay gigantic dividends to his joint-stock-company investors. He had also got himself knighted and had won the favour and confidence of the Queen. Besides, what could Ralegh do with his little fleet of men and ships when they were not actually embarked on voyages overseas? So Ralegh went in for "piccory." From 1595 until after the Armada, the official records are dotted with references to his captures. In 1585 he took 600 Spaniards with their ships at the Newfoundland fisheries. In 1586 he sent his ships *The Serpent* and the *Mary Spark* to fight the Spaniards at the Azores, whence they brought home three prize ships and captives, whose ransoms enhanced the total haul. In the same year he contributed a pinnace to a plundering expedition of the Earl of Cumberland to the South Seas. In the years 1589 and 1590 there are several charges against his men and ships for robbing French and Italian cargoes in Spanish bottoms; but Ralegh defended his claim to any prize that sailed under the hated flag of Spain. In the year 1591 alone, Ralegh, with eleven other adventurers, brought home prizes worth £331,150, with a profit to the partnership of £14,952.

No reader needs to be told that these were the years of the Armada excitement, but perhaps not all literary students will realize the connections between the death of Mary Stuart and Philip's anti-English policy, and the action of the Holy League on the Continent. A knowledge of these issues is, I believe, essential to an understanding of the play we are considering.

As I have already indicated, the fierce sixteenth-century quarrel between England and Spain was by no means confined to the issue of commercial rivalry, though that was probably at the bottom of the whole thing. As usual, however, the real issue was variously disguised, and never so successfully as under the oft-abused banners of religion. This was always true of Philip's policies, but in the last decades of the century it was true also of the machinations of the leaders of the civil wars in France. We have already alluded to this situation in our discussion of the *Massacre at Paris*. A somewhat closer view is now necessary, in order to recognize the various threads that seem to be woven together into the tangled web forming the plot of *The Jew of Malta*.

The following account may seem hackneyed to students of

sixteenth-century history; on the other hand, it may seem unnecessarily complicated to many. The fact is, nothing could be more complicated than the history of the Holy League, and it goes without saying that what follows is the merest outline of events and the roughest sketch of the personalities involved. Because it is necessary to my argument that the reader recognize in the *Satire Ménipée* and *The Jew of Malta* the hits at the Dukes of Guise and Mayenne, at Archduke Mathias and his

THE HOUSE OF GUISE

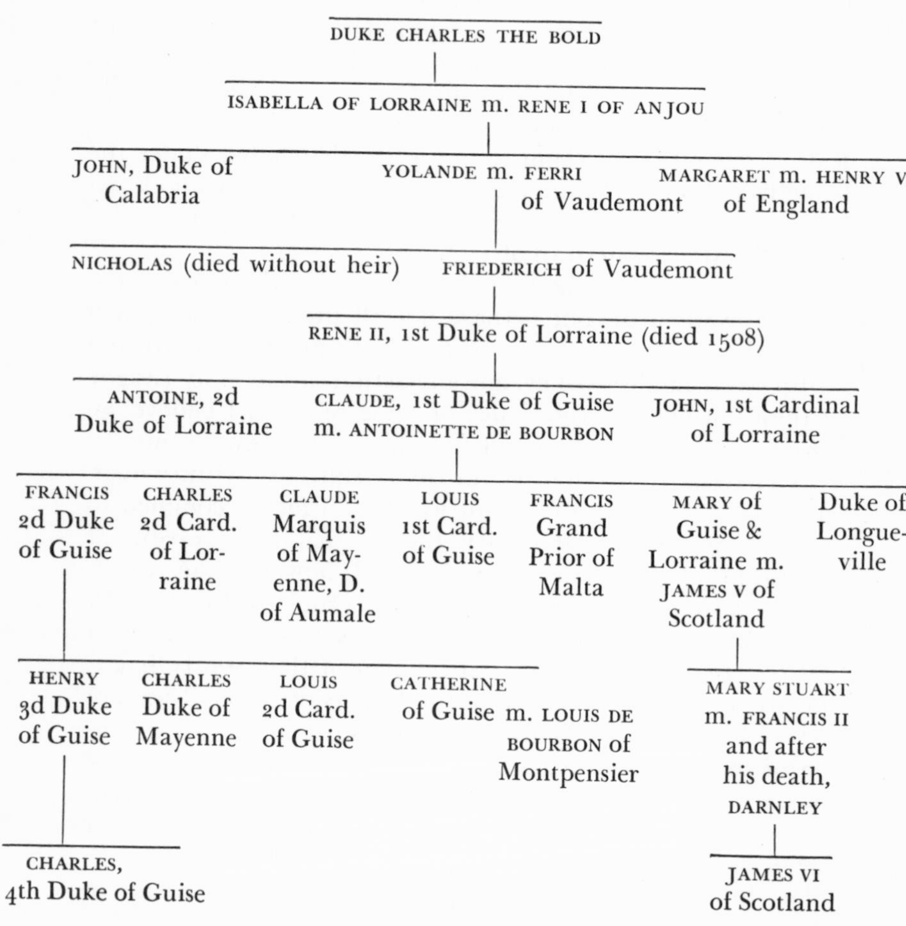

brother Ernst, at Farnese, Feria, and, of course, at Philip and the Infanta, I herewith make a special plea for patience during the perusal of this tedious background material.

When the first League was formed in 1576, it was ostensibly for the defense of the Catholic Religion in France against the Huguenot heresy; but the roots of this so-called religious war were embedded deep in the rocky subsoil of an old rivalry between the two most powerful families of France, namely, the house of Bourbon (allied ultimately with the house of Montmorency), and the house of Lorraine. A glance at a section of the family tree of Lorraine will help us to understand the elaborate pretensions of the House of Guise, first in their rivalry with the houses of Bourbon and Valois, and finally with that of Montmorency.

It may be seen that when Mary Stuart married Francis of Valois, eldest son of Catherine de Medici, the Guisans won precedence over their old rivals the Bourbons, for Francis of Valois became, in 1559, Francis II of France. The new king, influenced by his wife's relatives, was led to suspect the Bourbons because of their Huguenot leanings, and the Constable Montmorency shared the cool treatment meted out to these rival princes. He was compelled to give up his mastership of the royal household, and during the short reign of Francis II, the Guises (Francis, second Duke, and his brother, second Cardinal of Lorraine) managed France.

History, especially English history, has made a grim and perhaps unfair report of the character and career of this second Duke of Guise. The fact is that he has been made to share the odium that has justly clung to the memory of his brother, the Cardinal. It is true that he was ambitious to hold a place in the kingdom as important as that enjoyed by the elder branch of the family, the House of Lorraine. Again a chart will be the simplest aid in grasping the situation.

Thus, the older branch became allied to the ruling house by the marriage of Louise of Lorraine to Henry, Duke of Anjou and Prince of the House of Valois (third son of Catherine de Medici and Henry II); but the union of Francis II with Mary Stuart, the niece of the second Duke of Guise, brought to the cadet branch of the family, powers that were all but royal.

THE HOUSE OF LORRAINE

RENE II,
1st Duke of Lorraine

ANTOINE, 2d Duke of Lorraine m. RENÉE DE BOURBON	CLAUDE 1st Duke of Guise m. ANTOINETTE DE BOURBON	JOHN, 1st Cardinal of Lorraine

FRANCIS (d. 1545)	NICOLAS OF LORRAINE, 1st Duke of Mercoeur

CHARLES (the Great) m. CLAUDE, daughter of HENRY II of France	PHILIPPE EMANUEL (1558-1602), 2d Duke of Mercoeur	LOUISE of Lor-raine m. ANJOU (HENRY III) of Valois

Francis of Guise had aspired to the hand of Jeanne d'Albret, princess and heiress of Navarre, and had she been agreeable to the match, the Guise might have secured a connection that would have made him the friend rather than the rival to the houses of Bourbon and Valois. Jeanne married Antoine de Bourbon, who became in her right King of Navarre. Their son, who married Marguerite of Valois, was the first Bourbon king, Henry IV of France. So the Guise did not get Navarre, but the Bourbons did. This was a new cause of irritation, and henceforward the Guises sought more than ever to edge out these princes of the blood royal as well as the Montmorencys. As cadets of the sovereign House of Lorraine and as descendants of the House of Anjou, and as immediate relatives of the Queen, why should they give precedence to the Bourbons, whose royal ancestors were, after all, fairly remote, i.e., directly, as far back as Louis IX, and indirectly by marriage, as remote as the daughter of Louis XI?

Two more charts, which will clarify as well as short-cut the discussion of this fairly remote background material,* are here inserted.

* A readable account of this period of French history may be found in the second volume of *The History of France From the Accession of Henry the Third to the Death of Louis the Fourteenth,* by Nathaniel William Wraxall.

THE HOUSE OF BOURBON

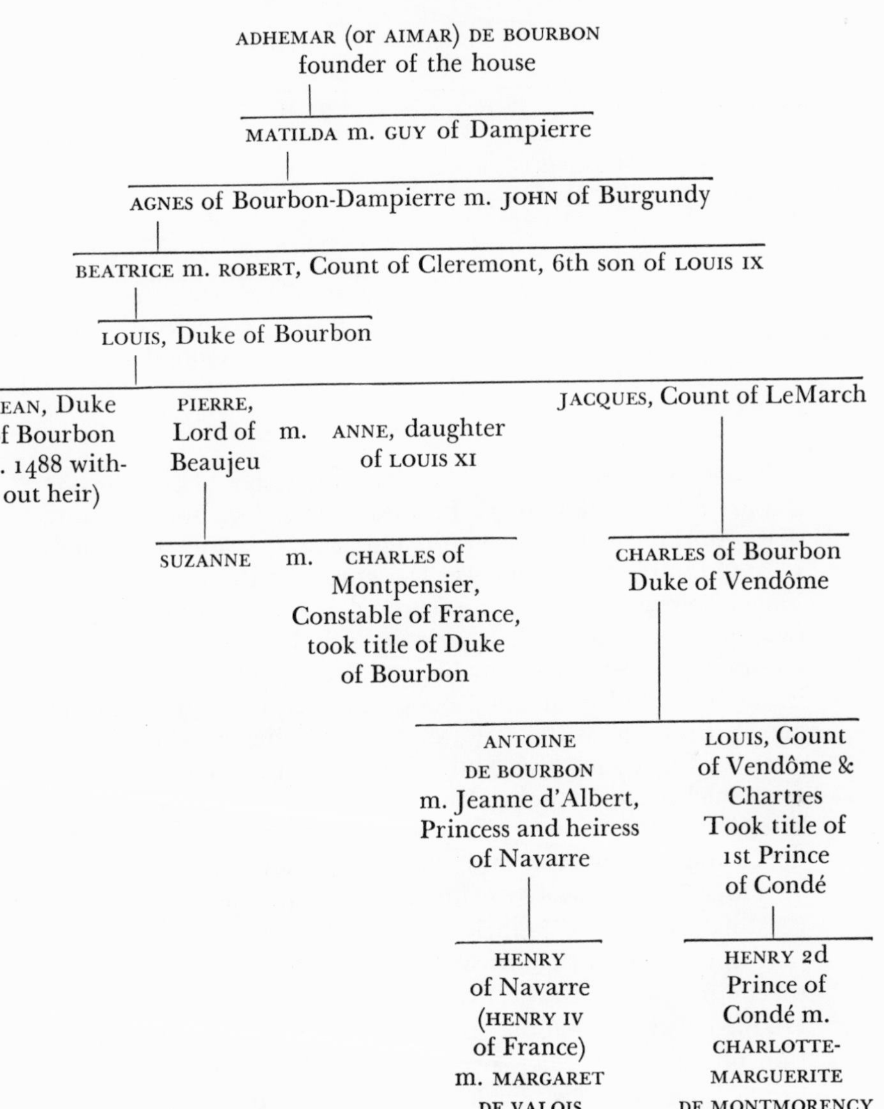

THE HOUSE OF MONTMORENCY

ANNE, 1st Duke of Montmorency

FRANCIS, 2d Duke of Montmorency 1530-1597	HENRY, 3d Duke of Montmorency 1534-1614	LOUISE DE MONTMORENCY m. GASPARD DE COLIGNY, (1519-1572) Marshal of France

Children of Louise de Montmorency and Gaspard de Coligny:

ODET, Cardinal of Chatillon	GASPARD DE COLIGNY, Admiral of France 1552	FRANCIS, Seigneur of Andelot

It was inevitable that this family rivalry should take on the colours of the religions of the two houses, for the Bourbons, both Antoine and Louis, were Huguenots, while the Guises were Catholic. The result was the horror of the Civil Wars of France. When Coligny came to court, a young man of twenty-two, he contracted at first a strong friendship with Francis of Guise. They were both capable and intelligent, had done well in the wars, and both stood out in marked contrast to the debauched retinue of the Valoise princes. Coligny was made Admiral of France in 1552, and as such could not but be largely concerned in the Catholic-Huguenot struggle then being waged throughout the country. The break between the friends, the Guise and Coligny, was brought about in several ways: first, in all France there was a growing disgust at the behaviour of the Cardinal, brother of Francis of Guise. He had abused his position as the Queen's guardian-adviser, both in his arrogance to the Bourbons and in the barbarous brutality meted out to the Huguenot victims of the struggle. The result was the formation of a popular party against him, led by Louis, Prince of Condé, but seconded by his brother Antoine, now King of Navarre. For a time Coligny wavered between the two camps, now showing Protestant leanings, now Catholic, but in the course of events he was discovered to be holding secret negotiations with the Huguenots, and, indeed, finally came into a frank alliance with their cause. His final choice was influenced largely by his Huguenot brother, Andelot, and by the political exigencies of the Prince of Condé's party. This meant, of course, a break with the Guises. The story of the Conspiracy of Amboise (1560), resulting in an open breach between the two houses, needs, happily, no more than a mention here. It was partly a plot, led by Louis of Condé, to get the young king out of the hands of his "uncles," that is, the uncles of his wife; but it was wholly unsuccessful. Condé's party was defeated, hundreds were captured, and the revenge of the Guises is too odious to relate, much more hideous, in fact, than the more famous massacre of the Huguenot congregation at Vassy, in 1562. This latter massacre the Guise tried to prevent; but the tortures of Amboise, while instigated and directed by the Cardinal, were at least assented to by Francis, the Duke. At all events, by 1563 the Guise was the successful leader of the Catholic party, idolized by army and populace alike, and he was proclaimed Lieutenant General of the kingdom. His career was cut short by his death, 24 February, 1563. He was shot by a Huguenot, Jean Poltrot de Méré; but Coligny was blamed for the murder.

Meantime, the Cardinal had lost his foothold at Court by the death of Francis II, in 1560, shortly after the tragedy of Amboise; for when Charles IX succeeded to the throne, his mother became regent and was henceforward the controlling factor in French politics, insofar as they were controlled at all. As a matter of fact, Catherine de Medici, like her great contemporary across the Channel, was more or less indifferent in religious matters, but she wanted peace in France, and so she undertook to steer a middle course between the two factions. Again like Elizabeth, she attempted the dangerous game of playing off one party against the other, the Bourbons and the Montmorencys against the Guise-Lorraine combination. Though remaining nominally Catholic, she flattered Antoine de Bourbon, first prince of the blood, into allowing her to act as regent, promising to effect religious toleration in general, and in particular to protect the Admiral Coligny from the revenge of the Guisans.

Francis of Guise was succeeded by his son Henry of Lorraine (1550-1588), who became the third Duke of Guise. This boy grew up under the domination of a passionate desire for avenging his father's murder; so he was naturally unsympathetic to Catherine. Therefore, when he returned to Court after a successful campaign against the Turks in Hungary, it is not surprising that he was received somewhat coldly, or at least, with caution. His proposal for the hand of Marguerite of Valois was repulsed with disdain.

Then, for many reasons too complicated to discuss in this summary, Catherine veered again and assented to the Massacre of St. Bartholomew, in 1572, where the young Henry of Guise satisfied his personal vengeance by superintending the murder of Coligny. Now he, like his father, became leader of the Catholic party; but, distrustful of Catherine, he sought to strengthen his party by alliance with powers whose loyalty and point of view could be counted on to remain constant. He chose the Jesuits and Pope Gregory XIII, with Philip II of Spain for financial backing. Henry's brothers, Charles, Duke of Mayenne, and Louis, Archbishop of Rheims and second Cardinal of Guise, were closely associated with him in this new organization of the Catholic party, known as the Holy League, in 1576.

Meanwhile Charles IX had died (1574), and Henry III, perhaps the most impotent of all the Valois kings, came to the throne. Dissolute and vacillating as he was, he feared the strength of the Guise and the League; but as a measure of control he made himself head of it, and, as soon as he possibly could, disbanded it (1577). The disappointed Guise then became a pensioner of Philip II, and thenceforward identified himself with his cause. One aspect of that cause was, I believe, the subject of *The Jew of Malta;* but more of that presently.

The death of Anjou, in 1584, gave the Guise a new foothold, for by it Henry of Bourbon, the Protestant King of Navarre, became heir to the throne of France. At this prospect, the Catholic party aroused itself anew. A second Holy League was formed, again subsidised by Philip, who agreed to furnish 50,000 crowns a month. Though coveting the throne of France for himself, Guise wisely deferred to the Bourbon claims, and agreed to recognize as heir only the old Cardinal de Bourbon, who was pledged to "extirpate heresy and receive the Council of Trent in France." The Cardinal, however, was only a puppet leader, while the real power remained in the hands of the Guises, Henry, the third Duke, and his brother, the Duke of Mayenne. The new League issued a manifesto from Peronne on 30 March, 1585, to the Princes of France, amounting almost to a declaration of war against Henry III. For a while Henry temporised, being afraid to do otherwise; but, while he was playing for time, an event happened for which all Europe had been waiting with anxious apprehension: Mary Stuart was executed by Elizabeth, 8 February, 1587. Immediately Philip II proceeded to use the organization of the League to help him in the great task of punishing England. It was the excuse he wanted for open war. By agreement with Philip, Guise sent the Duc d'Aumâle to overthrow the strongholds of Picardy, in order to assure by this means a way of retreat to the invincible Armada. (Wraxall, *op. cit.*, II, p. 149.) Such an action did not escape the notice of the English spies, and at once the Holy League flared out into the limelight of popular disapproval at the English court, sharing to the full the odium which England felt for Spain. From this year on, until several years after the dissolution of the League (1596), the English State Papers are dotted with animadversions which reveal the intense hatred felt toward any manifestation of the League's activity.

The pamphlets, from which we have quoted to illustrate certain aspects of anti-Spanish propaganda (see, p. 404) represent, of course, only a handful of those published during these years. The fact is that the "stationers at Paules," who, Kyd said, were Marlowe's special friends, throve on them. It will not be possible here to give a full account of this pamphlet propaganda, but it will be useful to note two or three cases in which the dramatists and stationer friends of Marlowe were engaged.

It was the boast of Greene's friends that he could "yarke up a pamphlet" in one or two nights. *The Spanish Masquerado,* published while the Armada was still the most burning topic of conversation, must have been one of these, "yarked up" to accompany a set of anti-Spanish emblems, now lost. The pictures, twelve in number, do not bear directly on the Holy League, but they are so very like those that do, particularly the one in the text accompanying *The Birth, Purpose, and Mortall Wound of the Romish Holy League* (see, p. 428), that I have ventured to include here the description of them (*Life and Works of Robert Greene,* ed. by Grosart for the Huth Library, V, pp. 242-45):

(1) First the Pope hauing put off his triple Crowne, and his Pontificalibus, sitting malcontented, scratching of his head, throwing away his keies and his sword, in great choller saith thus:
Neque Petrus, neque Paulus, quid igitur restat.

(2) *Phillip,* King of *Spaine,* attired like an Hermit, riding towards the Church on his Mule, attended on onely with certaine his slaues that are Moores, saith thus:
Iubet Ecclesia, dissentire non audeo.

(3) The Cardinals of Rome, seeing that the Pope was malcontented for the bad successe of the Spanish Fleet, appareled like Mourners, go solemnly singing *De profundis,* from Castel Angelo to S. Peters Church: to them is said:
Lugete quia cecedit Meretrix.

(4) The Cleargie of Spaine, mounted richly on their Iennets, ride vp and downe consulting, and at their wits end, fuming and fretting that their counsels had no better successe: to them is said:
Achitophelis consilium, Achitophelis laqueum.

(5) The rest of the rascall Rable of the Romish Church, as Monkes, Friers, and dirging Priestes, storming at these newes, sitting banquetting with the fair Nunnes, hauing store of daintie cates and wines before them, stall-fed with ease, and gluttony, grone out of their fat panches this passion:
Quanta patimur pro amore Christi.

(6) The Nobilitie of Spaine, grieued at the dishonour of their shameful returne: after great consultation, vow generall Pilgrimage to *S. James of Compostella,* in hope of his aide for reuenge: to them is said:
Si Petrus dormit Papae, num Iacobus vigilabit vobis?

(7) The Duke of *Medina,* Captaine general of the Armie and Spanish forces, rydeth on a Iennet, with one foote out of the Stirrop, his cappe pulde ouer his eies, and his points vntrust: to him is said:
Pillulae Britanicae in dissenteriam te coniecerunt.

(8) *Don Martines* de *Ricaldo,* chiefe Admirall of the Fleete, standing in the Hauen, and seeing his tattered Shippes, considering

what goodly Vessels were taken and drowned, and what store of men and munition they had lost, leaning backe against a broken ancker, and shaking of his head: saith thus:

O Neptune, quantas epulas vna caena devorasti?

(9) *Don Pedro de Valdes,* Generall of the Armie of *Andelosia,* now Prisoner in England, greeuing at his fortune, sitteth sad, and leaning his head on his hand, with a great sigh saith:

Heu quanta de spe decidi.

(10) The Princes, noble men, and other men of name that of their free will offered themselues aduenturers in this Spanish attempte: frustrate of their intent, walk at home muffled in their cloakes, as men disgraced, and say one to another in great passion:

Temeritatis nostrae cum Briareo poenas luimus.

(11) The Vicegerentes of his Indies, hauing lost by Sea and land, much of their Kinges treasure: sitting as discontented men on the hatches of their ships, to them is said:

Sic vos non vobis mellificatis Apes.

(12) The common Souldiours, haled forward, rather by commaund then courage, fearing at the first to attempt so dangerous an exploit, and grieued at the last with their hard misfortune, halfe mutinous, murmure this:

Quicquid delirant Reges, plectuntur Achiui.

In the gloss to the first picture, Greene praises "our mighty and famous princesse Elizabeth," who, taking upon her the Ecclesiastical supremacy, "hath vtterly raced and abolished all his [the Pope's] trash and traditions as absurdities & heresies." This, he says, stirs the Pope to new "tricks" and "pettie practices," such as Bulls, Excommunications, sending of Jesuits and Seminarians into England, etc. Worst of all, "he flieth to incense princes to bend their forces against our little Island, which defended by God, and gouerned by so vertuous a Princesse as God hath chosen after his owne heart, standeth and withstandeth their forces, without aide of speare or horse, hauing the wind and sea Captains sent from aboue to quell the pride of such hereticall enemies of the Gospell, so that the Pope seeing his purposed intent could not speede: as in a doubtful anguish to mind fell into his bitter passion."

In the second picture he concentrates his venom for an attack on Philip II, whom he describes as "ryding quietlie with a few Moores to heare Masse," while the clergy plot with the Pope to send " a great Armada" with "shippes huge and monstrous" to attack "a little Island, a handfull in respect of other Kingdomes." But "God hearing their great braves against him and his people, did put a hooke into their nostrilles and a Bridle into their Jawes, and brought them back the same way they came . . . [and] . . . scattered them as dust before the wind." The gloss to the second picture closes with a panegyric upon Drake, Frobisher, and M. Candish [Cavendish] who have so successfully, "with a few small Barkes and Pynasses," gone to his [Philip's] Indies, and "fetched from them gold and treasure for the enriching" of the best of Protestant princesses.

In the remaining glosses, he rings the changes on this theme, till it would seem that even a sixteenth century Englishman would have had enough. One passage in the eighth gloss, however, may be of special interest to Elizabethans, both because of the mention of Holofernes and Judith as a parallel for Spain and Elizabeth, and because of the nickname of "mice" for the gentlemen sailors, familiar to us in the ballad celebrating Drake's adventures. Some may even be interested in the appearance of Armado and Holofernes in close proximity.

The passage in the *Spanish Masquerado* is as follows (*ibid.*, p. 274):

> Provided thus, as might be supposed for the conquest either of Asia or Africa, hee bendeth his course against England, a little Island, where as S. Augustine saith, their be people with Angels faces, so the Inhabitantes haue the courage and heartes of Lions: which poore Don Martines tried true: for God using ELIZABETH his servant and her subiectes as his instruments, to punish the enemies of his truth, no sooner came the proud Holofernes into our seas, but the mice crept out of little Betulia: Judith sitting peaceably in her royall seat; & incountring fiercely with their Foes, taught them that God fought on their side, then not to be daunted with multitudes: and *Martines* fearfull, shrunke away.

The eleventh and twelfth glosses are also relevant to our discussion. He describes the Spaniard, established in the Country of the American Indies by violence and knavery, bringing in his yearly harvest of gold. He says (*ibid.*, p. 282):

The Spaniard . . . straight out the Mines of golde, & causing the remnant of the Moores as slaues to digge in the mines, sent yearly with a great Fleet, much treasure from them into Spaine: which being blazed abroad through all the world, the report coming unto England, there rose vp a man of high and hardie resolution, Sir Francis Drake, who sent by her Maiestie to discouer that Countrie, not onlie found it out, but brought home great riches, and the same time as a warriour went, and malgrado of the Spaniard landed, entred vp into the country neer *Carthagene,* & *Sancto Domingo,* putting the Spaniard to the foyle, & the sword, brought home store of wealth and treasure, and getting by his valour such endles fame and glorie, as far surmounteth such momentanie trash: using the Moores, conquered, with such courtesie, as they thought the English Gods, and the Spaniards both by rule and conscience halfe Deuils. Sir *Francis Drakes* happie success in *India,* and the late losse of their Soueraignes Fleete, ioned together, sore danted the mindes of the *India* generals, that they sit as men discontented in their heartes; to whom is obiected (as in derision) the verses that *Virgill* wrote against Batillus.

Sic vos non vobis mellificatis Apes,
Sic vos non vobis Nidificatis Aues,
Sic vos non vobis fertis aratra Boues,
Sic vos non vobis vellera fertis Oues.

Meaning, that as the Bees make honye themselues, yet not for themselues, but men reape it to their vse, so the Spaniard digged out sweete honye from the golden Mines, and Sir *Francis Drake* fetched it home to be tasted in England, reaping his profite out of their labours: so that the *India* Generals are faine to beare this scoffe, *Sic vos non vobis.*

The final gloss has also a special interest for its bearing upon what is probably the most famous of all patriotic speeches upon the English stage. The series is concluded with these words (*ibid.,* p. 287):

Seeing then wee are euery way blest and fauoured from aboue: that the Lorde our mercifull God maketh England like Eden, a second Paradice: let us feare to offend him, and bee zealous to execute terrour of his commaundementes, then shall we be sure his Maiestie will send our Queene long life, his Church to have faithfull Ministers, and our Realme perfect Subiectes, and shroude vs against Spaine, the Pope, and all other enemies of the Gospell.

It is interesting to note that although Greene is speaking much about the Indian mines, he studiously avoids any word of praise for Ralegh. This is, of course, entirely consistent with Greene's known prejudice against the whole School of Night. The pictures to which the *Spanish Masquerado* must have been once attached, are now lost, but the chart attached to the *Birth, Purpose, and Mortall Wound of the Holy Romish League,* published by the same publisher, Thomas Cadman, forms so close a parallel as to suggest something more than a casual relationship. Thomas Cadman, one of the most interesting of the stationers at Paules, whose shop was at the *Sign of The Bible,* at the Great North Door, appears to have been one of the most active of the band of stationers who defied the Masters and Wardens of the Company, and resisted the decrees of the Star Chamber. (McKerrow, *Dictionary of Printers and Booksellers,* p. 60.) He was one of those who sold John Day's *A B C;* he was fined for selling Powell's edition of *Nostradamus,* and was constantly in trouble for disorderly conduct and quarreling with other stationers. Whether his quarrel was caused by business rivalry, or prompted by his too strident "beating of the patriotic drum," I know not; but it is clear that he welcomed political plays and pamphlets, for he had printed Lyly's *Campaspe,* in 1584, Greene's *Spanish Masquerado,* in 1589, and in the same year the crude, but entertaining pamphlet against the Holy League. The title page states that it was written by "I. L." Inasmuch as it was published the same year as *Midas,* whose sentiments it echoes exactly, and since the verse section is in the same stanza as much of Lyly's poetry, I see no obvious reason why it may not have been written by Lyly himself, though it must be admitted that the reputation of that courtly poet would not be enhanced by the acceptance of this popular piece into the canon of his work. The unique copy of this work is in the Bodleian Library. The pamphlet is in two parts, one prose, and the other verse, but both are, like the glosses of the *Spanish Masquerado,* little more than explanations of the accompanying *Mappe* or cartoon, illustrating, according to the title page, "the envie of Sathan's Shauelings, and the follie of their wisdom, through the Almighties prouidence." The cartoon repre-

Reproduced from a photostat of the original by permission of the *Bodleian Library*.

Death apeareth
M
B
C
I
E
K

sents various phases of the League, set out in pictures numbered alphabetically *A* to *M*.

A represents the Pope and the Devil in colloquy with the "shavelings" hatching up the plot of the Holy League, to be directed against all the Devil's foes, but especially his "Arch-enemies, Elizabeth Queene of England, & Henrie King of Navarre."

B and *C* represent the "inhumane massacres" of the Huguenots, instigated and directed by the Duke of Guise, whose "necessitie" is being "supplied with Spanish and Romish superfluetie," which "the Pope's messenger to whet him on, powrde . . . at his feete."

D shows Navarre "fortified from heaven, armed at all points like a Christian Chevelier," defending the Gospel.

E shows Elizabeth "crowned with a wreath of peace (making Christ her hope) as a Rocke vnmoveable."

F represents the Pope "whetting on" Philip of Spain "to discharge his abundance of Indian earth [Is this a misprint for *wealth?*] in reward for which the Pope traps "his very horse" with Bulls and Pardons.

In *G*, to the right of the Pope stands "that catiffe Cardinall" Allen, the "English Arch traitor, discharging from his Cannon of corrupt conceipt . . . two seditious Libels against his Soueraign to which the English Friers and Seminarie Priests give fire."

H represents the "horned Moone of huge and mighty shippes" sailing to meet

I, the Prince of Parma, whose soldiers are fleeing from him because of their terror of

K, the English Fleet.

L represents the Spaniards raking "the finest golde . . . out of the wretched Indaes wombe, whose senseless bowells [they] (slaue-like) ceaselessely teare out."

M: "But all this is vaine: for the breath of the Lord's mouth hath dimmed the brightness of her Moone, and scattered those proud shippes, whose masts seemed like Cedars to dare the Sunne, the treacherous Libels of traiterous *Allen*, are with himselfe, held infamous to the world: The Guise also (one of the greatest helpers) is dead deservedly." So, the Holy League, "being with these sorrowes surcharged, and mangled with manie maimes, she languisheth in a consumption on her bed. The Pope (on earth her chiefe Patrone) promiseth his helpe in what he maie, & feeling her pulses, assureth her there is yet good hope. But the Deuill belike being the better Doctor, and not louing to dissemble where his daughter was Patient, protests after he had cast her water, there was euident signe of death. Thus is this deuelish League deuised by the Deuill, and confirmed by the Pope, weakened and wasted through the spirit of Truth, &, &."

If the Stationers at Paules chatted with their friend Marlowe about this chart, we should not be surprised to find reverberations in one or several of Marlowe's plays. That we do find such reverberations in *The Jew of Malta,* I hope to prove in the ensuing pages.

First, however, I should like to draw attention to another pamphlet on the subject by Anthony Munday, a dramatist who was constantly employed as a propagandist, particularly against the Catholics, and whom, on one occasion, we have seen writing a play in deference to the wishes of one of the Ralegh circle, Lord Cobham. This pamphlet, which was a translation of a French original, was printed in 1592 by John Charlwood for Richard Smith. Charlwood and Smith were, like Cadman, stationers at Paul's; Smith's address was "at the Corner Shop at the North West Door of St. Paul's Church." Like Cadman, Smith was often in trouble for printing objectionable literature. *The Masque of the League and the Spaniard Discovered* was, however, entirely orthodox. It was addressed by Smith to "Mistress Dorothy Edmondes: one of the Gentlewomen of her Maiesties most honourable priuie Chamber." This pamphlet is a part of that series already referred to in which the French are admonished to drive out from their land

> . . . the crueltie and barbarisme of these *Scithians, Gothes* by nature, these *Moores* & *Sarrasin* Spaniards, whose first Fathers had theyr originall from the *Gothes,* and from hence thys League (the Mother of all mischiefe) that is heer so louingly cherished, had her beginning.

Describing the effect of the League in France, the pamphlet states:

It hath made Fraunce a den of thieues, murderers, robbers, and spoylers, such Monsters hath thys League prodigiously brought foorth; among infinite of the very worst sort is ignorance, malice, deceit, guile, hypocrisie, robbing, theft, incest, feigned Religion, all kind of execrations, murder, sacriledge and parricide.

Frenchmen are called upon to . . . "detest thys *Scithia,* to fly from this *Lybia,* whose Monsters strangle liuing men, as hath bene known and seene."

The League is jeeringly asked,

Holdest thou still this ancient withered *Sarasin* for thy support? puttest thou thy hope in the Duke of *Parma* and his Spaniards, who by nature use crueltie even towards their own followers, because they loue the League no better then they doe theyre Kings? thinkest thou yet to help thyselfe with thy Monks coule and hoode, to bath againe thy parricide hands in the blood royal? . . . Thy old Caball and coverture of Religion is as good to thee as nothing, this drugge was long since uttered and returns thee no profit . . . heerein is no vertue left to shielde thee from falling; at thys hooke and line, angling for the estates, thou fastnest sundrie licorish baytes, of Crosses, Miters, Dignities, Prelat-ship, Partages of Prouinces, Offices, Governments, and Great prerogatives, which thou promisest to destribute among such, as with thee doe cast the Nets for so rich a Fish.

Speaking of Philip II and his ancestors, the pamphlet continues [italics inserted]:

The first Fathers of *this halfe crowned Jewe* (who to thy proper ruine, and his own advancement, pluckes the hart out of thy bellie), . . . tooke Spayne by the like bayte, *feigning themselves religious, and men of good behaviour; so this old Foxe,* seeing himselfe readie to succeede his forefathers, hath practised, and doth practise the like in the vsurpation of this Crowne, hoping to make a bootie of it, and to tyrannize therein at his own pleasure; but that our noble Prince makes him let goe his holde, and surrender up the estates he proudly vsurpeth, namely, the Realme and estate of Navarre, sometime troden down by Ferdinand of Castile and Arragon, one of thy grandfathers.

The Elizabethan reader will not need to be reminded of a bitter dramatization of this angle of Spanish history in Green's *Alphonsus, King of Arragon.* He may, however, be less conscious of a similar application to be made in the case of the anonymous *Alphonsus, Emperor of Germany*. Speaking of the grotesque distortion of history in this play, Professor Mark Parrott says *(Tragedies of Chapman,* p. 687):

> The motive that lay at the back of this wild distortion of the facts of history is plain enough to the student of Elizabethan literature. It is the fierce anti-Spanish and anti-Papal prejudice that burnt so hotly in England from a few years before the coming of the Armada till some time after the death of Elizabeth. To an Englishman steeped in this prejudice the mere fact that a Spaniard had once been the rival of an Englishman for the Imperial throne was enough to warrant the assumption that the Spaniard was a villain of the blackest dye, a perjurer, a poisoner, a stabber, in short, the perfect Machiavellian; and the picture of Alphonsus in this play has been drawn in perfect conformity with this prejudice.

Of the style and date of this play, Professor Parrott writes (*ibid.,* p. 688):

> This prosaic author is a playwright of no mean merit. *Alphonsus* is not, of course, a tragedy in the true sense of the word; it is crude, superficial, and notably devoid of characterization or internal struggle; but it has many of the merits of first-class melodrama, an interesting story clearly told, vigorous dialogue, thrilling climaxes, and a catastrophe at once surprising, overwhelming, and wholly satisfactory to the popular demand for "poetic justice." It is impossible to determine accurately the date of *Alphonsus,* but it must certainly have been written many years before the performance of 1636. The style of the blank verse, the choice of subject, and the dramatic treatment, all point back to a time not much later than the epoch-making work of Marlowe.

In other words, the play should be classed with *Locrine, Selinus, The Battle of Alcazar, Lust's Dominion, Edward I,* and, perhaps, *Titus Andronicus.* As Professor Parrott points out, fairness to history, much less to one's opponent, was entirely out of the question, and he rightly cites Peele's slander of the "good Queen Eleanor" as a case in point.

The relation of *Alphonsus* to the pamphlet under discussion is obvious. The author, now addressing the League itself, continues [italics inserted]:

Thy Masque cannot hide thee from being noted for a most disloyal and infernall Furie . . . thou doost but lye, when thou tearmest thyself a Christian and a Saint.

The mercinarie tongues of thy false Preachers, with all theyr Cosenage and impostures, are other sophisticall wares of slender valewe. . . .

Thus by Monkes thou inurest the estate which thou wouldest dismember and divide among those Coniurers. . . .

And because the Spanish hypocrisie, the shadow of Atheisme, is one of the principall pillars of thy contrived conspiracie, and thou makest men to believe . . . *that these Moores are good Catholics, and theyr followers religious* . . . *So many abuses & mischiefes hath been committed by these counterfeit hypocrites, these scellerous and hooded murthers* [that a man of great learning] both despised and disproved openly such Beggars, alleadging that their poverty was vowed without cause, and that he would maintaine such manner of life, to be but a pretext of Religion, and only fit for such beggars as desired to live in loosenes and idlenes. . . . But if wee would see how thay [the Spaniards] have imployed their industrie, *to make themselves renowned with the Prototype, first patterne and mould of all barbarous crueltie:* let us read the hystorie of the horrible insolencies and detestable tyrannies exercised by them of late memorie in the West Indiaes, vnder the raigne of Charles the fift, and Phillip his sonne, thy *Atlas* and thy chiefest Minnion. Thys Historie is written by a Spaniard himself named *D. F. Bartholemew de los Casas,* a religious man and a Bishop, and out of the Castilliane tongue, was turned into French,* . . . Was never seene such outrages, such impieties, wracke of Religion, corruption, licentiousness, and Atheisme? Thou prophanest iustice . . . thou makest the Catholic Religion the Goddess of Warre, that strikes, spoyles, and kylles.

It is difficult, from the wealth of illustration afforded in this pamphlet to make a judicious selection of just those passages which will best confirm the analysis which I am offering herewith for *The Jew of Malta.* In my choice, I have tried to emphasize the habitual merging of Jew with Moor and Turk, to signify Spanish cruelty and Catholic iniquity in general, and the ambitious knavery of Philip in particular; for these are,

* Munday adds, in a marginal note: "And is likewise in English by the name of *The Spanish.* . . ." The last word has been mutilated by the trimming of the margin.

I believe, the qualities which Marlowe intended us to see in Barabas, Ithamore, and the outrageous friars.

Before presenting to the reader an analysis of one more pamphlet, the *Satire Ménipée,* which was translated into English in 1593, it will be necessary to gather up a few threads in the history of the League.

The vicissitudes of the League's warfare against Henry III need not be told in detail. Suffice it for us to know that after the battle known as the Day of Barricades (12 May, 1588), the Guise was master of Paris, forcing Henry to treat with him. The latter actually signed the Edict of Union at Rouen on 10 July, 1588, by which he ratified the League, gave various offices of trust to the Guise, made him Lieutenant General of the Kingdom in opposition to the Protestants, barred Henry of Navarre from succession to the throne and promised the immediate convocation of the States General. When they assembled, however, at Blois (September-December, 1588), it became clear to the King that the Guise was leading not a religious, but a political movement, and against him, the King. Henry was treated throughout as "a sluggard king," while Guise was the idol of the whole party. At this, Henry determined to rid himself of his rival, and so on 23 December, 1588, the Guise was murdered by the King's guards. When the King was sure the Guise was dead, we are told, he left his apartment to kick the dead man in the face! On the same night Louis, the Cardinal, brother of the Duke of Guise, was also assassinated. This left the Duke of Mayenne as the only remaining Guise to be reckoned with. As Governor of Burgundy, Mayenne had raised his province for the League, and at his brother's death was still in command of a considerable army. The King, who was still officially on the side of the Catholics against Navarre, tried to negotiate with Mayenne against their common enemy, but the surviving Guise naturally distrusted the murderer of his brothers, and nothing came of the attempt at reconciliation. Before another year was out, i.e., 1 August, 1589, Henry III himself was assassinated by a crazed Dominican monk, Jacques Clement. Henry's mother, Catherine de Medici, had died eight months before (5 January, 1589).

The throne was now vacant, and both parties roused themselves for a final drive to establish the succession. Mayenne was the natural leader of the extreme Catholic group, and, like his brother, assumed the title of Lieutenant General of the kingdom. His most serious obstacle was not to be found in the troops of Navarre, but in a group within his own party, or rather, perhaps one should say, a group that was officially Catholic, but anti-Guisan, and so against the League. This Catholic minority group, known as *Les Politiques,* was led by Henry, third Duke of Montmorency, who was then head of the family most inimical to the House of Guise. The motives of Montmorency may have been largely personal animosity, but the emotion that cemented this group into a powerful opposition was hatred of Spain, whose acquisitive shadow had been lowering on the horizon ever since Philip undertook to finance the League. The *Politiques* now girded their loins for a desperate resistance to Philip's machinations to get the throne of France for Spain. Their political game was to oust the Spanish claimant by "converting" Navarre to Catholicism and so removing all possible objection to his succession, which had already been promised by the dying words of Henry III. It was, in fact, this intense anti-alien feeling that gave rise to the bitter anti-Spanish pamphlets to which we have referred.

Philip's claims must now be examined. When the nominal Catholic heir-presumptive, the aged Cardinal de Bourbon, died on 8 May, 1590, the Leaguers were truly embarrassed in having no candidate, and it was at this point that Philip stepped in to supply one. He would marry his daughter, the Infanta Isabella, who was the granddaughter of Henry II through her mother, Elizabeth of Valois, to Charles, the young son of Henry of Guise, now fourth Duke. She was born in 1566, so that in 1592, the latest possible date for *The Jew of Malta,* she was twenty-six years old and still unmarried. We are told that her father had quite a peculiar affection for her and that he initiated her into the gravest secrets of state and still called her on his death-bed "the light and mirror of his eyes." Brantôme says *(Le Grand Larousse, s.v., Isabelle Clair Eugenie):* "She was a princess of gentle spirit, who entered into all the schemes of the king her father, and was thereby much harmed."

As early as 1580, when Isabella was only fourteen years old,

Philip began scheming to secure a throne for her. His first choice was naturally James VI of Scotland, since by such a match she would not only be made Queen of Scots, but, in the event of James's succeeding to the English throne, would actually sit in the seat of the "arch-heretic" Elizabeth. The Spanish State Papers of 1580-1582 are filled with references to this proposed match. Philip had, of course, an eager ally in James's mother, Mary Stuart, but one whose hands were much tied as to the arrangements for her son's marriage. She not only lent the scheme her full approval while she had even that small power, but almost her last act was to "will" her son and her kingdom to Philip for the Infanta.* The obvious reason that the match was not effected during James's minority was that neither his mother nor her co-plotters (Philip, Don John of Austria, the Pope, and the third Duke of Guise) could actually manage to seize the person of the young King, who was so carefully guarded by the Protestant lords, his guardians, whose particular business it was to keep him from the influence of his mother. The Spanish correspondence shows that one of the chief instruments chosen for this difficult job of abducting the King, was Henry, third Duke of Guise; but, as all the world knows, nothing came of it, largely because there was no assurance that James would risk his succession to the English throne by marrying a Catholic princess, even though she happened to have a correct lineal line, through John of Gaunt.

By 1584 Philip had given up James as a forlorn hope and turned his attention to what he considered the second best throne on the horizon, namely, that of France. As we have seen, the death of Anjou, in 1584, made Henry of Bourbon, the Protestant King of Navarre, the most likely heir-presumptive to Henry III; and forthwith, with almost inconceivable impudence, considering that Navarre was both Protestant and already married to Margaret of Valois, offered him the hand of the Infanta, glibly guaranteeing to use his influence with the Pope for the divorce from Margaret that would be necessary.†

* These plans are referred to in various letters to be found in the *Calendar of State Papers, Spanish, 1580-1586,* pp. 4-6, 13, 309.

† These negotiations are referred to in Dryden's *History of the Holy League,* p. 183; in Edward Edwards' *Life and Letters of Sir Walter Ralegh,* I, pp. 255, 291-93; and in *The Last of the Valois,* by Catherine Charlotte, Lady Jackson, Boston, 1896, II, p. 167, *et passim.*

Navarre, however, proved as intractable as James had, and refused the offer; so once more the Infanta was placed in an unflattering situation. In retaliation for such ingratitude on Henry's part, Philip instructed his ambassador at the Conference of Soissons to urge that Navarre be excluded from the succession, on the ground of his being a Protestant. All Europe watched in a mood of cynical amusement to see where Philip would try next. Gossip was rife in England about a possible English husband for her, the suggestion reaching even as impossible a capture as Essex. Essex in his turn, did not scruple to charge Cecil with having intrigued to sell England to the Infanta's claims.

There remained on the Continent four possible candidates: Archduke Ernst of Austria; his brother Matthias, famed hero of the Turkish war; the Duke of Mayenne; and the fourth Duke of Guise. A word should be said concerning this possible Hapsburg alliance. Ernst was the second son of the Emperor Maximilian II, and Maria, daughter of Charles V. His older brother succeeded his father as Emperor Rudolph II, but his other brothers, Matthias and Albert, play a larger part in our story than either Ernst or Rudolph: Matthias, Governor General of the Netherlands, 1578-1581, was associated throughout his career with a policy of cruelty towards the Protestants; and Albert, who became Archduke of Austria at the death of his brother Ernst, in 1595. Their sister Elizabeth had married Charles IX of France. As to Matthias, there is no actual record of his being offered the Infanta, though he would have been a choice preferable to his young brother, who finally got her.

Now we must turn to the Conference of Soissons where Philip, while ruminating the question of the Infanta's husband, managed, through the instrumentality of the Duke of Feria, to insinuate that the throne of France really belonged to Isabella in her own right. To this end Philip finally made up his mind to offer her to the young Duke of Guise, believing that with his help the League would make the Guise King of France. This plan might actually have matured had the Duke of Mayenne not interfered, probably from jealousy at seeing the throne slip from his grasp; he would have been as good a candidate as Guise, if he had not been tied by a marriage which it would have taken some time to dissolve. He therefore frustrated the alliance between the Guise and the Infanta by securing passage of a decree of Parliament forbidding the transfer of the crown to any foreign princes or princesses, thus ruling out Philip's hopes forever. It was the first step in the banishment of all ultramontane pretensions in France, a goal which was not finally achieved until after the dissolution of the League and the signing of the Treaty of Cateau-Cambrésis, 2 May, 1598. Philip, however, admitted his defeat when, in 1597, he married the Infanta, at the sober age of thirty-one, to the Cardinal-Archduke Albert of Austria, the younger brother of Ernst and Matthias. Albert was then Governor of the Low Countries, which Philip gave as his daughter's dowry.

We must return now, in our survey, to the winter following the death of the Cardinal de Bourbon, 1590-91. As we have noted, the Leaguers were uncertain where the election would light, whether on Guise or Mayenne, on Ernst or Matthias; but one thing was certain: they would hold out till death against the Protestant King of Navarre. Especially loyal were the citizens of Paris, who had been under siege by Navarre's troops since 28 March, 1590. The city was under the temporary government of the Spanish Ambassador, Bernardino de Mendoza, acting for the Duke of Mayenne, who was at Meaux, trying to effect a juncture with Alessandro Farnese, the Duke of Parma, Governor, for the time being, of the Spanish Low Countries. This was the famous Siege of Paris, which was endured by the starving citizens for more than four months. Fantastic are the tales of their suffering and the exalted heroism of their stubborn resistance; but they need not be told here. Finally, on 23 August, word came that Farnese had joined Mayenne at Meaux, and Henry was compelled to raise the siege in order to meet these new forces at Chelles on the Marne. The city was revictualled, Navarre was compelled to retire without giving his soldiers the satisfaction of pillaging the richest city in the kingdom, and Mayenne entered Paris on 18 September, 1590. Arrangements were quickly set afoot for the election of a successor to the Cardinal-King, Charles X (by grace of the League); and the new Pope, Clement VIII, sent a legate to assist at the assembly of the States of Paris. Meanwhile the Vicomte de

Turenne was traveling through England, Holland, and Germany, negotiating in Henry's name and seeking aid in troops and money for the support of the cause of the Huguenot King of France. Elizabeth sent both, first secretly, then finally, in 1591, openly despatching an auxiliary force under Essex, who pursued a fruitless campaign there until he was recalled from the command in January, 1592. The last years of the League are full of events and personalities of intense interest to the student of Shakspere and Chapman: the defection of the Marêchal Biron, the reconciliation of Mayenne with Navarre; Navarre's capitulation to Catholicism at St. Denis on 23 July, 1593, with much else; but these events are subsequent to *The Jew of Malta,* and therefore must be ruled out of this brief account of what I believe to be the background, and indeed the subject of that play.

Before going on to give my application of all this material to *The Jew of Malta,* I should like to mention another treatment of this subject that offers, I believe, an exceedingly interesting parallel to our play. I refer to the *Satire Ménipée,* published in Paris, in 1593, and translated into English the same year. The full title was *Le Satyre Ménippée de la Vertu du Catholicon d'Espagne et de la Terme des Etats de Paris.* This was the joint production of a group of ex-Catholics, chiefly lawyers, and is a rowdy satire upon the assembly of the States at Paris when they met for the purpose of electing a successor to the Cardinal-King. The name is borrowed from the *Satira Menippea* of the Roman Satiric poet Varro, who had taken as a model the Greek cynic Menippus, Diogenes' pupil. The burlesque opens with a description of a drug such as that already aluded to in *The Masque of the League.* It is a magic charm, or "simple," imported from Morocco where it is known as *Higuiero;* but in Spain it is called *Catholicon.* It was brought thither by the King of Morocco and there "sophisticated" by the Jesuits in their College, "so well that by dint of touching, handling, refining, burning, and sublimating it," they had "composed from it . . . an infallible *electuaire,* which surpasses every philosophic stone." * It seems clear that Higuiero or Catholicon

* *Satyre Ménippée,* 1593 edition, p. 10. This and all passages that follow were translated by my friend and former pupil, Miss Eleanor Renner, Bryn Mawr, 1932.

stands for Catholicism in general (particularly the mysteries of the Sacraments) and for the League in particular. The opening harangue assures the audience that they may be as "nefarious," as "atheistic" as they like, for—says the speaker—you have only to "wash yourself with the water of Higuiero, and there you are, an immaculate lamb, and a pillar of the faith."

Somewhat earlier in this introduction, the speaker describes "two charlatons, one Spanish and the other Lorrain," sitting on daises in the Louvre. To the dais of the Spanish Charlaton was attached "a great skin of parchment, written in several languages, sealed with five or six seals of gold, and lead, and wax, with the titles in letters of gold bearing these words 'Letters of power of a Spaniard, and of the miraculous effects of his drug called Higuiero, or of compounded Catholicon.' "

Then follows what purports to be an account of the "States of the League assembled at Paris in the month of January, 1593." The Assembly is opened by a procession in which all the chief members of the League and their families march, "the Duke of Mayenne, Lieutenant of the State and Crown of France, the Duke of Guise, the Constable of Aumâle, the Princes of Lorrain, and other deputies from Spain, Flanders, Naples, and other cities of the Union, with Mme. de Nemours, representing the Queen Mother, or grandmother *(in dubio)* of the future king . . . Mme. the dowager of Montpensier [she who was said to advise exhuming the dead for food during the Siege of Paris], . . . and Mme. the wife of the Lieutenant of the State and Crown of France, followed by Mmes. de Belin and de Bussi le Clerc."

Following the account of this procession, there is a mock description of the tapestries with which the hall of the Assembly was hung, each tapestry portraying some betrayal of the French cause. A sample or two of these must suffice to give a notion of the quality of the satire and of the fustian under which it was bodied forth. One represented "the disasters of Icarus and Phaeton . . . exceedingly well worked out: it was very beautiful to see the sisters of this youth change themselves into poplar trees, one of them, who had broken her hip in running to save her brother, naïvely resembled the dowager of Montpensier, all disheveled and distressed."

The first piece of tapestry next to the dais, "was the story of the golden calf, as it is described in Exodus, xxxii, where Moses and Aaron were represented by the defunct King Henry the Third, and the late Cardinal de Bourbon: but the golden calf was in the form of the late Duke of Guise, raised loftily and adored by the people; the two tables bore the fundamental law of the States of Blois and the Edict of July, 1587, and at the base of the piece were written these words, *In die vltionis visitabo & hoc peccatum eorum.*

"The fourth represented mainly the feats of arms of ancient and modern assassins, otherwise called Bedouins and Arsacides, who did not fear to go as far as the chamber, and as far as the very bed to kill those whom their imaginary Prince Aloadin, surnamed the old man of the six or seven mountains, commanded them."

This refers, of course, to the murder of the Admiral Coligny. Another section of the fourth tapestry represented the murder of Henry III, "a king of France . . . struck by a knife by a debauched zealot, a Monk, who was on his knees, presenting a letter. On the forehead of the said monk was written in great letters the anagram of his name, brother Jacques Clement, 'It is Hell which has created me.' "

Many of these pictures and the comments on them are too obscene for quotation.

"The twelfth and last above the windows contained the portrait of M. le Lieutenant, very well drawn of his length, dressed as Hercules Gallacus, holding in his hand numberless reins, by which were haltered lambs also without number. . . . "

The long description of these tapestries is followed by a mock speech by M. le Lieutenant, in which he brags of all his crimes, particularly his part in the Siege of Paris, comparing himself to the Jewish zealots Simon and John, who also ". . . had more inventions and disguisements of motives to make the poor people of Jerusalem obstinately continue to die of famine than I have had to make thousands of souls within this city of Paris die the same death, even so that mothers have eaten their children as they did in that sacred city."

M. le Lieutenant claims further:

> Instead of its being necessary for me to go and seek and send a master to Flanders, it was there that I changed my French clothing for a Spanish cape, and gave my soul to the Southern Demons to deliver that which I hold more dear within this city: but I would have made myself valet to Lucifer, as well as to the Duke of Parma, to wreak spite on the heretics. . . . I would rather a hundred times make myself a Turk or Jew with the good grace and permission of our holy father, then see these relapsing into heresy, return to enjoy their goods, which you and I enjoy with just title, and with good faith by year and by day—even more.

Then Monsieur le Legat pleads for the Infanta:

> I know truly that you will have done a most gratifying deed for our Lord the Pope, and the sainted Apostolic seats and for my most Christian and Catholic benefactor, the king of Spain and of all kingdoms, if you save the leadership of the British "Amoricae" for his Infanta, his most illustrious daughter: the kingdom you surely assemble for some leader out of this family, whom that one will wish to choose as a husband, and the Crown of France is worthy for a dowery *"in solidum utrique competenti."* . . . In short, make a king, for the sake of my love. I do not care whom it may be, be he the devil, so long as it be a servant and vassal of his Holiness and of the Catholic King, through whose efforts I have been made Cardinal, thanks to the good Duke of Parma. But I say to you that my vote would be gladly given for the Infanta of Spain, because she is a worthy lady, and much loved by her father: nothing indeed could give such pleasure to the Signor Duke of Feria and M. le Lieutenant.

With Rabelaisian irony he scoffs at the notion that Philip might be grabbing for himself:

> Would you think, indeed, that he who is lord of so many kingdoms which he is unable to count by the letters of the alphabet, as Charlemagne could his monasteries, and so rich that he doesn't know what to make of his treasures, would wish to put himself only in the pain of longing for such a little thing as the sovereignty of France? All Europe, so to speak, is not to him a region of these new islands [of the Caribbean] won over from the savages. When he sweats, he sweats diadems: when he blows his nose, he blows crowns; when he belches, he belches sceptres: . . . [*causa pudoris*] . . . His demeanor toward the Low Countries and toward the New Lands ought to assure you that he thinks of no evil, no more than an old monkey. If it should happen thus, that he should have made all of

you kill one another, and perish by fire, sword, and famine, would you not be happy to be seated there high in Paradise above the Confessors and Patriarchs, mocking the Protestant soldiers whom you will see below you roasting and boiling in the steam boilers of Lucifer?

When M. de Lyon speaks, he refers to the followers of Guise who

. . . are obliged by gaiety of heart to follow their part, even had they made themselves Turks, as it is said: they prefer to be traitors to their king and to the country than fail in respect to the word of a master who himself is a valet and subject of a king.

All these mock speeches are followed by the intentionally serious remarks of M. le Rector Roze, formerly Bishop of Senlis. He takes the floor as spokesman against the Leaguers, and the general purport of his words is a warning against the Infanta (*ibid.*, p. 130):

They promise you this divine Infanta in marriage to make her a Queen of Spain *in solidum* with you; and take care that the Duke of Feria doesn't fill his blank notes without orders. He has a full case of them which he uses on all occasions, like a form for every shoe, and a saddle for all horses. He dates them or ante-dates them with his urinal when it pleases him. I fear something that he has proposed to us, which may be but an artifice to amuse when he has seen that we do not wish to listen to breaking the Salic law.

The text here is extremely obscure, and in the edition from which I have been quoting, is even obliterated in part; but the sense of the passage seems to be that he has heard that the Infanta has already been promised to the Archduke Ernst, and he adds: "Those of the House of Austria act like Jews, who marry only among themselves, and hold themselves together by the rump like may-bugs." He urges the delegates to dismiss the "vain hope" of this alliance, for it is nothing but a myth:

"Small children mock at it and already joke about it. I heard one the other day, who leaving a tavern, sang this quatrain quite softly:

The League had no wife. No excuse!
The Leaguers, astounded, uprose,
They bethought themselves of a ruse,
To create a king lacking nose."

It is evident from many of the jibes at Ernst that his countenance suffered from a deficiency of nose, and it is more than possible that an added insult was intended by implying that syphilis was the cause. The speech goes on to ridicule the Infanta as the "wife of the League":

What would you say of these impudent politicians who have put a likeness of you on a sheet of paper, already crowned as King of Diamonds in anticipation, and on the same sheet have put the likeness of the divine Infanta, crowned as Queen of France, like you, the two of you regarding one another face to face? And at the bottom of the said painting they have put these verses which I have learned by heart, because they are about you:

The Spanish Frenchmen made a king of France:
To the Infanta of Spain they promised this King—
Royalty, indeed, small, and of little importance,
For Paris enclosed is the France of their liking.
Do not bring this time for the cold marriage,
Oh Hymen! Nuptial God, your calm flame.
From these corpses, which both in love engage
With their eyes in the painting, we gather that same.
It is a royalty only in guise.
They are wed by the Pope, not by love.
To be king of France in a painting is wise,
When the queen is the picture above.

He then addresses Mayenne directly (*ibid.*, p. 135):

And you, M. le Lieutenant (to whom it is now necessary that I speak) what do you think you are doing? You are fat and dull; you are heavy and decrepit. You have a head big enough to carry a crown, but what! you say that you don't want it at all, and that it would burden you too much. The politicians say the fox spoke so of the grapes. What shall we do then? We must have a king; as the political doctors say, "Better be summoned than sought." You make the King of Spain believe that you protect the kingdom of France for him, and for his daughter, with this hope you collect from the good man all that which the Indies and Peru send him; he fills your plate for you. . . . Besides (*ibid.*, p. 139), you can not be king by marriage with the Infanta, if you don't do what you advised the legation; you are married and put your finger on the gap. For you have been astride the old girl, who guards herself well from the old buck; and then another chimney sweep, other than you, would be necessary for this bitch of thirty years, black as pepper, with an unreserved appetite, and dressed in what you will.

He describes Philip's character as that of a mean employer of servants (*ibid.*, pp. 261, 264):

For instead of master, you made yourself valet and slave of the most insolent nation under the sky. You are under the subjection of the most proud and ambitious man that you knew how to choose, as you have since experienced when he made you [amble? . . . the page is torn here] . . . after him and wait at his door, before making you an answer of little importance . . . and don't doubt that if through means of you he were made master of the kingdom, he wouldn't rid himself of you by poison, calumnies or otherwise, for that is the way he uses, and by which he ordinarily says that it is necessary to recompense those who betray their prince and their country.

The reader is asked to bear this passage specially in mind for later comparison with Barabas and Ithamore. Philip's reputation as a poisoner is further glanced at (*ibid.*, p. 267):

If they like the Catholic religion so much, and hate those who are not of it, how can he endure the Jews and the Marrans in his countries? How can he make peace with the Turks and the Mohammedans of Africa, from whom he accepts peace very dearly? His Spies, the Jesuit Scopetins, are no longer necessary, since we come to buy the trifles of Saint Jacques. The game is too clear. The Duke of Feria has revealed his memoirs gradually, a piece at a time, how he carried from Africa (a country rich in poisons and venoms), by the command of his master, a box full of different drugs of diverse qualities: one which kills rapidly, another which kills slowly, another more prompt in summer, another which takes effect better in winter, in order that he may avail himself of them in respect to us according to the occasions and the events: having charged that we be given one if he finds us disposed in one such humour, or another if he finds us otherwise. Before we had made clear that we would wish to retain the Salic Law (one which the kingdom of France has maintained for a thousand years in its strength and vigour), they told us of the rare virtues of this divine Infanta, in order to designate her as heir to the Crown. When they saw that we wished to keep this ancient custom of the cocks [succession through the male line only], they offered to give her to the Prince whom we shall elect king, and the above intrigues were for the

Archduke Ernst, whom she was destined to marry. Then when they perceived that this Ernst was not at all the armour that fitted us, they spoke of a Prince of France to whom they would marry the Infanta, and whom they would make king of France *in solidum*. For all this, there are memoirs and mandates apropos, signed by the king's own hand. M. le Legat serves as messenger to value the merchandise, for he has not come here for any other end than to ruin France or to make it fall in pieces, since he is Cardinal only through the favour of the King of Spain. . . .

This ends the serious speech; the tone changes again to the satirical burlesque of the introduction, this time describing the paintings on the staircase of the Louvre, with their legends. One of these shows *(ibid.,* p. 304),

. . . a king, entirely surrounded by crowns distributed here and there, and within his arms a daughter no longer young, who seemed to regard the combat of the woman and the doctor to await the issue. On one hand between the setting sun and the south scattered a little rain of gold which fell among these doctors, each of whom was amusing himself in gathering it, and others already had their hoods filled with it. I suspect that this portrait intends to represent the Salic Law, fought by Dom Inigo of Mandosse, with his harangue made and procured from Spain.

I subjoin a few of the verses attached to these pictures *(ibid.,* p. 314); they are particularly fatuous, though it is possible that the originals would strike a sixteenth-century French ear more tunefully than they do ours. If the situation were reversed, it is hardly likely that a Frenchman, even of the sixteenth century, would catch much melody or much sense from a political jingle like the following on Cardinal Wolsey:

Then was I led toward Court like
Dog in string,
And brought as beef, that Butcher-row
Must see.

So fell I sick, consumed as some
Did think;
So took in haste my chamber and my bed.
To fawning dogs sometimes I gave a bone,
And flung some scraps to such as nothing had,
But in my hands still kept the golden gad,
That served my turn, and laughed the rest to scorn.

Yet, when this poem was published in *The Mirror for Magistrates,* in 1587, its author, Thomas Churchyard, was so well esteemed as a poet that Nashe declared *(Foure Letters Confuted)* that his (Churchyard's) aged muse might well be "grandmother to our grandiloquentest poets at this present." *Sic transit gloria!*

On the Spaniards and their Doubloons

My God, how gold and beautiful
Are your doubloons!
You make them searching still
The darkened coons
Among your yellow, scoring dunes.
Indeed you are returning them,
After sun-burning them.
Paris, which is not your prey as you suppose,
Now shows
Your reflection with a hundred feet of nose.

Of Two Who Court Royalty [Ernst and Mayenne]

Two are in quest with a kingdom for goal,
But their appetite for it soon goes;
One 'cause his head is as big as a bowl,
While the other has too little nose.

The Doctors of the League

The Doctors of the League of Rome
By foolish doctrines hope
To make a Spanish mantel come
Out of religion's cope.

There is more nonsense about Higuiero, this time insinuating a terrific satire on the Blessed Sacrament, too blasphemous to quote. This whole Supplement strikes us as *Hudibras* did Pepys. We have tried to read it dispassionately, but the blasphemy and the obscenity so far outstink the wit that we forbear to quote further. The whole concludes (*ibid.,* p. 550) with a

. . . picture of the wife of the League or the Infanta of Spain, seated on high . . . [torn page] . . . ready to go and take to task the first who will be provided, confirmed, and recognized by the

Holy Union for the King of France; below the said portrait was written that which follows:

> Although I am dark-skinned, for such
> My friend, do not loathe me nor hate,
> For I long to love as much
> As one who is fairer by fate.

There is a final jibe at the Insignia of the League which is not at all clear, but which I quote for the possible parallel with the famous hat of Barabas *(ibid.,* p. 550):

> The sixteen, being reduced to the number of twelve, each one carried the favours of his future wife, such as follow: A collar of the order of the reprobate of the Apostles, from which hangs as an insignia the image of a purse, within which are some round pills, composed of the finest drug of the Catholicon of Spain, each of the weight and value of a dozen *tours livre* (worth about 10 pence); a bonnet of speckled scarlet . . . furred with the skin of . . . [torn page] . . . which served as a doubler for one of his old under-petticoats, to which bonnet was attached one of the plumes of the cock which sings at the spit to serve them as an alarm clock: all of which was sent from Spain for great excellence.

The *Satire Ménippée* not only gave the last blow to Philip's ambitious projects for his daughter, but made that poor lady forever ridiculous in the eyes of Europe, particularly those haunting the marriage-market.

It was, I believe, in the spirit of the *Ménippée,* with *The Birth* and *The Masque* in the background, that *The Jew of Malta* was written. It is rollicking satire, combining fierceness with fun, and, happily, in proportions that leave the fun far in the lead. This is not the *Tragedy* of the Jew of Malta, but, in the most classic sense of the words, a *Satiric Comedy,* and, so far as I know, the best example of it in the English language. Marlowe has been, I think, unfortunate in having attracted the attention of peculiarly heavy-gaited editors. For the most part, they are, like Theridamus and Usumcasane, quite incapable of catching the rich comic vein in much of the so-called romantic ecstasy of Marlowe's protagonists. Even after it has been pointed out, as at least in this case it has been, by Mr. T. S. Eliot (*Sacred Wood,* p. 84), they will have none of it. The fooling is on too big, too Rabelaisian a scale to be credible to their academic minds, or acceptable to their "modern finicky stomachs," and this in spite of the fact that Marlowe shows no penchant for the *obscénité érudite* of the French. In calling it a farce, Mr. Eliot came nearer the spirit of *The Jew of Malta* than anyone has; but it is more than farce. It combines the richest vein of ridicule, the subtlest *double entendre,* with a perfect farcical plot, utilizing the best of comic inventions in the final débâcle of the Jew, who had, up to the last moment, succeeded in outwitting everyone else. I feel that unless we approach this play with an understanding of the boisterous anti-Spanish, anti-Catholic temper that burned in the breasts of most patriotic Englishmen after the Armada, we shall miss the point of it altogether. At this point of our argument we need hardly emphasize the fact that this spirit was characteristic of Ralegh and his Devonian privateers.

Of the literary sources of *The Jew of Malta* even less is known than in the case of *Tamburlaine.* Certain scholars believe the inspiration for the character of Barabas came from the adventurous history of Juan Miques, a notorious Portuguese Jew of the sixteenth century. Mr. H. S. Bennet gives the following account of him *(The Jew of Malta,* ed. Case, 1931, pp. 9-10):

> We have no certain knowledge of any book or event which led Marlowe to write *The Jew of Malta,* but two important theses have been advanced to account for its appearance.
>
> The first of these, by L. Kellner *(Englische Studien,* 1887, X, 80ff.) is based on the adventurous history of a Portuguese Jew who achieved great notoriety in the sixteenth century. Juan Miques or Michesius is to be heard of in various countries. "The illustrious Republic of Venice, the mighty kingdom of Spain, the conceited government of France, and even the haughty Papacy, all saw themselves endangered by him." (Graetz, *History of the Jews,* IV, p. 632.) Finally he settled down in Constantinople about 1555, where he became an ally and friend of the Sultan Selim II, over whom he seems to have acquired great influence. He plotted continuously against the Christians, and was made Duke of Naxos and the Cyclades, assuming the name of Joseph Nassi. He was led to believe that he might become King of Cyprus and hoped to establish a new Jewish state in Palestine on the sea of Tiberias. We are told that on the strength of a half-promise given by the Sultan, he had prepared a

crown and a banner bearing the words "Josephus Rex Cypri." (Foglietta, *De Sacro Foedere in Selimum,* quoted by Kellner, p. 97.) He was undoubtedly a man of tremendous power, since he had the complete confidence of Selim II, but he was surrounded by enemies, many of them of European nationality, for Nassi's schemes offended and attacked many great states. Kellner argues that this brilliant figure arrested the attention of Marlowe and was the prototype of Barabas.

Others, notably Professor Tucker-Brooke, see a more likely model in David Passi, who was, in some way, concerned with the Turkish wars on Malta. His summary is as follows (*Times Literary Supplement,* June, 1922; Bennet, *op. cit.,* p. 11):

I believe that considerably more similarity to Marlowe's Barabas is found in the character of a later Jew of Constantinople, David Passi, whose career reached its culmination, after half-a-dozen years of European notoriety, in March, 1591, some eleven months before the earliest extant reference to *The Jew of Malta*. . . . This David, more distinctly than Joseph Nassi at an earlier period, was involved in the Turkish designs on Malta; and . . . instead of [adopting] Joseph's consistently anti-Christian attitude, he pursued a boggling policy, playing off Turk against Christian after the fashion of Marlowe's Barabas. He was closely connected with English diplomacy in the Mediterranean, and was a person of particular interest to English political observers. What I know of David Passi is derived chiefly from records digested in the Calendar of State Papers. These, of course, cannot have been known to Marlowe: but the essential facts about Passi are not likely to have been unfamiliar to Marlowe who had the privilege of conversation with such connoisseurs of English foreign policy as Ralegh and the Walsinghams.

Whether or not either of these famous Jews furnished Marlowe with the fustian for his satire on Philip and the Infanta has not been, perhaps cannot be, determined by documentary proof, but Professor Tucker-Brooke's suggestion seems a happy one, and far the likelier of the two, in spite of the modesty with which it has been broached. At all events, as in the case of *Tamburlaine,* the establishment of the precise literary sources is not essential to the discussion in hand, since it is abundantly clear, I believe, that the real prototypes were the Spanish King and his cruelly exploited daughter. The choice of Malta for his fustian scene of action is explicable on several grounds: (1) Malta was a Spanish dependency, and, during the years of the Holy League, especially identified with the policies of the Guisans, since the position of Grand Prior of the Knights of Malta was held by Francis of Guise, a younger brother of the second Duke of Guise; (2) Malta had recently been through a famous siege (1565) not unlike the one just terminated between the forces of the Holy League and Navarre; and (3) the adventures of David Passi in Malta were suggestive of Philip's shameless infidelities to his religious position for the sake of a politically advantageous marriage for the Infanta. At least to the English, his overtures to various Protestant princes would be so construed. Accordingly, he takes Malta for his scene, the siege for his situation, and Passi for his protagonist. So far, so good; but this contest of Malta against the Turks offers no opportunity for the anti-Catholic, anti-clerical jokes that have been so popular with English audiences ever since they had been presented in *The Troublesome Reign of King John,* where, for the delectation of the groundlings, the raiders of the monasteries discover not only chests full of priceless treasure in gold and gems, but those in which the "wanton" nuns are concealed in the monks' cells, and other such abominations. Accordingly, with admirable dramatic smoothness, he combines the story of the siege of Malta with an old favourite among the Norman *Fabliaux* of the thirteenth century, the story of *Le Segretain Moine,* better known to American story-readers as the *Legend of Martin Franc and the Monk of Saint Anthony,* so amusingly told by Longfellow in *Outre Mer.* The precise literary source used by Marlowe is unknown. (See, Bennett, *op. cit.,* p. 7.) Lest, however, the Maltese fustian be too esoteric for the popular element in his audience, Marlowe sprinkles about a few obvious names and clues. First he mentions the death of the Guise in the Prologue. Then, the city of Malta, threatened by siege from the Turks, is in the charge of "Fernese," the name of the man who forced Navarre to raise the siege of Paris, and "Martin del Bosco, vice-admiral of Spain." This Fernese, who is as mean, though not so clever a rascal as Barabas, and del Bosco, force Barabas to finance the siege, or rather, to buy off the Turks from laying siege to the city. This is fairly close to what happened in France, where Farnese and the Spanish Ambassador, Bernardino de

Mendoza, were holding out against Navarre by means of the crowns they had extracted from Philip. Marlowe makes this clue obvious again and again: one of Barabas' ships is the *Speranza;* his galleys were "wafted" to Malta under the protection of "a Spanish fleet that never left [them] till within a league" of Malta; and when Calymath takes the Maltese officers prisoners, he bids them "kneel for mercy to your conquering foe," and asks, "Now where's the hope you had of haughty Spain?" Barabas also admits that he had once been helping in the wars of Charles V. (*Ibid.,* p. 89.) Moreover, though Barabas, in conversing with the citizens of Malta, speaks their language, when alone he breaks out into Spanish and even into quotation from Terence in Latin, which, as Professor Tucker-Brooke observes, falls oddly from the lips of this Maltese Jew. True, but not so oddly as his oaths, which are not only Spanish, but of a sort which would be natural only to a Spanish Catholic: *"Corpo di Dio!"* could mean nothing to a bona fide Jew.

In the name of Matthias for one of Abigail's suitors, Marlowe has picked another League name, one well known in England because of his fame in the Netherlands as Philip's protégé and tool for extirpating the Huguenot heresy in these rebellious provinces. The name Katherine may have been suggested by Catherine de Medici, who spurned marriage alliance with the House of Guise, but in this case the parallel would be very remote and loosely applied.

But these are mere identification tags, catch-names to give one the key to the gloss. It is in the characterization of the Jew that the parallel is worked out so completely as to be inescapable to one familiar with the tenor of anti-Spanish pamphleteering of the last decade of the sixteenth century in France and in England. The character of Barabas is the Protestant idea of the character of Philip. The dishonourable citizens of Malta, who make treaties with the Turks and break them "on principle" because they are "heretics," force Barabas to give them money, and Barabas consents outwardly; but secretly he schemes to outwit them all by selling Abigail now to one suitor, now to another. Isabelle of Valois was, by the way, "A fair young maid, scarce fourteen years of age" (as Matthias says of Abigail) when she was first offered to Mary's son, James, and Barabas claims "she outshines Cynthia's rays." Take that, Elizabeth!

The whole parallel is extremely apt, especially when we note that Barabas forces Abigail to pretend a false religion "for policy." This, of course, is further laboured when he forces Abigail into the nunnery; but of that more presently.

As we have seen from the *Ménippée,* and as English students know from the charges against Philip in the case of Don Antonio of Portugal as early as 1586, his reputation as a poisoner was well established. So here, Barabas is shown as master of the art of poisoning by every subtle dodge known or imagined by a populace inflamed with anti-Spanish fever. Barabas says: "I ha' the poison of the city for him [Lodovico] and the white leprosy," and he brags: "Sometimes I go about and poison wells," and he actually poisons the nuns' porridge with

> . . . a precious powder that [he] bought
> Of an Italian, in Ancona once
> Whose operation is to bind, infect
> And poison deeply, yet not appear
> In forty hours after it be ta'en.

He asks Pilia-Borza to dine with him that he may "make the villain away." He poisons Bellamira and Ithamore by giving them a rose to smell, chuckling as he does so: "So now, I am revenged upon 'em all; the scent thereof was death: I poisoned it"; but later he regrets that he had not added "one dram of powder more," for that "had made all sure."

The *Ménippée* made much of the meanness of the office held by the leaders of the ultramontane faction—first the Duke of Guise, then the Duke of Mayenne, as pensioners of Philip. They were called valets, and were mocked for their acceptance of Philip's haughty treatment. So Ithamore is bought as a slave, his chief qualification being his aptitude for villainy, and he is made to wait on Barabas and do his filthy errands; but in the end he betrays him, just as Mayenne betrayed Philip by getting the assembly to rule out the Infanta by adhering to the Salic Law. The whole matter of the date of *The Jew of Malta* makes it impossible to draw these parallels too closely; but it may be that Marlowe was aware of the activities of the League even before they were published.

The insincerity of the Most Catholic King in assuming the task of exterminating heresy is pointed out again and again by the pamphleteers and by the authors of the *Ménippée*. The Leaguers say they must purge their domains of heresy, yet, while persecuting the Huguenots, they tolerate the Jews and the Turks and the Moors, not only in Malta, "from whom he accepts peace very dearly," but in Spain, France, and the Low Countries as well. So here, in our play, the officers make and break treaties with the Turks, sell the Moors as slaves, mistreat the Jews, but tolerate their presence and their heresy for the sake of the gold they bring into whatever realms they inhabit. How modern it all sounds!

After taking Barabas' money, Farnese says:

> Yet, Barabas, we will not banish thee
> But here in Malta where thou gott'st thy wealth
> Live still; and if thou canst, get more.

The pamphlets picture Philip as reeking with wealth: "when he sweats, he sweats diadems, when he blows his nose, he blows crowns, when he belches, he belches scepters"; indeed, he pretends to consider even the throne of France with all its revenue a mere bagatelle. So Barabas regards his wealth with an appalling greed, "singing over" his bags of gold and jewels like the "morning lark" as she hovers in the air, "singing o'er her young"! Yet he affects not to mind at all, or even to miss the amount of money required to pay the tribute demanded by the Turks, claiming that he had many jewels, "orient and round," any one of which "indifferently rated" would serve to "entertain Selim and all his soldiers for a month."

This hideous greed of Barabas both in commercial and marital affairs is matched only by the grotesque hypocrisy of his "conversion," all of which comic knavery is enormously enhanced, from a dramatic point of view, by the absurd connivance of the greedy, lascivious friars. Shylock is a guileless, ill-used, much-wronged, long-suffering man as compared with this Machiavellian monster of comedy, who opines, with a shrug of his shoulders, that

> Haply some creature hath a conscience
> And for his conscience lives in beggary.

It is precisely in this frivolous indifference to the ordinary moral values that Barabas out-tops Shylock. He is not only wickeder and cleverer, but incomparably funnier. Not even Swift could combine savagery with amusement in so devastating a formula of irony.

When Barabas offers to give Abigail, "his diamond," to Ludovico, the latter protests that he "will deserve it first"; but Barabas insists that the jewel is a mere nothing to pay in return for such valuable spiritual help as he has received from Ludovico's father:

> . . . Good Sir,
> Your father hath deserved it at my hand,
> Who, of mere charity and Christian ruth,
> To bring me to religious purity,
> And, as it were, in cathechising sort,
> To make me mindful of my mortal sins,
> Against my will and whether I would or no,
> Seized all I had and thrust me out of doors;
> And made my house a place for nuns most chaste.

But when Ludovico takes this for genuine gratitude, it is almost too much for the restraint even of a practised dissembler like Barabas. Ludovico says: "No doubt your soul shall reap the fruit of it," and Barabas answers:

> Aye, but, my lord, the harvest is far off:
> And yet I know the prayers of those nuns
> And holy friars, having money for their pains,
> Are wondrous . . . [*aside*] and indeed, do no man good.
> And seeing they are not idle, but still doing,
> 'T is likely they in time may reap some fruit,
> I mean, in fullness of perfection.

At this, the booby Ludovico, whom Barabas calls "this gentle maggot," mildly remonstrates: "Good Barabas, glance not at our holy nuns," and Barabas continues in shameless levity:

> No, but I do it through burning zeal.

Finally, when he and Ithamore have poisoned all the nuns, and they are congratulating each other, exclaiming,

> How sweet the bells ring, now the nuns are dead,
> That sound at other times like tinker's pans,

and Ithamore, who is no artist even in devilry, clamours to be allowed to poison the monks too, Barabas observes drily, but with insidious comedy,

> Thou shalt not need; for now the nuns are dead
> They'll die of grief.

Perhaps the climax of this witty irreverence comes when Barabas incites the two friars to fight over his conversion and residence in one of their monasteries:

Barabas *(aside to Ithamore):* ". . . I must dissemble." *(Then, to the friars):*

> O holy friars, the burden of my sins
> Lies heavy on my soul! then pray you, tell me,
> Is 't not too late now to turn Christian?

Then, to make their cupidity and hypocrisy the more outrageous:

> I have been zealous in the Jewish faith,
> Hard-hearted to the poor, a covetous wretch,
> That would for lucre's sake have sold my soul;
> A hundred for a hundred I have ta'en;
> And now for store of wealth may I compare
> With all the Jews in Malta; but [*with consummate irony*] what is wealth?
> I am a Jew, and therefore, I am lost.

After describing his wealth:

> Cellars of wine, and sollars full of wheat,
> Warehouses stuffed with spices and with drugs,
> Whole chests of gold in bullion and in coin,
> And I know not how much weight in pearl,
> Orient and round . . . [and so forth],

he exclaims:

> All this I'll give to some religious house
> So I may be baptized and live therein.

Then, when the friars have fallen to blows over the possession of this rich novice, Barabas jeers in the mock-reproof of absurd understatement:

> This is mere frailty, brethren, be content.

Finally, Ithamore goes off with Friar Bernadine, and Barabas chooses Friar Jacques, because, he says, "He converted Abigail," and so her father is "bound in charity to requite it." He gives a final leer by bragging that "the Turk shall be one of [his] godfathers."

The episode of the friar who is made to believe he has murdered his brother-in-religion, carries on the same line of flippant, irreverent irony. When Friar Jacomo protests against his arrest, Barabas declares, impudently:

> No, pardon me, the law must have its course,
> I must be forced to give in evidence,
> That, being importuned by this Bernadine
> To be a Christian, I shut him out,
> And there he sat: now I, to keep my word,
> And give my goods and substance to your house,
> Was up thus early, with intent to go
> Unto your friary, because you stayed . . .

Ithamore interrupts:

> Fie upon 'em, Master, will you turn
> Christian when holy friars turn devils
> And murder one another?

Barabas replies:

> No! For this example I'll remain a Jew.
> Heaven bless me! what, a friar a murderer!
> When shall you see a Jew commit the like?

Ithamore:

> Why, a Turk could ha' done no more.

When they proceed to carry him off, the friar cries out: "Villains, I am a sacred person: touch me not." Barabas mocks:

> The law shall touch you; we'll but lead you, we.
> 'Las! I could weep at your calamity!
> Take in the staff too—for that must be shown.
> Law wills that each particular be known.

This is obviously an ironical comment upon the procedure in cases of prosecution for heresy, implying of course, a charge of insincerity, with a particular glance at the flimsy grounds upon which confiscation of property was sometimes made by the Holy Office.

One wonders if the last comic jibe is not aimed at some particular hat, either Philip's high, black velvet hat which he wears so frequently in portraits, or the Bonnets of the League satirized in the *Ménippée*. Ithamore is baiting Barabas, unknowingly, by regaling Bellamira with the most impertinent and absurd slanders of his master, all of which are overheard by Barabas:

Ithamore: 'T is a strange thing of that Jew, he lives upon pickled grasshoppers and sauced mushrooms.
Barabas (aside): What a slave is this! The governor feeds not as I do.
Ithamore: He never put on clean shirt since he was circumcised.
Barabas (aside): O rascal! I change myself twice a day.

Then, to cap all, Ithamore declares:

The hat he wears, Judas left under the elder when he hanged himself.

The reader remembers that the Leaguers were said, in the *Ménippée,* to have taken their insignia "of the order of the reprobate of the Apostles." But Barabas insists that it was sent him for a present from the Great Cham.

Barabas' final brag of all the mischief he had been able to achieve during his lifetime is, again, in the same tenor as the mock boast of "inventions and disguisements" for the sake of working wanton destruction, made by M. le Lieutenant in the *Ménippée*. Like the Philip of the anti-Spanish pamphlets, Barabas has been the cause of civil strife within the city; he has set family against family, friend against friend, religious houses against each other, and had he but "escaped this stratagem" i.e., the boiling cauldron so often used for heretics, he "would have brought confusion on you all."

The parallel is complete, though the reader is cautioned against pressing too far for details. Of course, Philip did not end his days in a boiling cauldron; neither did the Guise ride in the chariot of the sun; both are fustian, and they represent an attitude on the part of the author and audience, not a fact of history. The "facts" are, indeed, hopelessly jumbled in the fiction.

I may conclude this discussion of the parallel between the *Ménippée* and *The Jew of Malta* by a last *caveat* to the reader, by reminding him that no inference is here made as to an actual literary relationship between the two. The matter of date makes this highly improbable. They merely represent similar satirical treatments of the Spanish King and his *confrères* of the Holy League; but the parallels are often so close that it would almost seem as if the authors of each had met.

Conclusion

Concerning *Dido* and *Edward II,* the two plays of Marlowe not considered so far, I have very little to say. In general, I believe *Dido* to have treated the same subject as *Tamburlaine,* that is, the founding of a new empire where wealth was heaped in shining radiance, as along the shores of "rich America."

Edward II is clearly a minion play, like the early *Richard II,* and if Marlowe is its author, it may represent Ralegh's indignation at the preposterous favouritism meted out to his rival Hatton. This is no more than a guess, based upon a possible parallel between the bequest to Hatton of the Bishop of Ely's palace at High Holborn, and the similar outrage perpetrated against the estates of the Bishop of Coventry in favour of Gaveston. With shocking impudence, the inflated minion of this play sneers: "What should a priest do with so fair a house?" It is not known that Hatton was guilty of any such ridiculous arrogance toward Dr. Cox, but the whole transaction concerning the lease was carried out with a ruthlessness hardly to be matched except by this dramatic incident in the play of *Edward II.* When Dr. Cox had recourse to the law for the protection of this property of his See, the Queen wrote: *

> Proud Prelate! I understand you are backward in complying with your agreement, but I would have you know, that I who made you what you are can unmake you; and if you do not forthwith fulfil your engagement, by God, I will immediately unfrock you.

Almost as good a parallel, however, could be drawn between Gaveston's appropriation of the Bishop's palace, and Ralegh's assumption of ownership, through an act of patronage, of the estates of Sherborne, long in the possession of the bishops of

* The authenticity of this letter is not above suspicion. Sir Harris Nicolas has the following note concerning it: "There are so many versions of this pithy letter that its authenticity becomes doubtful. No better authority has been found for it than the *Gentleman's Magazine,* vol. lxxix, pt. i, p. 136, where the above copy of it is printed from 'the Register of Ely.' " *(Life and Times of Sir Christopher Hatton, London,* 1847, p. 36.)

Salisbury. It is because I could find so little to point the parallel clearly to any particular group, that I have omitted further discussion of this play.

Perhaps, the reader will feel, there is as much base for a relationship clue here as in the case of the *Massacre at Paris.* If so, I should be inclined to agree with him. The "application" in both cases is merely suggested. Were it not that they seem to fill comfortably a gap in an otherwise complete pattern, their cases would not be worthy of mention. Needless to say, it is not necessary to believe that all of Marlowe's plays were expressions of Ralegh's point of view. Marlowe may have had more than one patron; and besides, it is always in the cards that he may have written some plays merely "for honest recreation."

However, for the thesis that *Tamburlaine, Doctor Faustus,* and *The Jew of Malta,* whether by actual assignment or by the poet's own initiative, do reflect the interests and issues and beliefs of the Ralegh circle, I feel there is abundant evidence, less well documented than such plays as *Believe As You List,* and the *Game at Chess,* only because these "arguments" of Marlowe's were not critical of the government, and so came into no collision with the Censor. The evidence may not be sufficient for proof, but it is, I believe, ample for establishing a strong plausibility. If this thesis is found to be acceptable, our knowledge of Marlowe will be amplified, and our pleasure in him enhanced in direct proportion to our increased understanding.

Naturally, the question framed by the reader upon finishing these pages is: How strong is the case? Are the threads which seem to draw Marlowe into the Ralegh circle, and thus to identify him with the interests of the group, too frail to trust with so heavy a burden as a fustian interpretation for all these plays? Or does the apparent presence of Ralegh-issues here add further proof to Marlowe's connection with the group?

Far be it from me to attempt to bolster the case with special pleading. My task ends with the presentation of the evidence; if this has not convinced the reader, a further expenditure of rhetorical energy on my part would only be wasted, would, in all likelihood, add prejudice to scepticism. My hope is that the further knowledge herewith presented concerning this distinguished circle will prove useful, even should certain of the inferences concerning the fustian element in Marlowe fail to be accepted. I, at least, have enjoyed the company of Marlowe's friends, and the intellectual association with men like Bruno, Hariot, Hakluyt, Chapman, Northumberland, and Ralegh, has well repaid me for the labour entailed in the writing of this book.

APPENDIX

A Note on the Acceptance of the Copernican Theory by Thomas Hariot

IT IS MATTER for the keenest regret that there has been so far no adequate history of the life and opinions of Thomas Hariot. In fact, few of his papers have been edited at all. He himself apparently was culpably negligent about his own fame. His friend and disciple, Sir William Lower, himself an eminent mathematician and astronomer, wrote thus to Hariot in February, 1610 (Henry Stevens, *op. cit.*, p. 122):

Do you not here startle, to see every day some of your inventions taken from you; for I remember long since you told me as much, that the motions of the planets were not perfect circles. So you taught me the curious way to observe weight in Water, and within a while after Chetaldi comes out with it in print; a little before Vieta prevented you of the gharland of the greate invention of Algebra. All these were your deues and manie others that I could mention; and yet too great reservednesse had robd you of these glories. But although the inventions be greate, the first and last I meane, yet when I survei your storehouse, I see they are the smallest things, and such as in comparison of manie others, are of smal or no value. Onlie let this remember you, that it is possible by too much procrastination to be prevented in the honour of some of your rarest inventions and speculations. Let your Countrie and friends injoye the comforts they would have in the true and greate honour you would purchase yourselfe by publishing some of your choice workes, but you know best what you have to doe. Onlie I, because I wish you all good, wish this, and sometimes the more longinglie, because in one of your letters you gave me some kind of hope thereof.

This all but godlike indifference on Hariot's side might have been remedied in part, had he a good literary executor; instead no one could have been less adequate than Nathaniel Torporley, so that we are still unable to say precisely when

Hariot came to a favourable decision concerning the new Copernican philosophy.

We are not, however, quite without data upon this subject; for although Hariot published little or nothing of his astronomical opinions, his friends and disciples who did publish their scientific studies, may be properly relied upon to reflect more or less the views of their revered teacher. Although Robert Recorde, the Welsh physician who attended Queen Mary Tudor, had published a short account of Copernicanism in his *Castle of Knowledge,* in 1551,* nevertheless, when Robert Hues published his *Tractatus de Globis,* in 1594, he gave no hint of his having accepted the new doctrine. Since, as we have seen, Hues was an intimate member of the Ralegh-Hariot group, this bit of negative evidence is of considerable importance.

Still stronger negative proof is furnished by the *Diclides Coelometricae, or Universal Gates of Astronomy, containing all the materials for calculation of the whole art in a moderate space of two tables, on a new general and easy system. By Nathaniel Torporely of Shropshire, in his philosophical retreat, printed in 1602."* Torporley had entered St. Mary's Hall the year Hariot graduated, and subsequently spent two years as private secretary to Francis Vieta, the great French mathematician. Before 1602 he had settled down in his vicarage in Shropshire and had become an enthusiastic disciple of Hariot, of whom he says, in the preface of the *Diclides Coelometricae* (Henry Stevens, *op. cit.,* p. 102):

For indeed by the delays and affected obscurity of authors, it was impossible, that in the first promulgation of the art, we should give the praise of invention and the credit of teaching, to the same individual; but while others were muttering, and waiting with excited minds to see who should rule the flock, whom so many herds should follow, our own champion has not been wanting to England. I mean

* This little dialogue shows that Recorde was deeply interested in and obviously sympathetic toward the new philosophy, but that he was not yet ready to stake his all in defense of it. In fact, his remarks (quoted by Dr. Dorothy Stimson in her study, *The Gradual Acceptance of the Copernican Theory,* p. 43) reveal an intellectual urbanity that would probably have caused him to withhold approval of the truculent Bruno, at least as discreetly as he condemned the militant ignorance of the opponents of the new doctrine.

Thomas Hariot, a most distinguished man, and one excelling in all branches of learning; a man born to illustrate Science, and, what was his principal distinction, to clear away by the splendour of undoubted truth those philosophical clouds in which the world had been involved for so many centuries; who did not allow the trophies of substantial praise to be wholly carried abroad to other nations. For he (while the arrow, which was to hit the bull's eye, was yet in the quiver) defined by an admirable method the limits of all that science; and showed it to me, amongst others of his friends, explained problems to us, enabled us to exercise our ingenuity in the profundities of this science.

Here again, there is no evidence of Hariot's having accepted or even seriously investigated the theories of Copernicus. As a matter of fact, the first hint of Hariot's interest in the new doctrine seems to associate his conversion with Kepler, and hence to fix the time of it somewhere in the first decade of the seventeenth century. The Kepler-Hariot correspondence dates from October, 1606 to September, 1609. From that time on, the new system is the burning question in Hariot's circle, as indeed it was in similar groups that gathered about Kepler, in Germany, and Galileo, in Italy. A brief review of the history of Copernicanism in Europe may help to show that not only had Hariot not adopted it before 1600, but that indeed very few of the great mathematicians or astronomers of Europe had done so. We have already shown how Bruno failed to get a hearing in England in 1583. In 1586, after he had returned to Paris with Castlenau, he lectured at the college of Cambrai. Here he had more success. Whereas in Oxford he had come up against a statutary provision that "Masters and Bachelors who did not follow Aristotle faithfully were liable to a fine of five shillings for every point of divergence, and for every fault committed against the logic of the *Organon,*" in Cambrai his anti-Aristotelian views were taken up with considerable enthusiasm. But the Promethean Titans of the world will never learn to be content with serving their brother man with the new-found fire, but must be ever thumbing their noses at the older Powers; and so Bruno. We have seen him indulging in the most violent ridicule and abuse in the *Spaccio* and the *Cena de le Ceneri.* Such indiscretion, of course, marked him out for clerical persecution. He was soon driven from Cambrai, and after a few years of wandering about the Protestant cities of Germany and Switzerland, finally returned to Italy in 1592. The inevitable happened. The Inquisition had been unable to lay hold of him while in the strongholds of Lutheranism, but the moment he started lecturing in Venice under the patronage of his young patrician friend Giovanni Mocenigo, he was arrested, thrown into prison, and, as all the world knows, was finally excommunicated and burned at the stake in 1600.

Meanwhile, however, the seed planted by Bruno in Germany had begun to sprout. When in 1588 John Kepler, aged 17, entered the University of Tübingen, he found Copernicanism not only a lively issue, but, at least secretly, an accepted doctrine. We are told that Kepler "imbibed Copernican principles from the private instruction of his teacher and life-long friend, Michael Mzestlin." At that time, however, he was little interested in astronomy, and it was not until he became professor at Gratz, early in 1594, that he seriously put his mind to astronomical investigation.

About the same time, or a little earlier, while Bruno lay languishing in one of the Inquisitional prisons of Rome, a young countryman from Pisa was preparing another shock for the "bigoted Aristotelians." Both because of mental capacity and personal initiative and indiscretion, Galileo Galilei was destined to be Bruno's most distinguished understudy. From the leaning tower of Pisa between the years 1589 and 1591, we are told *(Enc. Brit. sub, Galileo)* "he afforded to all the professors and students of the university ocular demonstrations of the falsehood of the Peripatetic dictum that heavy bodies fall with velocities proportional to their weights, and with unanswerable logic demolished all the time-honoured maxims of the schools regarding the motion of projectiles, and their elemental weight or levity. But while he convinced, he failed to conciliate his adversaries. The keen sarcasm of his polished rhetoric was not calculated to soothe the susceptibilities of men already smarting under the deprivation of their most cherished illusions." So he was forced to resign his professorship and withdraw to Florence in 1591, where he stayed till he was appointed to the Chair of Mathematics at the University of Padua, in

1592. A letter to Kepler dated 4 August, 1597, states that he had long since adopted the Copernican theory of the solar system, but that he was deterred from avowing his opinions by the fear of ridicule, a fear which apparently had more power to check him than any fear of persecution was able later to do. Until he could demonstrate the new theory, as he had done in the case of falling bodies by ocular proof, he lay low. The advent of the telescope, however, furnished him with the instrument he needed.

Apparently no two writers of astronomical history are agreed as to whom belongs the honour of this invention. Without attempting to settle the question, it is possible to believe that Hariot was using some kind of a telescope as early as 1585. He says in his *True and Brief Report (*Hakluyt, *Prin. Nav.* vol. viii, p. 378):

> Most things they [the American Indians] saw with us, as Mathematicall instruments, sea Compasses, the virtue of the loadstone and drawing iron, a *perspective glasse whereby was showed many strange sights* [italics inserted], burning glasses, wilde firewoorkes, gunnes, hookes, writing and reading, spring-clockes that seem to goe of themselves and many other things that wee had, were so strange unto them, and so farre exceeded their capacities to comprehend the reason and meanes how they should be done, that they thought they were rather the workes of gods than of men, or at the leastwise, that had been given and taught us by the Gods.

The possibility of regarding this "perspective glass" as one of the catoptric instruments referred to fairly frequently during the sixteenth century has been brought to my attention through the kindness of Professor Samuel C. Chew. The catoptric glass was some sort of an arrangement of mirrors which produced freak reflections, or "strange sights," and Catoptromancy was a species of divination by mirrors, which, during the eighteenth century, became a well recognized branch of occult science. Burton *(Anatomy of Melancholy,* 1651, I, p. iii; III, p. 211) says, " 'T is ordinary to see strange, uncouth figures by catoptricks." Dr. Dee refers to such an instrument in 1570 (*Math. Praef.,* 20; cited in the N. E. D. *sub, Catoptrics*); and Vangoose, the itinerant showman in Jonson's *Masque of Augers,* has one as part of his entertaining equipment. But Dr.

Dee uses the phrase "perspective glass" to mean some kind of a telescope. He says *(Elements of Euclid,* 1575, preface p. b. 1, quoted by R. T. Gunther, *Early Science in Oxford,* 1922, vol. ii, p. 291) that a commander of an army "may wonderfully helpe himself by perspective glasses. In which (I trust) our posterity will prove more skilful and expert, and to a greater purpose then in these dayes can (almost) be credited to be possible." The instrument referred to in this passage is obviously not a trick "for the amusement of philosophers," as catoptric glasses were; nor is there in the passage from *The True and Brief Report* any indication that Hariot was just "spoofing" the Indians.

Of course "perspective glasses" were in use in England before this. It is possible that Roger Bacon, in his experiments, had invented both telescopic and catoptric glasses, and that a part of his legend was caused by a confusion of the two in popular accounts. Thomas Digges, in his *Stratioticus* (p. 375), published in 1578, says that his father, Leonard Digges, "among other curious practices had a method of discovering by perspective glasses set at due angles all objects pretty far distant that the sun shown upon, which lay in the country round about." Leonard Digges himself states that he owed his knowledge of optics to the suggestions he found in Roger Bacon; and William Molyneux seems to agree in conferring upon this real, but too-much-legendized Oxford scholar of the thirteenth century, the honour of being really first in this discovery. Molyneux says, in his *Dioptrica Nova,* published in 1692 (Gunther, *op. cit.,* pp. 289ff), that Roger Bacon "did perfectly understand all kinds of optric glasses, and knew likewise the method of combining them so as to compose some such instrument as our telescope." Robert Recorde, in the *Pathway to Knowledge,* 1551, Preface, says (Gunther, *op. cit.,* p. 289):

> Great talk there is of a glass that he [Bacon] made in Oxforde in which men myght see thynges that were done in other places, and that was iudged to bee done by power of evill sprites. But I knowe the reason of it to bee good and naturall, and to be wrought by Geometrie (sythe perspective is a part of it).

However, Professor Gunther, the latest scholar to renew the investigation, says *(ibid.,* p. 291), "There can, I think, be no reasonable doubt that Leonard Digges, of University College, was the real inventor of telescopes both Refractory and Reflectory." Leonard Digges states that he had "at large in a volume by itself opened the miraculous effects of perspective glasses," and though the volume itself is now lost, we have an excellent description of the instrument described in it, furnished us by W. Bourne, in his *Treatise on the Properties and Qualities of Glasses for Optical Purposes* written sometime between 1580 and 1590. In chapter V, Bourne says (Gunther, *op. cit.*, p. 291):

> In what order to make a glass that you may looke thorow that shall further your sighte, and to have a small thynge to seem bigg, which is very necessary for perspective. And yt may be so made, that you may discerne a small thinge, a great distance, and especially by the ayde of other glasses.

In Chapter IX, he says:

> The effects that may bee done with these two last sortes of glasses, the one concave with a foyle, uppon the hilly syde, and the other grounde and polished smoothe, the thickest in the middle, and thinnest toward the edges or sydes . . .

Bourne then states that he himself is too poor to buy the apparatus necessary for extensive investigation of his own, but he adds:

> For that there is dyvers in this land that can say and dothe knowe muche more, in these causes, then I; and especially Mr. Dee and also Mr. Thomas Digges . . . I am assured that the glass that is grounde, beyinge of very clear stuffe, and of a good largeness, and placed so that the beame doth come thorowe, and so reseaved into a very large concave looking-glass, that yt will shewe the thing of a marvellous largeness, in manner uncredable to bee believed of the common people . . . So that those things that Mr. Thomas Diggess hathe written that his father hathe done, may be accomplisshed very well withoute any dowbte of the matter. But that the greatest impediment ys, that you can not beholde, but the smaller quantity at a tyme.*

It seems, therefore, wholly likely that Hariot had taken advantage of this knowledge for his earliest experiments with

* These passages were brought to my attention by Miss Edith White.

lenses, and that the "perspective glass" referred to in his Report on Virginia was in fact a telescope, whether or not identical with the one for which Galileo has received the credit. It is not clear where Galileo got his ideas for his instrument. He may have got them from Digges' early volume, or from Bourne, or from Johannes Lippershey, "an obscure optician of Middleburn, who, on 2 October, 1608, petitioned the States General of the Low Countries for exclusive rights in the manufacture of an instrument for increasing the apparent size of objects," for we are told *(Enc. Brit.,* 11th ed., p. 113) that he was refused a monopoly patent, "as many other persons had knowledge of this new invention." At all events, rumours of the invention reached Venice, so that in June, 1609, "after one night's profound meditation on the principles of refraction, Galileo succeeded in producing a telescope of three-fold magnifying power. Upon this first attempt he rapidly improved, until he attained to a power of thirty-two, and his instruments, of which he manufactured hundreds with his own hand, were soon in request in every part of Europe."

Henry Stevens, who is jealous for Hariot's honour, says *(op. cit.,* p. 113):

> Whether in the Tower, administering new scientific delicacies and delights to the prisoners; or at Sion, unlocking the secrets of the starry firmament by night, in his observatory; or floating between Sion and the Tower by day on the broad bosom of the Thames, prying into the optical secrets of lenses, and inventing his perspective trunks by which he could bring distant objects near, Hariot in foggy England of the north was working out almost the same brilliant series of discoveries that Galileo was making in Italy. To this day, with our undated and indefinite material, even with the new and much more precise evidence now for the first time herewith produced, it is difficult to decide which of them first invented the telescope, or first by actual observation with that marvellous instrument confirmed the truth of the Copernican system by revealing the spots on the Sun, the Orbit of Mars, the Horns in the Moon, the elliptical orbits of comets, etc. It is manifest, however, that they were both working in the same groove and at the same time.

How initiated we do not know, but the fact is that Hariot was corresponding with Kepler from October, 1606, to September, 1609, discussing the theories of refraction, exchanging observations on the "new comet" (now called Halley's); but we cannot say whether Kepler or Hariot or Galileo or all three made the first real verifications of the Copernican theory by actual observations. Kepler published his finding in 1609, in a book called *De Motibus Stellae Martis,* and Galileo did likewise in 1610, in a book published in Venice called the *Siderius Nuncius.* Hariot did not publish his at all. As we have already seen, his friends and pupils remonstrated with him in vain for his negligence of his own fame. From these same protesting letters, it is also plain that in Italy and Germany, as well as in England, the Peripatetics had been worsted and the New Philosophy was for the next decade the burning issue. Bruno's theories and the observations of Kepler and Galileo were alike being put through the fire of verification and analysis. Lower wrote to Hariot in June, 1610: "We are here so on fire with these things that I must renew my request and your promise to send me of all sortes of these Cylinders, etc." Even as late as 1618, Dr. Corbet, "the mirth-loving Bishop," in *A Letter sent from Doctor Corbet to Master* [Sir Thomas] *Ailebury, Decem. 9, 1618,* alludes to the intellectual furore caused by the advent of Copernicanism:

> Burton to Gunter cants and Burton heares
> From Gunter, and th' Exchange both tongue & cares
> By carriage: thus doth mired Guy complaine,
> His Waggon on their letters beares Charles Waine,
> And at this distance they both heare, and teach.
> Now for the peace of God and men, advise
> (Thou that hast wherewithall to make us wise)
> Thine owne rich studies, and deepe Hariot's mine,
> In which there is no drosse, but all refine,
> O tell us what to trust to, lest we wax
> All stiffe and stupid with his paralex;
> Say, shall the old Philosophy be true?
> Or doth he ride above the Moone, think You?

This, then, seems to be as near as we are likely to come to the truth regarding the formal entrance of Copernicanism into England, and the conclusion seems obvious that it happened nearer the first decade of the seventeenth century than in the late 1580's. Dr. Stimson mentions several other scholars who were interested in Copernicanism, both before and after Bruno's sojourn in England, but she concludes (*op. cit.,* p. 87), that "in 1600 when *De Magnete* was published, Sir William Gilbert (1540-1603) was apparently the only supporter of the earth's movement then in England, and he advocated the diurnal motion only."

It may be worth noting that Tycho Brahe (1546-1601) who is often called "the Phoenix among Astronomers," never accepted the Copernican theory, and it is certain that his scepticism accounts for the tardy acceptance of the doctrine by Kepler himself. Kepler was Tycho's chief assistant during the last two years of his life (1599-1601), and if he was slow to announce his "conversion," the caution of a scholar like Hariot, remote from the scene of experiment, is the more understandable. Therefore, the presence of Ptolemaic philosophy in Marlowe is not to be regarded as evidence that Marlowe did not know Hariot, or that he was not a member of the Ralegh group.

Index